2803

D1061718

THE MUMMY
IN ANCIENT EGYPT

Equipping the Dead for Eternity

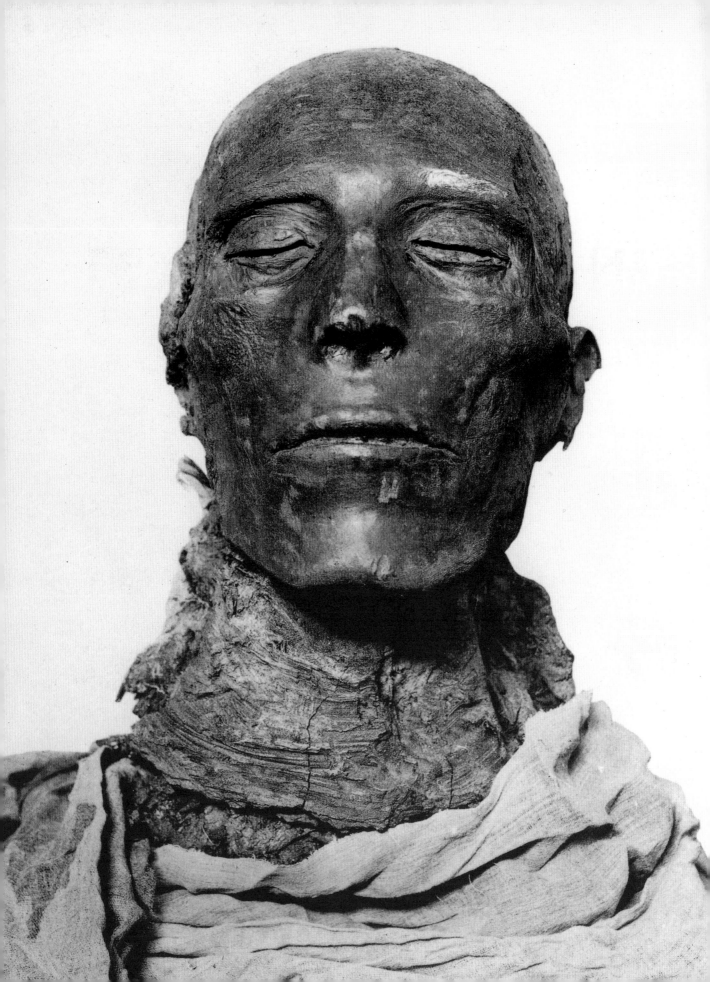

SALIMA IKRAM AND AIDAN DODSON

THE MUMMY IN ANCIENT EGYPT

Equipping the Dead for Eternity

With 485 illustrations, 37 in color

THAMES AND HUDSON

FRONTISPIECE: King Sethos I, one of the finest examples of
New Kingdom mummification.

Designed by Liz Rudderham

First published in hardcover in the United States of America in 1998 by
Thames and Hudson Inc., 500 Fifth Avenue, New York, New York 10110

Library of Congress Catalog Card Number 97-61993
ISBN 0-500-05088-0

Printed and bound in Italy

Contents

For Nicholas and Dyan

Preface

The idea for this book originated in 1992, when we both concluded that a comprehensive coverage of what one might call the Egyptian 'burial complex' was sadly lacking. There have been some detailed accounts of the history of mummification, but hardly any address the parallel developments in the corpse's external ornamentation, or the detailed evolution of its containers – the coffin, sarcophagus and canopic jar/chest. Other more general works cover these elements, but all in a summary fashion.

What was also apparent was that many of the standard works are obsolete, and/or inaccurate. For example, the British Museum's catalogue of its mummy collection (Dawson and Gray 1968) mis-dates many of its subjects, in some cases by 1,000 years. Wallis Budge's *The Mummy* is widely available, following repeated reprints, but was originally written in the 1890s, and suffers from its author's unfortunate habit of failing to check facts.

Accordingly, drawing on our respective doctoral interests of faunal preservation and funerary containers, the present work took shape. It aims to provide an up-to-date digest of what is known about mummies and their immediate appurtenances, with both an in-depth discussion of the physical preservation of the body, and a close look at the developments seen in its containers and adornments. Part I and the chapter on external ornaments are a joint effort between the authors; broadly speaking, the chapters dealing with mummification, amulets and wrappings are the work of Ikram; those covering coffins, sarcophagi and canopics are the responsibility of Dodson.

We should like to express our particular thanks to the following friends, colleagues and loved ones for their help in writing this book: Edwin Brock, Karen Brush, Cullum and Nightingale Architects, Rosalie Ðavid, D.S. and E. Dodson, Richard Fazzini, Joyce Filer, Renée Friedman, Katie Hecker, Dyan Hilton, Julie Hudson, S. and K. Ikram, Nasri Iskander, Sara Jones, Rolf Krauss, Mark Lehner, Nancy Llewellyn, Jane McPherson, J. Simon Marriott, Wendy Monkhouse, Nicole Mostafa (née Freeman), Sara E. Orel, Bob Partridge, Mohammed Saleh, Meredith Sarris, Margaret Serpico, J.J. Shirley, Emma Sinclair-Webb, Ibrahim Soliman, John H. Taylor, Angela M.J. Tooley, Daniel Vitkus, Roxie Walker, A. and J. Warner, Nicholas Warner, David West, and Pat Winker and the staffs of the Egyptian Departments at the Metropolitan Museum of Art and the Boston Museum of Fine Arts.

We are also indebted to the editorial staff of Thames and Hudson for their assistance and encouragement. Finally, we would like to thank all other friends not otherwise named for their help and support.

Cairo and Bristol   Salima Ikram and Aidan Dodson

Chronology

A Note on Egyptian Chronology

The scheme used by modern scholars for structuring the chronology of historical ancient Egypt is based upon one drawn up by the Egyptian priest, Manetho, around 300 BC. He divided the succession of kings into a series of numbered 'dynasties', corresponding to our idea of royal 'houses' (e.g. Plantagenet, Windsor). These broadly fit in with our knowledge of changes in the ruling family, but in some cases the reason for a shift is unclear.

Modern scholars have refined this structure by grouping dynasties into 'kingdoms' and 'periods', during which constant socio-political themes can be identified.

Ancient dating was by means of regnal years, not any kind of 'era' dating such as is used today. Thus, absolute dates, in terms of years BC, have to be established by various indirect methods. Some reigns can be fixed by relation to events linked to better-dated cultures, while others can be placed by reference to mentions of contemporary astronomical events. These allow other reigns' extent to be calculated by dead-reckoning. Nevertheless, there remain many areas of uncertainty, and while dating is solid back to 663 BC, margins of error before then may run in excess of a century in certain cases.

PREDYNASTIC PERIOD

Badarian Culture	5000–4000 BC
Naqada I (Amratian) Culture	4000–3500 BC
Naqada II (Gerzean) Culture	3500–3150 BC
Naqada III Culture	3150–3000 BC

Horus or Throne name	Personal Name	Conjectural Dates	Regnal Years
ARCHAIC PERIOD			
Dynasty 1			
1 Horus Narmer		3050–	
2 Horus Aha		:	
3 Horus Djer	Itit	:	
4 Horus Djet	Iti	:	
5 Horus Den	Semti	:	
6 Horus Anedjib	Merpibia	:	
7 Horus Semerkhet	Irinetjer	:	
8 Horus Qaa	Qebh	–2813	
Dynasty 2			
1 Horus Hotepsekhemwy	Baunetjer	2813–	
2 Horus Nebre	Kakau	:	
3 Horus Ninetjer	Ninetjer	:	
4 ?	Weneg	:	
5 ?	Sened	:	
6 Horus Sekhemib/ Seth Peribsen	Perenmaet	: –2709	
7 ?	Neferkasokar	2709–2701	8
8 ?	?	2701–2690	11
9 Horus and Seth Khasekhemwy	Nebwyhetepimyef	2690–2663	27
OLD KINGDOM			
Dynasty 3			
1 Horus Sanakht	Nebka	2663–2654	9
2 Horus Netjerkhet	Djoser	2654–2635	19
3 Horus Sekhemkhet	Djoser-ti	2635–2629	6

Horus or Throne name	Personal Name	Conjectural Dates	Regnal Years	Horus or Throne name	Personal Name	Conjectural Dates	Regnal Years
4 Horus Khaba	Teti?	2629–2623	6	**Dynasties 9/10**			
5 Nebkare	Seth?ka	2623–2621	2	1 Meryibre	Akhtoy I	2160–	
6 Horus Qahedjet?	Huni	2621–2597	24	2 ?	?	:	
				3 Neferkare	?	:	
Dynasty 4				4 Wahkare	Akhtoy II	:	
1 Horus Nebmaet	Seneferu	2597–2547	50	5 ?	Senenen . . .	:	
2 Horus Medjedu	Kheops	2547–2524	23	6 Neferkare	Akhtoy III	:	
3 Horus Kheper	Djedefre	2524–2516	8	7 Mery . . .	Akhtoy IV	:	
4 Horus Userib	Khephren	2516–2493	23	8 (Various)	(Various)	:	
5 Horus Kakhet	Mykerinos	2493–2475	18	9 ?	Meryhathor	:	
6 Horus Shepseskhet	Shepseskaf	2475–2471	4	10 Nebkaure	Akhtoy V	:	
				11 Merykare	?	:	
Dynasty 5				12 ?	?	–2040	
1 Horus Irimaet	Userkaf	2471–2464	7				
2 Horus Nebkhau	Sahure	2464–2452	12	**Dynasty 11a**			
3 Neferirkare	Kakai	2452–2442	10	1 Horus Tepya	Mentuhotep I	2160–	
4 Shepseskare	Isi	2442–2435	7	2 Horus Sehertawy	Inyotef I	–2123	
5 Horus Neferkhau	Neferefre	2435–2432	3	3 Horus Wahankh	Inyotef II	2123–2074	49
6 Niuserre	Ini	2432–2421	11	4 Horus Nakhtnebtepnefer	Inyotef III	2074–2066	8
7 Menkauhor	Ikauhor	2421–2413	8				
8 Djedkare	Isesi	2413–2385	28	**MIDDLE KINGDOM**			
9 Horus Wadjtawy	Unas	2385–2355	30	**Dynasty 11b**			
				5 Nebhepetre	Mentuhotep II	2066–2014	52
Dynasty 6				6 Sankhkare	Mentuhotep III	2014–2001	13
1 Horus Seheteptawy	Teti	2355–2343	12	7 Nebtawyre	Mentuhotep IV	2001–1994	7
2 Nefersahor/Meryre	Pepy I	2343–2297	46				
3 Merenre	Nemtyemsaf I	2297–2290	7	**Dynasty 12**			
4 Neferkare	Pepy II	2290–2196	94	1 Sehetepibre	Ammenemes I	1994–1964	30
5 Merenre	Nemtyemsaf II	2196–2195	1	2 Kheperkare	Sesostris I	1974–1929	45
				3 Nubkaure	Ammenemes II	1932–1896	36
				4 Khakheperre	Sesostris II	1900–1880	20
FIRST INTERMEDIATE PERIOD				5 Khakaure	Sesostris III	1881–1840	41
Dynasty 7/8				6 Nimaetre	Ammenemes III	1842–1794	48
1 Netjerkare	?	2195–		7 Maekherure	Ammenemes IV	1798–1785	13
2 Menkare	Nitokris	:		8 Sobkkare	Sobkneferu	1785–1781	4
3 Neferkare	?	:					
4 Neferkare	Neby	:		**Dynasty 13**			
5 Djedkare	Shemay	:		1 Khusekhemre	Wegaf	1781–	
6 Neferkare	Khendu	:		2 Sekhemkare	Amenemhatsonbef	:	
7 Merenhor	?	:		3 Sekhemre-khutowi	?	:	
8 Nikare	?	:		4 Sekhemkare	Ammenemes V	:	
9 Neferkare	Tereru	:		5 Sehetepibre	Ameny-Qemau	:	
10 Neferkahor	?	:		6 Sankhibre	Ameny-Inyotef-Ammenemes VI	:	
11 Neferkare	Pepysonbe	:		7 Smenkare	Nebnuni	:	
12 Neferkamin	Anu	:		8 Hotepibre	Hornedjhiryotef-sa-Qemau	:	
13 Qakare	Ibi	:	4	9 Swadjkare	?	:	
14 Wadjkare	?	:		10 Nedjemibre	?	:	
15 Neferkauhor	Khuihapy	:					
16 Neferirkare	?	–2160					

Throne name	Personal Name	Conjectural Dates	Regnal Years
11 Khaankhre	Sobkhotep I	:	
12 ?	Rensonbe	:	
13 Auibre	Hor	:	
14 Sedjefakre	Kay-Ammenemes VII	:	
15 Sekhemre-khutawi	Ammenemes VIII-Sobkhotep II	:	
16 Userkare/Nikhanimaetre	Khendjer	:	
17 Smenkhkare	Imyromesha	:	
18 Sehotepkare	Inyotef IV	:	
19 Sekhemre-swadjtawi	Sobkhotep III	:	
20 Khasekhemre	Neferhotep I	:	
21 ?	Sihathor	:	
22 Khaneferre	Sobkhotep IV	:	
23 Khahetepre	Sobkhotep V	:	
24 Wahibre	Iaib	:	
25 Merneferre	Ay (I)	:	
26 Merhetepre	Sobkhotep VI	:	
27 Mersekhemre	Neferhotep	:	
28 Merkaure	Sobkhotep VII	:	
29 Djedneferre	Dedumose	:	
30 Swahenre	Senebmiu	−1650	

SECOND INTERMEDIATE PERIOD

Dynasty 15

Throne name	Personal Name	Conjectural Dates	Regnal Years
1 Maaibre	Sheshi	1650–	
2 Meruserre	Yakobher	:	
3 Seuserenre	Khyan	:	
4 ?	Yansas . . .	−1585	
5 Nebkhepeshre/Aqenenre/Auserre	Apophis	1585–1545	40
6 ?	Khamudy	1545–1535	

Dynasty 17

Throne name	Personal Name	Conjectural Dates	Regnal Years
1 Sekhemre-wahkhau	Rehotep	1650–	
2 Sekhemre-smentawi	Djehuty	:	
3 Sankhenre	Mentuhotep VII	:	
4 Swedjenre	Nebiriau I	:	
5 Neferkare	Nebiriau II	:	
6 Seuserenre	?	:	
7 Sekhemre-shedtawi	Sobkemsaf I	:	
8 Sekhemre-wepmaet	Inyotef V	:	
9 Nubkheperre	Inyotef VI	:	
10 Sekhemre-heruhirmaet	Inyotef VII	:	
11 Sekhemre-wadjkhau	Sobkemsaf II	:	
12 Senakhtenre	Taa I	−1558	
13 Seqenenre	Taa II	1558–1553	5
14 Wadjkheperre	Kamose	1553–1549	4

NEW KINGDOM

Dynasty 18

Throne name	Personal Name	Conjectural Dates	Regnal Years
1 Nebpehtire	Amosis	1549–1524	25
2 Djeserkare	Amenophis I	1524–1503	21
3 Akheperkare	Tuthmosis I	1503–1491	12
4 Akheperenre	Tuthmosis II	1491–1479	12
5 Menkheper(en)re	Tuthmosis III	1479–1424	54
6 (Maetkare	Hatshepsut	1472–1457)	
7 Akheperure	Amenophis II	1424–1398	26
8 Menkheperure	Tuthmosis IV	1398–1388	10
9 Nebmaetre	Amenophis III	1388–1348	40
10 Neferkheperure-waenre	Amenophis IV/Akhenaten	1360–1343	17
11 (Ankhkheperure	Smenkhkare/Neferneferuaten	1346–1343	3)
12 Nebkheperre	Tutankhamun	1343–1333	10
13 Kheperkheperure	Ay (II)	1333–1328	5
14 Djeserkheperure-setpenre	Horemheb	1328–1298	30

Dynasty 19

Throne name	Personal Name	Conjectural Dates	Regnal Years
1 Menpehtire	Ramesses I	1298–1296	2
2 Menmaetre	Sethos I	1296–1279	17
3 Usermaetre-setpenre	Ramesses II	1279–1212	67
4 Banenre	Merenptah	1212–1201	11
5 Userkheperure	Sethos II	1201–1195	6
6 (Menmire-setpenre	Amenmesse	1200–1196	4)
7 Sekhaenre/Akheperre	Siptah	1195–1189	6
8 Sitre-merenamun	Tawosret	1189–1187	2

Dynasty 20

Throne name	Personal Name	Conjectural Dates	Regnal Years
1 Userkhaure	Sethnakhte	1187–1185	2
2 Usermaetre-meryamun	Ramesses III	1185–1153	32
3 User/Heqamaetre-setpenamun	Ramesses IV	1153–1146	7
4 Usermaetre-sekheperenre	Ramesses V Amenhirkopshef I	1146–1141	5
5 Nebmaetre-meryamun	Ramesses VI Amenhirkopshef II	1141–1133	8
6 Usermaetre-setpenre-meryamun	Ramesses VII Itamun	1133–1125	8
7 Usermaetre-akhenamun	Ramesses VIII Sethhirkopshef	1125–1123	2
8 Neferkare-setpenre	Ramesses IX Khaemwaset I	1123–1104	19
9 Khepermaetre-setpenre	Ramesses X Amenhirkopshef III	1104–1094	10
10 Menmaetre-setpenptah	Ramesses XI Khaemwaset II	1094–1064	30
a (Hemnetjertepyenamun	Hrihor	1075–1069	6)

Throne name	Personal Name	Conjectural Dates	Regnal Years
THIRD INTERMEDIATE PERIOD			
Dynasty 21			
1 Hedjkheperre-setpenre	Smendes	1064–1038	26
2 Neferkare-heqawaset	Amenemnesu	1038–1034	4
3 (Kheperkhare-setpenamun	Pinudjem I	1049–1026	23)
4 Akheperre-setpenamun	Psusennes I	1034–981	53
5 Usermaetre-setpenamun	Amenemopet	984–974	10
6 Akheperre-setpenre	Osokhor	974–968	6
7 Netjerkheperre-meryamun	Siamun	968–948	20
8 (Tyetkheperure-setpenre	Psusennes II	945–940	5)
Dynasty 22			
1 Hedjkheperre-setpenre	Shoshenq I	948–927	21
2 Sekhemkheperre-setpenre	Osorkon I	927–892	35
3 (Heqakheperre-setpenre	Shoshenq II	895)	
4 Hedjkheprre-setpenre	Takelot I	892–877	15
5 Usermaetre-setpenamun	Osorkon II	877–838	39
6 Usermaetre-setpenre	Shoshenq III	838–798	40
7 Hedjkheperre-setpenre	Shoshenq IV	798–786	12
8 Usermaetre-setpenamun	Pimay	786–780	6
9 Akheperre	Shoshenq V	780–743	37
'Theban Dynasty 23'			
1 Hedjkheperre-setpenamun	Harsiese	867–857	10
2 Hedjkheperre-setpenre	Takelot II	841–815	26
3 Usermaetre-setpenamun	Pedubast I	830–805	25
4 (?	Iuput I	815–?)	
5 Usermaetre-setpenamun	Osorkon III	799–769	30
6 Usermaetre	Takelot III	774–759	15
7 Usermaetre-setpanamun	Rudamun	759–739	20
8 ?	Iny	739–734	5
9 Neferkare	Peftjauawybast	734–724	10
Dynasty 23			
1 Sehetepibenre	Pedubast II	743–733	10
2 Akheperre-setpenamun	Osorkon IV	733–715	18
Dynasty 24			
1 Shepsesre	Tefnakhte	731–723	8
2 Wahkare	Bokkhoris	723–717	6
Dynasty 25			
1 Seneferre	Piye	752–717	35
2 Neferkare	Shabaka	717–703	14
3 Djedkare	Shabataka	703–690	13
4 Khunefertumre	Taharqa	690–664	6
5 Bakare	Tanutamun	664–656	8

Throne name	Personal Name	Dates	Regnal Years
SAITE PERIOD			
Dynasty 26			
1 Wahibre	Psammetikhos I	664–610	54
2 Wehemibre	Nekho II	610–595	15
3 Neferibre	Psammetikhos II	595–589	6
4 Haaibre	Apries	589–570	19
5 Khnemibre	Amasis	570–526	44
6 Ankhka(en)re	Psammetikhos III	526–525	1
LATE PERIOD			
Dynasty 27			
1 Mesutire	Kambyses	525–522	3
2 Setutre	Darius I	521–486	35
3 ?	Xerxes I	486–465	21
4 ?	Artaxerxes I	465–424	41
Dynasty 28			
1 ?	Amyrtaios	404–399	5
Dynasty 29			
1 Baenre-merynetjeru	Nepherites I	399–393	6
2 Usermaetre-setpenptah	Psamuthis	393	1
3 Khnemmaetre	Akhoris	393–380	13
4 ?	Nepherites II	380	1
Dynasty 30			
1 Kheperkare	Nektanebo I	380–362	18
2 Irimaetenre	Teos	362–360	2
3 Senedjemibre-setpenanhur	Nektanebo II	360–342	18
Dynasty 31			
1 –	Artaxerxes III Okhos	342–338	5
2 –	Arses	338–336	2
3 –	Darius III	335–332	3
HELLENISTIC PERIOD			
Dynasty of Macedon			
1 Setpenre-meryamun	Alexander III	332–323	9
2 Setepkaenre-meryamun	Philippos Arrhidaeos	323–317	5
3 Haaibre	Alexander IV	317–310	7
Dynasty of Ptolemy			
1 Setpenre-meryamun	Ptolemy I Soter	310–282	28
2 Userka(en)re-meryamun	Ptolemy II Philadelphos	285–246	36

Throne name	Personal Name	Dates	Regnal Years
3 Iwaennetjerwysenwy-setpenre-sekhemankhen-amun	Ptolemy III Euergetes I	246–222	24
4 Iwaennetjerwymenekhwy-setpenptah-userkare-sekhemankhenamun	Ptolemy IV Philopator	222–205	17
5 Iwaennetjerwy-merwyyot-setpenptah-userkare-sekhemankhenamun	Ptolemy V Epiphanes	205–180	25
6 Iwaennetjerwyperwy-setpenptahkepri-irimaetamunre	Ptolemy VI Philometor	180–164	16
7 Iwaennetjerwyperwy-setpenptah-irimaetre-sekhemankenamun	Ptolemy VIII Euergetes II	170–163	7
6 –	Ptolemy VI (again)	163–145	18
8 ?	Ptolemy VII Neos Philopator	145	1
7 –	Ptolemy VIII (again)	145–116	29
9 Iwaennetjermenekh-netjeretmerymutesnedjet-sepenptah-merymaetre-sekhemankhamun	Ptolemy IX Soter II	116–110	6
10 Iwaennetjermenekh-netjeretmenekhsatre-setpenptah-irimaetre-Senenankhenamun	Ptolemy X Alexander I	110–109	1
9 –	Ptolemy IX (again)	109–107	2
10 –	Ptolemy X (again)	107–88	19
9 –	Ptolemy IX (again)	88–80	8
11 ?	Berinike III	80	1
12 (?	Ptolemy XI	80	1)
13 Iwaenpanetjerentinehem-setpenptah-merymaetenre sekhemankhamun	Ptolemy XII Neos Dionysos	80–58	22
14 –	Kleopatra VI	58–57	1
15 (–	Berenike IV	58–55	3)
13 –	Ptolemy XII (again)	55–51	41
16 –	Kleopatra VII	51–30	21
17 (?	Ptolemy XIII	51–47	4)
18 (?	Ptolemy XIV	47–44	3)
19 (Iwaenpanetjerentinehem-setpenptah-irimeryre-sekhemankhamun	Ptolemy XV Kaisaros	36–30	6)

ROMAN PERIOD	30 BC–AD 395
BYZANTINE PERIOD	395–640
ARAB PERIOD	640–1517
OTTOMAN PERIOD	1517–1805
KHEDEVAL PERIOD	1805–1919
MONARCHY	1919–1953
REPUBLIC	1953–

Introduction

For most people mummies are synonymous with ancient Egypt. They have gripped the popular imagination both through archaeological discoveries and penny-dreadful horror movies pandering to people's morbid curiosity. However, to the scholar they are a key element of investigating the past.

This book aims to be of interest to both enthusiasts and scholars. Part I gives a broad survey of the development of the ancient Egyptian burial – the tombs and their contents – Egyptian funerary beliefs, and an account of the fate of the mummies and their sepulchres. Laid away by pious hands, many mummies were almost immediately violated by those in search of the objects and ornaments interred with them. Others rested undisturbed until opened in the name of knowledge, although in many cases this intrusion was almost indistinguishable from that of the ubiquitous tomb-robbers. Only in the most recent years have the tombs and their contents been treated with some degree of respect, their structures conserved, and the human remains investigated non-destructively.

Part II focuses on the various aspects of the burial. Working from the core of the burial, the mummy, outwards, the evolution of the methods for treating the body, wrapping it, and sheltering it are dealt with in turn.

Part III is a substantial reference section, consisting of a timeline, glossary, maps and gazetteer of the royal cemeteries, details of the royal caches, a descriptive catalogue of all the known royal mummies, and much else besides.

There was constant innovation and change in the way in which the Egyptians approached the various aspects of the 'burial complex'. Popular belief has it that the ancient inhabitants of the Nile valley were a supremely conservative people who changed nothing during the three thousand years of pharaonic civilization. To the casual observer, this may seem so: the artistic style seen on the Narmer Palette of around 3050 BC looks remarkably similar to that seen in the temple of Dandara, built in the first century AD. Likewise, the anthropoid coffins of 2000 BC seem to have much in common with those of 200 BC. However, close study shows the dramatic ways in which practice and underlying concepts changed over those centuries. A good example may be seen in the so-called canopic jars used to contain the viscera, removed from the body during the embalming process. When first found, they are simple, functional pots; two millennia later, they have a fundamental ritual significance so strong that even when their practical purpose had been removed by changes in embalming techniques, they still accompanied the mummy – as solid blocks of wood or stone.

Everything depended on the Egyptian belief in eternal life, and the need to provide for it. This had nothing to do with a morbid fascination with death. Far from it – it reflected a love of life and a need to ensure that it carried

1 (*above*) The mummy of King Sethos I lying in his coffin. CM CG 61077.

on beyond this world, where life could be all too short. It is worth remembering that the average age at death was about thirty. Thus, it was important that the full set of magical 'machinery' was available to ensure a smooth passage to the next world. For those of low status this was rather limited, being restricted to a tomb, a few commonplace grave goods, basic mummification, and, if feasible, a stela. For those of high status, the machinery comprised much more: a chapel, a tomb, a sarcophagus, coffins, masks and other adornments of the body, and canopic equipment, as well as furniture and further ritual objects.

The requirement for this assemblage led to Egyptian sepulchres being filled with some of the most stunning objects of all time, such as the gold coffin and mask of Tutankhamun. Aside from their religious significance, the tombs and all that they contain attest to the remarkable creativity and resources of a civilization that flourished in the Nile valley for thousands of years.

Part I

Chapter 1

The Ancient Egyptian Burial

The earliest surviving Egyptian burials are simple graves, scooped into the desert sand. They date from the period before 3000 BC, before the foundation of the Egyptian state, before any certain evidence of literacy, when the country was composed of numerous small polities. These early cemeteries are located near the settlements, in the margins of the desert that abuts the green fields that extend a few kilometres either side of the River Nile. The graves contained the body in a foetal position, surrounded by pots, knives, beads and other items of daily life. Although often reduced to mere skeletons, some of the bodies still retain their flesh and skin, the result of the desiccating effect of long contact with hot sand. This natural phenomenon was most probably the catalyst in the search for an artificial system for the preservation of the body – mummification.

THE EGYPTIAN CONCEPTION OF THE AFTERLIFE

You live again, you revive always, you have become young again, you are young again, and forever.

(Ancient Egyptian funerary text)

The continued existence of the body on earth formed but one part of the ancient Egyptian view of the necessities for the Afterlife. While our detailed knowledge of their conception of eternal survival is primarily based on New Kingdom and later evidence, the basic picture seen then is clearly valid for most of the earlier eras.

The physical corpse seems to have been the dead person's link with Earth: the conduit of the sustenance provided by offerings and the magical spells inscribed on the walls of the tomb or chapel. From this conception stemmed the requirement that the body be preserved from corruption and disintegration, which led to the whole development of the elaborate practices surrounding mummification. However, should the body be damaged, it was possible for its role to be taken over by a sculpted image; failing that, the deceased's name could be enough to maintain his or her eternal survival. This base of the hierarchy ties in with the Egyptian belief that to speak a person's name was to make them live: while even a verbal remembrance of an individual survived in the world of the living, eternal existence was guaranteed.

Any tomb ideally comprised two elements, the below-ground closed burial chamber (the substructure), and an above-ground offering place (the superstructure). In the latter, family, friends or employed priests of the deceased would leave foodstuffs, or commune with the departed on feast days. This offering place might simply be the ground above the grave, in front of a simple stela, or a huge free-standing or rock-cut complex, either above the burial place, or some distance away. At different periods the forms of these elements varied very considerably, but at all times the fundamental concepts remained constant: the burial apart-

2 *(above)* Dancers at a Nineteenth Dynasty funeral. Saqqara; CM JE 4872.

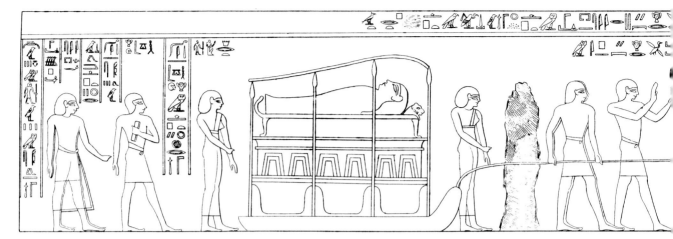

ment(s) centred on the corpse itself; the chapel centred on a 'false door', the interface between the two worlds, through which the spirit could emerge, and then return whence it came.

Egyptian funerals were important events, the last point at which the earthly body of the deceased could be viewed and bid farewell by friends and relations before the soul went to Amenti, the Otherworld. A stela in Theban Tomb (TT) 110 provides a vivid account of such a funeral:

> A goodly burial arrives in peace, your 70 days having been ful-filled in your place of embalming. You are placed on the bier…and are drawn by bulls without blemish, the road being sprinkled with milk, until you reach the door of your tomb. The children of your children, united of one accord, weep with loving hearts. Your mouth is opened by the lector-priest and your purification is performed by the *Sem*-priest. Horus adjusts for you your mouth and opens for you your eyes and ears, your flesh and your bones being perfect in all that apper-tains to you. Spells and glorifications are recited for you. There is made for you a 'Royal Offering Formula', your own heart being with you, thy heart of your earthly existence. You come in your former shape, as on the day on which you were born. There is brought to you the Son-whom-you-love, the courtiers making obeisance. You enter into the land given by the king, into the sepulchre of the west.
>
> (after Davies and Gardiner 1915: 56)

Egyptian funerary ceremonies were long and compli-cated. The prepared mummy would be retrieved from the embalmers and would be taken in procession with the funerary goods to the tomb. The procession included the mourning family and friends, priests, and, if the deceased were wealthy, a host of professional mourners who would tear their clothes, beat their breasts, and pour ash upon their heads, ululating all the while. Such hired mourners are known in Egypt today. The burial culminated in the cere-mony of 'opening the mouth', in which the dead body was reanimated, involving implements that recall those used at birth. The key item was the *pesesh-kef* knife; the set con-sisted of a flint blade that broadened to a fork at the end, and two sets of small vessels. Models of these are known from Old Kingdom tombs and continue to occur occasion-ally until the Eighteenth Dynasty. The knife was probably a model of one used to cut the umbilical cord of the baby, and as such was necessary for the soul's rebirth in Amenti, and its ability to eat and drink again, just as severing the umbilical cord means that the child must use its own mouth to eat and therefore live. Tutankhamun's tomb held a kind of bronze *pesesh-kef* knife, flanked by shrines con-taining four faience cups. The latter held natron and resin, both crucial elements in mummification. The adze and the foreleg of an ox were also used in the ritual, the latter com-ing from a sacrificial animal that probably provided the main part of the funeral meal. Once the mummy was reani-mated, it joined the mourners for one last time in a funerary feast. No doubt many of the fresh food-offerings were consumed during the course of this meal, with a share being set aside for the deceased.

Having feasted, the corpse was placed in the tomb with accompanying pomp and ritual, garlands and flowers often being placed on corpse and coffin. Meanwhile the spiritual aspect of the deceased had set out on its journey to eternity.

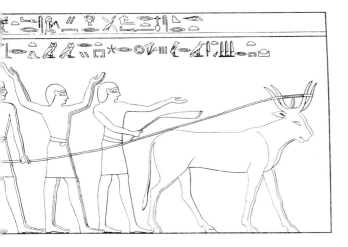

This entailed overcoming the obstacles placed in its way by the guardians of the various gates that lay between it and its goal, the Hall of Judgment. Aid in doing so was provided by the Book of Coming Forth by Day, better known as the Book of the Dead, or the more ancient Coffin Texts. These were essentially guidebooks to the hereafter, and supplied spells to negate the threats that lay between the dead person and resurrection.

The earliest such texts had been inscribed on the interiors of Fifth and Sixth Dynasty pyramids, for the benefit of the king's assimilation into the company of the gods. During the First Intermediate Period, a 'democratization' of ritual allowed some of them to be inscribed inside coffins (hence 'Coffin Texts'); occasionally these verbal aids were complemented by actual maps of the Underworld painted within the coffin. By the Second Intermediate Period, there had been an increasing codification of these texts into a

3 Funerary procession of Paheri. The mummy is shown resting upon a lion-headed bier, atop its wooden sarcophagus, which is drawn along on a canopied sledge, pulled by a combination of men and oxen. Tomb 3 at El-Kab.

4 The Opening of the Mouth ritual took place outside the tomb, with a priest, dressed as the jackal-headed god Anubis, and a *sem* priest, dressed in a leopard skin, being the main officiants. The deceased's female family members are weeping and saying their last farewell to the revivified mummy.

new composition: the Book of the Dead. Extracts appeared on coffins, sarcophagi and tomb walls, but more complete versions were inscribed upon papyrus rolls, often illustrated with vignettes. The spells enabled the spirit to negotiate successfully the various gates of the Underworld, until it reached the Hall of Judgment, where Osiris, King of the Dead, presided.

There, the final part of the ordeal comprised the weighing of the deceased's heart – regarded as the seat of intelligence and knowledge – against the feather of *maat*, the personification of truth, order and justice. If the pans of the scale balanced, the dead person would come before Osiris and pass into eternal life in what was visualized as a bigger and better Egypt. If the heart proved heavier, it would be fed to a monster named 'the Devourer', and the spirit cast into the darkness; however, the Book of the Dead contained spells designed to avoid such an outcome, thus guaranteeing the spirit of success in its great journey. In addition to their inclusion on papyrus rolls, similar texts, with accompanying vignettes, appear on coffins of certain periods, and on tomb walls; as has been mentioned above.

Once the deceased was safely in the Afterworld, the living could approach the dead and ask for supernatural intervention in their affairs, be it for advice, an increase in prosperity, or to help heal the sick. The most popular way of doing this was in letter form. Such 'Letters to the Dead' were inscribed on papyrus, or more often, on pottery bowls. The bowls contained food that would entice the deceased's spirit out of the tomb, and provide 'payment' for it to speed along the desired intervention. There were other festive occasions when the dead were remembered and visited by the living. One such was the 'Festival of the Valley', held once a year in Thebes. Similar tomb visits with family picnics continue in Egypt today.

The Gods and Goddesses of Death

Osiris was regarded as the prototype mummy. Myth had it that he had been murdered and later dismembered by his brother, Seth. The body was ultimately rescued and reassembled by his wife, Isis, embalmed by the jackal-headed god, Anubis, and resurrected to become ruler and judge of the dead. Osiris is almost always represented as a wrapped mummy, his arms crossed at the breast. The exposed flesh of the face is usually painted black or green,

both colours of fertility and rebirth: the former recalls the black silt that was annually deposited on the fields by the inundation of the Nile; the latter the resulting crops.

At various times during his posthumous ordeal, Osiris was watched over by his devoted sisters, Isis – who was also his wife and mother of his son, Horus – and Nephthys. These two goddesses are ubiquitous in funerary representations, and from the Middle Kingdom respectively guard the foot and head of coffins and sarcophagi. Two other goddesses, Neith and Selqet, regularly join them in their tutelary duties, along with four beings known as the 'Four Sons of Horus'. Named Imseti, Hapy, Duamutef and Qebehsenuef, they are regularly found linked with the four goddesses in coffin and related inscriptions, but were particularly linked with the internal organs, removed during mummification. For a period during the Middle Kingdom, the Four Sons of Horus seem to have been regarded as uniformly hawk-headed; they then became human-visaged until the New Kingdom, when they gradually obtained different heads – Imseti that of a man, Hapy that of a baboon, Duamutef that of a canid, and Qebehsenuef a hawk.

These gods form part of a large group of deities who are only found within funerary contexts. Some are variants of better-known gods, such as Anubis: two of his sub-forms, Imywet and Khentysehnetjer, are often found with the Four Sons upon coffins. Others are more obscure, and restricted to certain of the funerary 'books', of which the Book of the Dead is but one.

The Life Eternal

Although eternal life in the 'Fields of Iaru' – an even more perfect celestial Egypt – was a primary theme in the Egyptian view of posthumous existence, others were also present. The spiritual part of the dead person was believed to have a number of aspects, including the *ka*, the *ba*, the *akh* and the 'shadow'. Of these, the *ba* (ill. 7) was depicted as a human-headed bird, which seems to have been the form in which the spirit travelled within and beyond the vicinity of the tomb, flying around and able to sit before the grave, taking its repose in the 'cool sweet breeze'. The concept of the *akh* was somewhat more esoteric, being the aspect of the dead in which he or she had ceased to be dead, having been transfigured into a living being: a light in contrast to the darkness of death, often linked with the stars.

5 The Architect Kha, and his wife Meryet, adore Osiris, King of the Dead, on Kha's papyrus copy of the Book of the Dead. Reign of Amenophis III, from Deir el-Medina, TT 8; Egyptian Museum, Turin.

6 Embalming was under the patronage of the jackal-god, Anubis, shown here preparing the mummy of Djedhoriufankh. Early Twenty-first Dynasty, from Thebes(?); CM TR 23.11.16.12.

7 The form in which the spirit was believed to be able to come out into the world was known as the *ba*. In this incarnation, it was shown as a human-headed bird hovering over the mummy of Ani; Nineteenth Dynasty. Pap. BM EA 10470.

8 Here the human-headed *ba* appears on the coffin of Pediamun, Twenty-first Dynasty, from Deir el-Bahari; CM JE 29666.

9 (*right*) The *ka* was a kind of 'double', which accompanied a person from conception onwards. It was represented hieroglyphically as a pair of upraised hands, which were placed on the head when shown anthropomorphically. Thirteenth Dynasty, from the tomb of King Hor, Dahshur. CM JE 30948 = CG 259.

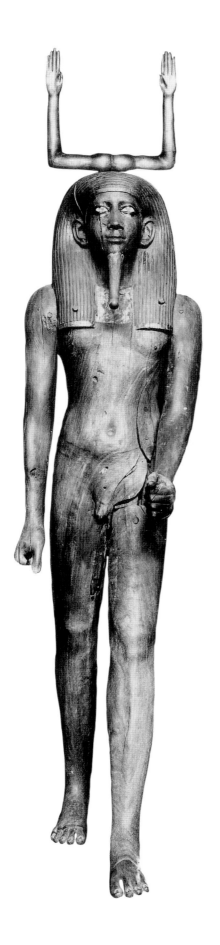

The notion of the *ka* was even more complex, being an aspect of the person created at the same time as the body and surviving as its companion. It was the part of the deceased that was the immediate recipient of offerings, but had other functions, some of which remain obscure. The *ka* was shown as an upraised pair of arms.

The foregoing represent beliefs concerning the eternal destiny of private individuals; kings, on the other hand, were already divine beings, who were viewed as joining their fellow gods after death. Thus, a dead king would journey with the sun-god through the skies and the Underworld, serving amongst his entourage: one text speaks of him acting as the sun-god's secretary. The distinction can be seen in the architecture, decoration and contents of royal tombs, although too much can be made of this. It is often said that private tombs bore scenes of 'daily life', while royal ones contained those of the Underworld. This misses the crucial point that it is the *chapels* of private tombs that contain the daily-life scenes, and the burial apartments of the royal ones that depict the Underworld. Most private sepulchral apartments are devoid of adornment, but where they are decorated, it is usually with purely ritual elements. Conversely, royal funerary chapels and temples bear some scenes analogous to those of private tomb-chapels: in particular, instead of the nobleman hunting game, we see the king hunting and defeating Egypt's enemies. It has been argued that these tomb-paintings depicting daily-life scenes can be interpreted on an allegorical as well as a literal level. Many hunting and fishing scenes not only show the tomb-owner successfully feeding himself in the afterlife, but show the triumph of human control and the maintenance of *maat* over the chaos of nature.

THE TOMB AND ITS CONTENTS

As already noted, an Egyptian's sepulchre had two basic elements, and it is important to be able to distinguish between them. They are the offering place, above ground and accessible to the living, and the burial place, below ground and sealed for eternity. Each have independent evolutionary chains, and depend, at least in part, on the topography of their locations for their physical forms, for example, flat desert as opposed to rising escarpment.

The Genesis of the Egyptian Tomb

Egypt became a single political entity around 3100 BC. The first properly constructed tombs date to shortly before this: brick-lined pits at Abydos and Hierakonpolis which formed the burial places of the last of the great regional chieftains. One example comes from the latter site, Tomb 100 being adorned with the earliest known tomb-paintings in Egypt.

Such brick-lined cavities continued to form the core of the sepulchres of the kings of the First Dynasty at Abydos, one or more wood-framed rooms being built within them. They were clearly intended to represent an underground palace, equipped with huge quantities of pottery, furniture and other objects. Their superstructures comprised two elements, separated by a considerable distance. Directly above the tomb-chamber there was probably a low mound, accompanied by a pair of stone stelae, giving the king's name. Nearly 2 kilometres away lay a great niched enclosure of sun-dried brick, which formed the centre for the royal cult. Within this were erected various buildings that became the prototype for later royal mortuary temples. These huge structures are the earliest of the monumental royal tomb-superstructures that were to develop into the breathtaking pyramids of the Fourth Dynasty, and the beautifully decorated mortuary temples of the New Kingdom.

While the royal cemetery lay in the southern part of Egypt, many high officials had tombs at Saqqara in the north. In these large tombs the two superstructure elements seen at Abydos were combined into a single one. Although much smaller than the Abydene enclosures, they are still most impressive monuments – so impressive that the archaeologist W.B. Emery thought that they belonged to the pharaohs themselves. The panelled exteriors perhaps betray some Mesopotamian influence. They certainly represent the façades of high-status dwellings and domestic enclosures, and initially contained store rooms. Such niching or panelling (sometimes called the 'palace-façade' or *serekh* motif) is also found on the coffins of the same date. The latter are squat in their proportions, the bodies are still in a contracted pose. Some bodies were swathed in bandages, showing indications of artificial preservation.

During the Second Dynasty private tomb-superstructures became solid, generally losing their panelling

decoration to more closely resemble the plain brick benches that give such tombs the Arabic appellation, *mastaba* (bench). Below ground, tomb-chambers are frequently to be found tunnelled deep into the bedrock, approached by stairways. Some royal substructures at Saqqara exhibit spectacular dimensions and elaboration.

The niched royal enclosure survives the end of the Archaic Period. The latest brick example is that of the pharaoh, Horus Khasekhemwy, at Abydos. It contains, along with traces of various buildings, a low mound-like structure, sheathed in brick, which would appear to be a representation of the primeval mound on which the sun-god came into being at the moment of creation. It formed the immediate prototype for the first ever example of that most Egyptian of monuments – the pyramid.

THE OLD KINGDOM

The transition from mound to pyramid occurred at Saqqara, where a great stone panelled enclosure (ill. 14) was built for King Djoser, second (?) king of the Third Dynasty. A square, mastaba-like massif lay in its centre, the whole ensemble being the first substantial stone structure erected by man. This massif was soon extended sideways, and then upwards into a six-stepped pyramid, to which two further stages were later added. The monument is known today as the Step Pyramid, and seems to have been intended as a symbolic stairway to heaven, to be trodden by the ascending king, on his way to join the sun-god, Re.

As we have already seen, unlike private individuals, the deceased god-king's fate was to serve amongst his fellow-deities in the entourage of Re. This solar destiny was made concrete in the form of the true pyramid that superseded the step pyramid at the beginning of the Fourth Dynasty. Probably intended as a representation of the sun's descending rays, this new form of royal tomb superstructure was accompanied by a revision of the surrounding enclosure: from then until the demise of the royal pyramid a thousand years later, a mortuary temple lay against the eastern face of the monument, linked to the desert edge by a causeway that led down to the so-called 'valley building' (ill. 16). The enclosure also contained a small 'subsidiary' pyramid, whose exact significance remains unclear. It was certainly not the tomb of a queen, and must presumably have had

10 *(right)* The substructure of the tomb of the Horus Den, showing the approach stairway, burial chamber and surrounding graves for subsidiary burials. The superstructure was completely destroyed. First Dynasty, Umm el-Qaab, Abydos.

11, 12 A range of superstructure-reconstructions have been suggested for tombs like Den's. Günter Dreyer has put forward the idea of a double mound *(above)*, with the possible further embellishment of a covering wood-and-reed shrine. The truly monumental elements of the Umm el-Qaab tombs were supplied by a series of large brick enclosures on the edge of the desert, over a kilometre away *(right)*.

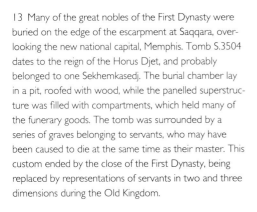

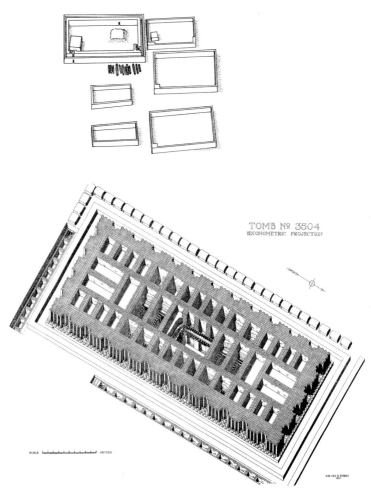

TOMB Nº 3504
AXONOMETRIC PROJECTION

SCALE ⊢⊢⊢⊢⊢⊢⊢⊢⊣ METRES

WALTER B EMERY

13 Many of the great nobles of the First Dynasty were buried on the edge of the escarpment at Saqqara, overlooking the new national capital, Memphis. Tomb S.3504 dates to the reign of the Horus Djet, and probably belonged to one Sekhemkasedj. The burial chamber lay in a pit, roofed with wood, while the panelled superstructure was filled with compartments, which held many of the funerary goods. The tomb was surrounded by a series of graves belonging to servants, who may have been caused to die at the same time as their master. This custom ended by the close of the First Dynasty, being replaced by representations of servants in two and three dimensions during the Old Kingdom.

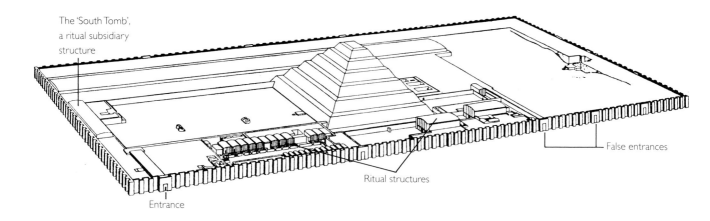

The 'South Tomb', a ritual subsidiary structure

False entrances

Ritual structures

Entrance

14 The enclosure of the Step Pyramid at Saqqara, the first of the pyramids, built by King Djoser, and based upon the Abydene brick enclosures. Its rectangular form was only used during the Third Dynasty, and occasionally in the late Twelfth Dynasty.

some ritual role, perhaps some symbolic relationship with the extent of the pharaoh's rule. However, from the early Fourth Dynasty, most queens had their own pyramids, normally lying close to the funerary complex of their husband.

Pyramids reached their peak of development early in the Fourth Dynasty, when the largest of the genre were erected by Seneferu, Kheops and Khephren, at Dahshur and Giza (ill. 15). Thereafter, the size and quality of stonework declined rapidly. All pyramids had originally been sheathed with high-quality stone, but after this was removed subsequently for re-use, most of these later pyramids fell into shapeless mounds of rubble (ill. 17).

Private tombs of the Fourth Dynasty mainly comprise rectangular mastabas, with subterranean burial chambers approached by deep shafts. These rooms are the first regularly to hold stone sarcophagi, a genus whose first exemplars occur irregularly in royal contexts of the Third Dynasty. They likewise have the first installations designed to contain the embalmed viscera; these are referred to as 'canopic', through a modern confusion between a Graeco-Roman human-headed jar linked with the Greek hero Kanopos and similar vessels later used to hold the internal organs. At the very end of the Fourth Dynasty come the first known set of canopic jars, simple stone vessels with flat lids.

This form of private tomb remains the standard for cemeteries lying on the desert plain down to the Middle Kingdom. The main variation is in the form of the offering place, which develops from a single niche or chamber into

an extensive complex of rooms and passages during the Fifth and Sixth Dynasties. The walls of the apartments were usually extensively decorated with scenes of life in Egypt, serving as part of the magical mechanism intended to provide the departed with all the produce and recreations that he or she had possessed in life, and desired in the hereafter.

Offering places always faced west, towards the abode of the dead, the site of the setting sun. The corpse itself was placed north-south, lying on its left side, facing east, i.e. back into the land of the living, to be able to 'see' the offerings that were made to it. Its ability to see was aided by the eyes that were painted on the side of the coffin late in the Old Kingdom, and the mask that often covered its face. The container(s) for the internal organs were traditionally placed at the foot of the coffin or sarcophagus.

COLOUR PLATES

I The mummy of Tutankhamun stands before King Ay, who performs the act of 'opening the mouth', to reanimate the corpse and allow it to take nourishment. This scene is unique in a royal tomb for naming the officiant: this seems to have been because it was upon this act that Ay owed his accession to the throne. As the one who acted *like* a dutiful son, burying his 'father', Ay became the legitimate heir. Eighteenth Dynasty, KV 62.

II (*overleaf*) The judgment of the dead. The heart of Hunefer is weighed against the feather of the goddess of truth, Maat. While Anubis adjusts the scales for accuracy, the Ibis-headed Thoth records the result. Nearby perches 'The Devourer', who would eat the heart if it proved heavier than 'Truth'. All this happens before Osiris, the patron deity and ruler of the dead. Nineteenth Dynasty, BM EA 9901/3.

15 The pyramids of Giza, from right to left, those of Kheops, Khephren and Mykerinos. In the foreground are the pyramids of two of Mykerinos' wives, and his satellite pyramid. Fourth Dynasty.

From the Archaic Period to the end of the Old Kingdom, mummification developed from simply wrapping the body and placing it in the desert sand to desiccate, to a chemical treatment, consisting primarily of natron-salt, and wrapping in an endeavour to help preserve the flesh (for a detailed explanation of mummification see Chapter 3). By the Fourth Dynasty evisceration was taking place, with the viscera placed in a separate container. Early on, the exterior of the bandages covering the body were covered with plaster, and the features of the body moulded and painted onto this. Around the end of the Old Kingdom, this mode of external adornment was superseded by the development of the helmet-mask, incorporating the features and head covering, that fitted over the head and shoulders of the wrapped mummy.

Typically, the body was enclosed in one or more rectangular wooden coffins, inscribed with the standard offering

COLOUR PLATE

III Part of the right-hand wall of the well-room of the tomb of King Horemheb. On the left is a seated figure of Osiris, his face painted green to represent the shoots of regeneration. He is attended by the embalming-god Anubis and the hawk-headed Harsiese. From the reign of Horemheb onwards, the decoration of the royal tomb was ideally carved as well as painted, ending the earlier practice whereby the burial chamber was decorated after the burial had taken place. Eighteenth Dynasty, KV 57.

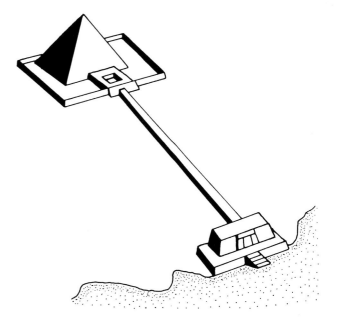

16 By the Fifth Dynasty, a standard pyramid complex had evolved, with a mortuary temple against the east face, and a covered causeway leading down to a valley building on the edge of the desert.

17 Many of the kings of the Fifth Dynasty built their pyramids at Abusir, south of Giza. Here we see the ruined pyramids of Sahure, Niuserre and Neferirkare, viewed from the southwest.

formula, in turn sheltered by a rectangular stone sarcophagus. Some examples followed early tombs and coffins in bearing the 'palace-façade' motif, but the majority are essentially plain. The sarcophagus lay at the western side of a burial chamber, with a canopic chest at, or to the east of, the feet. Such rooms' walls were usually plain: decoration was essentially restricted to the above-ground chapels. Only a few private tombs have their burial chambers adorned with depictions of offerings. The exceptions to this convention are royal burial chambers which, from the reign of Unas (last king of the Fifth Dynasty), were adorned with magical funerary compositions known as the 'Pyramid Texts'.

In locations unsuited to the construction of mastabas, the mortuary chapel, rather than being built into the interior of such monuments, was cut into the face of rocky escarpments. While found around the pyramid sites of the Memphite necropolis, as well as mastabas, the vast majority of rock-cut tombs are in Middle and Upper Egypt. These areas' complement of major tombs greatly increased in the later Old Kingdom, as more and more power passed into the hands of provincial governors. The decoration of such chapels closely followed the broad schemes found in mastabas, their burial chambers also conforming to the usual pattern of being cut into the rock below the chapel.

THE MIDDLE KINGDOM

Egypt's status as a unitary nation collapsed around 2160 BC; shortly afterwards, however, the situation stabilized, two power blocs now ruling the north and the south respectively. This kind of split was to become common in periods of disunity, with the country naturally dividing a little south of modern Cairo. This era is known as the First Intermediate Period and saw the display of considerable independence by the various provincial centres.

Cultural particularism, which continued after the reunion of the country under the Middle Kingdom, can be seen clearly in the funerary record, specifically in modes of coffin decoration. As compared with the largely plain Old Kingdom coffins, those of the following periods display extensive painted decoration, with long magical spells (the Coffin Texts, derived in part from the earlier royal Pyramid Texts) inscribed on the interiors, alongside friezes of all manner of funerary and other items. Around the same time canopic jars, originally equipped with plain covers, acquire the human heads that remained a characteristic feature until the middle of the New Kingdom.

A feature of burials at a considerable number of sites was the presence, usually upon the lid of the coffin, of

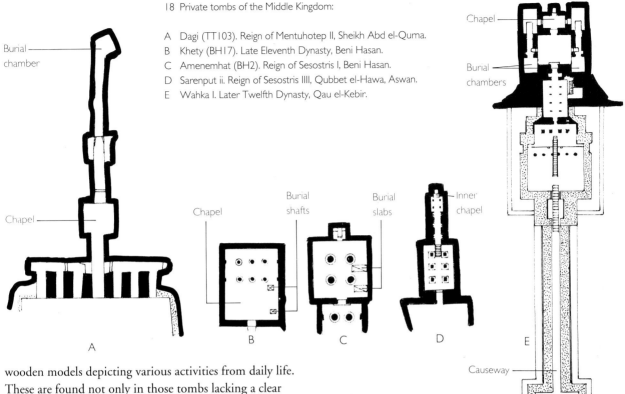

18 Private tombs of the Middle Kingdom:

A Dagi (TT103). Reign of Mentuhotep II, Sheikh Abd el-Quma.
B Khety (BH17). Late Eleventh Dynasty, Beni Hasan.
C Amenemhat (BH2). Reign of Sesostris I, Beni Hasan.
D Sarenput ii. Reign of Sesostris IIII, Qubbet el-Hawa, Aswan.
E Wahka I. Later Twelfth Dynasty, Qau el-Kebir.

wooden models depicting various activities from daily life. These are found not only in those tombs lacking a clear offering place, or possessing only a single crude stela above the burial shaft, but also in those with spacious chapels whose walls bear images of the self-same vignettes.

The Middle Kingdom saw significant innovations in all aspects of the Egyptian funerary complex. Concerning tomb superstructures, the basic private options of mastaba or rock-cut chapel remained constant. In the latter case, at Thebes the superstructures are usually 'T'-shaped, with a wide, but shallow, pillared fore-hall leading to a decorated passage and the principal offering place.

For the first half of the period, large private tombs appeared throughout the country, as well as around the royal cemeteries, where they had been concentrated for much of the Old Kingdom (ills. 19–22). In addition to the basic forms already noted, some rock tombs added further built structures to their exterior. At Qau el-Kebir, for example, some of the largest of all were created. The series of large provincial tombs came to an end towards the end of the Twelfth Dynasty, following a series of governmental reforms carried out by Sesostris III. These concentrated far more power, and hence high-status individuals, at the national capital, at this time Itjtawi, near modern Lisht.

While private tombs broadly conformed to a common pattern, kingly structures showed a number of major variations. The reunifier of the country, Mentuhotep II, and his immediate successors, adopted a scheme comprising a terraced temple, surmounted by a massif or mound, reminiscent of the Second Dynasty precursor of the pyramids (ills. 23-4). The Twelfth Dynasty kings readopted the actual pyramid, but after the middle of the dynasty, construction switched from being in stone, as in the Old Kingdom, to the more economic and easily manipulated mud brick.

Enclosures generally followed later Old Kingdom patterns, with the exception of two examples of the late Twelfth Dynasty, which seem to have been constructed as close copies of the ancient layout seen around the Third Dynasty Step Pyramid. The reigns of these pyramid-owners, Sesostris III and Ammenemes III, are replete with unusual artistic and practical innovations, which can be clearly discerned in their funerary monuments.

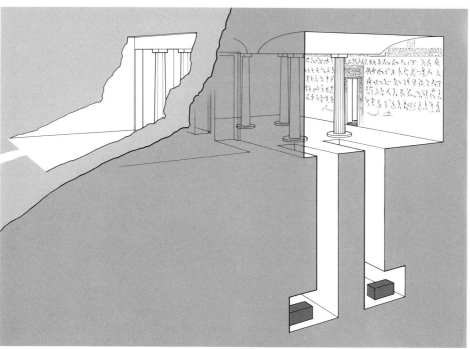

19 The rock-tombs of Beni Hasan, amongst the finest examples of provincial private tombs of the Middle Kingdom.

20 Reconstruction of a nomarch's tomb at Beni Hasan, showing the portico, pillaged burial chamber, statue niche at the rear, and burial shafts. Since these tombs lay on the east bank of the Nile, the 'false door' (not visible here), the gateway to the West, the abode of the dead, lay to the right of the chapel entrance, rather than, as usual, adjacent to the statue niche.

21 The Beni Hasan interiors contain many of the scenes of 'daily life' which typify private tomb-chapels; they probably combine both a desire to recreate their activities in the afterlife, together with more subtle, religious notions. Reign of Sesostris II, tomb of Khnumhotpe (BH 3).

22 The tomb of Sarenput ii is more linear, an unadorned pillared room giving onto a passage, at the end of which the chapel centres on a finely painted stela. Twelfth Dynasty, Qubbet el-Hawa (Aswan).

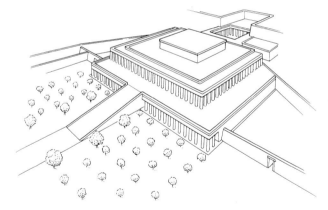

23, 24 (*left* and *below*) Section of the temple-tomb of Mentuhotep II at Deir el-Bahari (Eleventh Dynasty). The central edifice of the temple was originally restored as a pyramid; this now seems unlikely, and it is generally regarded as being a low platform, or perhaps even an earthen mound, topped with a tree.

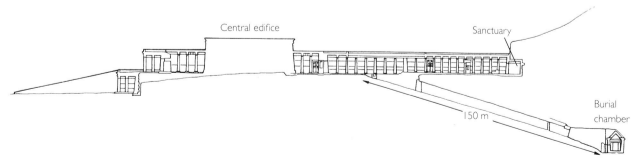

Central edifice   Sanctuary

150 m   Burial chamber

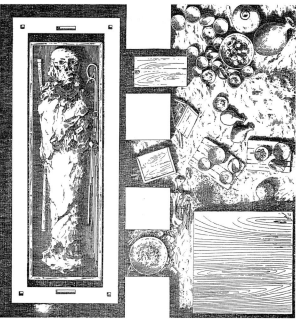

Although many sepulchres continued to use simple shaft-and-chamber, or sloping passage-and-chamber sub-structures, a wide variety of other designs may also be seen below Twelfth Dynasty tomb-chapels. Some are particularly complex, as a result of a heightened awareness of the need to safeguard the sepulchre from grave-robbers. This is particularly evident under the royal pyramids, where the entrance was moved from its customary northern position to a purely random location. The layout of the galleries became increasingly complex, with right-angle turns, dummy passageways and trapdoors in chamber roofs. The peak of such complexity is seen under an unfinished, anonymous, pyramid of the Thirteenth Dynasty, where such a labyrinth gave access to both a real burial chamber and a decoy-dummy. The burial chamber, well concealed, was carved from a single block of stone which included an integral sarcophagus and canopic chest. This room was sealed by a huge roof-block, moved into position by 'hydraulics' filled with sand.

Concerning the mummy itself and its adornments, the most notable development during the Twelfth Dynasty was the introduction of a full-length anthropoid covering around the body. This was essentially a downwards extension of the usual mask, and initially regarded as a substitute for such. Early examples were simply decorated to represent a wrapped mummy, and lay on their sides inside the rectangular inner coffin, as did the corpse itself.

During this period mummification techniques varied considerably, with a number of concurrent methods. While evisceration and desiccation continued to be employed, other methods, not involving evisceration, also prevailed. Some bodies seem to have been injected anally with an oleo-resin, which served to further dissolve some of their internal organs which had already been partially extracted from the rectal and vaginal areas. Some mummies had their

25 The tombs of the family of King Ammenemes II (Dynasty 12) at Dahshur were astounding stone constructions at the bottom of a huge pit. They were designed so that once sealed they became solid masses of masonry. Only by emptying almost the entire pit, and dismantling the stone work, would it be possible to reach the interment.

26 The burial of Princess Khnemet, daughter of Ammenemes II, at Dahshur. Her body lay wrapped up in her coffin, with staves and grave goods sharing the space. In the chamber adjoining her sarcophagus chamber lay an array of boxes, tables and pottery vessels filled with offerings.

27 The *shabti*-figures were often housed in wooden boxes bearing the name and title of the deceased, in this case the God's Wife of Amun, Maetkare (Dynasty 21). Although the boxes contained many *shabtis,* the quality of their production tended to be crude.

brains removed, while others did not; there was indeed very little consistency in embalming traditions.

Many fine examples of plain shrouds and mummy wrappings have been found from Middle Kingdom contexts. The most spectacular find was the intact tomb of Wah at Deir el-Bahari. He was wrapped in about 375 square metres of linen. The body was covered with spiral bandages, padded out with linen, and linen sheets, some bearing his name, were placed over him (ill. 170). Some mummies, such as that of Senebtisi from Lisht, had outer wrappings consisting of alternating shawls (some fringed) and bandages. All this extra padding served not only to display the individual's wealth, but also to better protect the body from any damage.

Since the earliest times, the body and its containers had been accompanied by all kinds of funerary equipment – furniture, vessels and ritual objects. During the Middle Kingdom, mummiform statuettes began to be placed in funerary deposits; these figures, known as *shabtis,* were regarded as substitutes for the dead, to carry out tasks in the hereafter for the deceased. Initially uninscribed, they soon acquired inscribed spells giving their posthumous role.

THE SECOND INTERMEDIATE PERIOD

A major decline in central authority followed the end of the Twelfth Dynasty around 1781 BC, the north of Egypt falling under Palestinian ('Hyksos') rule in about 1650. Few tombs of any significance survive from this epoch, the late Middle Kingdom and the Second Intermediate Period. Almost all the available evidence comes from Thebes, where the most important development is the appearance of anthropoid coffins as independent mortuary containers in the Seventeenth Dynasty. In addition, the coffins change from being merely painted imitations of the mummy within: instead, they are decorated so as to show the dead person as a human-headed bird – the *ba.* Known as *rishi* (arabic for 'feather', descriptive of the *ba* bird's plumage), this class of coffin's introduction also coincided with the definitive move of the mummy from lying on its side to on its back.

The royal tombs of the dynasty took the form of a chapel cut in the rock, surmounted by a small, brick, steeply angled pyramid. Their substructures were apparently simple vertical shafts, leading down to a single passage that gave access to the burial chambers. In at least one case a rock-cut sarcophagus was provided. In others, the coffin was simply placed on the floor of the chamber, covered with a linen pall. Funerary equipment was restricted to a canopic chest, and items actually placed on the mummy.

THE NEW KINGDOM

The Eighteenth Dynasty

The reunification of Egypt was begun by the kings of Thebes around 1560 BC, and completed by King Amosis, who expelled the Hyksos from their strongholds in northern Egypt and founded the Eighteenth Dynasty. From his reign date the first substantial tombs to be identified since the decline of the Middle Kingdom. Amongst them are some of the most famous sepulchres in the world, noted either for their superb decoration, or for their contents. The most spectacular example of the latter is the tomb of Tutankhamun, one of the tiny number of royal tombs found essentially intact (ill. 28).

The fundamental tomb type for the nobility, at first largely based at Thebes, was the rock-cut chapel.

Decoration of the Theban tombs was, in the vast majority of cases, in paint on plaster, contrasting with examples from elsewhere in Egypt, whose adornment was usually in carved and painted relief. The main reason for this was that the quality of much of the rock at Western Thebes was too poor for the execution of fine relief. Good rock *is* present at Thebes, but at a low level: in the early years of the Eighteenth Dynasty tomb-owners preferred an imposing, high altitude to the ability to decorate their chapels with relief.

The basic design of the tomb-chapels imitates the 'T'-shape seen at Thebes in the Eleventh Dynasty – indeed, some may be re-used Middle Kingdom sepulchres. During the Eighteenth Dynasty, the usual decoration of private tomb-chapels consisted of various scenes of daily life, although some may have had a rather more deep, ritual, significance. The burial-elements of the tombs were usually simple shafts and associated chambers. Some chapels have more elaborate substructures approached by sloping pas-

sageways and/or stairways, with additional rooms. Certain burial chambers have their roofs supported by columns. Decoration is rare, a few tombs having extracts from the mortuary compositions that become current during the New Kingdom, ultimately based on the Old and Middle Kingdom Pyramid and Coffin Texts. Only one or two are anomalous by being decoratively akin to their chapels, while another has a distinctive astronomical ceiling.

Most private tombs follow earlier examples in combining the chapel and burial chamber at the same site: the sepulchral room(s) lie underneath the public apartments. However, in some cases the two parts were separated by some considerable distance, to allow the body to lie close to that of the king whom the tomb-owner had served. Nevertheless, the chapel and burial chamber remained a conceptual whole.

Kingly interments lay in a wadi behind the cliffs of Western Thebes, the Wadi (Biban) el-Moluk, or Valley of the Kings. In contrast to private tombs, the separation of

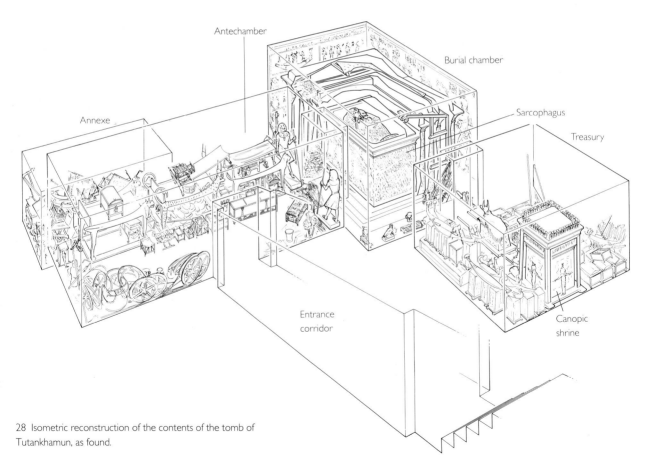

Antechamber

Burial chamber

Annexe

Sarcophagus

Treasury

Entrance corridor

Canopic shrine

28 Isometric reconstruction of the contents of the tomb of Tutankhamun, as found.

29 The walls of the chapels of the New Kingdom to the Ramesside Period were very similar to those of later Middle Kingdom tombs (cf. ill. 20). Here we see a mid-Eighteenth Dynasty version of the common 'fowling in the marshes' motif. From the tomb of Nebamun, probably at Dira Abu'l-Naga, BM EA 37977.

chapel and burial was *de rigueur* for kings from at least the time of Tuthmosis I (*c.* 1503–1491 BC) onwards. Pyramids had been abandoned for royalty at, or soon after, the end of the Seventeenth Dynasty. Regrettably, the first royal tombs of the Eighteenth Dynasty are unidentified. The earliest known sepulchre cut in the Valley of the Kings was that of Tuthmosis I. Its cutting is recorded in the autobiography of the official, Ineni, who proudly boasts of his sole responsibility for the project. The tomb comprised a long passageway, interrupted by stairways, that ultimately led to a rectangular burial chamber. It was later usurped, and extended, by the king's daughter, Hatshepsut. Succeeding kingly tombs were of a rather different form, much more regular and 'L'-shaped, giving access to a pillared, oval or cartouche-form burial chamber, which in turn contained a quartzite sarcophagus. The last-named are a feature of royal tombs for much of the Eighteenth Dynasty. In contrast with the situation during the Old and Middle Kingdoms, when stone sarcophagi were fairly universal, only a few

30 (*below*) Royal tombs of the New Kingdom display a steady developmental sequence: those of the earlier Eighteenth Dynasty have a bent axis; those of the late Eighteenth/early Nineteenth Dynasty had a jogged, but broadly straight, axis, before an entirely linear one appeared late in the Nineteenth Dynasty. Early in the Twentieth Dynasty, the sarcophagus became aligned with the axis, rather than across it.

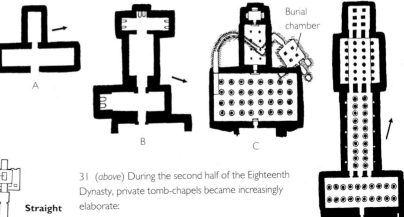

31 (*above*) During the second half of the Eighteenth Dynasty, private tomb-chapels became increasingly elaborate:

A The simple T-shaped tomb of Heqaerneheh (TT 64) Reign of Tuthmosis IV, Sheikh Abd el-Qurna.
B The sepulchre of Khaemhat (TT 57), an elaboration of the previous type. Reign of Amenophis III, Sheikh Abd el-Qurna.
C The tomb of Ramose (TT 55) essentially conforms to the old T-shaped design, but adds a large number of columns to both elements. It also possesses a pillared burial chamber, approached by a sloping passage, rather than the usual vertical shaft. Reign of Amenophis III/IV, Sheikh Abd el-Qurna.
D The chapel of Amenemhat-Surero (TT 48) is the largest of its era, a greatly extended elaboration of the traditional design. Reign of Amenophis III, Khokha.

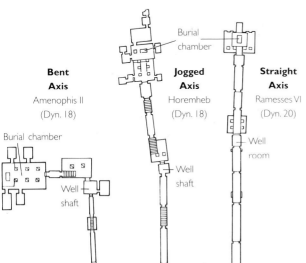

Bent Axis
Amenophis II (Dyn. 18)

Jogged Axis
Horemheb (Dyn. 18)

Straight Axis
Ramesses VI (Dyn. 20)

Burial chamber

Well shaft

Well shaft

Well room

Well shaft

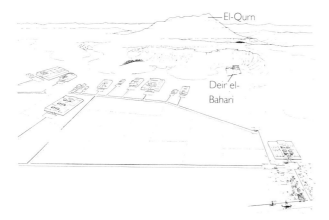

32 Reconstruction of the royal necropolis at Western Thebes, showing the royal mortuary temples that lined the edge of the desert.

33 Under Amenophis III, decoration in relief came back into vogue: amongst the finest reliefs ever to come from Egypt are those in the tomb of Ramose at Thebes (TT 55).

exceptionally well-placed individuals were to possess them during the New Kingdom.

The vast majority of private sarcophagi were made of wood, with their external colouration mirroring that of contemporary coffin designs. Of rectangular form, they take on an increasingly shrine-shaped appearance, later examples being mounted on sledges. Canopic chests usually form sets with the sarcophagi, taking the same basic shape.

The Valley of the Kings may have been chosen for royal tombs by the presence above it of El-Qurn, a pyramidal peak that may have been viewed as substituting for the man-made mountains of the past. With the tombs isolated in their valley, the chapel-element of the funerary complex was perforce separated from the burial. This lay instead on

the edge of the cultivation, the best preserved being the mortuary temple of the female pharaoh Hatshepsut, at Deir el-Bahari. Like most of the royal chapels of the earlier Eighteenth Dynasty, it is built in a series of terraces, and contains the basic elements that are to be seen in all such temples during the New Kingdom: a central chapel dedicated to Amun, with whom the dead monarch became fused, an open altar dedicated to the sun-god, and a further sanctuary in the name of the late ruler's father.

The first few years of the Eighteenth Dynasty saw the continuation of the use of the *rishi* coffin for almost all classes of burial. However, fairly early on, it began to be replaced in private burials by a 'white' design that once again imitated a simple wrapped, masked, mummy. This, in turn, was superseded during Tuthmosis III's reign by a 'black' type, still representing the wrapped mummy, but with the shroud overlaid by black resin. This design was to remain standard until the end of the dynasty for private individuals. Kings, on the other hand, were to retain the old *rishi* coffins for a further six centuries. Both kings and commoners now once again wore masks, inside single or multiple anthropoid coffins.

At the same time, royal sarcophagi assumed a cartouche form that they were largely to retain until the end of the New Kingdom. Under Amenophis II, there was a major expansion in the number of *shabtis* that accompanied the dead. Until then, a single figurine was usually sufficient, but Amenophis' tomb contained a considerable number, with subsequent burials including hundreds by the end of the dynasty (cf. ill. 27). Large quantities of other funerary equipment were deposited in both royal and private tombs during the Eighteenth Dynasty, including furniture and other household items, besides more ritual pieces (ill. 28).

The walls of royal burial chambers were decorated with compositions reflecting the posthumous destiny of the king. As in the Old Kingdom Pyramid Texts, he was visualized as joining the sun, and accompanying the divine entourage through the heavens. Thus, the Book of Amduat ('What is in the Underworld') depicts the episodes of the sun-god's nocturnal journey through the Underworld. This book forms the core of the decoration of royal funerary chambers for much of the New Kingdom, supplemented and supplanted by a number of new compositions along similar lines from the end of the Eighteenth Dynasty: the Books of the Gates, Caverns and the Earth.

34 The tomb-chapels of the short-lived Amarna Period bear wholly anomalous scenes centring on the activities of the royal family, in particular the worship of the sun. This block was found in the tomb of King Akhenaten himself, and shows, from right to left, Akhenaten, Nefertiti, and their elder daughters Meryetaten and Meketaten. It may represent a pattern-piece for those inscribing wall-surfaces. From Amarna tomb TA 26; CM TR 10.11.26.4.

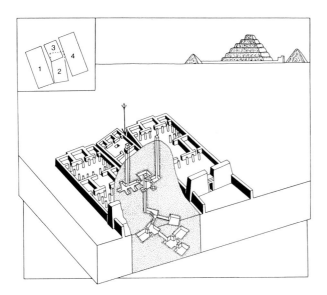

35 Schematic drawing showing the substructure of the tomb of Maya, one of the 'temple-tombs' that are characteristic of the late Eighteenth/early Nineteenth Dynasties at Saqqara. KEY: 1 Tomb of Horemheb; 2 Tomb of Tia and Tia; 3 Tomb-chapel of Ramose; 4 Tomb of Maya.

As the dynasty progressed, some of the highest-status private tomb-chapels, while following the basic 'T'-form, became more elaborate, with columned halls, and decoration that featured a wider selection of subjects than earlier in the period. They also favoured decoration in relief, and are thus located in the lower level, higher quality, rock strata on Sheikh Abd el-Qurna. This shift led to the creation of some of the most exquisite reliefs in Egypt, those of Ramose, vizier under Amenophis III (ill. 33).

A major funerary upheaval occurred during the religious revolution of King Akhenaten, who abolished the Egyptian pantheon in favour of a single sun-god, the Aten, whose theology was essentially unrelated to that of traditional solar deities. Although this religious reform or so-called 'heretic' period was short-lived, lasting only a decade, a number of tombs were constructed reflecting the new beliefs, principally at Akhenaten's capital city, Tell el-Amarna. Rather than the scenes of 'daily life' found in private tombs since Old Kingdom times, private chapel decoration centred on the doings of the royal family, who were now regarded as the sole interface between this world and that of the divine. The chambers of the royal tomb contained no reference to the traditional funerary books which, while solar, had no connection with Atenist theology. Instead, they contained a wholly different scheme,

focussed on the worship of the sun through the royal family and the mourning of the dead. Elsewhere, on the king's sarcophagus, the traditional gods of burial were replaced by the disc of the sun, and the four tutelary goddesses by representations of the king's wife, Nefertiti (ill. 34).

The return to orthodoxy under Akhenaten's son, Tutankhamun, saw a reversion to conventional decoration in private tomb-chapels. At the same time there seems to have been a marked upswing in the construction of non-rock-cut chapels. Most known examples are at Saqqara, the cemetery of the administrative capital Memphis. The chapels no longer followed the old mastaba form, but instead imitated small temples. The larger examples are fronted by pylon-towers (ill. 35), with pillared courtyards leading to the sanctuary in which the dead person's statue stood. Smaller chapels simply consist of the sanctuary, constructed of stone or brick. The substructures of these Saqqara tombs can be extensive, in at least one case with its burial chambers lined with stone and carved with scenes of the owner and his wife worshipping the mortuary gods.

The same post-Atenist, post-Amarna period saw a growth in the employment of stone for the production of anthropoid coffins. The first such pieces had essentially appeared under Amenophis III, in the pre-Atenist period, and closely followed wooden prototypes. The latter lost their black aspect in the post-Atenist epoch, becoming yellow-varnished confections, with various coloured vignettes that rapidly increased in quantity as time passed.

Another development of the end of the Eighteenth Dynasty and the following early years of the Ramesside Period was the disappearance of uniformly human-headed canopic jars in favour of those bearing the heads of the guardian-deities' faunal forms. The liver-jar of Imseti retained its human-headed stopper, but the lungs now had Hapy's baboon, the intestines the falcon of Qebehsenuef, and the stomach a canine Duamutef to close their containers.

Embalming methods of this period became fairly consistent and embodied what one might term 'classic mummification'. The brain was removed, generally via the nose, and the viscera through a narrow incision in the left side of the body, and placed in canopic jars, before burial of the body in dry natron.

The bandaging of the period was carefully executed with each individual extremity, such as fingers and toes, being separately bandaged before being bandaged as a whole element, e.g. as a hand. Prior to bandaging, the extremities were sometimes covered with gold caps in order to protect them. Mummies of this period were heavily wrapped using bandages and entire sheets, as well as linen pads for fleshing out the body. Shrouds were sometimes decorated with selected vignettes and spells from the Book of the Dead, all the better to protect the deceased and help him or her to reach the Afterworld.

The Nineteenth and Twentieth Dynasties

The Ramesside Period saw trends begun in the post-Amarna Period being carried forward. Royal tombs' decoration spread throughout their galleries, rather than being concentrated in the principal chambers, and in private sepulchres, chapel-murals became more ritual in their composition, the daily-life depictions of earlier times largely disappearing.

Private burial chambers contained either stone anthropoid, or 'yellow' wooden coffins, the mummies now being covered with full-length mummy-boards, rather than just masks. Rectangular wooden sarcophagi had the same yellow hue as coffins, although they maintained earlier shapes; the

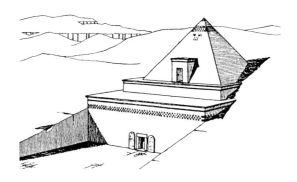

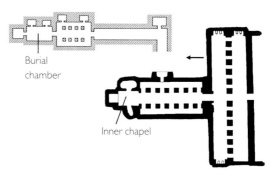

Burial chamber

Inner chapel

36 Reconstruction and plan of the tomb of Nebwenenef (TT 157). The superposing pyramid is typical of the Ramesside Period, as is the elaboration of the chapel plan through the use of pillars. An especially elaborate burial complex is also included. The tomb-owner, a High Priest of Amun, is unusual in also having a free-standing mortuary chapel on the plain below. Reign of Ramesses II, Dira Abu'l-Naga, Thebes.

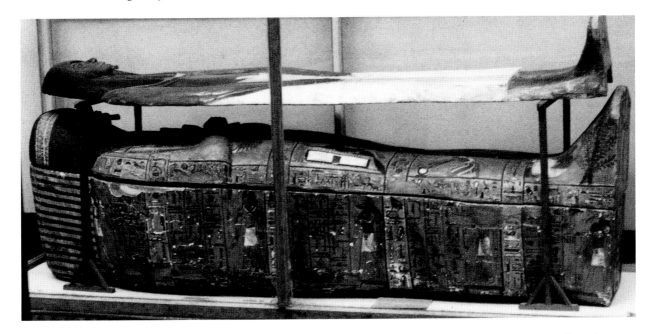

37 The coffin and mummy-board to Sennedjem. For a brief period around the beginning of the Nineteenth Dynasty, some *shabtis*, coffins and mummy-boards showed the deceased in the costume of life. Reign of Sethos I, from TT 1; CM JE 27308.

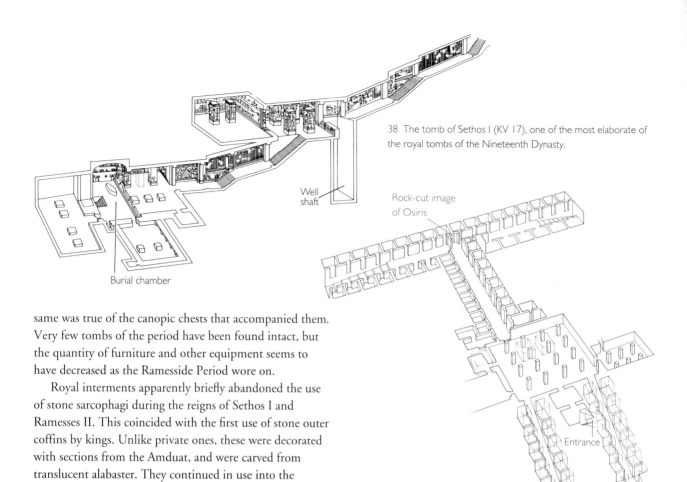

38 The tomb of Sethos I (KV 17), one of the most elaborate of the royal tombs of the Nineteenth Dynasty.

Well shaft

Burial chamber

Rock-cut image of Osiris

Entrance

39 Perhaps the largest subterranean tomb in Egypt, KV 5 was cut to contain the bodies of the sons of Ramesses II; although clearance is as yet incomplete, it has revealed fragments of princes' mummies, stone coffins and canopic jars.

same was true of the canopic chests that accompanied them. Very few tombs of the period have been found intact, but the quantity of furniture and other equipment seems to have decreased as the Ramesside Period wore on.

Royal interments apparently briefly abandoned the use of stone sarcophagi during the reigns of Sethos I and Ramesses II. This coincided with the first use of stone outer coffins by kings. Unlike private ones, these were decorated with sections from the Amduat, and were carved from translucent alabaster. They continued in use into the Twentieth Dynasty, but granite cartouche-form sarcophagi reappeared in the succeeding tomb of Merenptah, and later sepulchres. These are notable in their acquisition of a recumbent figure of the king on the lid, and for their sheer bulk. The royal tombs have a basically straight axis, and are decorated throughout with coloured reliefs of the various Books of the Underworld.

Miniature versions of these sepulchres were provided for members of the royal family, some of whom were granted rectangular stone sarcophagi. Royal wives and offspring thus acquired for the first time fully decorated tombs of their own, in the newly-founded Valley of the Queens. Previously, they had frequently shared their husbands' fathers' tombs or had to be content with more anonymous sepulchres. Certain princes continued to be buried near their fathers in the Valley of the Kings, most spectacularly in the reign of Ramesses II. Ramesses constructed a gigantic labyrinth, now numbered KV 5, with over a hundred chambers, intended to house at least some of his fifty sons. It is the largest subterranean tomb in Egypt, and fits in well with the grandiose nature of the monuments of the reign.

During the Twentieth Dynasty, increasing numbers of tombs of high-status individuals were built away from Thebes, following the relocation of the royal seat to the north-east Delta. Those constructed in the far north tend to be brick-vaulted chambers erected in cuttings within or near temple precincts. Chapels are almost universally lost, but may have been small brick structures erected directly above the burial chambers.

Nineteenth and Twentieth Dynasty mummification continued in much the same style as that of the Eighteenth

40 The right-hand part of the burial chamber of Ramesses VI (KV 9), showing extracts from the Book of Aker, one of the series of 'Books of the Underworld' that adorned Ramesside royal tombs. In the centre are pieces of the massive granite sarcophagus. Mixed with them were fragments of the king's outer coffin.

Dynasty. An interesting phenomenon of this period is that mats surrounded the shrouds of some fairly high-status individuals (including Sennedjem and family). Generally prior to this mats were found only in low-status burials.

Following the end of the dynasty, the royal residence remained in the north, while Thebes became effectively autonomous under a line of generals, who also held the High Priesthood of Amun, and occasionally royal titles as well. This transition to the Third Intermediate Period marked some major changes in burial practices.

THE THIRD INTERMEDIATE PERIOD

The Twenty-first Dynasty

The kings of the Twenty-first Dynasty were buried at Tanis, in stone chambers sunk in the ground just outside the local temple of Amun (ill. 41). Their sarcophagi were usurped older pieces, dating to the New and Middle Kingdoms; coffins at least initially followed the old *rishi* design. The tombs were furnished with a considerable quantity of equipment, including vessels in precious metals, boxes of *shabtis* and canopic jars. Gold masks lay over the faces of the royal mummies, together with a gold-covered mummy-board.

Mummification might well be said to have reached its acme in the Twenty-first Dynasty. This period saw a change in style of what was desired in a mummy. Instead of merely preserving the flesh, the embalmers attempted to make the mummy into a living image of the deceased. Sawdust, lichen, and the like were stuffed under the skin so that the mummy was 're-fleshed', and then painted to look more lifelike. The mummified internal organs were returned to the bodies, thus making canopic jars functionally obsolete, although they were retained by some individuals for their symbolic value. Bandaging was careful, although there was less padding as the body had been plumped up prior to wrapping. Shrouds became *de rigueur*, and most seem to have had a life-size figure of Osiris drawn on them in red ink, sometimes with lines of text commending the deceased to Osiris.

The deletion of canopics from the basic private burial ensemble was accompanied by the abolition of the sarcoph-agus. Most Twenty-first Dynasty interments comprised only a nest of 'yellow' coffins, with their mummy and mummy-board; an occasional accompaniment was a *shabti* box. Almost all known burials of the period come from Thebes, where they seemingly lack any kind of superstructure. A tiny handful of tomb-chapels were usurped by Twenty-first Dynasty individuals, but that seems to be all. Most burials appear to have been made inside older, robbed, tombs. At first mummies were interred singly, or in small groups, but as the dynasty progressed, large numbers of coffins were placed in one location. At one extreme, this led to the stacking of several coffins into a tomb-shaft, piled in total disorder; at the other, galleries were extended to produce a vast catacomb. The best known examples, both at Deir el-Bahari, are the Bab el-Gasus, which housed over one hundred and fifty priests of Amun, some of whom seem to have been reburied there, and TT 320, originally the family tomb of the High Priest Pinudjem II. Early in the Twenty-second Dynasty, the outer parts of TT 320 were used to rebury various New Kingdom kings and other royalty, rescued from robbed tombs in the Valley of the Kings and elsewhere.

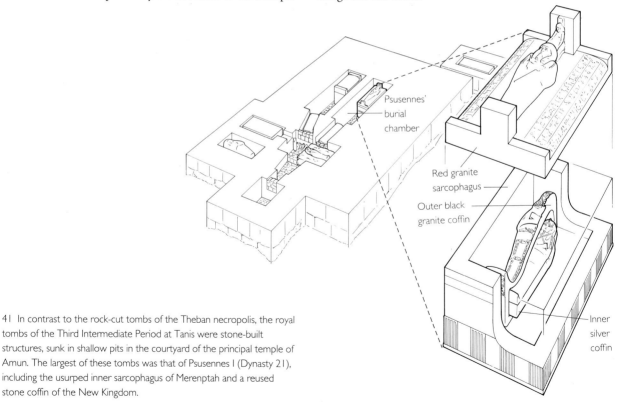

Psusennes' burial chamber

Red granite sarcophagus

Outer black granite coffin

Inner silver coffin

41 In contrast to the rock-cut tombs of the Theban necropolis, the royal tombs of the Third Intermediate Period at Tanis were stone-built structures, sunk in shallow pits in the courtyard of the principal temple of Amun. The largest of these tombs was that of Psusennes I (Dynasty 21), including the usurped inner sarcophagus of Merenptah and a reused stone coffin of the New Kingdom.

The Twenty-second to Twenty-fifth Dynasties

The first reigns of the Twenty-second Dynasty witnessed an effective reunification of the country, the Theban command being brought back within the direct control of the crown. However, before the middle of the dynasty, fissile tendencies had led to the establishment of a distinct Theban monarchy, itself riven at times by civil war. As before, the vast majority of surviving material comes from the south, only the royal tombs at Tanis providing an identifiable northern perspective.

The first part of the dynasty continued late-Twenty-first Dynasty norms. However, under Osorkon I, an important change in burial practices is seen. Mummy-boards were replaced by whole-body cartonnage cases, decorated in a new way, and enclosed in coffins that also show new styles of adornment. The royal tombs at Tanis also show changes in their coffins: the ancient *rishi* adornment finally disappeared in favour of a fresh design incorporating a falcon's head, before reverting to a human one again by the end of the Twenty-second Dynasty.

Sarcophagi continued to be recycled, in one case employing a complete Twelfth Dynasty example, in others merely using previously quarried stone as raw material. The latter were of a round-headed type that became standard until the Ptolemaic Period. Such stone sarcophagi, however, remained for the time being the prerogative of royalty; private individuals began once more to employ wooden ones.

Private Theban interments continued to be in various pit tombs around the necropolis. A number were found within the store-chambers of the mortuary temple of Ramesses II (Dynasty 19), the Ramesseum, including the sepulchres of some persons of considerable status. They comprised small brick chapels, sometimes lined with sandstone reliefs, surmounting tombs of shallow shafts, giving access to chambers little larger than the coffin(s) they contained. Such coffins were accompanied by limited quantities of funerary equipment, principally dummy canopics and wooden funerary figures.

Other burials, under the Eighteenth Dynasty temple at Deir el-Bahari, feature the reintroduction of wooden sarcophagi into the private funerary record, where they remained for the next millennium. A gradual evolution is seen among the coffins and cartonnages within the sarcophagi, decoration becoming increasingly dense over time. Cartonnages began to be superseded during the Twenty-third Dynasty by innermost coffins featuring pedestals under their feet. This was accompanied by the adornment of the mummies with nets of faience beads; small masks of beads or plaster appeared soon afterwards (ill. 44).

At about this time, southern, and then all, of Egypt was taken over by the kings of Kush, based at Napata in the Sudan. Fully Egyptianized, their assumption of power saw few major changes in funerary practices, apart from an increasing vogue for archaism in art. This manifested itself in certain coffins that were clearly meant to be copies of Twelfth Dynasty anthropoids, albeit with give-away pedestals and other features. More strikingly, the Kushite kings readopted the pyramid as their funerary monument. Once reintroduced, pyramids continued to be used in the Sudan until AD 350.

The contents of these tombs followed Egyptian practice, save that, with two exceptions, sarcophagi were replaced by rock-cut benches, on which the coffins lay on a bed. Bed-burials were a traditional Nubian custom that could not be obliterated by the Egyptian veneer of the Kushite kings. The Kushites were ultimately driven out of Egypt by an Assyrian invasion and native control was restored by a line of erstwhile vassals of the invaders, headed by Psammetikhos I of the city of Sais.

THE SAITE PERIOD

The Twenty-sixth Dynasty

The reunification effected by the Twenty-fifth Dynasty kings, and consolidated by those of the Twenty-sixth, led to a resurgence of monumental tombs amongst the highest-status individuals. The small-scale burials seen at Thebes since the early years of the Third Intermediate Period persisted, with continuing developments in the coffins and sarcophagi found in them. However, huge rock-cut tombs and tomb-chapels occurred once again both there and in northern cemeteries. A further revival was in the use of canopic jars to actually contain the internal organs, coupled with a wholesale revision of their texts. The former change was short-lived however, as the practice of enclosing the wrapped viscera in the body-wrappings, with dummy

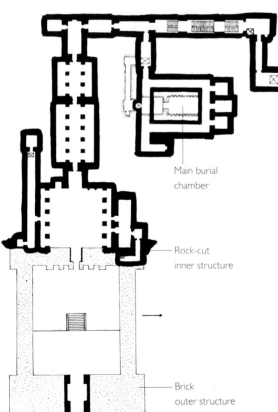

Main burial
chamber

Rock-cut
inner structure

Brick
outer structure

42 The brick pylon-gateway to the tomb of Montjuemhat (TT 34) on the Asasif at Thebes. A series of courts, decorated with scenes derived from earlier private tomb-decorations, give access to deep sepulchral chambers. Early Twenty-sixth Dynasty.

43 The largest of the Twenty-sixth Dynasty tombs is that of Petamenopet (TT 33). The inner chambers are decorated in the manner of royal tombs in the Valley of the Kings, with the burial chamber itself imitating a royal sarcophagus. Saite Period, Asasif.

canopics, was reverted to soon thereafter. It was clearly part of the age's archaism, already noted, and to be seen in other aspects of the funerary ensemble as well.

At Thebes during the Twenty-sixth Dynasty, specifically on the Asasif, pylon entrances gave access to a series of elaborately decorated courts and vestibules, and then burial passages that sometimes stretched over 100 metres into the bed-rock. Amongst these sepulchres were what were, until the clearance of KV 5, the largest known rock-cut tombs in Egypt, not excluding those of the Valley of the Kings.

Similar tombs were also constructed at Saqqara, but distinctive of the Memphite area are tombs built at the bottom of wide, deep, open shafts in the bed-rock. The kernel of the tomb was a built burial chamber, in the form of contemporary wooden sarcophagi, complete with corner posts. Inside this lay a simple rectangular stone sarcophagus, flanked by niches intended to contain canopic jars. The sarcophagus lid was lowered into place by props resting on sand-filled cavities; when released from below, the escaping sand allowed the lid to come down on the trough (ills. 45, 47). The latter contained a large stone anthropoid coffin, which in turn held the mummy, with or without an inner wooden case. The mummy was usually equipped with a bead net, and a very small gilt face-piece, wholly unlike the masks of earlier times.

These shaft tombs were designed to be entirely filled with sand after the burial, temporarily closed holes in the chamber roof being opened after the funeral to allow sand in from the main shaft to engulf the sarcophagus. Access to the burial thus became impossible, unless almost every grain of sand had been removed from the tomb first – running into thousands of cubic metres. Certain tombs added a series of concentric sand-filled shafts around the perimeter of the sepulchre. Nevertheless, robbers reached a number of such burials, but probably during post-pharaonic times; a number have, however, survived intact until the modern era.

Large stone sarcophagi and coffins are also found in more conventional tombs, which sometimes took the form of a whole series of underground chambers, each intended for one or more members of the family, or other owning group. The revived stone sarcophagi frequently found in tombs of this type adopted a round-headed form, often with the plan tapering towards the foot. Lids were heavy, with bevelled corners, and elaborate decoration, comprising elements from the funerary 'books' and deity-figures.

While the Twenty-third Dynasty types of wooden coffins continued to evolve, massive stone anthropoid cases also appeared. Some early ones are reminiscent of the New

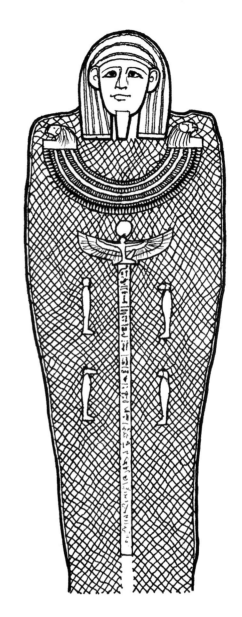

44 The gold mask and bead net that adorned Hekaemsaf's mummy. This kind of adornment was typical of the Twenty-sixth Dynasty. CM JE 35923 = CG 53668.

45 Roof of the burial chamber of Hekaemsaf, built in the shape of a contemporary wooden sarcophagus, with corner-posts, at the bottom of a deep shaft. The latter was filled with sand after the burial. Twenty-sixth Dynasty, Saqqara.

46 The mortuary chapels of the God's Wives of Amun at Medinet Habu, Thebes. These stone-built chapels are especially notable for being located within the temple compound. Twenty-sixth Dynasty. Burial chambers lay directly below their floors.

47 Cross-section of a typical Saite burial chamber at Saqqara:

(left) With main shaft filled with sand, but kept out of other parts of the tomb by pottery seals ('p' in diagram).

(right) With the seals broken, the props holding the sarcophagus lid open slide down in their shafts, and sand flows down, engulfing the closed sarcophagus, and filling the various passages. With the access shaft (on the left) filled, access is impossible without emptying both shafts completely.

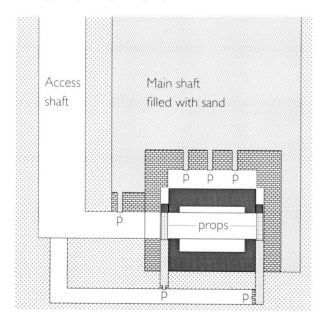

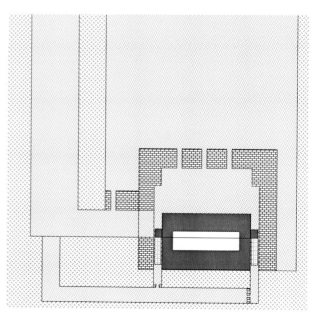

Kingdom in their proportions, but, like some wooden outer coffins, they rapidly became very wide in proportion to their length. Their influence is also seen on certain sarcophagi, which acquired three-dimensional faces on their lids, although otherwise retaining a normal sarcophagus design.

Although the burials of certain queens and princes have been found, they are of basically private type. No kingly tombs have survived from the royal necropolis of Sais, although near-contemporary descriptions indicate that they had been stone-built chapels, surmounting a burial chamber. They may have been very similar to the sepulchres of the God's Wives of Amun at Medinet Habu, which comprised decorated sanctuaries built outside the mortuary temple of Ramesses III (Dynasty 20), under the pavements of which lay a chamber, just large enough to hold the priestess' stone sarcophagi.

Mummification during this period was not as elaborate as in the preceding era. Less attention was paid to both the actual desiccation and the cosmetic aspects of the corpse; often the brain was not removed. The visceral contents moved back out of the body, and were often placed between or on the legs of the individual. Canopic jars often accompanied such burials, even though their use was once again more symbolic than practical.

THE LATE AND PTOLEMAIC PERIODS

The Twenty-sixth Dynasty was brought to an end by the invasion of the Persian king, Kambyses, in 525 BC. For the next century and a quarter, the kings of Persia were recognized as, and sometimes represented as, pharaohs. A number of burials of individuals who spanned the transition between the two regimes conform to Saite norms, but interments clearly datable to the Persian Twenty-seventh Dynasty are extremely rare.

Certainly, the production of stone coffins seems to have ended, and that of stone sarcophagi at the very least heavily curtailed. It is not until native rule was resumed under the Twenty-ninth and Thirtieth Dynasties that we can once again confidently identify burials. Royal tombs conformed to the type seen long before at Tanis, the sarcophagus of Nepherites I (Dynasty 29) at Mendes having been housed in a limestone chamber, its walls adorned with funerary

books. Private burials of various forms, including rock-cut chambers and pits covered with brick vaulting, have been found at various sites.

Stone funerary containers reappeared, with stone used for inner coffins alongside wood. The proportions of coffins from these dynasties are distinctive, and continued into the succeeding epoch: the face sinks down into the chest, with the shoulders appearing unnaturally highly placed. Stone sarcophagi continued Saite forms, with some high-status examples closely following New Kingdom prototypes in their decoration.

After a fairly brief renewal of Persian dominion, Egypt became part of the empire of Alexander the Great in 332 BC, and then an independent state under the rule of the

48 In Ptolemaic times, individuals could be buried in simple pits scooped in the soil, into which were inserted rough limestone sarcophagi, with anthropoid inner cuttings. The mummy lay with a simple stucco coating inside, without any coffin or other ornament. From Beni Hasan; present location unknown.

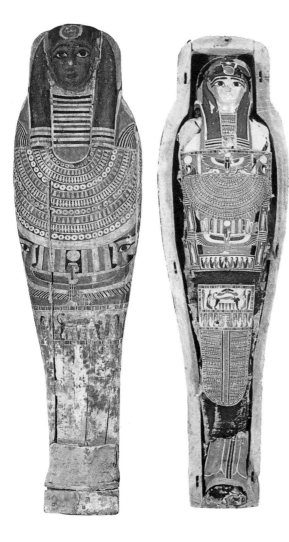

49 A typical coffin and mummy of late Ptolemaic date. The mummy is equipped with a gilded-faced mask, and painted cartonnage panels over the body and feet. This body possessed a false hand, shown in ill. 136. Provenance unknown; Oriental Museum, Durham.

sistent erosion of the Egyptian 'essence' of coffins and mummy-furniture. An increasing Hellenistic input is seen in various manifestations of Egyptian art, including that of death. The Hellenic conquerors, keeping to the spirit of Alexander's rule, adopted functionally Egyptian items without a true understanding of their use or fundamental symbolic meaning.

Ptolemaic tombs, at least from the first part of the period, continued Saite/Late practices, particularly as regards the provision for multiple burials. Nearly all lack stone sarcophagi, which effectively disappeared during the period. In addition, some tombs are reminiscent of the New Kingdom tradition of having the outside of the super-structure in the form of a miniature contemporary temple, for example the tomb of Petosiris. Its inner room is deco-rated after the manner of a Ramesside royal tomb; burial chambers lead off a shaft in the centre of the room. The outer part is adorned with daily life scenes in an unusual composite Egyptian/Greek style. Other tombs at the same site, Tuna el-Gebel, are more akin to houses, with doors, windows, and drain-spouts carved onto the exterior.

Fully Greek styles are found in the wholly Hellenized cities that were founded in Egypt, in particular, the new capital, Alexandria. There, tombs began to be built which combined debased Egyptian motifs with Classical art. This blurring of the divide between indigenous tradition and the alien culture of the Hellenistic overlords becomes particularly clear in the period that followed Egypt's annex-ation by the Roman Emperor, Augustus, after his victory over Mark Antony and the last of the Ptolemies, Kleopatra VII, in 30 BC.

THE ROMAN PERIOD

In Roman times, although some individuals continued to be buried in time-honoured ways, a fundamental change in practice may be observed in the heavily Hellenized Fayoum region. There, rather than being buried, mummies remained for considerable periods among the living. Very

Macedonian king, Ptolemy I. Basic funerary practices con-tinued much as before, but with an increasing debasement of motifs on coffins. The techniques used for the preserva-tion of the body were greatly simplified. Preparations were largely restricted to emptying the body cavities and pouring molten resin in them, before elaborately wrapping the corpse. Ill-prepared mummies returned to wearing full helmet-masks, made of cartonnage, with the addition of brightly painted segmented body-coverings of the same material. One aspect of the funerary ensemble which rapidly died out was the inclusion of (empty) canopic jars, for a time replaced by small, tall, painted canopic chests.

As this period of Greek rule, the Ptolemaic Period, con-tinued, the majority of high-status positions in society came to be held by non-Egyptians. There was, therefore, a con-

50 These Graeco-Roman tomb-chapels, at Tuna el-Gebel, designed to fulfil an Egyptian ritual function, exemplify the merging of Greek and Egyptian artistic traditions. The chapels resemble either temples or contemporary houses, and the decoration, although Egyptian in theme, is a mixture of the two cultures in execution.

elaborate outer wrappings and/or cartonnage casings had taken the place of coffins, superb painted portrait panels sometimes being placed over the face. Thus adorned, the mummies appear to have remained in the family home, perhaps housed in some kind of wooden sarcophagus or shrine, and/or in a public repository, where homage could be offered to them. Many show signs of rough handling over a considerable time. Periodically, groups of bodies would be removed to the cemetery, where they would be placed in mass burial pits, piled one on top of the other. This presumably reflected the need to make way for more recent dead.

Mummification techniques reached an all-time low during the Roman Period. Mummies were prepared by pouring molten resin over uneviscerated corpses, although in some instances, visceral removal was continued. The emphasis was placed on the wrappings, rather than the body. Mummy-wrappings were particularly complicated and, at their best, geometrical in their patterning.

A feature unique to portrait-panel mummies dating from about AD 140 to AD 250 is their apparent location, prior to burial in group graves. After the mummy was prepared it was placed in the house for an undetermined period of time, and brought out for religious and family festivals. Wooden cupboards with stable, or Dutch, doors have been found, and it is believed that the mummies would have been stored upright in them, so that the upper door could be opened, offerings made and advice solicited. According to Flinders Petrie, these mummies stood around a courtyard, playing the part of *imagines*, Roman ancestral

51 Encaustic mummy portrait of a woman, c. AD 98-117. From Hawara; BM EA 74712.

this practice had already occurred in the Late Period, and gave rise to keeping in-house mummies in the Graeco-Roman Period. Graeco-Roman mummies show evidence of being transported from one place to another, not only in the form of scuff marks on the portrait mummies, but also, more relevantly, of mummy labels, or tickets. These were wooden dockets attached to the mummy. Written in Greek or Demotic, a colloquial form of Greek, and later in Coptic, they bore the name, and sometimes the age, of the deceased. Often the death date as well as the burial date were recorded, and occasionally further identification as in daughter/son of whomever, or a brief message. The label on the mummy ensured that its identity was not lost when it was transported from the house to the graveyard, or even between cemeteries.

In general, cemeteries of this period show a move towards group burials in one tomb. Owing to the crowded conditions of sepulchres, the orientation of the body was very varied and depended more on space than on beliefs. Frequently several mummies were thrust not just into one tomb, but into one coffin. Occasionally, in these instances, the lid had to be forced down, damaging heads or feet.

In other areas, more conventional burials continued, but with Egyptian portraiture almost entirely superseded by that derived from Classical traditions. Coffins were largely discarded in favour of wooden sarcophagi and direct adornment of the wrapped mummy. This often featured a plaster portrait bust or mask of purest Classical type, yet juxtaposed with cartonnage casings of the foot and head which bore two-dimensional paintings of the time-honoured vignettes of burial. Thus, poor but recognizable depictions of Anubis, Osiris and the tutelary goddesses continued to appear in traditional style on the exteriors of mummies until the end of paganism.

Such images are also to be seen forced into a Classical straitjacket on the walls of Alexandrine tombs and catacombs. It is through this assimilation into Classical contexts that the continued survival of some of the ancient deities was assured. The iconography of Isis and her child, Horus, was transmogrified into that of the Madonna and Child, with the death and resurrection of Osiris providing a prototype for the Passion of Christ. And through various iconographic loops, Anubis emerged as Saint Christopher, through a late role as carrier of the moon, which ultimately became the young Christ.

portraits, in Roman houses in Egypt. Petrie noted that the foot and shin portions of the mummies had scribbles and knocks on them of the sort that might be acquired by being left in a courtyard which was used by adults and children alike, and many of them showed weakness in the bandaging around the ankles that could have been caused by years of being propped upright. Sometimes they were kept, standing upright, in above-ground visitable mausolea, such as might have existed at the cemetery of Hawara in the Fayoum. It is interesting to note that Herodotus, writing in the fifth century BC, mentions that models of mummies in their coffins were paraded through the banqueting hall towards the end of an evening of revelry and song so that people would be reminded of their own mortality. Its bearers would say, 'Look upon this body as you drink and enjoy yourself; for you will be just like it when you die.' Perhaps

IV The Step Pyramid at Saqqara, from the south-west. The pyramid is the oldest large stone building in the world. It was begun as a low, square massif, the outline of which is visible where the lower step has been broken away. Third Dynasty, reign of Djoser.

V (*overleaf*) The pyramids of Giza, from the south-east; to the left is the Third Pyramid, of Mykerinos, with the Second and Great Pyramids, of Khephren and Kheops, to the right. Kheops' pyramid is accompanied by the small pyramids of three of his wives. The area in front of the pyramids is occupied by private mastaba and rock-cut tombs. Fourth Dynasty.

VI East wall of the burial chamber of King Unas, showing the Pyramid Texts, inscribed for the first time inside this pyramid. They comprise a long series of spells designed to smooth the dead king's transition into the Hereafter. They include many elements that clearly date back to much earlier times, and contain many of the most basic statements of Egyptian mythology. End of the Fifth Dynasty, Saqqara.

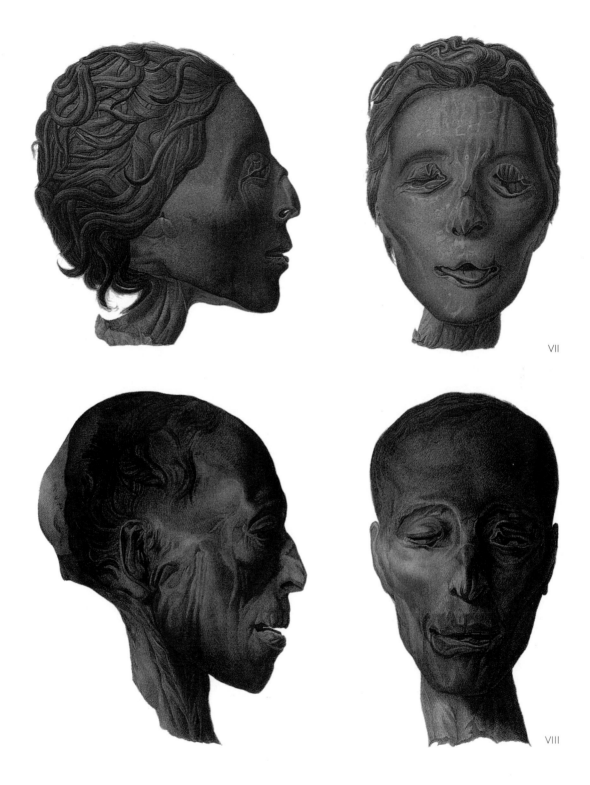

VII

VIII

VII, VIII Female and male mummies' heads, drawn by Napoleon's expedition.

IX

IX An early nineteenth-century view of the Kings' Valley at Thebes, showing the pyramidal peak, El-Qurn, that dominates the wadi. The half-buried tomb in the foreground is probably that of Ramesses VI (KV 9).

X Semi-perspective elevation and plan of the tomb of Sethos I (KV 17), as published by Belzoni. The calcite coffin is shown as found, athwart a mysterious corridor that extends below the burial chamber, possibly to the water table.

XI (*overleaf*) End wall of the burial chamber of Tutankhamun (KV 62) showing the First Division of the Book of Amduat ('What is in the Underworld'), with the barque of Khepri, its divine escorts and, below, eight baboons. The small cutting in the wall at the centre of the picture formerly housed one of the four 'magic bricks' that extended their protection to each side of the chamber. In the fore-ground, the king's gilded wooden outer coffin lies within the quartzite sarcophagus.

X

Chapter 2   The Resurrection of the Mummies

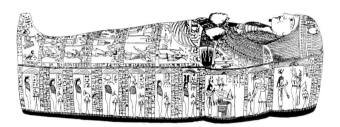

THE TOMB-ROBBERS OF ANCIENT EGYPT

When mummies were entombed in their coffins, sarcophagi and sepulchral chambers, it was intended that they should lie there for eternity. Fate, however, decreed otherwise, and by the present day only a tiny handful of bodies remain in their tombs, and even fewer are still as they were when interred.

This process of desecration began in ancient times, in some cases before the mourners had returned home: there are a considerable number of tombs in which the burial was despoiled by the undertakers themselves. Certain burial chambers have been found sealed, with no sign of penetration, yet with the funerary equipment smashed, and the denuded corpses lying in pieces around the chambers. In other cases, mummies have been found with their outer wrappings intact, but the inner ones disordered and some of their ornaments stolen: clearly they were robbed while they still lay in the embalmers' workshop.

> The mummies of Hent-towy, daughter of Iset-em-kheb, and of Nesit-Iset lay just as they had been placed in the grave, and we had every reason to believe that they were still intact. The tapes, the outer sheet, and the Osiris sheet were neatly and carefully folded on the bodies and stitched up the back. Everything was in perfect order at first, and then gradually, as we unwrapped them, we began to find more and more confusion among the bandages over the chest. The truth dawned on us when we found at last, on both mummies casts in the resin of the metal pectoral hawks, but the pectoral hawks themselves gone. Then we noticed that the heart scarabs in both cases had been taken out and then put back carelessly; that around the torn bandages on the chest there were the marks of fingers sticky with resin on layers of linen that should have been clean; and finally, that the left hand of Nesit-Iset had been laid bare in a search for finger rings.
>
> There can be little question as to what had happened here. The mummies had been rifled before they were even completely wrapped, and that must have taken place in the undertakers' own establishments. Fortunately for us, pieces of metal jewelry only were being sought, and papyri or heart scarabs were useless to the thieves. But what a picture do we get for the moralists! (Winlock 1942: 113–14)

Most tombs, however, were the victims of tomb-robbers who entered the sepulchre some time after the burial. In some cases this occurred within a few years; in others, not until modern times. It would seem that ancient robberies peaked during periods in which central authority

52 (*above*) The type YIIa coffin, mummy, and cover of Nesamun were presented to the Leeds Philosophical and Literary Society in 1827, and the publication of their examination is one of the earliest notable examples of such a work. The burial, originally found by Passalacqua, is one of the few datable to the late Ramesside Period. Probably from Deir el-Bahari; Leeds, City Museum D.426.1960.

53 The village of Sheikh Abd el-Qurna in the Theban hills. The settlement is built upon and among the tomb-chapels of the nobles of the New Kingdom, and for generations the inhabitants have been responsible for the robbery of ancient sepulchres here and elsewhere in the necropolis.

was weakened, and thus when necropolis guards were less well organized or honest. Certainly some of our best records of tomb-robbers and their trials come from the late Twentieth Dynasty, against a background of economic trouble and incipient national disunity. On the other hand, some robberies occurred in times of apparent stability. For example, in the Eighteenth Dynasty, graffiti in the tomb of Tuthmosis IV record its restoration, following robbery, in the reign of King Horemheb. The Twentieth Dynasty records, however, throw the period's situation into sharp relief. A series of papryi – in particular Ambras, Leopold II-Amherst, Harris A, and Mayer A and B – provide the basis for a reconstruction of events.

Following various rumours, the mayors of Eastern and Western Thebes (Paser and Paweraa, respectively) submitted separate reports to the vizier Khaemwaset, which led to the appointment of a commission to inspect parts of the Theban necropolis. Ten royal tombs in the el-Tarif/Dira

Abu'l-Naga/Deir el-Bahari area were examined, of which two showed signs of attempted penetration, and one – that of Sobkemsaf I of the Seventeenth Dynasty – had been robbed and the royal mummies burnt. Furthermore, the sepulchres of two priestesses of Amun and many lesser persons had also been thoroughly rifled.

Some forty-five people were arrested, tortured by various means, especially bastinado, and after confessing, brought to trial. The confession of the robbers of the pharaoh's tomb makes interesting reading:

We found the pyramid of King Sobkemsaf I, this being unlike the pyramids and tombs of the nobles that we were used to robbing. We took our copper tools and forced a way into the pyramid of this king through its innermost part. We found the substructure, and we took our lighted candles in our hands and went down. Then we broke through the blocking that we found at the entrance to his crypt, and found this god lying at the back of his burial place. And we found the burial-place of Queen Nubkhaes, his wife, situated beside him, it being protected and guarded by plaster and enclosed by a stone blocking. This we also broke through, and found her resting there in the same way.

We opened their sarcophagi and their coffins in which they were, and found the noble mummy of this king equipped with a *khepesh*-sword; many amulets and jewels were upon his neck, and his mask of gold was upon him. The noble mummy of the king was completely bedecked with gold, and his coffins were adorned with gold and silver inside and out and inlaid with all kinds of precious stones....

The survival of this record (in Papyrus Leopold II-Amherst), and the other trial records of the era, provides much information concerning legal proceedings, as well as the punishment for violating a royal tomb: impalement. The investigation seems to have been complicated by a feud between Paser and Paweraa: when the number of robberies appeared to be less than alleged by Paser, he was tried and convicted of malicious exaggeration.

Making an example of the robbers did not stem the tide of robbery. After only a year there are records of thefts from the Valley of the Queens, notably that of Queen Iset, wife of Ramesses III (Dynasty 20), whose burial was wrecked. Similar incidents down to the reign of Ramesses X are recorded, and also a trial under Ramesses XI, when Ramesses VI's tomb was found robbed.

A further confession of one of the thieves, recorded in the Papyrus Amherst, gives more information about the robbery of the tomb of Sobkemsaf I:

Now in Year 13 of Pharaoh my lord...I teamed up with the carpenter Sethnakhte [and others to rob the tombs in the necropolis] and we found the tomb of the king and the burial-place of the royal wife Nubkhaes, protected and sealed, but we forced it open...We opened their sarcophagi and their coffins... we found...many amulets and ornaments of gold at his neck, and his gold mask upon him...We also found the royal wife and collected all that we found on her as well. [We took] objects of gold, silver, and bronze, and divided them amongst us.

55 A nineteenth-century view of the burial chamber of Ramesses VII (KV 1), showing the curious deep lid that covered the rock-cut sarcophagus cavity. The tomb has stood open since ancient times, and had long been robbed of its mummy, through the breach in the foot of the sarcophagus lid.

54 The fate of the convicted tomb robber: the hieroglyphic determinative for the word 'to impale'.

In Papyrus Mayer A there is a description of the arrest and trial of the thieves:

There was brought the scribe of the army Ankhefenamun, son of Ptahemhab. He was examined by beating with the stick and fetters were placed upon his feet and hands, an oath was administered to him, on pain of mutilation, not to speak falsehood!

Certainly the mutilation that was threatened at the time – the five (or so) cuts which deprived the victim of nose, ears, and other major facial features – was a considerable deterrent to lying, and only used in extremely serious circumstances, such as violating the dead god-kings.

Despite all efforts to staunch the flow of tomb-robbing, the increasing number of robberies created a need for constant restoration of the burials that were still worth saving. By the Twenty-first Dynasty, the pressure was such that maintenance of individual tombs was increasingly abandoned in favour of cache burials where groups of bodies could be brought together in remote locations for protection. This was accompanied by the salvage of re-usable

items of funerary equipment – particularly if gilded – for recycling. The most significant caches were those of royal mummies, and the most important of these, now known as TT 320, near Deir el-Bahari, took its final form in the reign of Shoshenq I (Dynasty 22; see below pp. 77-9).

Following the final collapse of Egyptian civilization and religion in the face of the forces of Christianity and Islam, the old cities of the dead lost what sanctity and physical protection they still retained, many tombs falling victim to the monotheistic iconoclasts and treasure-seekers. Medieval Arabic accounts tell, often with wondrous embellishments, of ventures into the pyramids and tombs to recover their riches. However, by the sixteenth century the first real signs of European interest in ancient Egypt were becoming apparent, beginning the process that would culminate in the scientific resurrection of its monuments in the nineteenth and twentieth centuries.

MUMMIES IN THE OCCIDENT

From Herodotus to Napoleon

Speak! for thou long enough has acted dummy,
Thou hast a tongue – come – let us hear its tune;
thou'rt standing on thy legs, above ground, mummy,
Revisiting the glimpses of the moon,
Not like thin ghosts, or disembodied creatures,
But with thy bones, and flesh, and limbs and features.
From Mr Campbell, 'Address to the Mummy',
18 February 1835, in *London Morning Chronicle*

Mummies have excited considerable interest among all foreign visitors to Egypt. The earliest writings referring to them come from the fifth-century BC Ionian Greek historian, Herodotus, followed by the account of Diodorus Siculus in the first century BC. These ancient writers, who travelled to Egypt when a rudimentary form of mummification was still practised, provide fairly detailed accounts, describing mummies not as curios, but rather as manifestations of an ancient culture. It is later that they started to acquire a significance for the West that was far removed from their original purpose of buried bodies. The earliest Western interest, however, was not in the antiquity of the mummies, but their alleged medicinal properties. A confusion between

the black resins used in their preparation and *mum/mumia*, a Persian/Arabic word for bitumen, or mineral pitch, held to have therapeutic powers, led to ground mummy becoming a staple of apothecaries' shops in Europe during the sixteenth and seventeenth centuries.

Abd el-Latif, a twelfth-century Arab writer, records how *mum/mumia*, or mineral pitch, flows down from the 'mummy mountain' located in Persia, mixes with water and gives off an odour that is considered beneficial when inhaled, and is even more beneficial for certain diseases when ingested. This belief persisted well into the nineteenth century: the King of Persia sent Queen Victoria tiny quantities of treasured *mum* from the mummy mountain in Persia.

The earliest medieval record of mummy being used as medicine dates to the twelfth-century Arab-Jewish physician, El-Magar, a resident of Alexandria. Thereafter, its use as medicine was rapidly adopted by the West, and the word 'mumie' or 'mumia' starts appearing in Latin texts. Mummy had also featured prominently in ancient medical treatises, both oriental and occidental, with Dioscorides (AD 40–90), the Greek physician and pharmacologist, listing it for a few ailments, and Avicenna (AD 980–1037), the famous Persian physician and scientist, recommending it for even more, including abscesses, eruptions, fractures, concussions, paralysis, hemicrania, epilepsy, vertigo, spitting of blood from the lungs, throats, coughs, nausea, ulcers, poisons, and disorders of the liver and spleen. It was often taken mixed with herbs, such as marjoram, thyme, elder, and others. In addition to its use as a cure for these varied ailments, some authors also recommended it as bait to catch fish! Pierre Pomet, in a 1694 treatise on medicine, recommended that you choose your mummy with care; it should be black without bones or dust, with a good smell – that of something burnt, not of pitch or resin.

Several authors mention mummy in their medical and apothecarial works, such as Nicolas Lemery in his *Universal Treatise on Simple Medicine*, written in 1714. Francis Bacon (1561–1626), also a firm believer in the medicinal properties of mummies, wrote that 'mummy hath great force in staunching blood'.

Mummy became such an important drug in Europe that in 1549, to take one example, André Thevet, chaplain to Catherine de Medici, made forays to Saqqara in search of mummies for her medicine. Francis I of France never went anywhere without a packet of it mixed with pulverized rhubarb in case he fell or was injured. In 1564 the King of Navarre's physician, Guy de la Fontaine, visited Alexandria in quest of mummies for medicine. Alexandria was the main centre for all trade with Egypt, most notably that of mummies. De la Fontaine wished to make his purchase in bulk so he went to a major trader. The quantity and quality – especially the smell – made him suspicious, and he questioned the trader closely. It was revealed that the mummies were fakes. None was more than four years old, and all were the bodies of criminals and unclaimed people from Alexandria who had had pitch applied to them and had been buried in a group pit for a few years.

Apparently, due to the extreme demand in Europe, from about 1200 onward such fakes had been manufactured in Alexandria, primarily by Jews who were the only people allowed to indulge in this exercise. In the eighteenth century a severe tax was levied to deter the practice, as well as trafficking in dead bodies of any era.

Mummies were so popular in Europe in the Middle Ages and the Renaissance that they are frequently referred to in literature. Shakespeare's apothecary in *Romeo and Juliet* stocks mummy, and in *The Merry Wives of Windsor* Falstaff compares a drowned corpse to 'a mountain of mummy' (Act III, Scene 5). In *Othello* mummy was part of the magic potion that impregnated the fateful handkerchief:

> *The worms were hallow'd that did breed the silk,*
> *And it was dy'd in mummy which the skilful*
> *Conserv'd of maidens' hearts. (Act III, Scene 4)*

Several other authors also refer to mummy in their poems and plays: John Webster in *The Duchess of Malfi*, 1623 (Act IV, Scene 2), and again twice in *The White Devil*, 1612: once in Act II, Scene 1, and also in the previous act:

> *Your followers*
> *Have swallowed you like mummia, and being sick*
> *With such unnatural and horrid physic*
> *Vomit you up i' th' kennel. (Act I, Scene 2)*

Beaumont and Fletcher in *The Sea Voyage*, c. 1610 (Act III, Scene 1) invoke mummy, as does Falconer in *The Demagogue*, 1764, and J. Hale in his poems (c. 1646). Shirley the dramatist writes:

> *That I might tear their flesh in mammocks, raise*
> *My losses, from their carcases turn'd mummy.*
>
> *(The Honest Lawyer, 1616)*

56 Pietro della Valle (1586-1652), an Italian nobleman who lived in Baghdad from 1614 to 1626, and extensively explored the area around Cairo, including the various pyramid sites. This drawing allegedly shows him at Dahshur, although more probably at Saqqara, examining a newly-found mummy.

Protagonists often dramatically offer themselves for mummification in despair:

> *Make mummy of my flesh, and sell me to the apothecaries*
> *(Shirley, The Bird in a Cage, 1633)*

Not everyone believed that mummy was a beneficial medicine. At the height of the mummy-as-medicine mania, Ambroise Paré wrote his *Discours contre la momie*, in which he severely criticized its use, saying that it did more harm than good. Surprisingly, even until early in the twentieth century the Egyptians of Thebes were reported to use mummy powder mixed with butter for bruises, calling it 'mantey'. According to Bruyère, the French excavator of

Deir el-Medina, mummy was used to stop excessive bleeding. Indeed, some 'magical' stores in New York and Philadelphia still stock 'Mummy Dust' as a component of spells and magic potions – and in Walt Disney's animated *Snow White and the Seven Dwarfs* it is one of the ingredients listed in the evil step-mother's book of potions.

The critics were not restricted to those who regarded the use of mummies as unhealthy. In 1660 Sir Thomas Browne wrote: 'Mummy is become merchandise, Mizraim cures wounds and Pharaoh is used for balsam…avarice was then consuming the few Egyptian mummies which Cambyses or time had spared.' His view of mummies as valuable antiquities to be cherished was unusual for the time. From the sixteenth century onwards, visitors to Egypt went there to view mummies, mainly at Saqqara, where vast subterranean corridors and side chambers reportedly contained thousands of bodies. However, very few of the tourists felt any concern for conservation: the supply in Egypt seemed endless.

The early-nineteenth-century adventurer, Giovanni Battista Belzoni, served only to confirm this idea with his account of exploring a sepulchre in Thebes. He entered a passageway and sought a resting-place; but when his weight bore down on a mummy it 'crushed it like a band-box'. He sank among broken mummies with a crash of bones, rags and wooden cases. Every step he took he trampled and crushed a mummy. Amongst them he found papyri and statues which he promptly acquired. The mummies he found were not just of human beings, but also of animals such as bulls, cows, cats, crocodiles and birds.

The first mummy to enter the British Museum had been brought out of Egypt as a curio in 1722 by William Lethieullier (it was once contained in the coffin number EA 6695 but remains untraced since its unwrapping by Dr J. Blumenbach in 1792). A mummy may have arrived in England even earlier, if a tradition that attributes EA 6957 to the possession of Charles II's mistress, Nell Gwyn, is true.

A key event in the growth of popular interest and scientific investigation of ancient Egypt was Napoleon Bonaparte's invasion of Egypt on behalf of the French Republic in 1798. In addition to his soldiers, the Emperor-to-be took with him a commission of scholars to record the monuments, geography, fauna and flora of the country. Nearly all the ancient material collected soon passed into the hands of the British through the articles of capitulation

57 Giovanni Battista Belzoni (1778-1823), the former circus strongman-cum hydraulic engineer, whose discoveries included the burial chambers of kings Khephren, Ay, Ramesses I and Sethos I. Although rough and ready in his techniques, Belzoni was ahead of his time in the attention he gave to smaller, more commonplace, objects.

of Alexandria, and was surrendered by the French General Menou on 30 August 1801. However, the commission's multi-volume illustrated account of the country, the *Description de l'Égypte*, was instrumental in pushing Egypt to the fore in the consciousness of the educated élite.

Mummies, coffins and sarcophagi were amongst the items recovered or recorded by the French, including the last purely Egyptian royal sarcophagus to be made – the huge monuments of King Nektanebo II (Dynasty 30), found in use as a bath in the mosque, formerly the church, of St Athanasius in Alexandria and now in the British Museum. The heads of two mummies were given to Napoleon and his wife, Josephine, detached respectively from a male and female corpse. Other complete mummies collected by the expedition were taken back to the Louvre.

58 Napoleon Bonaparte being shown a mummy during his Egyptian expedition.

In early 1830, these started to smell and deteriorate in the damp air of Paris. It was decided that they should be buried in the palace gardens near the avenue Perrault. Victims of the revolution of the same year, which overthrew Charles X, were also buried in the Louvre garden. Some time later, the heroes of 1830 were moved from the garden to be re-interred under a column at the Bastille and it is probable that several Egyptian mummies accompanied them there at the same time.

Mummy mania

In addition to instigating the first large-scale excavations (discussed below), Napoleon's expedition prompted a further surge in the popularity of mummies amongst the European public. The growth of the great public collections brought Egyptian artifacts before an educated audience as never before. As the nineteenth century progressed, Egypt was more and more opened up to tourism, and the affluent visitor, with a retinue of agents and servants in attendance, was eager to bring back souvenirs of his or her time by the Nile.

The abundance, accessibility and wholly Egyptian character of mummies made them prime targets for souvenir hunters. As Father Géramb remarked in 1833 to Mohammed Ali, the ruler of Egypt, 'It would be hardly respectable, on one's return from Egypt, to present oneself in Europe without a mummy in one hand and a crocodile in the other.' Many people shared this view, and as they went into sepulchres filled with mummies, they wrenched off hands, feet, arms, heads, and indeed, sometimes removed entire bodies, which were taken back to Europe to reside in libraries and salons as peculiar mementos of a trip to Egypt.

Taking mummies from Egypt to Europe was not always straightforward. A pair of ladies, who had smuggled one

59 Most mummies ended up in people's libraries until they began to smell, when they were often relegated to the attic. Other, more fortunate, mummies formed a core part of museum collections, such as that of the British Museum, London, where legions of mummies lay in glass cases for perusal by visitors.

60 This posed nineteenth-century photograph shows some of the mummies that tourists would just 'happen' upon during the course of their visit to Egypt.

aboard their house boat (*dahabiyeh*) and were taking it out of Egypt, lost heart at the last minute due to its stench and threw it in the river at the dead of night. Other more daring souls who succeeded in removing their souvenirs out of Egypt, were faced with troubles on the way home. One gentleman who was transporting two mummies by train across Europe was stopped by the authorities and narrowly escaped arrest for being a murderer trying to dispose of his recent victims. He was fortunate that his mummies were indeed ancient Egyptians. Flinders Petrie, the 'father' of modern Egyptian archaeology, reports in his book, *Funeral Furniture*, that a tourist bought a mummy from Aswan that was eventually identified as the body of an English engineer who had died there, and not an ancient Egyptian at all. Despite these scares, Europeans continued to collect Egyptian mummies or their fragments.

'Discovering' mummies became an important element of a high-class tour of Egypt. To avoid disappointment, areas were 'sown' with bodies to allow a guaranteed 'spectacular find'. During his 1869 tour, the Prince of Wales, later King Edward VII, was shown what was alleged to be the great unearthing of some thirty mummies (Dynasties 25 and 26) in a tomb in Western Thebes. The bodies and coffins were brought back to England, and distributed among a number of collections. However, as has now become clear, the cases had been previously gathered together in a long-known tomb simply for the delectation of the distinguished visitor. The coffins had been placed in a 30-metre pit (Deir el-Medina 2005), in which lay the former sarcophagus of the Twenty-sixth Dynasty God's Wife Nitokris. This shaft had been originally found, devoid of any other contents besides the sarcophagus, in the 1830s. Not only princes were treated to this kind of 'find'. As mass-tourism took root later in the century, Thomas Cook and other pioneers also laid on such entertainments, albeit not on the same scale.

The Great Unwrappings

Once the mummies got to Europe they provided people with further ghoulish entertainment: unwrappings. These became social events and were very much a part of Victorian parlour entertainment, with special invitations being issued for them. Mummy unwrappings did not start in the nineteenth century; many curious individuals had staged such shows in previous years. One of the earliest recorded occurred in September 1698, when Benoit de Maillet (1656–1738), Louis XIV's consul in Cairo, unwrapped a mummy before a group of French travellers. Unfortunately he, as with most

61 In Egypt more 'scientific' unwrappings were conducted in the Museum confines. These were attended not only by scholars and scientists, but often by the Khedive himself. However, for the most part, none of these unwrappings proved to be methodical enough to be of use, and thus a great deal of information was lost. Here, Gaston Maspero (bearded, in a tarboush) and Daniel Fouquet unwrap a mummy from Deir el-Bahari.

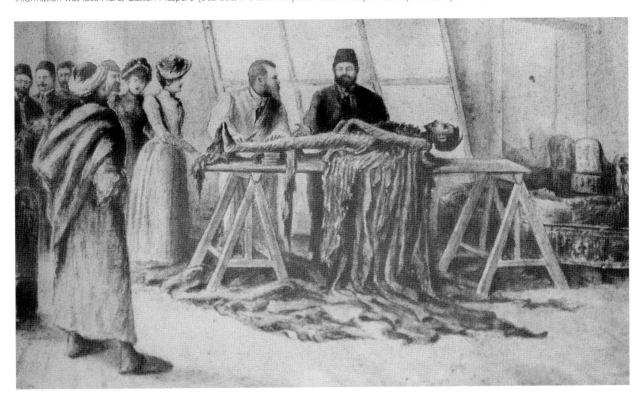

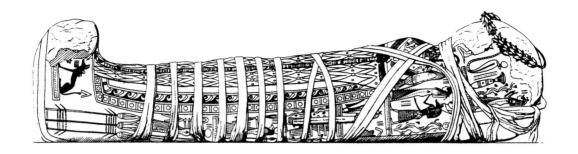

62, 63 Mummy of Petamenophis, son of Soter and Kleopatra, brought to Paris by Frédéric Caillaud (1787-1869): before (*above*) and after (*below*) its unwrapping on 30 November 1823. The mummy came from a brick-lined pit-tomb, found by Antonio Lebolo (1781-1830), a sworn enemy of Belzoni, before 1823, and containing thirteen burials. The eyes and mouth of the corpse were covered with thin gold plates. Time of Hadrian, from Sheikh Abd el-Quma, Thebes; Louvre Museum E 13048.

of his successors in this exercise, did not record anything concerning the mummy; he only mentioned some of the amulets found on it.

Similar emphasis was placed on amulets and precious metals by Frédéric Caillaud (1789–1869), who on 30 November 1823 unwrapped the mummy of a boy called Petamenophis, born on 12 January AD 95. Petamenophis sported a metal olive branch on his head and gold plates on his eyes and mouth, but Caillaud reveals very little about the method of embalming.

Not all unwrappers were solely interested in the trappings of the mummies; some expressed scientific interest in the bodies themselves. In 1718, C. Hertzog, an apothecary, unwrapped a mummy and published some of his findings. After that, being an economically minded man, he ground it up and sold it as medicine. Johann Friedrich Blumenbach (1752–1840), a German physician and anthropologist, spent much of the 1790s in England unwrapping mummies

belonging to both private individuals and museums (including the Lethieullier mummy, mentioned above). He frequently found both ancient and modern fakes: odd bones, animals, or rags that were bound up to give the appearance of children's mummies. Clearly the embalmers of ancient Egypt were as eager as the more modern dealers to package up and sell false mummies for a profit. The first mummy ever to be submitted to a professional chemical analysis by a group of scientists was the 'Leeds Mummy', belonging to one Nesamun (end of Dynasty 20), that was studied in 1828. Although the results raised more questions than answers, it was the first truly scientific investigation of a mummified body. The Leeds Mummy was just a foretaste of the scientific unwrapping fever that was to sweep Britain. In the early nineteenth century Belzoni had unwrapped a few as a public spectacle, assisted by one of his friends, Thomas Pettigrew (1791–1865). Intrigued and inspired by Belzoni's example, Pettigrew now started to unwrap mummies himself. He purchased one from Sotheby's for £23 and a friend bought another for £36 15s. Pettigrew began by unwrapping such purchases privately, taking notes on his observations and results, before starting public unrollings.

These public events, to which Pettigrew sold tickets, were conducted in the lecture-theatre of Charing Cross Hospital, the first taking place on 6 April 1833. They were attended by antiquarians, excavators, Egyptologists,

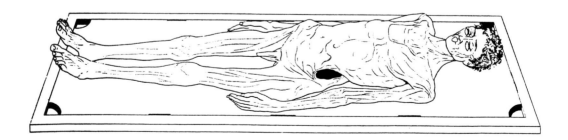

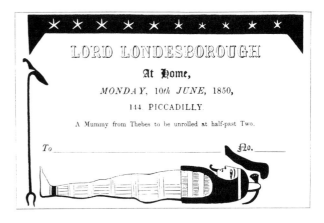

Members of Parliament, artists, authors, peers, princes, statesmen, diplomatics, physicians, army officers, as well as anyone else who could purchase a ticket. 'Mummy Pettigrew's' unwrappings proved such popular events that on one occasion the Archbishop of Canterbury had to be turned from the door, there being no space left. He subsequently had a command performance at Canterbury. Pettigrew became famous for his expertise and his six public lectures in 1837, each culminating in the dramatic unwrapping of a mummy were in great demand. On one occasion the mummy was so firmly fixed in its resinous cocoon that Pettigrew had to resort to a saw to free the body from the bandages. Amateur as such exploits may now seem, his researches provided Pettigrew with a great deal of information concerning different types of mummies and modes of mummification. In 1834 he published one of the earliest scholarly tomes on the subject, entitled *History of Egyptian Mummies*. Although Pettigrew's work involved examination of the bodies and the mode of mummification, it was as yet far from sufficient to clearly establish how mummies were made. Alexander, tenth Duke of Hamilton, nevertheless made out a will requesting that Pettigrew mummify him in the ancient European fashion and inter him at his family seat in Hamilton Palace. When the duke duly died in 1852, his body was taken by Pettigrew, mummified, and placed in a specially purchased Egyptian sarcophagus inside a huge mausoleum in the grounds of Hamilton Palace. When the tomb became structurally unsound, the sarcophagus and its occupant were re-buried in the local graveyard. It would be interesting to exhume the body to see how far Pettigrew succeeded in preserving it, but attempts at locating the sarcophagus have been foiled by sub-soil movements. Recently Bob Brier, an American academic, has experimented with mummifying a cadaver. Two years after his experiment the corpse was in a relatively good state with only some damage to its back.

Mummies Abused

In the nineteenth century mummies were so abundant that despite the mania for collection and unwrapping, there still remained sufficient in Egypt for what might be termed 'useful purposes'. A special paint, called Mummy Brown, was derived from fragments of mummified bodies and used in oil painting. One singularly pious artist was so upset to find that actual bodies of humans had been used to manufacture his paint, that he took all his tubes of Mummy Brown into the garden and gave them a decent burial. In the nineteenth century Augustus Stanwood, an American paper manufacturer from Maine, used linen mummy wrapping to make brown paper. This was sold to butchers and grocers who used it to wrap produce. An outbreak of cholera followed, the cause of which was traced allegedly to the paper, and the trade in mummy wrappings ceased.

Cat mummies were shipped from Egypt to Europe for a twofold purpose: first, they helped provide a bit of ballast for the boats; second, they were used as fertilizer until public outcry put a stop to it. Mummies suffered many ignominies in Egypt. They were burnt as firewood, since wood was scarce and mummies plentiful, and their arms and legs were used as torches when people wished to explore sepulchres or see their way at night. Mark Twain reports (one suspects with his tongue firmly in his cheek) that they were even used as fuel to fire locomotives.

Despite the varied wholesale attacks, many mummies have managed to survive the ravages of time and human greed and curiosity. Most museums in Europe and many in the United States boast one specimen, or at least a fragment thereof. An unusual survivor, now residing in the Rosicrucian Museum at San José, made its way to California under very curious circumstances. In 1971 a catalogue from Nieman-Marcus, the department store, offered 'His and Hers' mummy-cases that were 'approximately 2,000 years old'. These 'companions from the past richly adorned, but gratefully vacant' were coveted by the museum. An anonymous donor provided the funds and two cases were awaiting shipment when the museum received an apologetic telephone call from Nieman-Marcus to say that one of them actually contained a mummy. The museum officials replied that they would happily accept an inhabited case, and are now the proud possessors of two coffins, in one of which resides a mummy.

Some years earlier, in the 1950s, the Brooklyn Museum purchased a cartonnage case containing a mummy from the Metropolitan Museum of Art. Brooklyn was interested in the cartonnage, but not the mummy, so tried to separate the two. Once this was accomplished, museum officials endeavoured to dispose of the offending corpse by burying it in the garden, but were rudely interrupted by a police officer who wanted to examine the 'murder victim'. Once the mummy's identity was established, and the museum

officials no longer under suspicion, they were informed that they could not carry out a burial without a death certificate, something difficult to obtain for a 3,000-year-old corpse from Egypt! Attempts to give the mummy away to other museums were also foiled as it was illegal to ship bodies out of the state of New York without a death certificate. Finally a museum official decided to unwrap and study the mummy, and out of this grew a television programme starring this mummy, nicknamed 'Melvin' by the museum staff. The mummy also featured in a show, 'The Mummy Complex', that appeared at the Armstrong Circle Theater in New York in 1958. 'Melvin' is now on display at the Brooklyn Museum where he is a permanent resident, still lacking a death certificate.

The Curse

Since the nineteenth century there have been several mentions of the 'Mummy's Curse', either attached to a mummy or to entering a tomb. None is more famous, however, than that associated with the discovery of the tomb of Tutankhamun in the 1920s. The Tutankhamun curse was a result of journalistic intrigue; the only slightly odd death associated with the opening of the tomb was that of Lord Carnarvon, the patron of the excavation. His death, attributed to an infected mosquito bite, was marked by a blackout in Cairo (quite common, especially at the time), and the anguished howling of his dog in far-off England at the moment of his death. No actual curse, however, was found in the tomb of Tutankhamun, and only two have been recorded from other tombs. These read: 'As for any people who would enter this tomb unclean and do something evil to it, there will be judgment against them by the great god', and, 'As for any one who enters this tomb unclean, I shall seize him by the neck like a bird, he will be judged for it by the great god!' Such curses were aimed at tomb-robbers who sought to despoil the tomb without honouring the dead; Egyptologists, it might be said, make the name (and therefore the soul) of the dead live, and thus would escape punishment. Whatever the case, these curses stopped neither the scientist nor the thief.

Some scholars have suggested that illness or infections that affect people present at the opening of a sealed tomb are the result of poisonous moulds and bacteria rather than any supernatural element. Poisonous gases have also been

66 The Fifth Earl of Carnarvon: his death, attributed to an infected mosquito bite, was marked by a blackout in Cairo (quite common, especially at the time), and the anguished howling of his dog in far-off England at the moment of his death.

When Mohammed Ali, a man avid for Western technology and diplomatic and commercial relations, gained control of Egypt in the early years of the nineteenth century, he encouraged a large influx of Europeans. Particularly important figures were the Consuls and Consular Agents of the Great Powers. Apart from their broader diplomatic roles, many of these individuals also took it upon themselves to gather collections of antiquities for national, and more importantly, personal enrichment.

Two of the most prominent figures in this Consular activity were Giovanni Battista Belzoni (1778–1823) (ills. 57, 65), working for the British representative Henry Salt (1780–1827), and Bernardino Drovetti (1776–1852), Consul-General for France. Belzoni was by far the more careful worker – although by no means a scientific archaeologist – publishing a very fair book on his adventures. Apart from exploring communal tombs from which came a number of Late Period mummies, he discovered some of the most important examples of New Kingdom coffins and sarcophagi. Working in the Valley of the Kings, one of his spectacular finds was the tomb of Sethos I (Dynasty 19), containing the alabaster outer coffin of the king, the only example of its kind to survive in such a complete condition. Amazingly, the British Museum was not prepared to purchase this superb item; instead, it was bought by the architect, Sir John Soane, for £2,000, and remains on display in his house, now a museum, in London (ill. 68).

From another royal tomb, that of Ramesses III (Dynasty 20), Belzoni removed the coffer of the king's sarcophagus, which was sold by Salt to France, where it now stands in the Louvre Museum. Later, Belzoni recovered the lid, which had remained buried in flood-debris; it is now in the Fitzwilliam Museum, Cambridge. In a much less spectacular tomb, a shaft-grave cut for a member of the nobility, Belzoni seems to have found the earliest known example of a stone anthropoid coffin, dating to the Eighteenth Dynasty, discovered under the auspices of the Earl of Belmore (1774–1841). The coffin passed into the Earl's collection, and then to the British Museum.

A most significant find took place in the western branch of the Valley of the Kings, where Belzoni located two tombs. One, perhaps begun for Amenophis IV (Akhenaten) (Dynasty 18), was unfinished and contained a number of Third Intermediate Period mummies. The other was the tomb of King Ay, which held a sarcophagus of a design

thought to cause illness amongst archaeologists. When the archaeologist Sami Gabra was working in the ibis-necropolis of Tuna el-Gebel during the 1940s, he and his team were suddenly seized by violent headaches and shortness of breath. The workers blamed a curse placed on the tombs by the ibis-headed god of wisdom, Thoth, but Gabra diagnosed the cause as noxious gas, and returned to work in the catacombs after three days.

DIGGING FOR THE DEAD

Napoleon and after

As we have seen, an upsurge in interest in ancient Egypt followed on from Napoleon's great expedition. Apart from the souvenir-hunting of casual travellers, the early years of the nineteenth century saw the start of organized excavation and plundering, which was to continue into the next century.

only found in the last years of the Eighteenth Dynasty. It remained *in situ* until 1896, when it was broken into fragments by a Moroccan treasure-seeker. The pieces were moved to Cairo and partially restored in 1908, where the sarcophagus remained until 1994. It was then returned to its tomb and reunited with other fragments found during the full excavation of the sepulchre in 1972.

Belzoni worked in Lower Egypt too, clearing a way into the Second Pyramid at Giza where he discovered Khephren's plundered sarcophagus. To commemorate the event he scrawled his name in lamp-black across one of the walls of the chamber where it can still be seen today. Also working at Giza was Colonel Richard Howard Vyse (1784–1853) who, together with the engineer J.S. Perring (1813–1869), carried out the first systematic archaeological work in the area in 1836–7, including the discovery of the sarcophagus of Mykerinos (Dynasty 4), a coffin made for his reburial, and what may be part of his mummified body. This sarcophagus was sent off to England by ship but never reached its destination owing to a storm off the Spanish coast which sank both ship and sarcophagus. Perring also carried out a major survey of the pyramid fields to the north and south of Giza; his work still remains of considerable importance.

A contemporary and sworn enemy of Belzoni was Antonio Lebolo (1781–1830). Before 1823 he made an important discovery somewhere on Thebes' Sheikh Abd el-Qurna hill: a shaft tomb containing the sarcophagi, coffins and mummies of some fourteen individuals, apparently members of a single family. They provide excellent examples of Roman Period funerary equipment, some items being precisely dated within the reign of Hadrian. The majority of these are now in Turin.

Later expeditions proved more professional. Some formed parts of scholarly commissions, such as a French one in 1828–9, led by Jean François Champollion (1790–1832), decipherer of hieroglyphs. There was also a contemporary Tuscan one under Ippolito Rosellini (1800–1843), and the great Prussian expedition, under the leadership of Karl Richard Lepsius (1810–1884), which covered the whole of Egypt and Nubia in 1842–5. In each case large volumes were published with plans of monuments and drawings of their decorations, while massive quantities of antiquities were shipped back to Paris, Turin and Berlin. Amongst them many were important examples of coffins and sarcophagi.

Other foreigners, following the examples of Salt, Belzoni and Drovetti, came to the country with the rather more commercial intention of amassing collections for sale at a profit. One of the most remarkable stories is that of the horse-dealer, Giuseppe Passalacqua (1797–1865). Unsuccessful in his own business in Egypt, he changed trade to that of excavator and made a number of interesting discoveries in the Dira Abu'l-Naga area of Western Thebes, including perhaps the first intact burial to be properly described. Having sold his collection to Prussia, he became Conservator of the Berlin Egyptian Museum for the rest of his life.

67 An important early discovery was that of the intact Theban tomb of the Steward Mentuhotep by Giuseppe Passalacqua, a former horse dealer, in 1823. It provided an excellent example of middle-class burial of its date, with pottery, food offerings, tomb models and three-fold coffins. This find, and others, was to lead to the excavator becoming the first Conservator of Egyptian Antiquities in Berlin. Late Twelfth Dynasty, from the Asasif; Berlin 9-22.

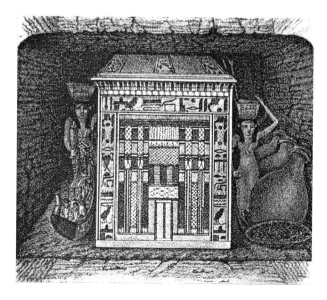

68 Belzoni acquired the calcite sarcophagus of Sethos I in the hopes of selling it to Salt and/or the British Museum. Neither would have it, so Belzoni transported it to Britain at his own expense where he displayed it in one of his exhibitions in the Egyptian Hall, near Piccadilly Circus. Fortunately for Belzoni the sarcophagus found a buyer in Sir John Soane in whose London house (now a museum) it still stands.

69-71 Three of the labels found by Rhind, together with the mummies of a series of reburied princesses. They respectively name Tia and Pyihia, daughters of Tuthmosis IV, and Wiay. From Sheikh Abd el-Qurna, RMS 1956.163-5.

Towards True Archaeology

Alexander Henry Rhind (1833–1863) worked on his own account in Egypt from 1855. He had come for health reasons, but soon became interested in antiquities, adopting a scientific approach that was before its time. Although he undertook some work in the Wadi el-Moluk (the Valley of the Kings), his principal activities were on the Sheikh Abd el-Qurna hill at Thebes. Two of his discoveries are of particular interest. Both were re-uses of earlier sepulchres, one being the last resting place of Montjuemsaf, who lived under Kleopatra VII (the famous Cleopatra) and Augustus in the first century BC.

The other find was even more interesting and, although unrecognized for many years, provided the first example of a cache: a type of deposit of which two even more spectacular examples were to be found later in the century. It lay near the previous tomb, but unlike its companion, it had been penetrated by robbers. Rhind first found his way into a large rectangular chamber, its roof supported by six pillars, from which a lower chamber could be reached by a passage. This had formerly been closed with the Seal of the

Theban Necropolis. The chamber contained a number of rifled mummies, with rough wrappings and a number of wooden tags, inscribed in hieratic script. The tags make it clear that the bodies were those of a series of late Eighteenth Dynasty princesses, including a daughter of Tuthmosis IV, reburied here in the twenty-seventh regnal year of Psusennes I of the Twenty-first Dynasty. During the late Twentieth Dynasty, many tombs suffered severely from robbery, as a result of which many high-status mummies were collected together and cached, in the hope that concentration would improve security.

Some order began to be imposed on the antiquarian free-for-all in 1858, when Auguste Mariette (1821–1881) was appointed the first head of the Egyptian Antiquities Service. Unofficial digging was suppressed, and official excavations were begun around the country. Unfortunately, supervision was poor, and led to a near-major disaster in 1859, when the gilded coffin of Queen Ahhotpe (Dynasty 17) was found by Mariette's men at Dira Abu'l-Naga. The local governor seized the mummy, broke it up to extract its jewellery, and sent the latter as a present to the Khedive, in Cairo. Aware that this was a test-case for the supremacy of the antiquities laws over arbitrary government, Mariette intercepted the governor's steamer and confiscated the jewellery, safeguarding it for the new Cairo Museum at Bulaq.

The coffin itself is an important, and virtually undamaged, example of its type. It had been hidden during the Twenty-first Dynasty in the rubble at the bottom of the cliffs, as had the contemporary coffin of King Kamose (Dynasty 17) found shortly before. Further up the cliffs, during the 1840s, the intact tombs of at least three Seventeenth Dynasty pharaohs had been found by local inhabitants. The mummies had fallen to pieces owing to rough handling, but the coffins found their way to the British and Louvre Museums, and a canopic chest to the State Museum of Antiquities in Leiden.

The Kamose coffin had been found while work was being carried out in advance of the projected visit to Egypt of Prince Napoleon, cousin of the French Emperor, Napoleon III. The idea had originally been to ensure that material was 'found' wherever the Imperial party visited, as we have seen was arranged for the Prince of Wales' visit.

Kings and Brigands

Perhaps the most spectacular of all mummy-finds occurred in the early 1870s, although not revealed to the world until the beginning of the next decade. In 1871, according to one of the many versions of the story, Ahmed Abd el-Rassul of Qurna (d. 1918/19) went in search of a lost goat near Deir el-Bahari and found that it had fallen into a tomb-shaft. Descending, he discovered some antiquities lying at the bottom half-covered with sand. As he scraped away the sand from the treasures, he came upon the outline of an opening that had been hidden by debris in the shaft. The opening proved to be a sealed doorway. With growing excitement he chipped a small hole through it and peered into the darkness where he saw coffins: dozens of them. He had found the tomb of Pinudjem II (Dynasty 21; tomb TT 320) which not only contained several members of the priest's family, but also the coffins and mummies of over thirty individuals who had been placed there for their protection in antiquity.

72 The location of TT 320, at Thebes, the cache-tomb which contained the mummies of some forty kings, queens and other high-status individuals.

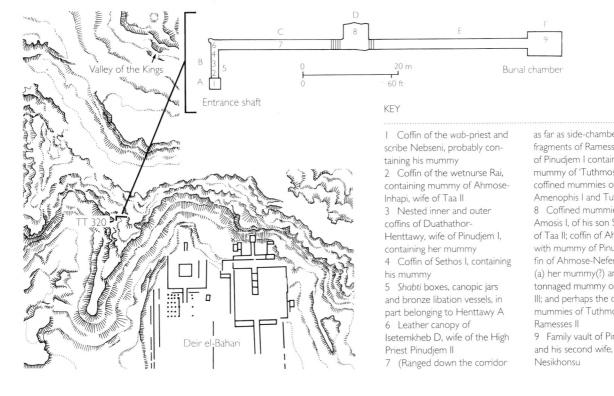

KEY

1 Coffin of the *wab*-priest and scribe Nebseni, probably containing his mummy
2 Coffin of the wetnurse Rai, containing mummy of Ahmose-Inhapi, wife of Taa II
3 Nested inner and outer coffins of Duathathor-Henttawy, wife of Pinudjem I, containing her mummy
4 Coffin of Sethos I, containing his mummy
5 *Shabti* boxes, canopic jars and bronze libation vessels, in part belonging to Henttawy A
6 Leather canopy of Isetemkheb D, wife of the High Priest Pinudjem II
7 (Ranged down the corridor as far as side-chamber D): coffin fragments of Ramesses I; coffin of Pinudjem I containing the mummy of 'Tuthmosis I'; coffined mummies of Amenophis I and Tuthmosis II
8 Coffined mummies of Amosis I, of his son Siamun, and of Taa II; coffin of Ahhotpe I, with mummy of Pinudjem I; coffin of Ahmose-Nefertiry, with (a) her mummy(?) and (b) cartonnaged mummy of Ramesses III; and perhaps the coffined mummies of Tuthmosis III and Ramesses II
9 Family vault of Pinudjem II and his second wife, Nesikhonsu

73 Funerary papyrus of King Pinudjem I, from the cache; CM SR 11488.

74 The inner coffin and mummy cover of Maetkare A, daughter of Pinudjem I, had been damaged by robbers before being placed in TT 320, who had removed its gilded face and hands. Both elements conform to type YIIc. Early-mid Twenty-first Dynasty; CM CG 61028.

For the next ten years Ahmed, his brother Mohammed (d. 1926), and a few other members of the Abd el-Rassul family steadily removed smaller objects from the cache and sold them, piece by piece, to dealers in Luxor, notably Mustapha Agha Ayat, who traded extensively abroad. Particular examples were papyri and canopic jars from Pinudjem's family. This flood of antiquities, which were especially noticeable as some bore royal cartouches, came to the attention of Gaston Maspero (1846–1916), the Director General of the Antiquities Service. He ordered an investigation, and on 4 April 1881 the Abd el-Rassul brothers were arrested. Both pleaded their innocence and were freed due to insufficient evidence.

After their temporary incarceration, the brothers had a disagreement over the apportioning of profits from their illicit trade. The quarrel became exceptionally heated, and the secret of the tomb's existence became public. Mohammed Abd el-Rassul, after obtaining some guarantees from officialdom, decided to make a full confession. On 6 July 1881, he took the Antiquities officials, Emile Brugsch (1842–1930) and Ahmed Kamal (1851–1923), to the tomb, along with their colleagues and policemen. Reached by a 12-metre shaft, the tomb extended for many metres into the mountainside. Its first corridor was crammed with coffins, *shabti* boxes, canopic jars, and metal libation vessels; at its end lay a leather tent belonging to Isetemkheb D, one of the original inhabitants of the tomb. The second corridor,

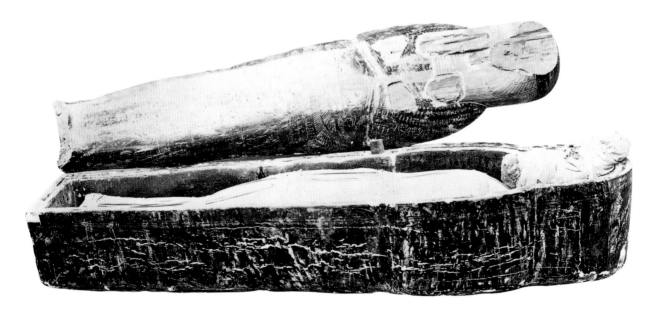

75 Removing the mummies and burial equipment discovered in the cache of Deir el-Bahari to the boat that would carry them to Cairo.

at right angles to the first, contained many more coffins, with a large stack of them in a chamber to one side. Beyond this side chamber a long empty corridor led to the burial chamber of Pinudjem II and his family. In all, the tomb contained mummies, statues, jars, shrines, and other objects from the burials of fifty-four individuals, many royal, and dating in the main from the New Kingdom. Among others the bodies of Amenophis I, Tuthmosis III, Sethos I, Ramesses II, Merenptah, and Ramesses III were recovered.

Some three hundred workmen were hired to remove the contents of the cache and to load the forty mummies and their paraphernalia onto a steamboat for passage to Cairo. As the boat passed settlements along the Nile the villagers would come out and wail, ululate, and fire guns in tribute to the dead monarchs. The atmosphere of these events is recaptured by the greatest of all Egyptology-inspired films:

Shadi Abd el Salam's *El Mumia* or *Night of the Counting of the Years*, made in 1969.

The mummies from the Deir el-Bahari cache and tomb of Amenophis II (discovered in 1898: see below) were initially displayed in the first Cairo Museum, located in the suburb of Bulaq (ills. 76–7). From there they were moved, with the other contents of the museum, to Giza (on the site of today's Cairo zoo), before being transferred to Room 52 in the current museum at Qasr el-Nil, opened in 1902. This was not the end of their wanderings, however, since in the 1930s the then Wafd Party Prime Minister moved these ancient monarchs to the mausoleum of his rival, Saad Zaghlul, the late Nationalist leader. This was an effort to diminish Zaghlul's stature by raising that of the pharaohs. The move achieved nothing, and the next (Nationalist) Prime Minister returned them to the museum.

76 A gallery at the Bulaq Museum, showing a closely-packed collection of sarcophagi, coffins and canopic chests. Through the doorway can be glimpsed one of the queens' coffins found in TT 320.

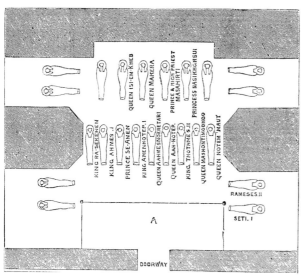

77 The royal mummies in their new resting place in the Eastern Hall of the Bulaq Museum. The public was only allowed into the area marked 'A' whence they had to strain to see the mummies in the back. The unmarked cases belong to priests and nobles.

In 1980, Room 52 was locked by order of President Sadat who wished the dead kings of Egypt to remain in peace in a new mausoleum. This was never constructed because of Sadat's subsequent death. Finally, however, after several years' wait, a selection of the pharaohs are once again on view in a new mausoleum-like room in the Cairo Museum.

Kings and Pyramids

After the pyramid explorations of Belzoni, Vyse and Perring, little was done with these great monuments until late in Mariette's regime. Under the (apparently justified) assumption that pyramids were 'mute' (uninscribed), and unlikely to reveal historical/religious texts, Mariette had given little priority to opening the unexplored examples that dotted the Saqqara necropolis. Nevertheless, in early 1880, a French grant was given to the Antiquities Service for the specific purpose of their excavation.

In May 1880, a Saqqara villager penetrated the burial chamber of the pyramid of Pepi I (Dynasty 6), a monument so devastated that the roof of the burial chamber was exposed. Far from being mute, hieroglyphic texts adorned the walls. With the help of Service workmen, Emile Brugsch entered and made preliminary copies which were sent to France for study by Mariette (on leave there) and Gaston Maspero, then Professor at the Collège de France. At the end of the year, the Antiquities Service *reis* (head worker) opened the nearby pyramid of Nemtyemsaf I (Dynasty 6), which was also examined and partly copied by Brugsch and his elder brother, Heinrich (1827–1894). They were able to announce to Mariette, shortly before he died in Cairo-Bulaq on 18 January 1881, that the existence of the famous Pyramid Texts was confirmed.

This was not all that the Brugsch brothers were able to present to the dying Director of the Service: in the sarcophagus in Nemtyemsaf's pyramid they found a naked mummy, intact apart from a missing lower jaw, wearing a side-lock (the symbol of youth). The mummy was carried to the local railway station in a wooden box. Unfortunately, the train stopped short of Cairo so that the Germans had to

78 Head of the mummy found in the pyramid of Nemtyemsaf I in January 1881. It is usually regarded as a New kingdom intrusion, although a number of fragments of other late Old Kingdom kings were found in their pyramids; CM Ex. 3107.

79 Early unwrappings of the royal mummies were not particularly careful; here, Tuthmosis III lies with his wrappings cut open by Maspero at Bulaq in 1881; note the disarticulation of the king's hips, from his original robbery.

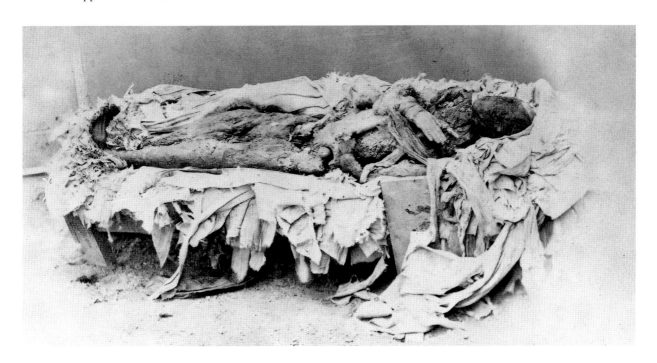

walk the last few kilometres. The box proving too heavy, the mummy was then carried on its own – until it broke in half! One brother carrying each part, they eventually caught a cab to the museum, paying customs duty on their burden as 'pickled fish' when they crossed into the city via the Qasr el-Nil bridge.

This mummy, now in the Cairo Museum, has been much discussed, and is generally felt to be a later intrusive burial, rather than an Old Kingdom royal mummy. However, Pepi I's sepulchre revealed a mummified hand, and some of the king's inscribed bandages. The former was not found by the Brugschs, or Maspero, who succeeded Mariette in his Directorship, but by the archaeologist Flinders Petrie (1853–1942). Petrie had been working further north at Giza, but had entered Pepi's pyramid while on a reconnaissance trip to Saqqara. There he had examined the interior of the pyramid (without asking permission), and had found the hand (now apparently lost). He also made copies of the texts, which he sent to Samuel Birch (1813–1885), Keeper of Oriental Antiquities at the British Museum. Thus, the first publication of the famous Pyramid Texts took place in a British periodical in April 1881, beating the official accounts to the press.

Most of the remaining pyramids at Saqqara were opened in February to April 1881 (Unas and Pepi II) and May (Teti), revealing more texts and mummy fragments in the burial chambers. Unas was represented by pieces of his skull and left arm; Teti's remains comprised a shoulder and arm. All were once displayed in the Cairo Museum.

The Theban City of the Dead

Another important find of the 1880s was that of a small tomb-chamber at Deir el-Medina, above the site of the village that had housed those who built the royal tombs in the Valley of the Kings. It proved to be the beautifully decorated sepulchre of Sennedjem, one of the workmen who had lived during the time of Sethos I (Dynasty 19). Its significance lies in the six intact burials found within, providing a well-dated sample of the sarcophagi, coffins, mummy-covers, masks and canopic equipment current during the first few decades of the Nineteenth Dynasty.

The last decade of the nineteenth century marked a great upsurge in archaeological work in Egypt. One great find again featured Ahmed Abd el-Rassul who, after his

part in the episode of the Deir el-Bahari royal cache, was employed by the Antiquities Service. Early in 1891 he went to his chief, Eugène Grébaut (1846–1915), a most unpopular head of the Service, with information concerning the location of a tomb just outside the Hatshepsut temple at Deir el-Bahari. Men were set to work there and found several large stones lying beneath the sand. The stones were removed and revealed the mouth of a pit. Lower down they found mud brick and other debris including sand, stones and vegetable matter. Work continued, and on 4 February 1891, Georges Daressy (1864–1938), another senior Service official, went to Luxor to oversee the proceedings. Having

80 The painted doorway of the tomb of Sennedjem, found by Maspero in 1882. The top register shows Sennedjem, a workman in the royal tombs, together with his wife, Iyneferti, and their daughter, adoring Osiris and Maat. In the lower register, the falcon mortuary god, Ptah-Sokar-Osiris, together with Isis, receive the homage of relatives of the deceased. Reign of Sethos I, from TT 1; CM JE 27303.

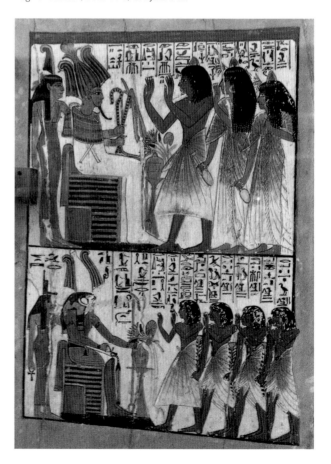

81 The family catacomb of Sesostris III: Jacques de Morgan supervises the opening of a cavity in the floor in which had been hidden the parure of a princess. Her plundered sarcophagus stands mutely in the background.

breached a wall the workers came upon another cache, a gallery filled with coffins. Daressy spent the night guarding the tomb. Removal of the contents began the next day, and continued for a week, when everything was transferred to a boat bound for Cairo. The principal gallery measured 52 metres long and 1.5 metres wide. The total subterranean length of the sepulchre was 155 metres. The cache, known as the Bad el-Gasus, included, besides 153 sets of coffins and mummies, 110 boxes of *shabtis*, 77 Osiris figures, the majority of which contained a papyrus, statuettes of Isis and Nephthys, and a handful of canopics. Food offerings of fruit were also found, in addition to funerary wreaths and bouquets. The burials belonged to lower level priests of Amun, all dating roughly to the Twenty-first Dynasty. Embarrassed by the sheer scale of the discovery – there was no room in the Giza Museum to house all the coffins – the Antiquities Service presented a considerable number of foreign museums with one or more coffins from the tomb.

De Morgan at Dahshur

In 1892, Jacques de Morgan was appointed Head of the Antiquities Service. He was far more of a 'field man' than his predecessors, and had ambitious plans for a proper archaeological survey of the Nile valley – cut short after one volume had been published – as well as for excavations of hitherto virgin sites.

One of these was the necropolis at Dahshur, dominated by two huge Fourth Dynasty pyramids and a series of ruined Middle Kingdom pyramids. It was around three of these that he devoted his efforts in 1894–5. The three pyramids themselves, belonging to Ammenemes II and III, and Sesostris III, of the Twelfth Dynasty, were completely stripped by robbers. However, the surrounding tombs yielded some of the finest treasures of ancient Egypt (ill. 83).

A series of galleries constructed for the family of Sesostris III had been plundered, but contained caches of fine jewellery, together with sarcophagi and some of the most beautifully-made canopics to survive. The best, however, came from the temenoi of the two kings Ammenemes. A private tomb beside the pyramid of Ammenemes III had been extended as the sepulchre of the Thirteenth Dynasty king, Hor. Amazingly, it had been only partly robbed, and still contained the denuded mummy of the pharaoh, together with his intact canopic equipment, and much of his funerary furniture, including a large statue of his *ka*, still within its original shrine (ill. 9). Next door was the burial of the Princess Nubheteptikhered – completely intact. These were the first individuals of such status whose burials had been found in anything like a pristine state.

The next season was even more successful, with four daughters of Ammenemes II being found completely intact. Their tombs were constructed so as to embed the sarcophagi entirely in solid stone (ills. 5–6). Thus, canopics, masks, coffins, sarcophagi and funerary offerings remained as they had been left around 1900 BC. Unfortunately, most had suffered badly from water penetration, with only a few pieces now surviving in the Cairo Museum. These include, however, two of the most wonderful diadems known, found upon the brow of Princess Khnemet (ills. XII, 82).

Once More into the Valley

In 1897, soon after his Dahshur triumphs, De Morgan took up a new post excavating in Iran. He was replaced by Victor Loret (1859–1946). Although more of a library-scholar, Loret also undertook excavations in the Valley of the Kings, where he found a number of tombs. As well as that of Tuthmosis III, and the largely untouched tomb of the noble, Maihirpri (Dynasty 18), they included, in 1898, a second cache of royal mummies in the tomb of Amenophis II (KV 35). The body of King Amenophis lay in his sarcophagus, while one side-room contained three mummies, probably members of the king's family. Another room held nine more mummies, all royalty, including Sethos II, Amenophis III and Ramesses V. They had been hidden away there in the Twenty-first Dynasty.

Most of these mummies were removed to Cairo in 1901 with the exception of Amenophis II and his three family members. Unfortunately, not long after the bulk of the mummies had been removed, despite the precautions of the Antiquities Service, the guards to the tomb were overpow-

ered by robbers who proceeded to despoil Amenophis II's mummy in search of jewellery. Howard Carter, who was then the Antiquities Inspector for the area, traced the crime with the help of a spoor-man (footprint-tracker) to the infamous Abd el-Rassul family, although he could not conclusively prove their guilt.

After Loret's resignation in 1899, Maspero returned to the Directorship-General of the Service, which he reorganized, with the installation of a new series of Inspectors in Upper and Lower Egypt. The key appointments were of Howard Carter (1874–1939) at Thebes, and James Quibell (1867–1935) at Saqqara. Carter had earlier worked as an epigrapher at Beni Hasan, Deir el-Bahari and other sites. He now oversaw the monuments and excavations of southern Egypt. From 1903, this included the work being financed by the American Theodore Davis (1837–1915), but under the auspices of the Service. Working with him, Carter discovered the robbed tombs of Tuthmosis IV, Hatshepsut and others in the Valley. He was succeeded by Quibell, and others, who also found a number of important tombs while being funded by Davis.

The first of these finds, in 1904, was the burial place of Yuya and Tjuiu (KV 46), parents-in-law of Amenophis III. Although partly ransacked, the tomb still contained much of its fabulous furnishings, including the bodies, coffins and sarcophagi of the deceased, all currently displayed in the Cairo Museum. Until 1922, and the discovery of the tomb of Tutankhamun, it was to be the richest tomb found in Egypt. It also enjoyed the notoriety of having almost entrapped the portly figure of the Director of Antiquities, Maspero himself. As he attempted to enter through a robbers' hole he became stuck, and was only freed by the exertions of Messrs Weigall and Davis.

During the clearance of KV 46, Quibell, who had moved back to Saqqara, had been succeeded as Inspector-General by Arthur Weigall (1880–1934). At around the same time Davis acquired the services of a full-time archaeologist, Edward Ayrton (1882–1914) for his next discovery. This was the tomb of King Siptah (KV 47; Dynasty 19), unfortunately largely wrecked by flooding. A series of tombs found shortly afterwards, however, held a series of well-preserved animal mummies, principally apes and dogs, probably royal pets. Another still contained the plundered mummy of the vizier Amenemopet, who lived under Amenophis II.

In 1907, a tomb (KV 55) was opened which contained a badly rotted coffin and mummy, plus canopic jars and a disintegrating gilded shrine. The owner had been deprived of his identity in antiquity by the effacement of his royal names from the coffin, and poor archaeological techniques meant that many important clues to the deposit's meaning were lost. Thus was born the 'mystery of Tomb 55', which still generates much argument today. It is clear, however, that the body found in the tomb belonged to one of the late Eighteenth Dynasty's 'heretic' kings. The first 'heretic' pharaoh was Amenophis IV (Dynasty 18), who abolished, in state religion, all the gods but the Aten, or solar disc. In

82 De Morgan triumphantly raises the golden diadem from the mummy of Princess Khnemet, daughter of Ammenemes II.

83 M. and Mme. de Morgan on horseback, accompanying the Dahshur finds. The procession is headed by outrunners and a drummer. Various workmen fire guns, both to express joy and excitement, and to scare away brigands.

honour of this deity Amenophis changed his name to Akhenaten. The evidence from the coffin seems to point towards Akhenaten's short-lived successor, Smenkhkare/ Neferneferuaten as being the occupant, but debate continues. The bones to which the mummy had been reduced by damp were at first casually identified as female, but subsequent examinations have determined them to be male.

The final tomb discovered in the Valley before 1914 was that of the pharaoh Horemheb (KV 57). Badly robbed, it contained the bones of four individuals, but these remains now appear to be lost, and whether any might have belonged to the king (whose mummy is missing from the caches) is unknown.

Egyptology International

Apart from the work sponsored by the Antiquities Service itself, expeditions were mounted by many European and American institutions, as well as by wealthy individuals who had managed to obtain a permit. Amongst the earliest teams into the field were those working on behalf of the London-based Egypt Exploration Fund (EEF, founded in 1882, later Society (EES)), and those led by William Matthew Flinders Petrie. The latter worked periodically for the EEF, independently, and for the British School of Archaeology in Egypt, based at University College London, where he held the first Chair of Egyptology in England.

During the last decade of the old century and the first two of the new, Petrie, generally regarded as we have seen as the father of scientific archaeological practice in Egypt, excavated cemeteries ranging in date from the Roman mummy-pits of Hawara, which revealed to the world the glory of the Fayoum mummy portraits, right back to the prehistoric cemeteries at Naqada and Ballas. In between lay the royal tombs of the Archaic Period at Abydos, the gigantic mastabas of the early Fourth Dynasty at Meidum, the Middle Kingdom Tomb of the Two Brothers at Rifeh, the Third Intermediate Period burials at the Ramesseum, and countless other sites from other periods. Key discoveries for the history of mummification were made at Meidum, where a number of broken mummies of the Fourth Dynasty were found. Some gave rise to considerable controversy, as they appeared to have been defleshed before wrapping. Others were more conventional, showing the contemporary technique of moulding external features in

84 Sir William Matthew Flinders Petrie, first Edwards Professor of Egyptology at University College London, and often termed the 'founder' of scientific archaeology. Shown in his last years of field work, at Tell Farah South in Palestine.

plaster-soaked bandages. From these excavations came the mummy of Ranefer, believed at the time to be the oldest extant mummy. It survived in London's Royal College of Surgeons until 1941, when it was destroyed by bombing.

Associates of Petrie worked through the Egyptian Research Account at various sites, while the newly-founded Institute of Archaeology at Liverpool sponsored the work of John Garstang (1876–1956) at Abydos, Esna and Beni Hasan. The last-named site revealed over four hundred middle-class tombs of the Middle Kingdom, making it one of the key sites for the study of the period. Unfortunately – and typically for the time – the excavator took less care and interest in the description and study of the mummies than in the accompanying grave goods.

Other tombs and aspects of the Middle Kingdom (as well as other periods) were revealed by the work of Ernesto Schiaparelli (1856–1928) and Giulio Farina (1889–1947) for the Egyptian Museum, Turin, at Gebelein, Asyut and Qau el-Kebir. Many of the objects and bodies recovered from their campaigns reside in the Turin Museum. In addition, large numbers of Middle Kingdom coffins and associated material came from Antiquities Service work, and from that of the Boston Museum of Fine Arts (MFA) working at El-Bersha. The highlight of the latter project was the discovery in 1915 of the tomb of Djehutynakhte, with its unusual mummy, superb coffins and tomb-models.

The focus of the MFA's work, however, was the great Old Kingdom necropolis at Giza. Directed by George Andrew Reisner (1867–1942), vast numbers of tombs were discovered and recorded, including the famous tomb of Hetepheres, mother of Kheops. This contained the queen's sarcophagus, intact canopics – the oldest known – and gold-sheathed furniture, but mysteriously no mummy.

Others working at Giza were the Italians, led by Schiaparelli, as well as the Vienna Academy under Hermann Junker (1877–1962), and the Egyptian Antiquities Service/Cairo University under Selim Hassan (1886–1961). Between them they cleared the majority of the necropolis. Saqqara was largely an Antiquities Service site, with

85 George Andrew Reisner (1867-1942), the excavator of much of Giza, Naga el-Deir and the Nubian pyramids, to name but a few sites.

86 The shaft-tombs at Beni Hasan, excavated by John Garstang in 1903-4 on the slope below the great rock-cut tombs. They produced very large numbers of intact burials, material from which has been dispersed around the museums of the world.

Quibell, Cecil Firth (1878–1931), Jean-Philippe Lauer (1902–), Selim Hassan and Gustave Jéquier (1868–1946) opening tombs and pyramids of every conceivable date. Amongst items found were a plywood coffin and mummy-fragments from below the Step Pyramid. Earlier, Quibell had opened Second Dynasty tombs with the earliest known bodies to have been properly wrapped, albeit without chemical mummification.

Yet another major set of investigations was carried out by Ludwig Borchardt (1863–1938) at Abusir in 1903–8. The enclosures and environs of the Fifth Dynasty pyramids were cleared, revealing a series of Middle Kingdom tombs. A number of these were largely intact, their assemblage of coffins and models providing useful Lower Egyptian comparisons to the material from Beni Hasan, Asyut and other Upper Egyptian sites. Although the Germans worked extensively at Abusir, they left much work to be done. This has been taken up by the Czechoslovak (now Czech) Institute, which has worked there from the 1960s onwards.

In addition to these academic, reputable excavations, there were others of rather more dubious pedigree, if not legality. A number of individuals, lacking archaeological grounding but blessed with official permits, excavated and shared their finds with the Cairo Museum. Although most such enterprises were to be found in provincial cemeteries, a pair of Copts were allowed to work in part of the Valley of the Kings in December 1900. They were closely watched by Carter, who actually undertook the clearance of their principal discovery, the tomb of Tuthmosis II. Half their finds were sold, some now being in Hanover.

Wholly illegal were the continued time-hallowed activities of the tomb-robbers, who continued to operate throughout Egypt. Some academic institutions continued to patronize these individuals, and none more so than the British Museum, through the Keeper of Egyptian and Assyrian Antiquities, (Sir) Wallis Budge (1857–1934). Budge made regular visits to Egypt, and had equally regular tussles with the Antiquities Service and the Egyptian police, almost always securing his prizes. A particularly important group of mummies and coffins were acquired at Akhmim in 1896, dating to late Ptolemaic times and representing very unusual forms of cartonnage mortuary containers. Their true date was only recently ascertained, by Mark Smith of Oxford, through analysis of handwriting found on some of the cartonnage cases.

The Theban Necropolis

Apart from the work in the Valley of the Kings, the hills of Western Thebes provided the richest sources of mummies, coffins and related material. Since the earliest years of Egyptology, the great bay in the cliffs at Deir el-Bahari has been a major source of antiquities, both architectural, from the temples of Mentuhotep II (Dynasty 11) and Hatshepsut (Dynasty 18); and funerary, from the myriad interments that were either associated with their construction, or were drawn around their hallowed portals. A considerable number of late Third Intermediate Period burials were discovered by Mariette under the floors of the Hatshepsut temple, with more found by the Egypt Exploration Fund in the 1890s, under the direction of Edouard Naville (1844–1926). The same expedition's discovery of the Mentuhotep temple in 1903–6 revealed a series of Middle Kingdom tombs, including the very important shrine tombs of priestesses of Hathor. Together with others found later by the Metropolitan Museum of Art (MMA), their contents included some unique sarcophagi and certain bodies which proved to be of the greatest importance for the history of mummification.

During the years leading up to the First World War, a series of essentially intact tombs revealed much about the funerary assemblages of the New Kingdom. One of the finest was the tomb of Kha at Deir el-Medina (TT 8), found by Schiaparelli. The Overseer of Works and his wife lay surrounded by a wide range of furniture and other material, providing us with a perfect example of a 'typical' noble's tomb under Amenophis III. The Italian expedition was also responsible for the clearance of the Valley of the Queens, including the famous tomb of Queen Nefertari. Most of the tombs had long been despoiled of their original occupants – only Nefertari's knees and a broken sarcophagus lid remained – but some mummies were found, most importantly that of a princess of the early Eighteenth Dynasty, aside from many Third Intermediate/Late Period intrusive corpses.

Howard Carter and the Earl of Carnarvon (1866–1923) (ill. 66) made a spectacular discovery in 1910, when tomb HC 37 was found in the Asasif, on the west bank at Thebes. Originally cut in the Middle Kingdom, it had been re-used at the very beginning of the Eighteenth Dynasty, and contained no fewer than sixty-four mummies and coffins of this period. Further burials in the area were subsequently found by the MMA to be of the same date.

From the other end of the Eighteenth Dynasty came Georges Daressy's (1864–1938) find in 1896 of the tomb of Hatia, datable to the earliest years of the heretic king, Akhenaten. Although parts of its contents had been destroyed by a rock fall, two very fine coffins are today in museums, Hatia's in Cairo, and that of his wife(?) Henutwedjebu in St Louis, Missouri. In 1928–34 the French Institute team led by Bernard Bruyère (1879–1971) found a number of tombs of a similar date that represented the artisan class.

The 1920s and 1930s saw some important work amongst the private tombs on Sheikh Abd el-Qurna by Sir Robert Mond (1867–1938) and Walter B. Emery (1903–1971). Much of this was aimed at conserving the superbly decorated and justly celebrated tomb-chapels of the hill, but also included the clearance of various substructures. A particularly significant quantity of material came from the tomb of Amenemhat (TT 97), including a contemporary mid-Eighteenth Dynasty coffin, plus a large number of late Ramesside/early Twenty-first Dynasty intrusive burials, which provide a good complement to the higher-status examples found in the Bab el-Gasus.

The key excavation area of Deir el-Bahari was extensively worked by the MMA after the First World War under the direction of H.E. Winlock (1884–1950). While concentrating on the temples, a large number of tombs were opened, and recorded to a standard seldom seen before, although in most cases never fully published. Highlights included the uncovering of the tomb of Amenophis I's queen, Meryetamun (Dynasty 18), containing her mummy, carefully rewrapped in the Twenty-first Dynasty, along with two of the finest coffins ever made.

Queen Meryetamun also had a 'lodger', the Twenty-first Dynasty princess, Nauny. Her burial formed part of a set, a number of other interments of the same date being found nearby. One of the most interesting was tomb MMA 60. It had been intended to hold three members of the family of the High Priest Menkheperre, but over successive generations had been repeatedly opened and more and more coffins added around and above the original occupants. The venality of these later undertakers was such that the gilded faces and hands of the princesses' coffins were wrenched off for their value. The same damage was suffered by the coffins of Nauny – in her case the culprits seem to have been her own burial party. The mummies robbed by their embalmers, referred to at the beginning of this chapter, come from this tomb. In general, the Twenty-first Dynasty burials found by the Metropolitan are a sorry indictment of the embalmers and undertakers of their age.

A further key tomb group found by the expedition dates to the early Eighteenth Dynasty. Found in 1934–5 under the direction of William C. Hayes (1903–1963), it housed the family of Neferkhauet, an official in the household of Hatshepsut before her accession. Its importance lies in the selection of coffin types found within, which show how one supplemented and then replaced the other in the early part of Tuthmosis III's reign. It also provides an excellent example of an upper-middle class burial of the time.

The Intact Royal Tombs

Of all the royal tombs excavated in Egypt, none had ever been found completely intact. Some private tombs which had escaped the attention of robbers had come to light, including a large number of middle-class examples from all periods and a few of junior royalties. However, of the pharaohs, only Hor had been found in anything vaguely approaching pristine state. This all changed, however, in 1922 when Carter opened the almost intact tomb of Tutankhamun (KV 62), in the Valley of the Kings (ill. 87). Although a private tomb adapted for a king, it at last enabled Egyptologists to see the extraordinary range of objects that accompanied a king to the grave. The material also allowed sense to be made of the tantalizing fragments found by Belzoni, Loret and Davis in previous decades. The full adornments of a royal mummy were now revealed in all their splendour, including an innermost coffin and mummy-mask of solid gold. The only disappointments were the poor preservation of the body – due to the over-enthusiastic application of anointing unguents – and the lack of papyri, religious or historical.

Remarkably, only six years after work ended on the excavation of Tutankhamun's tomb, another, more intact sepulchre of a pharaoh came to light. This lay at the opposite end of Egypt, at Tanis in the Delta. In 1939, Pierre Montet (1885–1966) noticed that the enclosure wall of the city's temple did not run consistently parallel with its axis. Clearing a group of mud-brick structures in order to

87 The west wall of the antechamber of Tutankhamun (KV 62), showing the animal-headed beds that represented those used in the embalming process.

investigate, a limestone structure was found below. Initially taken for a store chamber of some kind, investigation showed it to be a tomb. It consisted of several rooms and, although plundered, still contained important material, including the debris of the burial of Prince Harnakhte, son of the tomb's owner, the Twenty-second Dynasty King Osorkon II.

A second, adjacent, tomb proved to be intact. On 20 March 1939, Egypt's modern king, Farouk, came to witness the opening of a solid silver coffin, revealing a gold mask upon the face of King Shoshenq II (Dynasty 22). The walls of the tomb bore the name of Psusennes I (Dynasty 21), and Montet at first believed that Shoshenq II had been cached in the earlier king's robbed tomb. However, the

west wall contained two hidden doorways. One was dismantled to show a short corridor with a granite plug in place. On 21 February 1940, a pink granite sarcophagus was revealed, which held a black granite coffin, and, in turn, another silver coffin, with the decomposed body of Psusennes I with gold mask and jewellery. 16 April saw another visit by Farouk and the opening of the neighbouring chamber, which contained the burial of Amenemope, the successor of Psusennes I.

Seven tombs were ultimately identified, dating to the Twenty-first and -second Dynasties. Six of these were robbed and/or empty, but Psusennes' (NRT III) actually held the remains of five kings, plus a contemporary general. All were severely damaged by humidity, which had reduced the mummies to skeletons. The discovery's impact was diminished by the outbreak of the Second World War; the royal tombs of Tanis represent nevertheless a fundamental find in the study of Egyptian funerary practices.

A set of intact princely tombs was also discovered during the war years, when Ahmad Badawi (1905–1980) uncovered a group of them within the temple enclosure at Memphis. In position and design they closely resembled the contemporary (Twenty-second Dynasty) tombs at Tanis, and revealed a considerable quantity of material. This included a silver coffin, canopics, *shabtis* and jewellery, but the level of the water table had largely destroyed the organic remains.

The First Golden Age of Physical Anthropology

The discovery of the royal mummies at Deir el-Bahari (above, p. 78–9) and their transport to the Bulaq Museum were followed by the unwrapping of many of the bodies. The first such unrolling was carried out by Maspero on the body of Tuthmosis III in 1881. No attempt was made to

unwind the bandages carefully; instead, they were slit through from head to foot. A pathetically broken body was revealed, its limbs and head detached by tomb-robbers and held in place only by the new wrappings which had been applied by the priests who had restored the body around 1000 BC (ill. 79). Disheartened by the sight, the investigators hurriedly rewrapped the mummy, and no more examinations were attempted until 1886.

In June of that year, the body of Ramesses II was unwrapped in the presence of the Khedive; it proved to be in a far better state, and over the following months nearly all the bodies were divested of their outer layers. The only major exceptions were the mummies of Amenophis I and the Lady Isetemkheb D, which were so beautifully wrapped that Maspero decided to leave them undisturbed. Only with the advent of X-rays were their bodies to be revealed for study.

The fate of some of the unwrapped royal mummies was unfortunate: that of Queen Ahmose-Nefertiry began to decompose and had to be buried under a shed for some

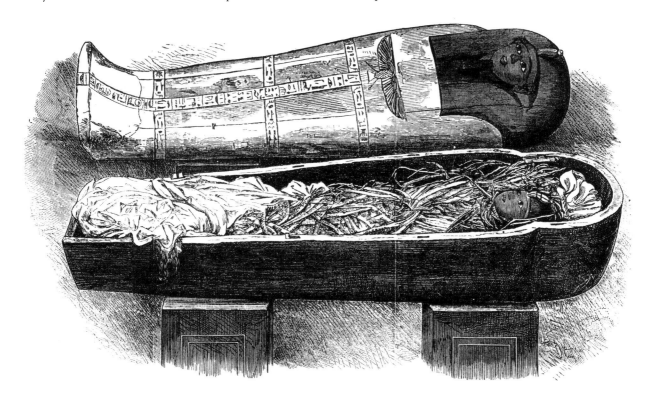

88 The body of Amenophis I had been so beautifully rewrapped in antiquity that Maspero did not have the heart to open it, although it was later X-rayed. The king's body still lies in the Cairo Museum with its burial garlands around the neck. CM CG 61005 and 61058.

years to become stabilized. Even worse, some mummies appear to have been lost. That of Pinudjem I, as well as others lacking identification, cannot now be traced. It is possible that they were 'mislaid' during the two transfers experienced by the contents of the Cairo Museum.

Many of the early unrollings were attended by a qualified anatomist, Daniel Fouquet (1850–1914), a Cairo resident. He remained a consultant to the Antiquities Service into the 1890s. During the early summer of 1891, he undertook the examination of many of the mummies from the Bab el-Gasus, which had been unwrapped by Daressy. In 1895, he reported on the remains of the Middle Kingdom corpses found at Dahshur by De Morgan. His approach showed little consideration for the antiquity of his subjects, King Hor's cranium being sawn open for examination. Fouquet produced a lengthy memoir on mummification which was, however, 'full of erroneous observations and inferences' (Dawson, Uphill and Bierbrier 1995: 155).

The next major group of royal bodies, the kings found cached in Amenophis II's tomb (KV 35), were the subject of research by a far better observer, Grafton Elliot Smith (1871–1937), Professor of Anatomy at the Cairo School of Medicine. His efforts concluded with the production of a great catalogue of nearly all the royal mummies (Smith 1912), plus a number of major works on mummification in general. He also studied human remains from Nubia, the Valley of the Kings, and numerous other sites, found between 1900 and 1909.

Elliot Smith's place as Egyptology's anthropologist was taken by Douglas Derry (1874–1961), who likewise occupied the Cairo chair of anatomy. During his tenure at the Qasr el-Aini hospital's medical school, he undertook the examination of the vast majority of mummies found in Egypt. These included that of Tutankhamun and all those discovered by Winlock's team, such as Queen Meryetamun and the Twenty-first Dynasty princesses. Derry was also responsible for the royal remains found by Montet at Tanis, although their very poor condition meant that he had little to assess other than crumbling skeletons.

By the time he retired, Derry had placed knowledge of mummies and mummification on a much higher plane than any of his predecessors. Among his activities was the first use of X-rays upon a wrapped mummy, that of Amenophis I. In addition, chemical and experimental work by Alfred Lucas (1867–1945) did much to elucidate how the mummification process was actually carried out. Thus, by 1945, a very effective base-line had been established regarding the study of mummified remains, which could realistically only be advanced with the advent of newer scientific techniques – which duly came in the 1960s.

Discoveries since the Second World War

The 1939–45 war marked a watershed in Egyptian archaeology. Political and economic changes affected both the funding and organization of excavations. Conceptual changes gradually led to the favouring of non-funerary sites, together with the adoption of much more careful techniques, replacing industrial-scale clearances. Nevertheless, many new tombs and their contents have come to light in Egypt during the last fifty years.

Although much work had been carried on around them, the interiors of a number of Old Kingdom pyramids remained without proper clearance when Abd el-Salam Hussein (d. 1949) and Alexandre Varille (1909–1951) began work on a hitherto anonymous structure at South Saqqara in 1945. They established that the pyramid had been built by King Isesi (Dynasty 5), and within it they found a smashed sarcophagus, amongst whose fragments lay more than half of the king's mummy. Before his premature demise, Hussein had also, in 1947, cleared the interior of the Red Pyramid at Dahshur, the tomb of Seneferu. In it, he found pieces of a mummy that seem most probably to have been those of the king himself. Both these sets of remains were examined by the anatomist Ahmed Batrawi (1902–1964), and were deposited in the Anatomy Department of Cairo's Qasr el-Aini hospital, along with many remains examined by his predecessor, Douglas Derry. The latter included almost all the mummies discovered in the period since the First World War.

During and directly after the Second World War, a number of important tombs of the Saite Period were found at Saqqara by the Egyptian Antiquities Service. Protected by their ingenious design, most were found intact, thus giving an excellent picture of high-status burials of the period. Of the same period was the intact burial of the Saite queen, Takhuti, found by Shehata Adam (1917–1986) at Athribis in 1950.

Zakaria Goneim (1911–1959) made an exciting but ultimately disappointing find at Saqqara, in 1952, in the

89 The sarcophagus of the Horus Sekhemkhet, in his burial chamber under his unfinished step pyramid at Saqqara. For some unknown reason, the sarcophagus proved to be empty, in spite of being sealed shut.

unfinished pyramid of the Third Dynasty king, the Horus Sekhemkhet. The burial chamber contained a sealed calcite sarcophagus of unusual design, with what appeared to be the remains of a funerary wreath on top. When opened, the sarcophagus proved inexplicably to be empty. Goneim was found drowned in the Nile in 1959; more work on the pyramid was subsequently carried out by Lauer, who revealed a subsidiary tomb, containing the body of a six-year-old boy.

The pyramid of Princess Neferuptah (Dynasty 12) at Hawara, identified by Naguib Farag in 1955, certainly once contained a mummy. Excavated with the aid of Zaki Iskander (1916–1979), the tomb proved to be intact. Unfortunately an elevated water table had entirely destroyed the body, only a few chemical traces showing that it had once been present. However, remains of gilding allowed the reconstruction of the rectangular and anthro-

poid coffins that lay within the magnificent sarcophagus, while items of jewellery and other funerary equipment were recovered from the tomb and are now displayed in Cairo.

Saqqara has remained an important source of finds, ranging across Egyptian history. A great cemetery of the nobles of the Archaic Period was excavated by Emery throughout the 1950s, merging with the discovery, at the opposite chronological extreme, of the Sacred Animal Necropolis (mainly Graeco-Roman), in which mummified creatures had been interred in kilometres of catacombs. Work still continues there.

In 1967, one of the very oldest intact mummies was found by Ahmed Moussa, in the Fifth Dynasty tomb of Nefer. Still in the tomb, it has a moustache modelled on its upper lip, has all its limbs free, and is a perfect example of a mummy of its time.

Until the 1970s, little of the New Kingdom had been known from Saqqara, apart from a few poorly recorded discoveries of the nineteenth century. This all changed with the inception of an Anglo-Dutch expedition under Geoffrey Martin, Hans Schneider and Jaap van Dijk; a French expedition under Alain Zivie; and an Egyptian team under Sayed Tawfik (1936–1990). These brought to light a whole series of tombs in areas previously little investigated. Tawfik's discoveries included the tomb of Ramesses II's vizier, Neferrenpet. The French team identified Amenophis IV's vizier, Aperel. Although damaged, the coffins of the vizier and his family still lay in the tomb, with canopics and other funerary equipment, making it one of the most important discoveries of its kind. The Anglo-Dutch work has now uncovered a considerable number of tombs of the late Eighteenth and Nineteenth Dynasties. They include that of Ramesses II's sister, Tia; Tutankhamun's Treasurer, Maya; and most important of all, the sepulchre of the general Horemheb – later to become pharaoh – whose royal tomb lies in the Valley of the Kings. Although the humid conditions and robbers had left the human remains in a pitiful condition, skilful work by the anthropologist Eugen Strouhal produced evidence to show that Horemheb's queen, Mutnodjmet, had died in childbirth, and had been buried with her baby. At the opposite end of the social scale, a mass of Ramesside burials intruded into the tomb of Iurudef provided a unique opportunity to study the bodies and coffins of lesser folk of New Kingdom Memphis.

Recent Discoveries

Work continues on sites throughout Egypt, with probably more expeditions working than ever before. Finds of fundamental importance are made on a regular basis by archaeologists working for the Supreme Council for Antiquities (SCA) (the latest incarnation of Mariette's Antiquities Service), Egyptian institutions, and those of almost every European country, North America, Japan and other nations.

It is impossible to mention more than a handful of projects with a bearing on funerary archaeology, but Polish excavations at Marina el-Alamein, and by the SCA at Bahriya Oasis, have harvested key information on Roman Period interments. Two First Intermediate Period family tombs were found by the Australian expedition led by

90 Rock-cut Osiris-figure at the end of the main corridor of the tomb of the sons of Ramesses II (KV 5).

Naguib Kanawati at El-Hagarsa in January 1989 (D 11 and D 30). The mummies were examined by Rosalie David's Manchester team, and provided important DNA evidence. One discovery showed that certain mummies had been mixed up, causing a mismatch between the gender depicted on the masks and that actually revealed by the mummy.

Following the clearance of Tutankhamun's tomb, the Valley of the Kings has seen very little archaeological activity. Since the 1970s, however, work has resumed to some extent, not in the hope of finding new tombs, but properly clearing and recording those long known. Thus, John Romer cleared the tomb of Ramesses XI; Donald Ryan has worked on some of the small, private, tombs there; Edwin Brock has devoted years to the study and reassembly of the broken Ramesside royal sarcophagi; and Otto Schaden cleared the tomb of Ay and has begun to empty the debris from the tomb of Amenmesse. Hartwig Altenmüller has undertaken similar work in the tomb of the Chancellor Bay, and Kent Weeks has started clearing and recording the tomb of some of the sons of Ramesses II (KV 5). These excavations have brought to light much material of importance for mummy studies. Perhaps the most extraordinary discovery in the Valley has been that by Kent Weeks of the inner parts of KV 5. Over one hundred chambers have so far been reached, some littered with the broken remains of mummies, sarcophagi and canopics: it appears to have been the largest and most spatially complex tomb in Egypt.

Another ongoing piece of work has identified the youngest known pharaonic royal tomb in Egypt. Back in the 1880s, a large sarcophagus lying exposed in the ruins of Mendes was found to contain some bones and a *shabti* figure of King Nepherites I (Dynasty 29). It was not until 1992–3, however, that excavations by Donald Redford uncovered the remains of the walls of the chamber that had once surrounded the sarcophagus, bearing the funerary texts of Nepherites.

By a coincidence, in 1988, only a few years earlier, Günther Dreyer had found at Abydos perhaps the earliest tomb of a named king. Numbered U-j, it provided a rich harvest of material, standing at the beginning of the 3,000-year sequence of mortuary practices that form the subject of this book.

SCIENTIFIC RESEARCH

Over the last century, and especially during the last thirty years, mummies have been subjected to an increasingly sophisticated battery of scientific tests. X-rays, CAT-scanning, endoscopy, scanning electron microscopy, histopathology, as well as blood group and DNA testing of mummies have all been performed in an effort to understand better the diseases from which the ancient Egyptians suffered, their diet, family relationships and methods of mummification.

Mummies and Medicine

The earliest medical interest in mummies during the late nineteenth and early twentieth centuries mainly concerned the racial type of the ancient Egyptians, and concentrated on cranial measurements which were popular in physical anthropology at the time. Phrenology – determining the personality and character of an individual from the shape and bumps of the skull – was also a favoured 'science' a century ago, which gave further impetus to the study of mummy-crania. The popularity for phrenology (and therefore mummy-crania) luckily dissipated when it was shown

---

DRUGS IN ANCIENT EGYPT

Whether or not the Egyptians used 'recreational drugs' is a question that has occasionally been asked. Recent controversial scientific tests on mummy samples (notably hair) have shown evidence of the presence of nicotine and/or hashish, and/or cocaine in some mummies, including that of Ramesses II. Soft tissue samples of the mummy Henut-tawy, and six other mummies of Third Intermediate Period to Roman date (now in Germany) examined by Svelta Balabonova tested positively for hashish, nicotine and cocaine. The presence of hashish is not surprising as hemp plants, the basis of hashish, grew in Egypt as well as throughout the Near East, and are known to have been used as drugs, both medicinal and recreational. However, both coca and tobacco come from the New World, and were not introduced into the Old World until the fifteenth century A D. Unless some species of these plants grew in Africa it is difficult to explain their presence in the mummies sampled, though there are several possibilities. The samples might have been contaminated either by incorrect sampling procedures, or by tobacco being absorbed by the mummies from nearby smokers (surely a very unusual case of secondary smoking?). Sometimes tobacco leaves are used to keep away insects, and this could have been practised in the museum in the nineteenth century. It is also possible that some other chemicals used in mummification have broken down with time in such a manner that they can be mistaken for the residues of tobacco, hashish and cocaine. Perhaps if the tests were carried out on other mummies one could better determine the reason for these extraordinary results.

---

to be inaccurate and unreliable. Although these measurements, together with long-bone measurements, have provided various ideas about the ancient Egyptians' origins, there is still no clear racial type that has been identified as being typically ancient Egyptian. Rather, it seems that the population was a mixture of a number of physical types.

In 1895 Roentgen, a German physicist, discovered the rays that were to form the basis for the X-ray method. While early investigations meant unwrapping and in effect, destroying the mummy, X-rays proved an effective and non-destructive means of finding out what was in the wrappings in terms of amulets, artificial eyes, jewellery, as well as the actual mummy. Diseases that manifested themselves in the bones were likewise easily identifiable, as were fractures, breaks and the like.

W. Koenig X-rayed the first human and animal mummies in Frankfurt in 1896 at the request of a Dr Bloch. The next X-ray autopsy was performed by Petrie in 1898 on a mummy from Deshasheh. Petrie was thrilled by the results, especially as the mummy did not suffer from the examination. Tuthmosis IV was the first royal mummy to

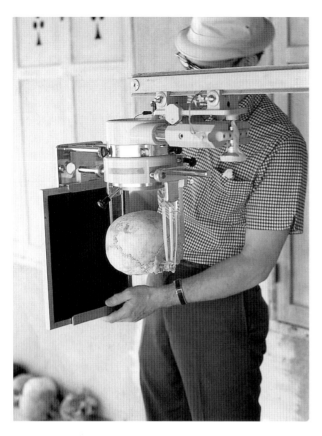

91 Part of the project sponsored jointly by the universities of Michigan and Alexandria consisted of measuring skulls and teeth, together with making X-rays of the royal mummies.

be X-rayed in Cairo, Elliot Smith carrying the late monarch to a private nursing home in Cairo in 1903 in a horse-drawn cab. Here, the only X-ray machine in Cairo was used by Dr Khayat to gaze inside the ancient shell. In 1913 Barlotti used X-rays to locate amulets and jewellery on an Eleventh Dynasty mummy, as well as identifying an anomaly in the vertebral column of a mummified six-year-old. By the 1920s and 1930s X-raying mummies was an established form of investigation for amulets and jewellery as well as disease. In 1924 the Field Museum of Chicago examined a Twenty-sixth Dynasty mummy, and in 1931, R.L. Moodie X-rayed much of the museum's remaining collection, including mummies from Peru. P.H.K. Gray (1913–1984) and Frans Jonckheere (1903–1956) X-rayed over two hundred mummies in Europe, Gray becoming the established expert in the field.

By the 1950s X-rays were increasingly used to identify diseases rather than to locate amulets in the wrappings, and both the Liverpool and Manchester Museums employed the process on most of the mummies in their collections. The great X-ray investigations culminated in the 1970s project sponsored by the University of Michigan and the University of Alexandria. James E. Harris, Kent Weeks, Edward F. Wente and their team investigated most of the royal mummies held by the Cairo Museum, with special attention being paid to their teeth. Animal mummies have also been examined in this manner, and extensive X-rays of the cat mummies in the British Museum are under way. (Thus far the cat mummy study has revealed several ancient fakes consisting of odd limbs or rags beautifully wrapped and sold as votive offerings to pious pilgrims.)

The most common disease identified by X-rays is arthritis: Amosis, Ramesses II, Amenophis II, Merenptah and a host of others suffered from it. Osteoarthritis is the most common form of arthritis. Age and stress on the bones is responsible. Through continual use the cartilage between the joints wears away so that the bones rub together and under the stress start to lip (grow) at the edges. Arthritis is one of the commonest diseases found in ancient Egyptian mummies of all periods, irrespective of class. In Maya's tomb at Saqqara nearly 550 individuals were found, of which about 350 were adults. They date from the New Kingdom and the Late Period. Almost all individuals over thirty years of age suffered from arthritis.

Fractures and breaks can easily be identified by X-rays, as well as violent trauma wounds, such as blows to the head, and of course injuries that punctured the bone, such as those found in the bodies of the sixty veteran soldiers buried near the tomb of Mentuhotep II at Deir el-Bahari (ill. 95). The soldiers have usually been regarded as having fought with Mentuhotep II in his efforts to reunify Egypt after the chaos of the First Intermediate Period, although it has been recently suggested that they are somewhat later. Their remains were studied by Derry. Many of them had received head wounds earlier in life which had healed, thereby establishing their status as veterans. In many instances the more recent cause of death was clearly visible: the wooden tip of an arrow embedded in an eye socket penetrating the skull, shattered skulls, gashes made by axes and daggers on the face and head. Some skulls from Kerma also show evidence of trauma or violent injury such as cuts or

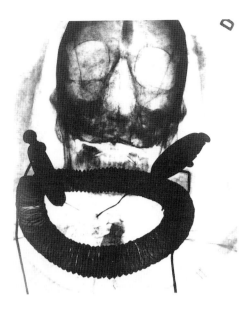

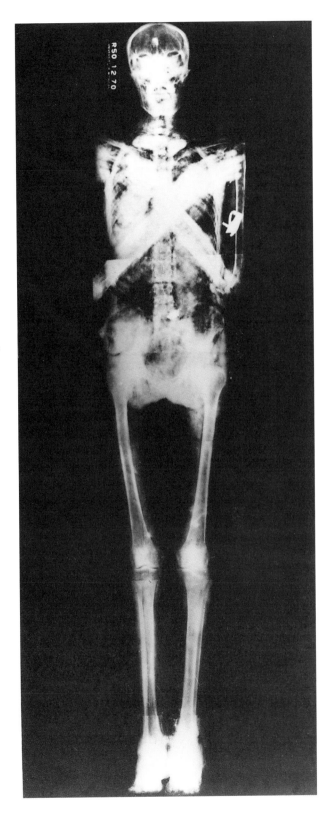

92 The architect Kha, discovered in 1906 by Schiaparelli, was X-rayed by the Egyptian Museum of Turin. The X-rays revealed gold earrings and an elaborate gold collar. They also show a snake's head amulet resting on his brow. Turin Supp. 8431.

93 (*right*) X-ray of the mummy of King Sethos I, showing the *wadjet*-eye that remains hidden in the inner bandages that still adhere to the body.

94 (*below*) X-ray of a severed mummified head, with a cartonnage moulding affixed to the face. Probably Roman Period; Chicago. Field Museum 1115200.

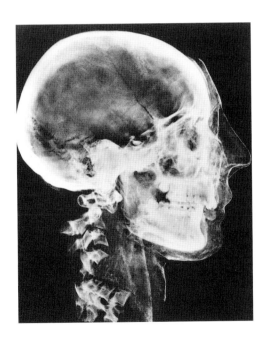

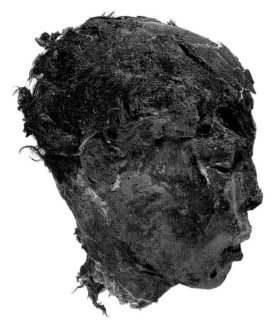

95 The wounds on the bodies of a group of soldiers buried near Mentuhotep II at Deir el-Bahari revealed whether or not they had been veterans and how they had died.

blows from weapons. In recent years Joyce Filer has worked on cranial (and post-cranial) injuries found on Egyptian and Nubian bodies in an effort to determine the types of weapons, wounds and cures prevalent in antiquity.

Teeth are one of the best indicators of the age of the deceased, as well as providing information on dental health and even dentistry. X-rays are particularly helpful in studying them. The ancient Egyptians had, due to their diet, very bad teeth, as has been established by F.F. Leek (1903–1985) and James Harris, amongst others. The mummies they examined suffered from dental caries, abscesses, and severe attrition. Caries is the progressive loss of tooth substance, a decay process associated with sugars in the diet. It is the least common of Egyptian dental problems, as honey was the only, and very expensive, sweetener used. Abscesses occur when infected teeth spread decay through the root of the tooth into the bone. They can also be caused by excessive wearing away of the crown, exposing the pulp cavity to infection. They are very painful, and Amenophis III, who had them, must have suffered for much of his life. The mummy of Mutnodjmet, the wife of the Eighteenth Dynasty pharaoh Horemheb, showed that the lady had lost all her teeth before death and was probably restricted to a diet of soup or mashed food.

The most common dental problem of the ancient Egyptians was attrition, or the wearing down of teeth which resulted in dental complaints, such as abcesses. Diet was primarily responsible for this. Ancient Egyptian bread, which had grit mixed into it to ease the grinding process, has long been thought the cause for the high rate of attrition of teeth. Once worn down with the dentine exposed, they were more susceptible to infections and diseases. Modern scholars have found that the high rate of tooth-attrition has made it difficult to use tooth-wear as a criterion to age skeletons. Now new methods are being developed for estimating age using teeth in Egypt, most notably by Corinne Duhig.

The study of Egyptian teeth has naturally led to a study of the practice of dentistry. The titulary of Hesire, a notable of the Third Dynasty, includes the apparent title of dentist. A few others also held this title, specialized and different from that of 'doctor' or indeed 'veterinarian', both common in ancient Egypt. Cures that could be used by all sorts of doctors are found in the many Egyptian medical papyri, notable of which are the Ebers, Edwin Smith and Kahun papyri.

Most interesting, however, is possible evidence of the work of Egyptian dentists. A few examples of attempts to steady loose teeth have been found. On a Late Period mummy (T 121) from Tura el-Asmant, one of the teeth was fixed with a wire made of silver with some copper impurities. Holes had been drilled in the neighbouring teeth, and the wire had been passed through them. A similar case has been reported from Giza, shaft burial 984, dating to the Fourth or Fifth Dynasty. There, gold wire was used to join a badly worn lower third molar to the second. There has been some debate as to whether this is an ancient example or not as there was some confusion surrounding the finding of the teeth. What has been termed a true dental bridge was found in a Fourth Dynasty tomb, 90, in the cemetery of el-Qatta, near Imbaba, where a few pieces of gold wire held together three teeth. Again, however, there is a question as to whether the wired teeth were really dental work, or were removed from someone's mouth, wired together, and worn as a charm. This latter explanation is more plausible since the method of tooth-wiring indicates that it was not done in the mouth. The study of ancient Egyptian dentistry is still in its infancy.

A combination of X-rays and physical examination can reveal significant information not just about teeth, but about disease and the entire individual. One of the mummified foetuses from Tutankhamun's tomb has been examined and tentatively diagnosed to have Sprengel's deformity. Examination of the still-born female foetus, aged approximately eight months, shows that the left clavicle is longer and more curved than the right, and the left scapula is wider and higher than the right, both indicative of this complaint.

CAT-scans (or CT-scans) have also provided a non-destructive way of studying mummies. CAT-scanning, which became popular in the 1960s, is the acronym for Computed Axial Tomography scanning, and is an advanced form of X-ray in the round. The body is passed through a machine and the X-ray film and ray-source are moved simultaneously in opposite directions. The advantage of this sort of study is that pictures can be taken of slices through the body which can then be joined together, producing a three-dimensional image. In this way density differences are easily noted, so that soft organs can be viewed, something that cannot be done by simple X-rays which concentrate only on bone. Furthermore, in CAT-scanning, the images recorded are taken from different angles which can be viewed together or separately. Thus, mummies in cartonnage cases can be studied with no damage being done to the cases or occupants. CAT-scanning can determine a mummy's age, sex and some pathologies that might be visible. Several human and animal mummies have been scanned successfully, including the mummies in the Pennsylvania University Museum (PUM II and IV), 'victual' or meat mummies from the tomb of Meryetamun, the body of the Chantress of Amun, Tjentmutengebtiu, and seven Roman and Ptolemaic mummies from the British Museum. An added interest of scanning is the possibility of creating a three-dimensional reconstruction of the face and entire body of the subject by using information from the scanned images.

Endoscopy is another method of studying the internal spaces of mummies. It involves introducing a narrow tube into the body through one of its natural orifices or through a small incision in the abdominal or chest wall. This allows one to look inside without damaging the body itself and to see structures that are not otherwise easily visible. It is an excellent technique for examining the stomach, especially for ulcers. Endoscopy can determine the need to take specimens and perform biopsies to identify what, if anything, the mummy had suffered from, or even the cause of death.

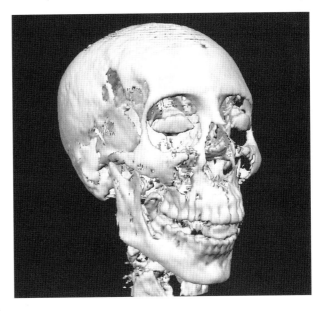

96 CAT-scan of the head of the wrapped mummy of the priestess Tjentmutengebtiu. Twenty-second Dynasty; BM EA 22939.

Although taking specimens from mummies for study is destructive, it can be very rewarding, especially with today's technology which requires only a mere 10 grammes or so of tissue, as well as sometimes bone, for a test. One of the first people to study mummy tissue was Marc Armand Ruffer (1859–1917), who coined the phrase, 'palaeopathology', the study of ancient diseases. He examined many samples from mummies and managed to identify diseases as well as organs that had dried beyond recognition. Nowadays, using small samples one can identify other diseases such as malaria, schistosomiasis, and trichinosis.

Schistosomiasis, or bilharzia, is a parasitic disease caused by *schistosoma haematobia*, a parasitic worm which uses water snails found in the Nile and canals as an intermediary host. Once the parasite enters the body, it lays eggs which are released into the bloodstream, gaining access to the intestines and bladder, from which they are eventually emitted. Symptoms include enlarged genitalia, blood in the urine, and baldness. The earliest finding to date of bilharzia is from a Predynastic body that was naturally desiccated and is now in the British Museum. Several new tests have been developed that enable identification of the disease and over ninety-five mummies have been tested for it by Robert Miller, with a very high percentage of positive results. Most

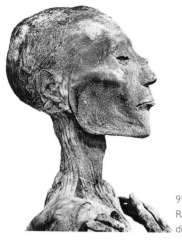

97 The pustules on Ramesses V's face have been diagnosed as smallpox.

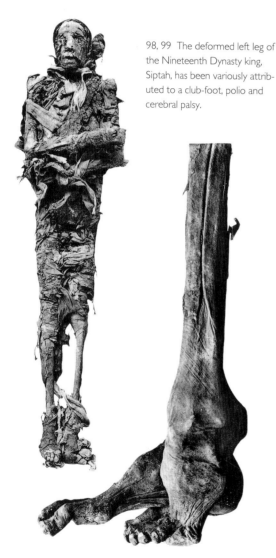

98, 99 The deformed left leg of the Nineteenth Dynasty king, Siptah, has been variously attributed to a club-foot, polio and cerebral palsy.

sufferers were of the poorer classes, especially fishermen, farmers and housewives, all of whom would have been regularly exposed to stagnant or slow-moving water. Other parasites carrying disease have also been found from Egypt: in Canada, the Royal Ontario Museum's mummy ROM I is reported to have suffered from trichinosis, as did the mummy of the weaver Nakht. This is most commonly transferred by pork, thus confirming the faunal evidence that the ancient Egyptian diet included pork. Malaria, also found in Egypt, is caused by the bite of the female Anopheles mosquito. The plasmodium parasite enters the victim's body while the mosquito withdraws blood. Severe fever and sometimes death are the results. Miller has done some work on identifying malaria in mummies and has found that the Granville mummy, now in the British Museum, suffered from it.

Other diseases have also been identified in mummies, all of which shed light on the ancient Egyptian environment, diet, and health. Several mummies, such as Nakht, PUM II, and Nakhtankh (Manchester), suffered from anthracosis, a lung disease caused by inhaling smoke from fires and oil lamps in poorly ventilated places. Sand and dust inhalation is also responsible for similar complaints, such as pneumoconiosis or perhaps silicosis, from which the weaver Nakht suffered. Evidence of tuberculosis has also been found in ancient Egyptian mummies dating from the Predynastic period as well as from the Nineteenth and Twenty-first Dynasties. Leprosy has also been found in Egypt, primarily in the Ptolemaic Period where some examples have been found in male burials. Furthermore, a possible case of poliomyelitis has been recorded in the mummy of the pharaoh Siptah. Polio is a viral infection of the central nervous system which manifests itself in the paralysis of one or more muscle groups: Siptah has one short and withered leg. The same symptoms, however, can result from certain types of cerebral palsy. Smallpox has also been suspected on the mummy of the pharaoh Ramesses V. Arteriosclerosis, or calcification of the arteries, seemed to be a common complaint amongst pharaohs and commoners during all periods of Egyptian history: PUM I, Lady Teye, Ramesses II, and Merenptah are among those who suffered from it.

The most recent scientific advances employed to study mummies are tests for blood-groups and DNA. DNA testing is used to identify gender, family relationship, genetic

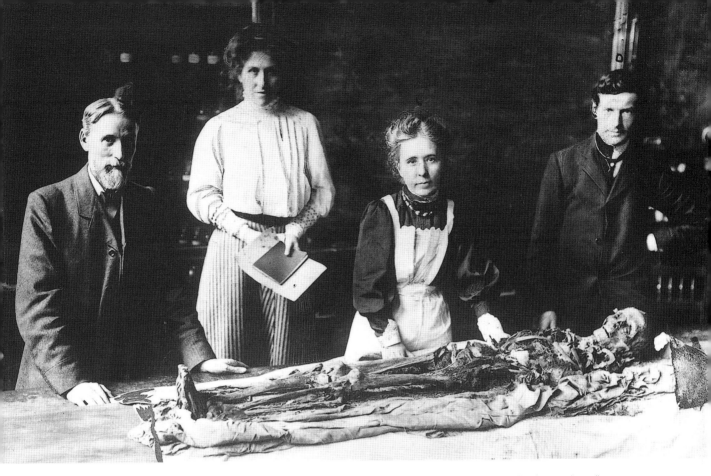

100 Manchester University's museum has had a long tradition of scientific examinations of mummies. One of the earliest large-scale studies was conducted in 1908, when the Twelfth Dynasty 'Two Brothers', from Riqqeh, were unwrapped, with Margaret Murray (second from the right) as the presiding Egyptologist.

and infectious diseases, and in the case of animals, species. So far only small portions of genetic information that are encoded in the DNA have been studied. DNA testing for mummies is in its infancy, and its full potential has yet to be explored and, indeed, determined. Some interesting work on the history of viruses is currently being undertaken in conjunction with DNA testing on the baboon and other monkey mummies recovered from the Sacred Animal Necropolis in north Saqqara. The research focuses on trying to detect virus DNA in the primate tissues that might have been the viruses' original hosts. The viruses would not have affected the monkeys adversely, but are now harmful to humans as, for example, the HIV virus. The study and identification of blood groups in mummies aids in determining familial relationships. However, the results of these tests are, thus far, not beyond question. Such serological tests have been undertaken with tissue from mummies from the Amarna group, notably Yuya, Tjuiu, Amenophis III, and Tutankhamun, but their precise relationships cannot

be clearly determined without the body of Akhenaten. Thus, although these methods have great potential, so far they suffer from grave drawbacks.

From the late 1960s onward there has been a trend to study mummies using as many techniques as possible. The starting point for this holistic research was Manchester where Rosalie David launched the Manchester Museum Mummy Project which studied all the mummies in the collection. The Manchester Museum has a long history of interest in mummies, the first study there being conducted in 1908 by Margaret Murray (1863–1963) on the mummies of Nakhtankh and Khnumnakhte, from Rifeh and two of the mummies that form the core of the Manchester collection. The holistic trend was carried on in Canada at the Royal Ontario Museum in Toronto, and by the University of Pennsylvania Museum. These all-inclusive and relatively non-destructive projects are currently providing us with a wealth of knowledge about ancient Egyptian diseases and embalming techniques hitherto unachievable.

CHRONOLOGY OF SIGNIFICANT MUMMY, COFFIN AND SARCOPHAGUS FINDS

1816–19	Belzoni	Western Thebes: various.
1817	Belzoni	Valley of the Kings: tombs of Ay (KV 23), Ramesses I (KV 16), Sethos I (KV 17).
1818	Belzoni	Giza: pyramid of Khephren (G II).
1822/5	Passalacqua	Dira Abu'l-Naga: Djehuty canopic.
1823	Passalacqua	Asasif: Mentuhotep.
pre-1823	Lebolo	Sheikh Abd el-Qurna: Pedamenopet et. al.
1827	Locals	Dira Abu'l-Naga: Inyotef VI.
1832	French	Deir el-Medina: Ankhnesneferibre sarcophagus.
1837	Vyse; Perring	Giza: pyramid of Mykerinos (G III); 'Campbell's Tomb' (LG 84).
1844	Lepsius	Asasif: Saite Tomb (L 27).
1845/9	Locals	Dira Abu'l-Naga: Inyotef V and VII.
1855	Rhind	Sheikh Abd el-Qurna: Montjuemsaf, Princess' Cache
1857	Mariette	Dira Abu'l-Naga: Kamose.
1858	Mariette	Deir el-Bahari: Priests of Montju.
1859	Mariette	Dira Abu'l-Naga: Queen Ahhotpe.
1871	Abd el-Rassul	Deir el-Bahari: Royal Cache (TT 320).
1881	Brugsch;	Saqqara: Late Old Kingdom pyramids.
1883	Dufferin; Graham	Deir el-Bahari: Queen Tem (DBXI.15).
1885	Maspero	Deir el-Medina: Nitokris sarcophagus.
1886	Maspero	Deir el-Medina: Sennedjem (TT 1).
1888	Petrie	Hawara: portrait mummies; Ammenemes III.
1889	Petrie	Lahun: Sesostris II.
1891	Petrie	Meidum: various.
1891	Grébaut; Daressy	Deir el-Bahari: Priests of Amun (Bab el-Gasus).
	Naville	Deir el-Bahari: Djeddjhutefankh.
1894–5	De Morgan	Dahshur: Complexes of Sesostris III, Ammenemes II and III.
1896	Daressy	Sheikh Abd el-Qurna: Hatiay.
1896–7	Quibell	Ramesseum: Nakhtefmut; Iufenamun; Hori.
1896	Locals; Budge	Akhmim: various.
1898	Loret	Valley of the Kings: tombs of Tuthmosis III (KV 34), Amenophis II (KV 35), Maihirpri (KV 36).
1900	Petrie	Abydos: Archaic royal tombs.
1900	Barsanti	Saqqara: Saite Tombs.
1907	Edgar	Masara: Udjashu.
1907	Edgar	Tell-Moddam: Kama.
1901	Carter	Valley of the Kings: tomb of Tentqerel (KV 44).
1902–4	Davies; Carter	Valley of the Kings; Tuthmosis IV; Hatshepsut.
1903–4	Garstang	Beni Hasan: various.
1904	Davies; Quibell	Valley of the Kings: tomb of Yuya and Tjuiu.
1904–7	Naville	Deir el-Bahari: Princess' Tombs (DBXI.7–11).
1905–9	Davies; Ayrton	Valley of the Kings: KV 55; Siptah.
1906–7	Mace; Winlock	Lisht: Senebtisi.
1905–25	Mond	Sheikh Abd el-Qurna: various.
1907–13	Carnarvon; Carter	Asasif/Dira Abu'l-Naga: Tomb 32.
1908–9	Petrie	Qurna: Seventeenth Dynasty lady.
1911–13	Möller; Anthes	Ramesseum area: Tabekentaashket; Ankhpakhered.
1914	Petrie; Brunton	Lahun: Sithathoriunet.
1914	Carter	Dira Abu'l-Naga: Ahmose-Nefertiry.
1916	Carter	Wadi Siqqat Taqa el-Zeide: Hatshepsut.
1916–23	Reisner	Kurru, Nuri, Meroë: Kushite royal tombs.
1917	Lansing	Asasif: various Seventeenth Dynasty.
1920–38	Hassan	Giza: various.
1921	Winlock	Deir el-Bahari: Princess' Tombs (DBXI.17–18).
1922	Carnarvon; Carter	Valley of the Kings: tomb of Tutankhamun (KV 62).
1924	Winlock	Deir el-Bahari: Henttawi (MMA 59); Three Princesses (MMA 60).
1924–32	Reisner	Giza: various.
1925–35	Junker	Giza: various.
1925	Gauthier	Tell Basta: Hori family.
1925	Reisner	Giza: Hetepheres (G 7000X).
1926–35	Bruyère	Deir el-Medina: various.
1927	Winlock	Deir el-Bahari: Soldiers of Mentuhotep II (MMA 507).
1928	Winlock	Deir el-Bahari: Queen Meryetamun (TT 358).
1933	Hölscher	Medinet Habu: Harsiese (MH 1).
1935	Hayes	Asasif: Neferkauet (MMA 729).
1936	Lansing; Hayes	Sheikh Abd el-Qurna: Ramose and Hatnefer.
1939–40	Montet	Tanis: tombs of Osorkon II, Psusennes I.
1941	Saad	Saqqara: Amentefnakhte.
1942	Badawi	Mit Rahina: High Priests of Ptah.
1944	Habachi	Tell Basta: Hori family.
1944	Hussein	Saqqara: Isesi.
1949	Hussein	Saqqara: Kanefer and family. Saqqara: Isesi.
1950	Adam	Athribis: Takhuti.
1950	Goneim	Saqqara: Horus Sekhemkhet.
1951	Drioton and Lauer	Saqqara: Neferibresineith and Wahibremen.
1955	Farag; Iskander	Hawara: Neferuptah.
1965	Moussa	Nefer.
1963–7	Lauer	Child from Sekhemkhet South.
1980	Zivie	Saqqara: Aperel.
1984	Martin	Saqqara: Irudef.
1988	Weeks	Valley of the Kings: tomb of the sons of Ramesses II (ICUS).
1989	Kanawati	El-Hagarsa: Hefefi and Bekhen.
1980	Verner	Abusir: Udjahorresnet.
1992–3	Redford	Mendes: Nepherites I.
1995–	Arnold	Dahshur: complex of Sesostris III.

Part II

Chapter 3

Mummies and the Art of Mummification

Thanks to the excavations and discoveries of the last two centuries a great deal is now known about the evolution of mummification from Predynastic times to the Roman Period. The bulk of this chapter will be concerned with a detailed survey of this 3,000-year history. First, however, we need to look at what the ancient and classical texts tell us about the process of mummification itself, before turning to the physical evidence of the mummies (*saah* in ancient Egyptian).

The Ancient Sources

There is, alas, no ancient Egyptian 'how to' book for mummification, although the Rhind Magical Papyrus (*c.* 200 BC) provides some information on the rituals associated with it. Three papyri, respectively in the Cairo, Durham Oriental, and Louvre Museums, all dating to approximately the first century AD, provide some spells to be recited whilst bandaging up each part of the body. Another papyrus, in Berlin, gives some instructions about the order in which limbs were to be wrapped, amulets inserted and spells recited. More detailed and clearer information, however, comes from Herodotus' *Histories* of the fifth century BC. In Book II, he provides a detailed account of the procedure as it was performed in his time. This, coupled with the accounts of other later writers such as Diodorus Siculus (*c.* 80 BC) and Porphyry (*c.* third century AD), has long provided the basis for the study of mummification techniques.

Herodotus' description of mummification, although relatively late in date, describes three types of embalming:

> When a body is brought to the embalmers, they produce specimen models in wood, graded in quality... They ask which of the three is required, and the family of the dead, having agreed upon a price, leave the embalmers to their task.
>
> The most perfect process is as follows: as much as possible of the brain is removed via the nostrils with an iron hook, and what cannot be reached with the hook is washed out with drugs; next, the flank is opened with a flint knife and the whole contents of the abdomen removed; the cavity is then thoroughly cleaned and washed out, firstly with palm wine and again with an infusion of ground spices. After that, it is filled with pure myrrh, cassia, and every other aromatic substance, excepting frankincense, and sewn up again, after which the body is placed in natron [see below], covered entirely over, for seventy days – never longer. When this period is over, the body is washed and then wrapped from head to foot in linen cut into strips and smeared on the underside with gum, which is commonly used by the Egyptians instead of glue. In this condition the body is given back to the family, who have a wooden case made, shaped like a human figure, into which it is put.
>
> When, for reasons of expense, the second quality is called for, the treatment is different: no incision is made and the

101 (*above*) Anubis bending over the mummy. Nineteenth Dynasty, from KV 47.

intestines are not removed, but oil of cedar is injected with a syringe into the body through the anus which is afterwards stopped up to prevent the liquid from escaping. The body is then cured in natron for the prescribed number of days, on the last of which the oil is drained off. The effect of it is so powerful that as it leaves the body it brings with it the viscera in a liquid state, and as the flesh has been dissolved by the natron, nothing of the body is left but the skin and bones. After this treatment, it is returned to the family without further attention.

The third method, used for embalming the bodies of the poor, is simply to wash out the intestines, and keep the body for seventy days in natron.

(trans. after de Sélincourt and Burn)

Natron, or *netjry*, 'divine salt', is nominally a mixture of sodium bicarbonate, sodium carbonate, sodium sulphate, and sodium chloride. The composition of the various samples that have been tested, however, varies widely. It is found naturally in Egypt, most commonly in the Wadi Natrun some 64 km north-west of Cairo. It has desiccating and defatting properties.

For the most part Egyptian texts agree with Herodotus that mummification took a total of 70 days, with 40 days or so being used for the drying, and the remainder for wrapping and entombment. In the Theban tomb of Djehuty (TT 110) a text reads: 'A goodly burial arrives in peace, your 70 days have been fulfilled in your place of embalming'. *The Bible* (Genesis 50) agrees with a period of 40 days for the actual drying when referring to the burial of Jacob. There is, however, an interesting inscription from the tomb of Queen Meresankh III at Giza (Dynasty 4) that states that she was buried 272 days after her death – far in excess of the usual 70-day period mentioned in other texts. This might have been due to the need to finish off the tomb before interment, or even for political reasons. Another individual, Pasheredenptah, a High Priest of Memphis in the Late Period, also had an embalmment lasting for 200 days, again for unknown reasons. The usual 70-day limit for embalming perhaps derives from the 70-day disappearance and reappearance cycle of the star Sirius. Sirius was associated with Osiris, god of the Afterworld, who, like the star vanished for 70 days before being resurrected.

Regarding Herodotus' 'second quality', it seems that the oil injected into the corpse would more often have been

102 The mummy of the Lady Rai. Early Eighteenth Dynasty, from TT 320; CM CG 61054.

juniper, rather than cedar, although both were probably used (see below for a discussion of these two oils). It is noteworthy that wrapping does not seem to have been included in this 'second quality' of preparation. Herodotus adds that the bodies of women of rank were not given to the embalmers until a few days had passed and they had started to putrefy, to prevent necrophilia. This might be a possible explanation for the unpleasant odour that emanated from the mummy of Ahmose-Nefertiry (Dynasty 18) when she was first unwrapped: perhaps she was embalmed after putrefaction had started.

Diodorus Siculus has a few things to add to Herodotus' description of the most expensive method of mummification. He writes that once the body was stretched out, a person called the 'scribe' traced the length of the incision on its left side so that the cut could be made accurately. He also says that the body was filled with aromatic substances for 30 days, emptied, and then filled once again, before being bound and coffined. Neither writer mentions what happened to the viscera, and Plutarch (first to second

103 Wadi Natrun was the main supplier of natron salt to the ancient Egyptians. The water at the edges of the lake and around it would evaporate, leaving natron that could be collected.

THE WORK OF THE EMBALMER

Several examples of embalmers' deposits have been recovered from Egypt, as well as embalmers' agreements, contracts between the embalmer and the client, dating to the Graeco-Roman Period. The deposits, found from almost all periods of Egyptian history, consist of the debris of the embalming process, such as linen fragments, natron, chaff and other fillers, lamps, brooms, clay vessels, lumps of resin, oils and embalming tables. Apparently the equipment used in mummification was not employed again, so it, like the body, was buried. A Graeco-Roman Period papyrus has been found that includes an embalmer's price list, which tells us how much each of the items found in the embalmers' caches cost at the time. The prices are in drachmae and obols (a Greek monetary unit, generally silver), and include some enig-matic items, such as a dog. The food items were either part of the funeral feast, or intended for the hired mourners and embalmers.

earthenware pot	4 ob	barley	16 dr
red paint	12 ob	leaven(?)	4 dr
wax	20 ob	dog(?)	8 dr
myrrh	4dr, 4ob	little mask(?)	14 dr
tallow	8 ob	loaves	21 dr
linen cloth	136 dr	pine cone/garland	16 ob
mask	64 dr	mourners	32 dr
cedar(?) oil	41 dr	carriage by donkey	8 dr
medicament for linen	4 dr	chaff(?)	12 ob
good oil	4 dr		
Turbon's wages	8 dr		
lamps	24 dr		
old tunic	24 ob		
sweet wine	20 ob		

THE BASIC MATERIALS NECESSARY FOR MUMMIFICATION

INCENSE *snetjer* was regarded as a crucial offering to the mummy and the gods. It was used to fumigate the corpse and played an intrinsic part in the Opening of the Mouth ceremony.

NATRON *netjry* or divine salt, comes from the Wadi Natrun, about 64 km north-west of Cairo, also from Barnugi district in the Beheira province (about 70 km north of Wadi Natrun, near Naucratis), and from el Kab in the south. It is the prime desiccating agent in mummification.

SALT was used as a desiccant in the Christian period, although there have been some misidentifications of its use in earlier eras.

SAWDUST, CHAFF, SAND, RAGS, CHOPPED STRAW were used to fill the body cavity, and to stuff other parts of the body in the Twenty-first Dynasty. Sawdust was also sprinkled on the skin to aid desiccation.

MYRRH and **FRANKINCENSE**, *antiyw* in Egyptian, were fragrant gum-resins in the shape of small yellow-red lumps. These resins come from Somalia and southern Arabia, and were most commonly used in the New Kingdom to stuff and massage on and into mummies. They were most valued for the fragrance that they imparted to the corpse.

RESIN Several varieties of resins were used in mummification. Resin is the sap secreted from fir and pine trees, especially. It was used, in a melted state, to fill the cranium, body cavity, and to coat coffins. It deodorizes and reduces the chance of bacterial activity, as well as . being sweet smelling. It has sometimes been confused with PITCH and BITUMEN, the latter coming from the Dead Sea area, and both of which were used occasionally in the Late and Graeco-Roman Periods.

OIL Various oils were used in mummification. Classical writers mention cedar oil as being the mainstay of mummification oils. Tests have proved that the cedar oil referred to is more often juniper oil. The difficulty in identification arose as both are coniferous trees found in the Syrio-Lebanon region, with juniper being more common and more resinous. Ancient writers rarely differentiated taxonomically between the two, often perhaps not knowing that they are two different species, especially since their scent is so similar. The oils of either tree cannot serve as adequate enemetics to dissolve the viscera; rather they serve to deodorize and scent the corpse. Often, a less expensive oil merely scented with the juniper oil was used. Rich scented oils were used to massage the body, and then, after mummification, were often applied to the wrapped corpse. The body of Tutankhamun was so thickly covered by oils and resins that it had to be cut out of the coffin with hot knives before unwrapping could be completed.

PALM WINE is 14 per cent ethyl alcohol, and one of the most sterile alcoholic substances available at the time. According to Classical authors it was used to wash out the body cavity; however, this cannot as yet be tested because it leaves no trace that can be scientifically detected.

CASSIA and **CINNAMON** *Cinnamomum cassia*, and *Cinnamomum zeylanicum* are spices from India, Ceylon and China. Classical authors list them amongst mummification materials, but thus far they have not been satisfactorily identified on or in a mummy. They would be used to make the body smell sweet.

BEESWAX has occasionally been found covering the mouth, nostrils and other orifices of New Kingdom and Late Period mummies, with occasional examples of use in the Middle Kingdom. In the Third Intermediate and Late Periods wax images of the Four Sons of Horus were included in the visceral packets. Bees were precious insects with magical as well as economic prestige attached to them, and this would have extended to their wax.

ONIONS were found from the New Kingdom until the Third Intermediate Period in body cavities, near feet and as false eyes. Onions are antiseptic and play a large part in medical mixtures, which might account for their use in mummification.

LICHEN *Parmelia furfuracea*, was used to fill out body cavities, especially in the New Kingdom. Why this was used remains a mystery.

century AD) says that they were thrown into the Nile. Porphyry is the only ancient source to state that they were removed from the body and placed in a (canopic) chest.

The Physical Evidence

Although not mentioned by the ancient writers, it is clear that after the body had been embalmed and coffined, all the waste material from embalming was carefully buried. Many such embalmers' caches from Thebes and Saqqara have been found, including that belonging to Tutankhamun. These deposits are very valuable as they contain many, if not all, of the materials used in mummification: labelled pots and jars containing coloured powders (ochres) for colouring the mummy; resin for filling, deodorizing and sanitizing; linen for stuffing and wrapping; natron for desiccating; wax for covering the body and some of the orifices; various oils for curing and scenting the body, and making it supple; terebinth resin as deodorant and perfume; and sawdust and chaff for stuffing cavities. Lamps, fragments of the funerary feast, and brooms used to sweep the last person's footprints from the tomb are also often found in such deposits.

Some embalmers' caches also included a table on which embalming was performed. The tables are quite low since much of the embalmer's work was done while squatting. Many of them consist of a rectangular piece of wood, measuring 2.41 × 1.28 m, with four narrow rectangular wooden blocks laid horizontally across it to support the body and allow for natron to lie above and below it. The tables are often stained with oils and natron. Some stone embalming beds, about 2.30 × 1.15 m and 0.26 to 0.46 m high, have also been found. They are generally of limestone with a basin at the foot. The ends of the table are in the shape of lion heads, and the body and legs of the lion flanked the side. The tables are about 6 cm lower at the foot end to allow for drainage. It is thought that the liquid emanating from the body was caught in a bowl and buried along with the caches. Embalming tables for sacred Apis bulls have also been found at Memphis. Another piece of furniture, frequently confused with an embalming table, is the funerary bed. These are often pictured on coffins of Third Intermediate Period or later date, as well as in tomb-paintings which show Anubis bending over the mummy lying on such a couch. Made of wood with elaborate finials featuring the fore and end parts of lions or semi-mythical beasts, these beds were used either for the lying in state of the mummy, or for the final wrapping ritual, which was a clean procedure and could therefore be performed on such elaborate beds. In some cases the coffin was actually placed on such a bed in the tomb, notably that of Tutankhamun where the coffins lay on a bier within the sarcophagus. In the kingdom of Kush (seventh century BC to the fourth century AD), in what is modern Sudan, kings as well as private individuals were actually entombed on beds.

Not much is known about the people who actually embalmed the bodies, save that the wrapping was performed by priests, one of whom was dressed and masked as Anubis, god of mummification. He bandaged the body, while others helped him and chanted appropriate spells at certain times. According to Herodotus, the embalmers were a special group of men belonging to different workshops, who, as with any trade, had an hereditary calling. Documents from the third century BC describe different embalmers' guilds, and sometimes the amounts they

104 Embalming table. MMA 30.3.45.

105 Embalming table. It was thought that these calcite 'beds' were used in embalming the Apis bulls, but some doubt has been cast upon this theory recently. Third Intermediate Period; from Memphis.

charged for embalmment. Diodorus records that they were honoured and respected men – after all, they were responsible for one's eternal preparation and last viewing on earth. Diodorus mentions one unfortunate member of the group, called the 'slitter', responsible for making the flank incision. According to Diodorus, the slitter was ritually required to flee immediately after making the incision, chased by the

106 A rare illustration of the mummification process is pictured on the coffin of Djedbastiufankh in the Pelizaeus-Museum, Hildesheim. The body is being washed and wrapped, with a priest dressed as Anubis conducting some of the funerary rites.

other embalmers and passers-by who all hurled stones and abuse at him for violating a corpse.

The embalming itself took place in or near the necropolis in a series of workshops and temporary shelters. The *per ankh* (house of life) was the building which probably contained the written knowledge concerning mummification and the religious rituals surrounding it. Embalming started at the *ibw*, a temporary tent-like structure where the body was initially washed; it was conveniently located near a body of water, either the river or a canal. A structure called the *seh netjer* (divine booth) might be the equivalent of the *ibw* in royal burials. Some scholars have suggested that for royalty, at least in the Old Kingdom, the *ibw* was located at or next to the valley temple. Once the body was purified it was taken to the *wabt wat* (pure place) or *per nefer* (beautiful house), the embalmer's workshop, where, in the course of seventy days, the actual evisceration, desiccation, stuffing, wrapping and coffining of the body took place. Excavators have found temporary buildings made of mud brick located at the entrance to some tombs; they have tentatively identified these as embalming workshops, *wabt net wet*, for the nobles buried there. Such structures have been found in front of the tombs of Nefer and Kai at the site of Giza.

Summary of the Development of Mummification

The idea for mummification probably dates back to the Predynastic when bodies were interred in sandy pits with a few grave goods. The bodies became naturally desiccated in these arid conditions and the ancient Egyptians would have observed this phenomenon when the burials were accidentally uncovered by shifting sands, or disturbances due to jackals, dogs or other scavengers. The Egyptians believed that the intact body was necessary for the afterlife and as burials became more elaborate, so did their efforts to preserve the body. In the Old Kingdom the trend was to wrap the body carefully and mould it in plaster-soaked linen so that it almost resembled a statue.

The Middle Kingdom saw some examples of mummification that resemble Herodotus' second method, with evisceration becoming increasingly popular, while the New Kingdom saw the regular removal of the brain from the body. It is possible that after the brain was removed, it was

107 Wrapping the mummy and putting the finishing touches to the mask and trappings.

wrapped in a bundle called the 'Tekenu', together with other mummification detritus, and placed in the tombs. In the Third Intermediate Period mummification achieved new heights, the body being stuffed and cosmetically enhanced to look life-like. In the Late and Graeco-Roman Periods the quality of preservation decreased; vast amounts of resin were used instead of a careful process of desiccation. Coptic mummies were often preserved in common salt rather than natron, and were not eviscerated.

A general point worth making is that, although a particular mummification method might be prevalent at any given time, the Egyptians did not necessarily use it exclusively. At any period a variety of techniques were often employed; perhaps this was, as Herodotus suggested, something to do with economics as well as fashion.

However, our understanding of Egyptian burial practices may have to be modified in the light of excavations started in 1997 at Hierakonpolis which revealed a large Predynastic cemetery full of mummies. The bodies were found in shallow pits dug in the desert sand and were laid on their sides in a flexed position with their heads to the east, looking south. They were wrapped in linen bandages, with additional pads of linen inserted to flesh out the bodies. The bodies showed no evidence for evisceration and have yet to be tested for natron; however, resin was applied both to the body and the linen wrappings. The bodies were wrapped in shrouds, and might even have worn linen and leather clothing originally. Pottery found in conjunction with these burials is of Naqada II date, thereby radically revising the date of the first mummies found in Egypt.

THE ARCHAIC PERIOD AND THE OLD KINGDOM

Few mummies, and indeed bodies, survive from the Early Dynastic periods. The few examples to do so were wrapped in linen and placed in rectangular clay or wooden coffins or stone sarcophagi, in a flexed position. Some bodies, dating to the First Dynasty from Tarkhan, were placed on beds. In all these the viscera were left intact. It is possible that the bandages were treated with natron and liquid resin, but unfortunately none of the bodies found from the First Dynasty have been closely examined. In fact, the bandaged and bejewelled arm of King Djer, or perhaps his wife, which was recovered in 1900 by Petrie from his tomb at

108 The earliest preserved bodies were naturally dried by the hot, dry desert sand. They lay on their sides in the foetal position and were surrounded by their grave-goods, such as pots, knives, and beads.

Abydos, was sent to the Cairo Museum, divested of the bracelets, and was then discarded by the curator, Emile Brugsch. Fortunately the mummy of a woman from the Second Dynasty, found in 1911 by James Quibell at Saqqara, was more closely examined and provides further information about mummification in this period (ill. 109).

The Saqqara body, which had probably been treated with natron, was lying flexed on its left side in a wooden coffin, and was wrapped in more than sixteen layers of bandages. Each limb was separately wrapped, and the outermost layer was worked to indicate the genitalia. This sort of detailed modelling became the norm in the Old Kingdom. Fragments (portions of the arm, torso and the complete left foot) purportedly belonging to King Djoser were recovered in 1934 from the granite sarcophagus chamber of his Step Pyramid at Saqqara. The foot, including all its toes, was still partially wrapped in linen. After removal of the upper layers it was found that the embalmers had 'sculpted' the tendons while the toes had been modelled so that they overlay the actual toes below. The corpse had been closely wrapped in fine linen, which had then been covered in plaster and moulded to the form of the underlying body. Currently, following carbon-14 tests, there is much debate about the date of the remains, which are being studied by M.F. Gaballah and Eugen Strouhal.

This method of mummification continued in use throughout the Old Kingdom, except for a few innovations made in succeeding dynasties. One improvement came in

the Fourth Dynasty, when the practice of evisceration was apparently first introduced. The earliest evidence for it derives from the Fourth Dynasty burial of Queen Hetepheres, the mother of Kheops. Although Hetepheres' mummy, which had lain stretched out, either on her side or on her back, as is attested by the length of her sarcophagus, had vanished, her canopic chest was found. The chest has four compartments, each containing a flat package wrapped in linen. In three of the compartments the viscera were preserved in a weak solution of natron in water; the fourth compartment was empty due to a leakage. Clearly, the embalmers had realized that once divested of its internal organs, the body would be much less susceptible to putrefaction. Other private individuals from the Fourth Dynasty onward were eviscerated through an incision made in their left side, with the resulting cavities filled with linen.

Following the introduction of evisceration, the basic method of mummification used in the Old Kingdom continued with the elaborate wrapping and painting of the mummy, transforming the body into a virtual linen statue that would serve as a house for the *ka*, or double, of the deceased. Two famous Fifth Dynasty examples of bodies thus prepared are the mummies of Waty or Nefer from Saqqara, and Ranefer from Tomb 9 at Meidum. Ranefer lay on his left side, with his head to the north, and his face to the east. The linen surface covering his body was modelled and painted, the hair being black, the eyes and

109 This Second Dynasty mummy, found by Quibell in Saqqara, lay in a crouched position on its side. It was quite decayed when found, and only wrapped limb-fragments and the skull remained.

110 This foot, with its modelled bandages, comes from the burial chamber of the Step Pyramid, and on archaeological grounds should belong to the mummy of King Djoser, together with a number of other fragments of the same body. Qasr el-Aini Al. 490.

eyebrows green, and the mouth reddish brown. His genitals were carefully modelled and show that circumcision had been performed. His brain remained in his skull, which rattled when the head was shaken. He was eviscerated and the viscera placed in a chest wall recess in his tomb. The mummy was taken to Britain where it was studied and stored in the Royal College of Surgeons. Sadly Ranefer's remains were destroyed in a bombing raid during the Second World War.

Waty or Nefer was found at Saqqara buried in a wooden coffin in the tomb of Nefer in 1966. As the tomb was for Nefer's whole family and the coffin provides no clue, the name of the short stocky mummy is uncertain. The body was tightly swathed in linen strips and impregnated with light green stucco plaster, the face detailed in the plaster surface and painted, even down to a debonair moustache and wig. The body was carefully moulded, showing such details as genitalia and even a callus on one of

the feet. In the 1970s, it was X-rayed by a team from the University of Michigan. This showed that Waty or Nefer had been about forty years old at the time of death and had remarkably good teeth; however, the actual flesh within the wrappings was partially decayed. Another similarly pre-pared but nameless mummy lay in Shaft 5 of Nefer's tomb. It differs from 'Nefer's' mummy mostly in its position, lying semi-flexed on its left side (like Ranefer), while 'Nefer' was found on his back. It is probable, however, that 'Nefer' had once lain on his side, but had fallen onto his back. 'Nefer's' body was not flexed – perhaps because his short height made flexing unnecessary for the coffin.

Another interesting Fifth Dynasty burial comes from Giza. Mastaba G 2220 contained a cedarwood coffin with a small female mummy lying on her left side. Each limb and extremity was individually wrapped in over thirty-seven lay-ers of linen bands into which linen pads were inserted to give it a more lifelike appearance. The breasts were made of narrow bandages criss-crossed and moulded using wet resin, with small wads of linen attached as nipples. She had not been eviscerated. This mummy was dressed in a mid calf-length tunic with a 'V' neck (ill. 174). Other mummies, until the Sixth Dynasty, if not a little later, that have been recovered from sites all over Egypt appear to have been treated in a similar manner: ill-preserved flesh carefully wrapped in plaster-impregnated linen which was moulded over the body into its exact form before being painted and dressed in kilts or dresses.

A group of more than a dozen bodies from Giza, also dating from the Fifth and Sixth Dynasties, were treated slightly differently. The corpses were carefully wrapped with plaster-impregnated bandages, and then covered with stucco-plaster, forming a sort of case. Sometimes only the head, but in a number of cases the rest of the body, also was covered. These bodies all lay on their backs with a wooden headrest carefully placed under their necks. The plaster was

applied when the wrapped mummy was already in the coffin, since it covers only the top and sides of the body, and not the back. This plaster casing made the mummy resemble a statue even more than the linen casings did.

Virtually all the mummies found from the Old Kingdom retain their brains. There are however a few exceptions which indicate that the Egyptians had started to experiment with brain removal as early as the Fourth Dynasty. The mummy from Mastaba 17 at Meidum was divested of its brain, perhaps through the foramen mag-num. A skull found in the North (Red) Pyramid at Dahshur, possibly that of King Seneferu, contained no brain, but resin had been introduced into the cranial cavity (perhaps suggesting a later date for this mummy).

Furthermore, Leek found a very few examples from Giza that show that the brain was removed via the nose after breaking through the ethmoid bone, the method that became common in the end of the Old Kingdom.

In the case of Old Kingdom mummies there is some discussion as to the amount of attention that was paid to the body as opposed to its wrappings. The main question concerning Old Kingdom mummification and, indeed, to some extent later practices, is the degree to which natron was used for 'curing' the mummy, and whether it was used in a solid or liquid state. Another issue of the period concerns 'defleshing', an idea put forward by Petrie.

The Use of Natron

The question regarding the degree to which the body was manipulated prior to wrapping is the hardest to answer. This is mainly due to the inattention of early scholars. According to several excavators many bodies from the Early Dynastic and Old Kingdom, notably from the cemeteries at Deshasheh, Beni Hasan and Tehneh, seem to have merely been dried without evisceration or the benefit of natron or salt. It is quite possible that in this early period some bodies were indeed dried in the sun and then wrapped, the emphasis being placed on the wrapping. This would have been the cheaper form of mummification at the time, but it is more probable that most bodies were treated with natron, however cursorily, prior to wrapping. As this does not leave much of a trace, it would have been hard to identify. No doubt evisceration occurred most frequently in the mummies of wealthy and important individuals.

Early modern works on mummification in Egypt state that the mummies were placed in a natron bath, thereby clearly indicating that natron was used in a liquid state. This belief originally sprang from a mis-translation of Herodotus, implying that the mummy was placed in a *bath* of natron. The word that Herodotus actually uses is the same word used to describe the preparation of dried and salted fish. (This is particularly appropriate since, in the nineteenth century, many of the mummified bodies brought to Cairo from Saqqara and Thebes, including the royal mummies, were taxed as dried and salted fish before being permitted into the city.) However, despite the correction of Herodotus' translation, some scholars remained convinced that liquid natron was used. There is some basis

for this belief: Hetepheres' canopic chest had a little liquid in it when it was found, and Brunton found natron solution in a Twelfth Dynasty canopic jar from Lahun. Furthermore, the mummy of Ptahshepses, dating from the end of the Sixth Dynasty or early Seventh, was found in a sarcophagus (ill. 339) filled with liquid that, when analyzed, proved to contain natron. This seemed to provide conclusive proof that natron was used in a liquid state. However, once the mummy of Ptahshepses was carefully analyzed it was found that the liquid was probably ground water that had entered the sarcophagus after a rainstorm, and the natron in it had come from the body. Ground water or rain water might be the real reason why liquid has been found in coffins and canopic chests. Experimental work by Alfred Lucas, Zaki Iskander and Renate Germer using dry and liquid natron to mummify mice and birds showed that those preserved in natron solution lost their skin and feathers or fur, while those preserved in solid natron remained intact; thus it is far more likely, given the state of many mummies, that solid natron was used. It is remotely possible, however, that in the early Old Kingdom mummies were immersed in natron solution – this might account for the poor preservation of some of the bodies – but that the practice was quickly discontinued. Certainly by the Middle Kingdom solid natron was used. It has been suggested that salt rather than natron was favoured for mummification. This might be true for very poor burials, but not for the majority of mummies studied. Any salt found on the bodies comes from the natron, which had salt as one of its components.

Finally, there is the issue of 'defleshing': having all the flesh removed from the bone prior to bandaging. The existence of this practice is hotly debated by Egyptologists, as the evidence is somewhat sketchy. Some alleged examples come from Junker's work at Giza, and from that of Petrie at Meidum, Deshasheh, and in some Predynastic cemeteries. In both the Giza and Meidum cemeteries several bodies showed that the bandages were in direct contact with the bone and in some cases the skeletons were not properly articulated. Thus the excavators hypothesized that they had been ritually 'defleshed' – in fact, for some of the Predynastic burials Petrie even went so far as to suggest that the flesh might have been removed for consumption as food in some ancient ritual. This is possible, especially when taken in conjunction with some of the ancient Egyptian funerary texts such as the Pyramid Texts and the

113 Third Dynasty wrapped corpse from Beni Hasan; for a coffin of the same type of burial, see ill. 236.

Book of the Dead, both of which contain incantations that refer to dis-and re-membering the parts of the body and consuming portions of it. Recently the question of 'defleshing' has once again been raised by the archaeological work of a French team at Adaima (located between Esna and Edfu). Thus far the team has explored 130 tombs dating to the Predynastic Period. Some of the bodies recovered seem to have had their heads cut off, while others appear to have been cut into pieces, and then reassembled (after a fashion) in the tomb, akin to what Petrie found at Deshasheh, Naqada and Ballas. This new evidence tends to support some of Petrie's theories about defleshing, and perhaps even consumption of the deceased at an early period. Certainly such evidence is virtually non-existent in the pharaonic period. However, until more research is done, the practice of defleshing must remain only an intriguing possibility. The more likely and much less sinister reason for the disturbed condition of the body and the lack of flesh between bone and wrappings is that natural decomposition, often perhaps due to the lack of evisceration, caused the flesh to crumble and the bandages to slip from their original position covering the flesh adhering to the bone. Certainly, enough mummies from the Old Kingdom (even some royal ones, such as those of Unas and Isesi) retain enough hair and skin to belie the idea of 'defleshing', at least in the Old Kingdom and later.

THE FIRST INTERMEDIATE PERIOD AND THE MIDDLE KINGDOM

Although there is relatively little evidence from the First Intermediate Period, one can say that bodies continued to be cured in dry natron, eviscerated, and bandaged, with the viscera being separately cured and placed in canopic chests. The practice of moulding the wrappings into a virtual

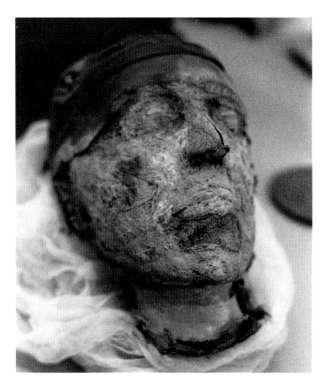

114 The head of Djheutynakht, now in the Museum of Fine Arts, Boston, is unusual for the Twelfth Dynasty in that facial features are painted on the bandages. From Deir el-Bersha. MFA 21.11767.

statue of the deceased ended for the most part by the end of the Sixth, or the beginning of the Seventh, Dynasties. There is an unusual example of an Eleventh Dynasty mummy, that of Djehutynakht from Deir el-Bersha, whose head is treated in a manner similar to that of Old Kingdom mummies. The face is covered by linen moulded over it and painted with eyebrows. This head is also notable for having had its brain removed through the nose. However, most mummies of the period did not involve facial modelling in linen. Certainly the Ninth Dynasty mummy of Pepiseneb from Sheikh Farag consisted only of a desiccated and eviscerated body, still containing the brain, and heavily wrapped in linen bandages like a cocoon. A cartonnage mask covered the face and chest. The mask had black-painted linen threads attached to its sides and back to represent hair, with cartonnage ears attached to it. Thus, although the wrappings were not creating a *ka* statue, the cartonnage mask was. The use of such external trappings is the subject of Chapter 6.

Middle Kingdom mummification is particularly remarkable for the variety of methods used to embalm the dead, as well as the additions to the external trappings of mummies and burial goods. Cartonnage masks appear, as do *shabtis*, the small figurines placed in tombs to do the deceased's work in the Afterworld.

Several mummies have been recovered from the Eleventh Dynasty. Many of these were eviscerated in the traditional fashion via an incision made in the left flank. There were, however, some that seem to have been treated to something approximating Herodotus' second method, that of an enema of so-called cedar (more probably juniper – see below) oil. Most of these mummies come from Thebes and were related to Mentuhotep II. Although fragments of Mentuhotep's jaw and skull were also found from his tomb at Deir el-Bahari, they do not reveal whether he was treated in the same manner as were his dependants.

At Deir el-Bahari, Herbert Winlock and Edouard Naville found several tombs of Mentuhotep's female relations: Sadhe, Henhenet, Kawit, Kemsit, Mayt and Ashayet, as well as some of their servants. The bodies of many of these were relatively well preserved – elaborate tattoos are visible on the arms and abdomens of certain dancing girls buried there. The princesses were found lying in rock-cut tombs adjacent to their king's. Their bodies were dried with natron, with the surface of the skin (of most of them) coated with resin. They bore no signs of evisceration through the flank. However, some of them show evidence of having their viscera dissolved and partially extracted through the rectum. Princess Henhenet and Queen Ashayet, and the burials in DBXI.24 and 26, all had dilated recta and vaginae, and some had bits of tissue, mainly intestines, projecting from the anus. It has been postulated that an oleo-resin, akin to turpentine, was injected into the anus in order to dissolve the organs, with partial success. Turpentine is made from resin, and could easily have been produced and used for this purpose. According to Herodotus, cedar oil was used for this type of mummification; it is more probable that juniper, rather than cedar, oil was used to perfume the turpentine, as the scented oil by itself would not have been effective in dissolving the viscera, but certainly would have provided the pleasant odour so prized by the Egyptians. Furthermore, it has been suggested that the bodies might have been filled with resin through the anus. This is because some shiny particles were found adhering to Ashayet's rectum, though analysis of the particles shows that this theory is doubtful. However, there is some debate as to whether the dilated recta and vaginae, and tissue projections, were due to a particular mummification technique or to other reasons. It is possible that the bodies had partially decayed prior to mummification, and the changes in physiognomy were due to this decay. All of the skulls contained brains.

Although Herodotus lists the anal injection as a cheaper form of mummification, it is doubtful that it would have been used for princesses who had rich burials. Surely it cannot have been due to an effort to economize? This is especially dubious as there are so many other contemporary mummies that were eviscerated from the flank. Perhaps, in the Middle Kingdom, anal injection was an expensive experiment which later began to be regarded as an economical way of preserving bodies. Certainly, the Eleventh Dynasty mummy of the Steward Wah, found intact and unwrapped in 1935, was eviscerated from his side. However, only the liver, stomach and intestines were removed; the lungs and heart remained in place. This mummy is also notable for the position of the hands. Predynastic bodies had flexed arms with their hands in front of their faces; Old Kingdom mummies tended to have their arms at their sides, as do many Middle Kingdom examples. Wah's is one of the earliest to have the arms folded over the chest, the right over the left, an arrangement that is unusual at almost all periods except for New Kingdom kings, and in the Roman Period.

An interesting sidelight on quick mummification in extenuating circumstances comes from the Eleventh Dynasty. Tomb MMA 507, located near the tomb of

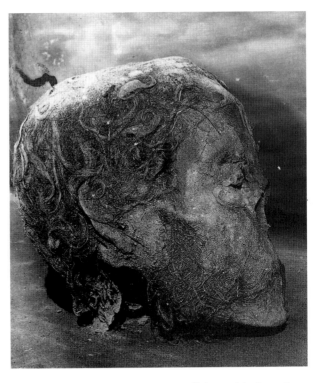

115 Head of the Twelfth Dynasty mummy of Ipi, one of the few well-preserved examples of the period. Note the beard, a short-lived early Middle Kingdom fashion that can also be observed on contemporary masks (see ill. 194). From Beni Hasan 707, formerly in Liverpool.

116 The skin of this woman was so well preserved that one can make out her tattoos. Tattooing was a form of ornamentation in ancient Egypt, and has sometimes been equated with dancing girls. Bedouin women in Egypt are still tattooed. Eleventh Dynasty, from Deir el-Bahari.

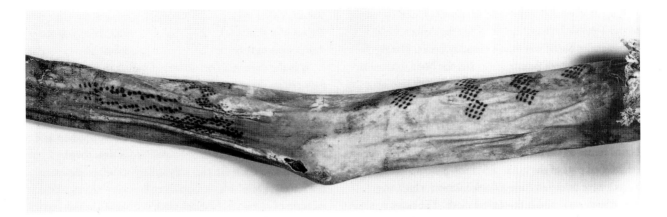

Mentuhotep II in Thebes, contained sixty corpses wrapped in layers of linen. These have generally been identified as the bodies of soldiers who had fought with Mentuhotep II in one of his many battles that brought about the successful reunification of Egypt after the First Intermediate Period. However, new research suggests that they may belong to the time of Ammenemes I. The bodies of the soldiers had been scoured with sand and wrapped in linen; certainly none of them had been eviscerated. Most of them had died violently in battle some distance from Thebes. This was attested by the arrow-tips protruding from the chest of one, and the crushed skulls and knife marks of others. The veterans had lain on the battlefield for some time, for at least six bodies showed evidence of having been ripped and pecked by birds of prey. Once they had been gathered up by their comrades, they had been hastily buried in the sand (grains of which still adhere to their bodies) and after this hurried but effective desiccation they were entombed with honour in their pharaoh's necropolis (ill. 95).

Although several mummies of Twelfth Dynasty date have been found in Dahshur, the majority of excavators provided inadequate descriptions of the remains. When found, the mummies were decayed, and only a few bare bones can be traced today. All that is known from the remains of several princesses from Dahshur is that they lay with their arms at their sides, and were heavily coated with resin. There is no information available concerning their viscera or brains, with the exception of Princess Menet (reign of Sesostris III) who it is known had her skull emptied. It is interesting to note that these ladies' arms lie at their sides: the arms of some mummies from this period, both male and female, are found crossed over the chest, while others have them lying over their pudenda.

One of the most remarkable mummies found that dates to the Twelfth Dynasty is that of Senebtisi from Lisht, whose entire burial was found virtually intact. Dating to around the reign of Ammenemes III, the body, like most others of Middle Kingdom date, lay on its left side with the head to the north and the face to the east. The arms and legs were individually wrapped. The brain remained within the cranium; some other contemporary mummies had their brains removed via the nose, but clearly this was not yet an established part of the mummification process. Senebtisi's viscera were removed from a flank incision which was sealed with resin and resin-soaked cloth. The heart was

wrapped in linen and replaced in the body, with linen and sawdust and resin-soaked bandages filling out the body cavity. According to the excavators, the most striking feature of the mummy, inside the inner, anthropoid, coffin, 'was a thick layer of pitch, which must have been poured on after the body had been laid in position, just prior to the burial, for the pitch had for the most part run down to the left side of the body, and must therefore have been introduced only just before the coffin was closed and laid on its side' (Mace and Winlock 1914: 17).

Few mummies have been found from the later Middle Kingdom. There was, however, the spectacular find of the burial of the Thirteenth Dynasty pharaoh, King Hor, at Dahshur. The tomb had been violated, but it still contained many grave goods and fragments of his body. His head, containing the brain, is on display in Cairo. The mummy had been treated with natron and resin, but was so damaged that it is impossible to tell if he had been eviscerated. Likewise, the body of his daughter(?), Nubheteptikhered, had been reduced to a skeleton.

The Use of Resin

Resin, poured in a semi-liquid state over mummies, appears to be common from the Twelfth Dynasty onward, although there are a few isolated examples from previous eras, such as one from the Fifth Dynasty at Deshasheh. Winlock hypothesized that the resin was poured over the body of Senebtisi to protect and hold in place the ornaments that were set on the mummy. If this were the case, it was an unsuccessful ploy. Resin was also poured into her canopic jars, and bits of resin were placed in front of the eyes, and the lids drawn down over them. In an Eleventh Dynasty burial in Deir el-Bahari, DBXI.23, resin had been smeared over the closed eyelids of a woman. Clearly, next to natron, resin was the most important material used in mummification.

It is the dark resin on preserved bodies in Egypt that gave rise to the word 'mummy', as the Persian/Arabic word for wax, bitumen and pitch, *mum*, was used to describe the black substance on mummies. Until the twentieth century people believed that this black substance was bitumen and that mummies were created by pouring it over them. Bitumen and resin are two very different things. Bitumen is a viscous liquid which originates from petroleum and a mixture of minerals. Natural pitch is bitumen which has become solid by exposure and is found in the neighbour-hood of the Dead Sea. Artificial pitch/bitumen is obtained by the destructive distillation of coal or wood. Resin, how-ever, comes from trees. The resin-producing trees found near Egypt in Lebanon and Syria were cedar, fir and pine. However, eighteenth-, nineteenth-, and early twentieth-century investigators used the terms bitumen, pitch and resin indiscriminately, with bitumen being the favoured term. This is partially because Diodorus, in his description of the Dead Sea, says that bitumen was sold to the Egyptians for embalming, and Herodotus mentions bitu-men, although he does not say that it was ever used in mummification. It was not until Alfred Lucas, the Egyptological chemist, conducted tests on the black mater-ial recovered from several mummies that the identification of the dark material as resin rather than bitumen was clearly established.

There are, however, three or four tested examples of human and animal mummies from the first century BC to the second century AD that contain traces of bitumen rather than resin. Bitumen was probably sometimes used in the Graeco-Roman Period instead of resin as it was traded from the Dead Sea area. Resin was popularly used on mummies because it inhibits bacteria and deodorizes. An Egyptian text, *The Admonitions of Ipuwer*, probably dating to the First Intermediate Period, underlines the importance of resin in mummification: 'No one sails north to Byblos today. What can we do for pinetrees for our mummies?'

Although most mummies were covered in resin, one of the Middle Kingdom is reported as having the surface of the body and thighs covered with a layer of beeswax. Wax would certainly act as a preservative. In the New Kingdom it was often used to cover the mouth, eyes and ears of an individual, but it is rare to find it coating an entire body.

THE SECOND INTERMEDIATE PERIOD AND THE NEW KINGDOM

The Seventeenth Dynasty

It is unfortunate that examples of mummies from the Hyksos Period (Dynasty 15) are scarce; it is thus difficult to determine if the Hyskos made any changes or innovations in the practice of mummification, or adopted what was

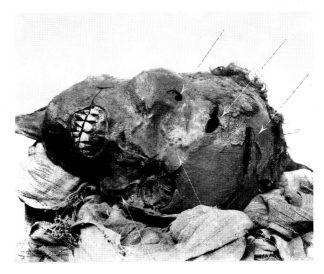

117 The head of the mummy of King Taa II is the most dramatic part of the body, showing its deep head wounds which caused the pharaoh's death. From TT 320; CM CG 61051.

being done by the Egyptians. Detailed examination of the skeletons that have been recovered from Tell el-Daba (the Hyksos capital, Avaris) may shed light on this issue. Most of those that have been recovered from the Second Intermediate Period are pure Egyptian and come from Thebes. Many were in a very poor state when discovered, and the majority seem to have disintegrated immediately on discovery, including four of the five kings whose bodies had been found. However, several mummies belonging to members of the royal family from the end of the Seventeenth Dynasty onward have come to light from vari-ous caches and been examined. In fact, it is the first time in Egyptian history that clear differences between royal and private mummies can be established.

The few examples recovered from the Second Intermediate Period tend to have empty crania, although this is not always the case. There is also quite a lot of resin used on the body, albeit not necessarily poured on in a semi-liquid state, as occurred on Senebtisi. Each limb is individually wrapped, and the arms are laid along the sides, with the hands often placed on the front of the thighs for women, and over the genitals for men. These arm positions continue on into the Eighteenth Dynasty. The mummy of King Taa II, perhaps the most dramatic ever found in Egypt, comes from this period. Literary sources identify

Taa II as the king who instigated the fight against the Hyksos in an attempt to drive them out and to reunite the country. His mummy was recovered from the Deir el-Bahari cache, and in some ways is reminiscent of those of the Middle Kingdom soldiers buried at Deir el-Bahari.

Taa's body is poorly preserved, the skeleton largely disarticulated, with only part of the skin surviving. It is the state of the head which grips one's attention. The skull is covered with horrific wounds: a dagger thrust behind the ear, mace-blows on his cheek and nose, and a cut above his forehead, perhaps caused by an axe. Until quite recently it was believed that Taa suffered these wounds in battle. However, recent examinations show that the cut above the ear might have occurred earlier as it had started to heal. Perhaps the weakened king was assassinated in his palace, rather than on the battlefield, as the initial injury would have rendered him too unsteady to command troops. On the other hand, analysis of the wounds suggests that they were inflicted with Palestinian weapons, although this cannot be proven incontrovertibly. Nevertheless, the king's final injuries are obvious on his body, and his anguish is apparent for all to see as his lips are drawn back over his teeth in an agonized grimace. The body is poorly preserved owing to hurried embalming, something that helped support the idea of a hasty burial amidst battle. Now, however, it seems that the hasty burial might be due to other political reasons. His brain remains in his head, although the viscera were removed and the body cavity filled with linen. The mummy was sprinkled with powdered aromatic wood, of the sort that might have been used for temporary desiccation, prior to wrapping.

Not all Seventeenth Dynasty royal mummies were as hastily prepared as Taa II. The body of a woman (Unknown Woman B) recovered from the Deir el-Bahari cache and tentatively identified as Queen Tetisheri, was carefully mummified and bandaged. As she was quite old and balding the embalmers had braided artificial hair into her own white tresses. The mummy of Ahhotpe might also have shown such care, but when her body was discovered there was a disagreement over who owned it, and in the ensuing confusion the mummy was stripped of her jewels and her body disposed of by the Governor of Qena Province. A similarly unfortunate fate overtook the body of King Kamose. His body was found by chance when Mariette and Brugsch were collecting antiquities in order to

'stage' a find for the visit of Prince Napoleon, cousin of Emperor Napoleon III. The encoffined body contained daggers and other objects which were removed, but according to Brugsch, on opening the coffin the mummy 'fell to dust'.

The Eighteenth to Twentieth Dynasties

The majority of New Kingdom mummies found date to the Eighteenth and Nineteenth Dynasties, a time when mummification achieved what can be called its 'classic' phase. This carried on through the rest of the New Kingdom, while some splendid innovations subsequently occurred in the otherwise rather chaotic Third Intermediate Period. Royal, noble and poor bodies of New Kingdom date demonstrate the simultaneous practice of different types of mummification.

Removing the brain through the nose by breaking the ethmoid bone became a standard procedure in the Eighteenth Dynasty. Once the ethmoid bone was broken and the brain accessible, a long thin metal tool was inserted through the left nostril and gyrated. The mummy was then held upright, or turned on its belly so that the liquefied brain would come out of the nose. It is only Amosis, the first pharaoh of the dynasty, whose brain was removed in an unusual manner. It seems that an incision was made on the left side of the neck, the atlas vertebra removed, the brain extracted through the foramen magnum, and the empty cranium packed with linen. There were a few isolated occurrences of this method in the Old and Middle Kingdoms, but it never gained any popularity.

Lavish use of resin is common in the New Kingdom. It was carefully applied to the face and body, poured, via the nose, into the emptied cranium, stuffed up nostrils, moulded into little balls and used to plug ears, and, occasionally, the anus. Tutankhamun's mummy had so much resin and sacred oil spread over the body that heated knives had to be used to free the body from its coffin in the final stages of unwrapping. Flank incisions were covered by smears of resin, and, in the case of the wealthy, with a rectangular or oval piece of metal, frequently gold. The location of this incision changed during the New Kingdom. Prior to the mummy of Tuthmosis III, it was a vertical incision down the left side perpendicular to the rib cage; then it became a diagonal cut from the hipbone to the pubes. Tuthmosis

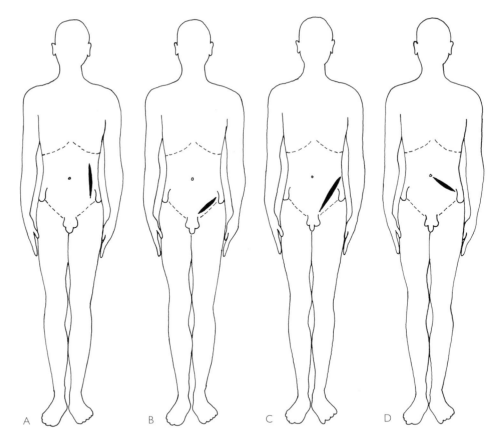

118 The mummy of Tutankhamun was so embedded in solidified unguents, poured over it in the funeral ceremonies, that the wrappings had to be removed piecemeal.

119 The position of the evisceration incision changed over time. Prior to the reign of Tuthmosis III it was vertical, along the belly (A); during and after Tuthmosis III's reign it was diagonal, parallel to the thigh (B). Occasionally, in less well-prepared mummies, the cut was bigger (C). Tutankhamun had an unusual evisceration incision, going toward his navel (D).

III's incision is neatly stitched rather than held together with resin. After his reign, both stitching and resining of incisions continued; it was not until the Twentieth Dynasty that stitched incisions became the norm.

Once the embalmers had inserted their hands through the incision and removed the liver, stomach and intestines, they cut through the diaphragm and pulled out the lungs. During this operation the heart might be inadvertently removed, but it was then replaced, occasionally after having been wrapped separately. In the case of Sethos I, it was acci-

dentally loosened and found lying on the right side of the body. It was imperative to keep the heart in the body because it would be used in the final judgment to weigh the soul of the deceased and thus grant everlasting life. The viscera that were removed from the body were treated with natron and spices, and then wrapped up, sometimes looking very much like miniature human mummies, and placed in canopic containers. During the Twentieth Dynasty, however, one first finds the practice of returning the internal organs to the body cavity. This would subsequently become much more common. Occasionally, as in the case of the mummy of Unknown Woman D from the Deir el-Bahari cache (perhaps Queen Tawosret), bits of epidermis that had fallen off in the mummification process were wrapped up and placed in the coffin with the mummy.

The body cavity would then be washed out with water, followed by palm wine, before being packed with natron for desiccation, myrrh for scent, resin for disinfection and bacterial control, linen for absorbing liquids, and possibly frankincense for scent. The body would be covered with

CORN MUMMIES AND OSIRIS BEDS

An Osiris bed consists of a wooden outline figure of Osiris, crowned with the *atef* crown, carrying sceptres, and facing right. The figure was filled with earth and planted with grain which had just started to germinate before being put into the tomb. These cereal beds, symbolizing growth, fertility and rebirth, belong to the New Kingdom, although earlier examples in the shape of rectangles, rather than Osiris, are known from the entrance of the Lahun pyramid of Sesostris II, found by Petrie in 1920. Cereal beds in the shape of Osiris were possibly inspired by Coffin Text 269: 'Becoming Barley of Lower Egypt' where the deceased is identified with this plant growing on the ribs of Osiris who nourishes both. Osiris beds were probably the precursors of the corn mummies.

Osiris corn mummies are a type of artifact peculiar to the later periods of Egyptian history, and consist of mummiform objects, 35–50

120 Corn Osiris, from tomb of Tutankhamun; CM JE 60703.

cm long, wrapped in linen bandages and placed in falcon-headed coffins. The mummies themselves are wrapped in the shape of a miniature figure of an ithyphallic Osiris, and contain a grain and clay-sand mixture reflecting the idea of sprouting cereals and rebirth. They were often provided with a wax mask which was painted green with details picked out in gold leaf. The text on the falcon head of the coffins indicates associations with the popular syncretized funerary deity, Ptah-Sokar-Osiris, master of resurrection, and also with the solar cult. A variant on these mummiform figures is a recumbent clay Osiride figure wrapped in linen and placed on a linen bed stuffed with grains of barley, the whole ensemble being wrapped with rush matting. Barley (*it* in Egyptian) and emmer (*bdt*) were fundamental to the Egyptian diet, providing the basis for beer and bread. Therefore, they had many symbolic connotations including food, the basis of life, wealth, the vegetal cycle of rebirth and a host of deities associated with rebirth and fertility. These mummies, placed in tombs, would act as an amulet promoting rebirth and regeneration. A series of texts from the Ptolemaic temple at Dandara concern themselves with the symbolism of the germination and sprouting of cereals and are related to the corn mummies.

121 Corn mummies were put into tombs as allusions to Osiris and his regenerative forces as exemplified by the crop-cycle. Third Intermediate Period; CM JE 36544.

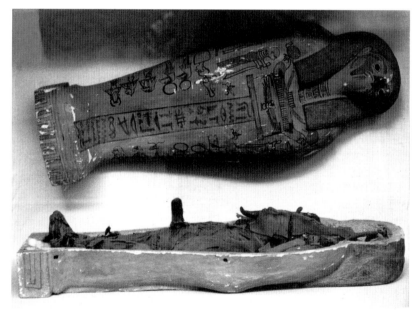

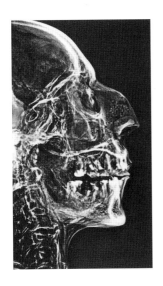

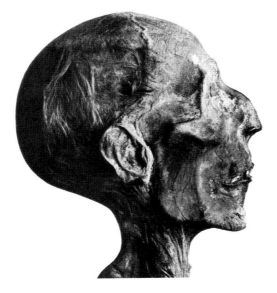

122 X-ray of the head of the mummy of Ramesses II. CM CG 61078.

123 The nose of Ramesses II's mummy is remarkable for being so well preserved. The reason for this is that it was packed with seeds and an animal bone in order to hold its shape.

natron. The natron and incense filler as well as the external natron would no doubt be changed during the drying period. Bob Brier, who experimentally mummified a human body in the mid-1990s without changing the natron, found that it took over ninety days to dry, and even so the results were not completely satisfactory. Successful (and expensive) mummification would entail changing the natron whenever it became damp from the body's secretions. When the final wrapping took place the body cavities would be filled with resin-impregnated linen to hold its shape and to deter insects.

In addition to an elaboration in desiccation methods, many New Kingdom mummies show signs of the cosmetic care lavished on them by embalmers: balding women have false hair woven into their own sparse locks; nails, especially of the royal mummies, are hennaed; from the Nineteenth Dynasty onward black lines are painted on foreheads to indicate the hairline (e.g. Siptah, Ramesses IV, etc.), and sometimes lines are drawn to emphasize the eye-brows. Occasionally the hair has been hennaed and, in the instance of Yuya and Tjuiu, the parents of Queen Tiye, it is blond, perhaps due to a reaction between henna and the chemicals used in mummification, or faded henna on white hair.

From the latter part of the Eighteenth Dynasty small pieces of linen with cursory eyes drawn upon them were placed over the eyes, providing new 'eyes' for the mummies. In the Twentieth Dynasty, Ramesses IV had small onions used as eyes. Onions were a popular addition to the items used in mummification: Ramesses IV also had onions placed in his ears, and each nostril which had been filled with resin was covered by a fragment of onion-skin. Other mummies of the Third Intermediate Period have onions placed on the chest, in the pelvic area, or scattered through the wrappings. Perhaps this was because onions are antiseptic agents, or because their strong odour might aid the mummy's nose to function well in the Hereafter. One mummy, that of Nesikhonsu of the Twenty-first Dynasty, had onions placed on her person, as well as lotuses, symbols of resurrection, wrapped around her feet.

From the Nineteenth Dynasty onwards, the body was stuffed very carefully so as not to be squashed by the bandages and to better retain its shape. Ramesses II's distinctive nose had been packed with seeds and a small animal bone to make it withstand the pressure of the bandages applied during mummification. The abdomens of Merenptah, Siptah and Ramesses IV, amongst others, were filled with dried lichen to better preserve the body's shape. Ramesses V was filled with sawdust, an adumbration of practices that became common in the Twenty-first Dynasty.

A curious feature of New Kingdom embalming is that finger- and toe-nails show evidence of having been tied onto the digits with string for the duration of the natroning process. This practice saved the nails from falling off the extremities when the surrounding skin shrank due to desiccation. Unusual care was also occasionally taken with male genitalia – the penis of Tutankhamun was mummified as though fully erect. Strangely, some time after the unwrapping of the boy-king this member vanished from the mummy, and has yet to be relocated. It is possible that the theft of this part occurred during the Second World War, when other acts of vandalism took place in the Theban necropolis. Other damage to the mummy seems to have occurred at the same time. On the other hand, the phalluses of Tuthmosis III and certain other Tuthmoside royalty were bound tightly against one thigh, so that they effectively disappeared from view, perhaps to avoid the loss of this important piece of the royal anatomy. The king's virility is made explicit in his title of 'strong bull'.

Frequently, when members or extremities of corpses fell off owing to desiccation or speedy decomposition, the embalmers tried to provide the dead with reproductions in resin and bandages so that they would not be deficient in the Afterworld. Embalmers of the Twenty-first Dynasty were particularly gifted in this respect. Certainly, when the New Kingdom mummies of the Deir el-Bahari cache were restored, the embalmers sometimes had to provide virtually new bodies since the robbers had so violently savaged them. Tuthmosis III's mummy was so badly damaged that the restorers of antiquity had to use narrow wooden splints to hold the body together. Princess Sitamun's restored mummy consisted of the skull, a few broken bones and three palm sticks constituting the axis of the body. Ramesses VI was so badly destroyed that the ancient restorers had tied the various parts of the body to a piece of the king's coffin to give it some form. Of course, embalmers were known to make mistakes other than losing bits of people. The mummy of Baki, from tomb MMA 729 in the Asasif at western Thebes, was the victim of a particularly unfortunate error:

> It is clear that, when about halfway through the application of the wrappings, the persons charged with the bandaging of the mummy suddenly lost track of which was its front and which its back, and, hazarding a guess as to which was which, guessed wrong, completing the wrapping with the unfortunate Baki lying on his face. Doubtless puzzled, but not in the least daunted by the fact that, as the wrapping progressed, the body looked less and less like the usual Eighteenth Dynasty bandaged mummy, these ingenious souls calmly imitated the totally lacking projection upward of the feet and the bulges over what should have been the chin, chest, and arms by the skilful and liberal use of padding – with the result that, though the fully bandaged body was placed in its coffin actually lying on its stomach, from the exterior it appeared to be in the usual and proper position, lying on its back. (Hayes 1935b: 20–1)

124 The Eighteenth Dynasty mummy of Yuya, one of the best-preserved examples known. His hand position is apparently unique. From KV 46; CM CG 51190.

The New Kingdom saw the regularization of arm positions. Men's and women's arms lie along their sides with their hands covering their genitalia. An exception to this is the superbly preserved mummy of Yuya, the father of Queen Tiye. His arms were bent at the elbow and crossed under the chin. Perhaps this was due to his semi-royal status as the father of the Queen? After Amosis, whose arms were extended along his body with the hands inward at the sides of the thigh, and starting with Amenophis I, kings had their arms crossed over the breast with their hands clenched to grasp the royal sceptres.

The mummy of Sethos I is the first royal mummy to have the palms flat. This royal arm position is one of the reasons why there is very serious doubt as to the true identity of a mummy frequently attributed to Tuthmosis I: his arms are stretched down the side of his body, and the hands are broken off. Few royal women have been found, and the arms of many of these have been torn off by thieves in search of jewels. For the most part, royal women's arms, like those of their noble counterparts, lie at their sides with the hands covering the pudenda. One mummy from the KV 35 cache, which has been claimed to belong to Queen

125 The mummy of King Amosis, interesting in that the brain was removed via the base of the skull, rather than the nose. CM CG 61057.

126 The mummy of Sethos I is one of the best preserved of the royal mummies; the family resemblance between Sethos I and his son Ramesses II is very prominent. Sethos was the first royal mummy to have the hands laid flat on the chest.

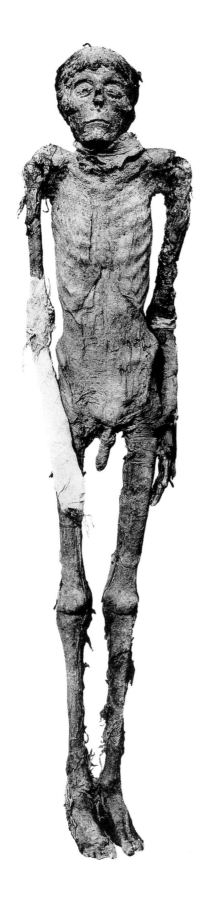

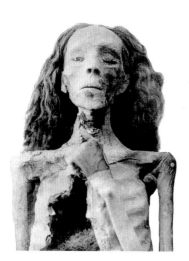

127 This female mummy is notable for her arm positions: one bent at the elbow, and the other straight. In sculpture and painting this is the 'classical' pose of women, but is hardly ever found on actual mummies. This particular body, in KV 35, was identified as Queen Tiye on the basis of the similarity of its hair to a lock of that of the queen herself in the tomb of Tutankhamun. However, on archaeological grounds, she is more likely to be a member of the family of Amenophis II. In KV 35; CG 61070.

position of both males and females is slightly unusual in that some have their arms crossed over the lower abdomen rather than lying over the pubes.

The two mummified female foetuses found in Tutankhamun's tomb are also very unusual. They were well preserved, probably only with natron. The larger one (of about eight months gestation) was eviscerated from the left side and the cranial cavity filled with linen impregnated with natron. The other (of about four or five months gestation) was probably uneviscerated, but dried with natron. The pads placed over the eyes of one of the foetuses were resined.

FROM THE THIRD INTERMEDIATE PERIOD TO THE LATE PERIOD

The Twenty-first Dynasty witnessed the acme of the embalmer's art, which then gradually deteriorated over the course of the Third Intermediate Period. The embalmers of the Twenty-first Dynasty concentrated on making the corpse itself look as life-like as possible – a contrast with Old Kingdom mummification where the wrappings were made to resemble the idealized person. This was done by making incisions in the skin and stuffing the desiccated corpse with sawdust, sand and mud in order to return it to the shape it had enjoyed in life. The location of the incisions is described in the Rhind Magical Papyrus, written nearly a thousand years later; it lists seventeen cuts: seven in the head, four in the thorax, two in the legs, two in the arms, one in the abdomen, and one in the back. Most mummies have fewer than this, about five, although the alleged mummy of Butehamun in Brussels, purchased from Mrs Belzoni, is reported to have all seventeen. Unfortunately, it has been questioned whether the mummy actually belongs to the coffins in which it came to the museum; its date is thus uncertain.

Typically, a slit was made in the left side for evisceration and for refilling the body cavity, including the back. Sometimes the cut would be made in the umbilical region. Often, through the same cut, the neck area was filled with semi-liquid mud or sawdust and plugged with linen tampons to prevent the stuffing from falling out as the mummy was manipulated to fill out the rest of the body. The pelvis was often filled with sawdust, and with women the genital orifice was sometimes plugged with linen, or sewn up, to

Tiye, although this is debatable, has the left arm crossed diagonally over the chest, and the right arm lying at her side. This 'queenly' pose – often seen on statues of royal women – is frequently found on women's coffins of the Nineteenth Dynasty, but most of the mummies of the period continue to have the arms placed over the pubes.

Several noble, artisan and poor burials have been found which do not fit the pattern of 'classic' New Kingdom mummification. The majority of these come from the cemetery at Deir el-Medina, attached to the village of the artisans who fashioned and decorated the tombs of the pharaohs. Often, although the bodies are well wrapped and entombed with rich grave-goods, the mummies themselves are neither eviscerated nor de-brained. Even the mummy of Hatnofret, mother of Hatshepsut's favoured architect Senenmut, contained her brain and bits of her viscera. There is some suggestion that instead of evisceration, she was covered with a layer of beeswax in order to enhance preservation. A few of the bodies of the period might have had their viscera dissolved by rectal injections of oleo-resins. Despite this, several of the burials are equipped with canopic jars. All these bodies were desiccated using natron, and often resin is smeared liberally on them. The hand

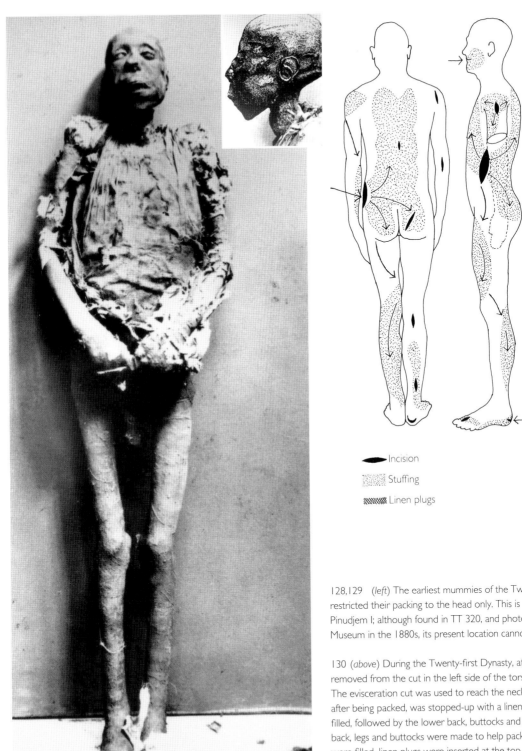

Incision
Stuffing
Linen plugs

128,129 (*left*) The earliest mummies of the Twenty-first Dynasty restricted their packing to the head only. This is the body of King Pinudjem I; although found in TT 320, and photographed in the Bulaq Museum in the 1880s, its present location cannot be confirmed.

130 (*above*) During the Twenty-first Dynasty, after the viscera were removed from the cut in the left side of the torso, the body was stuffed. The evisceration cut was used to reach the neck of the mummy which, after being packed, was stopped-up with a linen plug. Then the torso was filled, followed by the lower back, buttocks and legs. Additional slits in the back, legs and buttocks were made to help pack them. Once the legs were filled, linen plugs were inserted at the top of the thighs to keep the stuffing in place. Separate slits were used to stuff the arms, shoulders, feet and lower abdomen. The mouth was used to fill out the face.

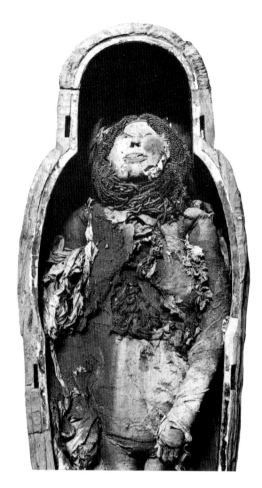

prevent the filler from leaking. Occasionally females' breasts were packed from here, although they were generally left unstuffed. The thighs were also accessible from this incision with the aid of sticks to push the filling down, although sometimes they were filled from a cut made in the back of the knees, an incision that was generally used to fill the calf. To stuff the buttocks, two vertical incisions were made, one on each buttock, although on some mummies, they were stuffed through the pelvis. Incisions at the ankle as well as down the sole between the first two toes were used to stuff the feet. Arms were packed through horizontal incisions made in the ventral and dorsal sides of the shoulders as well as sometimes in the arms at the elbows. There is only one example of a packed hand.

The embalmers of the Twenty-first Dynasty clearly took great pride in their work and were meticulously careful in their efforts to make the mummy look better than it had in its last days of life (ill. 134). The Lady Nesitnebtawy had probably been ill in bed for a long time prior to her death and suffered from bedsores. The resulting holes were used to stuff her buttocks, and then gazelle leather was cleverly used to patch up her wounds. Another man's scrotum was a hollow sack, perhaps due to a hernia. This was filled out with mud so it was better than it had been in life.

Occasionally the embalmers were over-zealous in their efforts at stuffing: Queen Henttawy's face was so full of a fat and soda mixture that her cheeks exploded. Her mummy is remarkable for having false hair made of string, rather than of real hair. The body of the High Priest Masaharta was also so overstuffed that his cheeks almost exploded and it was impossible for his hands to cross over his belly to be placed over his genitals. Perhaps this reflects corpulence in life.

Overstuffing has also proved the ruin of reputations. The body of Maetkare (Dynasty 21), God's Wife of Amun, was stuffed in such a manner that it looked as though she might have been pregnant until shortly before death.

133 Nodjmet, wife of the Priest-King Herihor. Nodjmet looks startlingly alive, through the use of inlaid eyes. CM CG 61087.

134 The mummy of Pinudjem II, a Twenty-first Dynasty High Priest of Amun. His is perhaps the finest of the bodies embalmed using the method involving subcutaneous packing, avoiding the 'bloated' effect which is seen on some earlier bodies of the dynasty. From TT 320; CM CG 61094.

Furthermore, a small mummy found in her coffin was believed by early investigators to be a still-born child. Early writers thus cast many aspersions on the character of Maetkare who, as God's Wife of Amun, was supposed to be a virgin – or at least not pregnant. When she and her baby were finally X-rayed and carefully examined the baby turned out to be a pet baboon, and her pregnant appearance apparently due to the over-packing of enthusiastic embalmers. Her character has thus now been vindicated.

The carelessness of embalmers is also responsible for some strange inclusions in mummies. One woman's viscera were lost during the mummification process, so the embalmers made false intestines from rope, a liver from cowskin, and the other organs from leather and rags.

After a body had been desiccated and finally packed, it was then coloured, red for men, and yellow for women, with the cheeks and lips of some of the women tinted with red. The face was cosmetically enhanced further, including the introduction of false eyes made of stone or glass, as well as continuing the tradition of false eyes made of painted linen. The glass or stone eyes render the mummies particularly life-like. Wigs and hair-extensions are commonly

found. A few such attempts had been made prior to the Third Intermediate Period when Amenophis III's body and face were packed with resin and linen fragments so they could be moulded into a life-like shape. Ramesses V's face had been painted red, and eyebrows had been painted on to the flesh of Merenptah.

Although the mummy itself continued to be cured in the same way as it had been in the New Kingdom, in the Twenty-first Dynasty, once the mummy was desiccated and ready for wrapping, visceral packages containing small wax or faience figures of the relevant Son of Horus were returned to the body cavity so that the body was complete. The incision was frequently vertical, rather than diagonal, as it had been following the time of Tuthmosis III. It was generally sewn up and covered with a metal or wax plate decorated with the *wadjet* eye. There are two unusual mummies belonging to a wife and husband, Tabes and Nesptah, who have two embalming incisions each instead of one. The first is in the stomach region, and the second in the left pelvis, both of which were covered with metal plates, albeit carelessly. Wax, rather than resin, was often used to cover eyelids, plug ears and nostrils, and in one instance peppercorns were introduced into the nose to hold its shape better, somewhat reminiscent of the mummy of Ramesses II. The brain continued to be removed by breaking through the ethmoid bone, and finger- and toe-nails were tied on to prevent their loss.

A peculiar Twenty-first Dynasty burial from Thebes consisted of the bandaged body of a girl, Henttawy. The body was recovered from tomb MMA 59 at Deir el-Bahari, usurped from an Eighteenth Dynasty owner. The girl had not been mummified, just wrapped in bandages and placed in a fine coffin with mummy-board. The lack of mummification is difficult to explain, given the very high quality of her coffins.

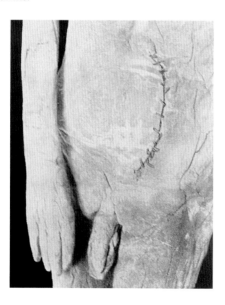

135 In later periods the eviscerating incision was neatly sewn up with linen thread.

Resin continued to be used in mummification. From the Twenty-second Dynasty, on through the Late Period, there was a trend to anoint the wrappings and sometimes the enclosing cartonnage with liquid resin which probably was transparent when new, but has blackened with time. Molten resin continued to be poured into the cranium after the removal of the brain, and often into the body cavity to prevent bacterial activity. Some instances of powdered resin have been found scattered over the entire body to enhance preservation. There are instances where pitch and bitumen have been found on Late Period mummies, sometimes together with resin.

The arms were generally left lying alongside the body with women's hands placed on the front or inside of the thighs almost on their pudenda, and the men's hands in front of their pubes. This held true for both royal and non-royal bodies. It became common for mummies of this period to have rolls of papyrus Books of the Dead or the Underworld placed between the legs.

The Twenty-fifth Dynasty to the Late Period

The Twenty-fifth Dynasty initiated changes that would become part of the repertoire of the Saite Period, and also heralded the decline of fine mummification. Mummies were not particularly well prepared, with several examples of hasty mummification in evidence. After the end of the Twenty-second Dynasty, there was a sharp decrease in the incidence of stuffing and painting the entire mummy to make it life-like, although the body cavity was still filled with earth and sawdust. In the case of better-quality mummies, body shape was provided by pads of linen and extra bandages. Although limbs were individually wrapped, the extremities, except in cases of expensive mummification, were not. Faces were not painted as often, but false eyes remained in vogue.

The brain continued to be removed through the nose. The major change was the placing of the four visceral packets on top of the thighs rather than in the body cavity. From the Twenty-sixth to the Thirtieth Dynasty, they were placed between the thighs or lower down, between the legs. Sometimes empty canopic jars accompanied these burials, clearly retained for their symbolism, although in a few cases they seem to have been used as real visceral containers once again (see Chapter 9). In the Saite Period the brain was not always removed, and there are at least two examples of evisceration incisions being made on the right side. Resin was used over-generously so that the body was often covered in it even before it had been completely dried, and being entirely covered, there was less effort made for competent mummification. Indeed, one mummy now in Newcastle was thought to be preserved using Herodotus' third type of mummification.

Examples of the second type are also found during this period, with portions of the internal organs removed via the anus. Hands for males and females are extended along the side and placed in front of the pubes or inside the thighs, with a few examples from Abydos having them crossed over the chest. No royal mummies from this period have been recovered, so it is impossible to tell if and how their arm positions differed from those of nobles.

Late Period mummies often lie with their head to the west and the feet to the east instead of being traditionally orientated north-south. Frequently there is no embalming incision, but portions of the viscera were extracted from the anus with a sharp instrument that was used both as a probe and a hook, as lacerations of the orifice attest. Nothing was used to dissolve the organs, and large framents of many were left *in situ*. The body-cavity was filled, either anally, or via the incision when extant, with resin, mud, plant material, and, in one instance, feathers. The area between the legs was often also filled with similar packing mixtures. The brain continued to be removed through the ethmoid bone via the nose and the cranium was partially filled with molten resin. The mouth was often packed with resin-soaked linen. Surprisingly, the embalmers sometimes continued to carefully tie on the finger- and toe-nails with string so as not to lose them. Other instances of careful mummification are evident. The genital organs of a man were lost so, to provide a substitute, a round sack-like piece of stiff linen filled with some vegetable powder had been rammed into the pelvic cavity through the perineum to close the cavity. Other mummies show the use of the central hard piece of a palm leaf, the rib, to hold unstable heads in position and to reinforce weak ribs so that the bodies retained their proper shape.

Whilst wrapping the mummy, resin was applied liberally to the bandages, although the bandaging itself was often hasty with fingers and toes not separately wrapped. There are one or two examples of bitumen being found on mummies in addition to resin. This is less surprising as it occurs on mummies of the Persian Period when trade with the bitumen-producing Dead Sea regions was particularly regular. Furthermore, Persia was where the 'mummy' mountain, a major source of bitumen, was found. Both men and women of the period lay on their backs with their hands arranged in a variety of ways: arms over the chest; the left arm folded to the breast and the right arm lying alongside the body; both hands covering the genital region. Some mummies who have the arms across the chest have their right hands open and the left clenched.

THE GRAECO-ROMAN AND EARLY CHRISTIAN PERIODS

With the final end of Egyptian independence until modern times, mummification practices suffered their ultimate decline, and came to an end in the Christian Period. Although the mummies of Graeco-Roman times are less well cured than those of preceding eras, they are far more splendidly wrapped, often in bandages forming lozenge patterns, each lozenge centered over a gold spot, with a portrait-mask painted on a wooden panel covering the face (see Chapter 6).

Most mummies continued to have the brain removed through the nose, although this practice was abandoned towards the end of the second century AD. When the brain was removed, resin was poured into the cranium, as was, in at least two instances, wood pitch. Ptolemaic texts mention packing the cranium with salt, cedar and other materials, although no physical examples have been examined. Throughout the Ptolemaic Period the nostrils were plugged by resin. In the Ptolemaic and early Roman Periods, when the viscera were removed from the body they were often placed between the legs with empty canopic containers occasionally present in the tomb. Other burials of the period have the viscera placed within the very last examples of canopic jars. During the Ptolemaic Period both traditional evisceration through the left flank and the anal purging methods were used. A typical feature of late Ptolemaic and early Roman mummies is the heavy use of liquid resin both inside the body cavity as well as on the surface. Many mummies of the third and fourth centuries AD show that the bodies were neither eviscerated nor de-

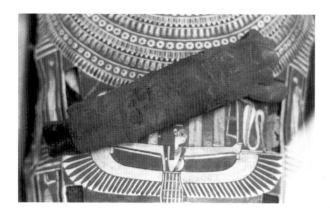

136 A man who had lost his arm traumatically during life had it restored for use in the afterlife. Ptolemaic Period; Durham Oriental Museum.

brained; instead they were thickly covered with resin. The presence of maggots in the body, among other things, indicate that women's mummies of the period were partially decayed before the rudimentary embalming was performed, perhaps to prevent necrophilia in the necropolis.

The arms lay along the sides of the body with the hands resting on the front of the thighs, or crossed over the chest particularly in Roman times. A few mummies from the Ptolemaic Period had their finger-nails tied on with string, but this did not last into the Roman Period. A delightful innovation of the early Roman Period was gilding the mummy. Fingers, toes, eye-lids, lips, hands, feet, genitals, and on occasion the entire body, were covered with a fine layer of gold.

In the Graeco-Roman Period some embalmers, especially in Nubia, continued to attempt to care for their creations: a head of a mummy had become disconnected from the torso, so it was reconnected with a stick; similarly a child's body had a stick passed through its entire length to strengthen it. Some Roman mummies from Giza had reeds placed between layers of wrapping to keep the mummy stiff. This provided mummies with additional protection if they were buried without a coffin, as was the case for many of the period. At the same time other embalmers would create 'dummy' mummies, a feature of the Ptolemaic and Roman Periods, although the phenomenon was not unknown in preceding eras. A body, wrapped to look like an infant, in an infant's coffin, when unwrapped revealed 'an old muddy thigh-bone, to make up the length, with a shinbone and an old skull, full of mud, picked up in some

deserted cemetery, to give the weight and substance requisite for the body. The whole fraud was decently put in a neat wooden coffin, and duly buried. It may have been mere indolence that led to this, or – sad to suggest – such bogus bodies may have been made up in healthy times when work was slack, and kept ready to serve out whenever a press of business came in' (Petrie 1889: 14).

Several mummies have been found that appear to date from the Graeco-Roman Period, but are atypical of the style of mummification for this time. Two quite unusual examples of Roman date (one in the British Museum, EA 6704) combine elements of Roman Period and Old Kingdom methods. The features over the skeleton are modelled in plaster which is covered by a linen 'skin' on which are painted eyebrows, eyes and a beardline in black, while the nostrils, mouth, ear details, a dot on the chin and another in the centre of the forehead, and two marking the inner and outer corner of the eye, are all painted in red. The style of painting with its caterpillar-haired eyebrows points to the Roman Period, though the idea of the technique is purely Old Kingdom. Such bodies are wrapped in linen bandages tightly and carefully in a typically Roman lozenge pattern, and gilded toe- and finger-nails are fixed on in their appropriate positions, outside the wrappings. Another mummy, PUM II, c. 100–170 BC by carbon-14 dating, shows a harking back to Third Intermediate-style mummification. The brain was removed via the ethmoid, and the cranial cavity filled with molten resin. The internal organs were removed from the body, wrapped and then returned to the cavity, and the body carefully wrapped in linen clearly belonging to the Ptolemaic Period. Perhaps this was a restoration of an earlier burial? Or a conscious reversion to an earlier period? The penis was intact and held in an erect position, like that of Tutankhamun, with support from a small piece of wood. The nails were coloured red with henna.

Manchester Museum 1770, the mummy of a fifteen-year-old girl, could also be a Ptolemaic restoration of an earlier body, as the carbon-14 dates for the body suggest. All the internal organs are missing, and, most strikingly, its lower limbs. Fake wooden legs and feet were made as substitutes. The curious thing is that the Ptolemaic embalmers were unsure of the mummy's gender, so they provided it with nipple covers as if it were female, and a false phallus, in case it were male. Maybe the body was of an unknown individual and found in an advanced stage of decomposition when it was prepared. If this were so, the question of why it was so carefully prepared and bandaged arises. Perhaps the body had been found in the Nile, partly devoured by crocodiles, a fate that semi-deified an individual, and would explain the elaborate wrappings. Certainly there are very few plausible reasons for elaborate restorations of non-royal mummies.

A unique way of preserving bodies which supposedly comes from the fourth century BC is the use of honey. The most famous person who, it is thought, was preserved this way was Alexander the Great. Unfortunately, as his body is still lost to us there is no way of verifying it. Certainly honey is a preservative often used in food preservation (on hams and ducks), and a few other examples of it being used for humans are known. Abd el-Latif, the Arab historian, relates that a child's body was found preserved in a jar of honey near the pyramids. Alas, no example of such sweetly preserved bodies has ever been seen in modern times to deny or confirm the reports.

There is very little information about Christian or Coptic mummies. From the limited amount we have it appears that Christian mummies dating approximately from the fourth to sixth centuries AD were only cursorily cured. They lay on their backs with the head to the west, and were covered thickly in salt, and very occasionally some natron. There was no evisceration or brain removal practised, and the use of resin was also abandoned. The arms invariably lay by the side of the bodies, and they wore their own clothes, along with a winding sheet and shroud. An unusual Coptic mummy, now in the Alexandria Museum, is elaborately wrapped with criss-cross bandages, and could easily be identified as Roman were it not for the small black cross painted on the throat. Church leaders seemed, however, to be violently against mummification as it was a strong tie to the earlier polytheist religion. St Anthony, on his deathbed (AD 356), launched a diatribe against the practice and made his followers swear that he be buried in the desert sand and not mummified and brought into the church or house as an object of veneration. It is ironic that, despite this, many important religious figures were embalmed after a fashion, and buried within churches and monasteries which are now sites of pilgrimage.

Islamic burials in Egypt have almost come full circle back to the Predynastic. The bodies were washed, wrapped in plain shrouds, occasionally coffined, and placed directly into the hot dry preserving desert sand, marked only by a small mound of earth.

ANIMAL MUMMIES

The Egyptians were famous in antiquity for mummifying not only humans, but also animals. These were sometimes faked for sale to tourists, both in antiquity and also more recently. Animal mummies are of four varieties: food for the deceased in the Hereafter; pets of the deceased; cult animals; and votive offerings. The first three types occur throughout Egyptian history; the last is largely restricted to the Graeco-Roman Period.

Animals that were buried as food were generally not buried whole, but were jointed. Until the Eighteenth Dynasty these 'victual mummies', in the form of joints of meat or entire fowl, were placed in the burial chamber, sometimes in pottery dishes, so that the deceased could enjoy them in the Afterlife. From the Eighteenth to the Twenty-first Dynasties the 'victual mummies' consisted of joints of meat or of entire birds that were treated with salt and/or natron and then wrapped in linen bandages. These were placed in individual sycamore-wood 'coffinettes' shaped to the form and dimensions of the meat. Some of these mummies are coloured brown; it is possible that a roasted appearance (browning) was given to them by the

137 This victual mummy consists of a leg of a bovid that was preserved in salt, wrapped up, and encoffined, before being put in the tomb of Yuya and Tjuiu in the Valley of the Kings (KV 46).

application of very hot resin on the wrapping which no doubt cooked the exterior surface, while preventing bacterial infestation. Close investigation would suggest, however, that it is more probable that the resin on the mummies came from the pitch applied to the interior of the coffinettes rather than to the mummies themselves.

Mummified pets have also been found in several tombs. It is unclear if the pets were killed when their owner died or perhaps more likely, interred when they had reached their natural end. Certainly the Egyptians were very fond of their pets and had them depicted in their tombs and sometimes even on votive stelae. Isetemkheb D (Dynasty 20) had a pet

138 This gazelle (or perhaps an ibex?) comes from the burial of Isetemkheb D in TT 320. It was probably a dear pet which died and was buried with its owner. CM.

139 Mummified dog from KV 50, perhaps a royal pet. CM JE 38640.

gazelle or ibex buried with her, and Ankhshepenwepet (Dynasty 25/6) also had a gazelle in her tomb. A certain Hapymen, buried at Abydos, was so fond of his pet dog that it was mummified and wrapped in linen, and placed at the side of his feet in his coffin. In the Valley of the Kings, tombs KV 50 and KV 51 were found to contain several mummies of monkeys, dogs and ducks. In the corner of tomb KV 50 a baboon and a dog were found glaring at each other as if in preparation for battle. This 'tableau' seems to have been the work of tomb robbers. It is unclear whose pets the baboon and the hound were, although they seem to belong to a cemetery associated with the tomb of Amenophis II. At Heliopolis there is a Predynastic cemetery which contains tombs of small herbivores, perhaps gazelles, as well as dogs. These might be pets, or, conceivably, an early cemetery for an animal cult.

Animal cults were common in Egypt throughout its history, although they reached an acme of popularity in the Late and Graeco-Roman Periods. Animal cults focused on one specific animal in whom the spirit of the god would reside and be worshipped as such for the duration of the animal's life. Upon its death it was mummified, and another one, chosen for its special markings, would take its place. The most common and long-lived cults were the bull cults, often having solar connections. There were several such cults in Egypt, but the most important were the Apis bull at Memphis, the Mnevis at Heliopolis, and the Buchis bull at Armant. It is unclear when the cults started; perhaps as early as the First Dynasty, if not before. Evidence for them comes mainly from the New Kingdom onward. It is unknown when the Mnevis cult died out; probably in the fourth century AD, along with the other bull cults. The Buchis cult survived until AD 362, while the cult of the Apis bull was the last to survive until the Emperor Honorius banned it and caused the destruction of the Serapeum, the cult and burial place of the bull, in AD 398. Several Buchis bull burials have been found intact, most from the Late and Graeco-Roman Periods. The earliest intact Apis burial is from the reign of Horemheb. When the rectangular coffin containing the bull was opened, the 'mummy' proved to be a surprise. It consisted only of a bull's head, devoid of flesh and skin, resting on a large black mass. When examined, the mass proved to be a bundle of resin, broken bovid bones, and fragments of gold leaf, all wrapped in fine linen. The canopics of the bull seemed to be filled with indeter-

140 The Serapeum at Saqqara was the burial-site of the Apis bulls. It was discovered by Mariette, who celebrated the event by having a party at the site during which he served champagne.

minate resinous material. Excavations under the floor of the burial chamber yielded a dozen large crude pottery jars, containing ashes and burnt bones. Similar jar-deposits were also present in a few other Apis tombs. This evidence has suggested that, during the New Kingdom at least, the body was cooked and eaten by the pharaoh and the priests before its interment. A connection has been suggested between this occurrence and the so-called 'Cannibal Hymn' of the Pyramid Texts (Utterances 273–4), which speaks of the king devouring the gods to take on their powers. It is possible that this hypothesis has some truth in it, but it is more likely that there is some other explanation. Certainly, no other sacred animals seem to have been devoured by their erstwhile caretakers. Later Apis bulls were definitely fully mummified. There is a papyrus dating from the Twenty-sixth Dynasty that describes the method used to embalm an Apis bull. It is similar to Herodotus' second method, and involves enemas and douches that melt the entrails, myrrh and resin applications for the exterior, and specific instructions for wrapping the bull.

Late Period examples of mummified Buchis bulls from Armant provide more information about the mummification of cult animals, although this too is limited due to the water-damaged state of the bodies. The mummies were prepared by removing the internal organs through the anus, possibly with the help of turpentine or some other oleoresin which would be injected into the body cavity. The

141 This stela shows the adoration of the Apis bull. Such stelae were placed in niches within the Serapeum. Nineteenth Dynasty; Louvre Museum.

142 Skeleton of a Buchis bull from Armant. The Buchis bull was held in place by a series of metal clamps fitted into the wooden base board.

143 These enemas, resembling those used in modern times, were probably used in embalming the Buchis bulls.

anus was then plugged until the viscera had softened and could be removed. An enema, a douche, and two vaginal retractors of bronze were recovered from the site. The animal was possibly then packed in natron to dry it out, before being wrapped. It would generally be fastened to a board with metal clamps through which bandages were passed to secure it to the board, and then wrapped, as the relative position of bandages to board indicates. The animals were arranged in the position of a recumbent sphinx, a position not natural to bulls. This was done by cutting the tendons, thus releasing the legs without breaking any bone. The tail was placed under the right hind leg. A wooden chin-rest supported the head, and the wrapped animal was covered by a shroud. The bulls wore masks covered by gold leaf, with artificial eyes inserted. There are also some other Late Period animal cults with cemeteries of mummified animals such as the Mothers of Buchis and Apis bulls. Each burial concentrates on an individual animal.

144 The 'mummy' of a Mother of Apis, comprising the cow's head fitted into a plaster-covered model of the beast.

The Late Period and especially the Graeco-Roman Period saw the advent of votive animal mummies given as gifts to the gods. These mummies were probably prepared at cult centres, purchased by pilgrims, and then placed in catacombs devoted to such gifts to particular gods. In the Graeco-Roman Period all sorts of deities gained importance, and consequently the animals associated with each deity were mummified and given to the god as offerings. Unlike cult animals, these had no intrinsic divinity – they were just gifts to the god. The most famous catacombs are Tuna el-Gebel, sacred to Thoth whose animals were the ibis and baboon; Abydos with ibis burials and burial of dogs and jackals for Khentyamentiu and Wepwawet, both canid deities; Bubastis, sacred to the goddess Bastet, filled with cat mummies, some of which were exported to Europe in the nineteenth century as fertilizer; and Saqqara, with catacombs for several deities, all containing different animals. This period in Egyptian history saw every imaginable creature embalmed: cows, bulls, sheep, cats, dogs, baboons, jackals, ibises, falcons, hawks, fish of all varieties, crocodiles, shrews, scorpions, snakes, and a Greek text even mentions a necropolis of lions at Saqqara. The most curious are mummified birds' and reptiles' eggs, and scarab beetles.

The various methods of mummifying and wrapping these animals are interesting, and by no means uniform. Late Period mummies of hawks and other birds of prey used to be identified as children until they were unwrapped. This was because the embalmers wrapped the mummy with a mass of bandages so that it looked baby-sized, and covered the head area with a cartonnage mask of a human face. The use of a human mask ceased in the latter part of the Graeco-Roman Period. Ibis mummies and those of birds of prey were often given the same treatment. The birds were grasped by the feet and plunged into a vat of liquid resin, before being wrapped elaborately in bandages, then perhaps sold to the pilgrims who wished to give these as offerings to the gods, and put into ceramic jars, often three or four to a jar, which were placed in the catacombs. Lengths of palm-rib were often used to make them rigid, as was done with some human mummies of the period. A few ibis mummies were eviscerated, but this does not seem to be the rule. It is estimated that at Saqqara alone over 10,000 birds were buried annually in the ibis and falcon catacombs.

Like their human counterparts, animal mummies were sometimes faked in antiquity. Fakes composed of cloth,

145 Baboons were also sacred to Thoth. Study of baboon DNA in a quest for the AIDS virus is currently underway.

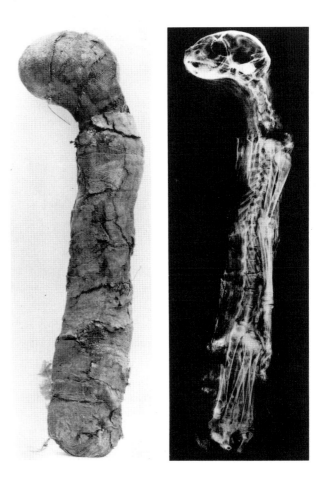

146,147 X-ray of mummified cat, now at Liverpool; LUSACOS E.537.

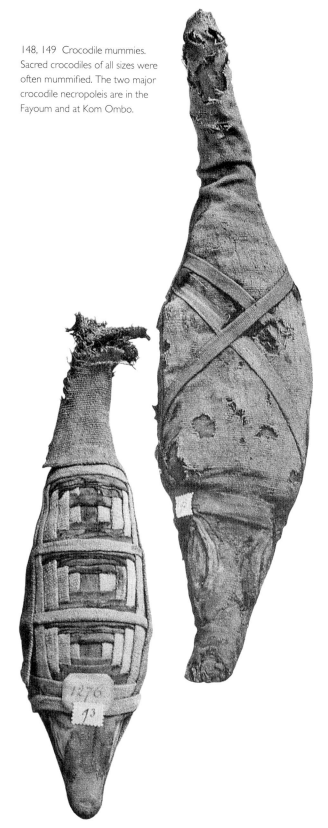

feathers, odd bones, brick or pottery would be beautifully wrapped and sold to unsuspecting pilgrims as offerings. Probably many of these had been produced when business was slow.

Fish, usually Nile perch, were mummified and placed in cemeteries. The mummies vary in size from a few centimetres to almost 2 metres. Early excavators suggested that they were plunged into a natron solution, air-dried, and then wrapped, sometimes with the eyes indicated in paint. Or they might have been packed in dry natron and then wrapped; it is difficult to determine. Some of them are slit down their bellies, thus indicating evisceration, and filled with mud and sand to hold the shape. Fish mummies are especially interesting as some of them are of species that no longer exist in the Egyptian Nile.

Mummified crocodiles, sacred to the god Sobek, were also common in Egypt. These were probably cured with natron or even salt and wrapped. They do not show signs of evisceration. Some burials not only included juvenile and adult crocodiles but their eggs, containing recognizable foetuses, in some instances over fifty. Crocodile mummies were often faked with reeds and bones.

The very number of all these mummies raises the question of whether the animals were bred specifically for mummification, and how they were killed. Given the vast numbers of animals buried, often within the space of a year, they were undoubtedly bred on the site as offerings. Unfortunately in the case of most mummies it is unclear as to how they were killed. The ibis and birds of prey were possibly killed by being immersed in vats of molten resin, while the fish would have died just by being removed from water. However, it is still to be determined how the dogs, baboons and other animals were disposed of. The only mammals whose mummies have been closely examined are cats. Ptolemaic cat mummies in the collection of the British Museum (now in the Natural History Museum, London), from the Museum of Fine Arts, Boston, and the Bubasteion at Saqqara that have been X-rayed show that several were strangled, since their necks were broken, while others were hit over the head. Some show evidence of natron or salt in their preparation, while others indicate the use of resin.

Further studies on animal mummies, including those currently being excavated in Saqqara and Tuna el-Gebel, should provide more information on whether the animals were wild or domesticated, and how they were killed.

Chapter 4 Amulets, Jewellery and Other Ornaments

Desiccating the mummy was only part of the embalming procedure. Linen wrappings (see Chapters 3 and 5) were an important part of the preservation process, as was the placing of amulets on the corpse, interspersed with the wrappings. Such amulets could range from a handful of protective charms to vast quantities of exquisite jewellery, as found on the mummies of Tutankhamun and other royalty.

AMULETS

An amulet can be many things, but may be described basically as a charm, often inscribed with a spell, magic incantation or symbol, and believed to protect the wearer against evil, or to provide aid and magical benefits. These benefits could include confidence, healing, luck, protection or even an ability to act as a double or replacement for an organ or limb. The ancient Egyptians had several words for amulet, most notably *sa* and *wedjaw*. The former means amulet, and is also very similar in sound to the word meaning 'protection'. The latter has the same sound as the word for well-being and prosperity, and is probably related to it.

The ancient Egyptians, much like their modern counterparts, were firm believers in wearing amulets for protection or aid for both the living and the dead. Several would be placed on a corpse and scattered amongst the wrappings in an effort to keep the body intact and ensure a safe passage to, and existence in, the Afterlife.

Tutankhamun had over 140 amulets scattered through his wrappings. It is ironic that these self-same protective amulets were primarily responsible for the destruction of the bodies that they were supposed to protect. It was the robbers' quest for the heart scarab, generally a large, finely carved scarab of a dark stone, that was responsible for the holes in the chests of many mummies. Often the entire mummy would be stripped or even burnt in an effort to divest it of its amulets. Frequently made of precious materials, they were portable and easily saleable to tourists, scholars and collectors alike.

The power inherent in an amulet was transmitted not only by its shape, but also by its material and colour, all of which helped to endow the wearer with power, protection and special capabilities. The use of the correct material guaranteed magical benefits. Green and blue stones or faience signified resurrection and rebirth; hematite meant strength and support; carnelian, jasper, red glass or red faience were used for any amulet that symbolized blood, energy, strength and power. The type of material utilized depended on the individual's wealth.

Throughout Egyptian history amulets were incorporated into the wrappings of mummies. Indeed, the Book of

150 (*above*) Heart scarab of King Sobkemsaf I or II, of green jasper mounted on gold base inscribed with Chapter 30B of the Book of the Dead; the scarab has a human face. Allegedly found on the mummy of King Inyotef VI; Seventeenth Dynasty, from Dira Abu'l-Naga; BM EA 7876.

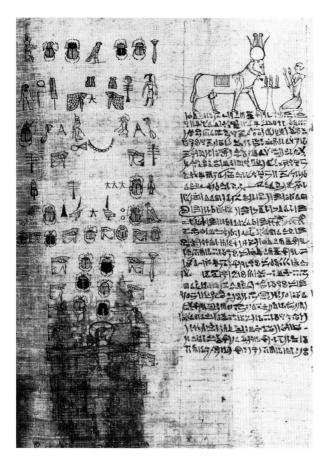

151 Sheet 12 from the Funerary Papyrus of Men shows a schematic plan of the position of amulets in the Ptolemaic Period. BM EA 10098.

152 The *wadjet* eye, or the eye of Horus, was one of the most potent and popular charms in ancient Egypt. It protected the wearer from all types of dangers and kept away the evil eye. The concept has endured in the culture, although the form that the modern amulet takes is that of a blue bead.

the Dead specifically mentions certain ones that have magical obligations to the deceased, notably the headrest and *wadj* pillar. These are the amulets that are the most commonly found on mummies and are also mentioned in one or two papyri that deal with wrapping the body after embalming. The Book of the Dead, which was included in the burials from the late New Kingdom onward, can itself also be regarded as a funerary amulet; it is a guidebook through the many pitfalls of the Underworld, and a key to all the questions that must be answered correctly by the deceased if the Afterlife is to be reached.

Funerary amulets continued to be important throughout Egyptian history, but their type and number changed over time, with a few exceptions. The location of the amulet on the body also changed, but unfortunately, due to the imprecise accounts and rapid unrollings of mummies in the past, the exact locations and changes are impossible to document clearly. The *wadjet* eye was one amulet that was extremely popular with both the living and the dead from the Old Kingdom well into the Graeco-Roman Period, and beyond. It is quite possible that in Egypt some of the Coptic and Islamic protective charms against the evil eye are derived from the *wadjet* eye. It was supposed to represent the eye of Horus or of Re and protected the wearer against all evils by taking on the powers of the god. From the New Kingdom onward this amulet was placed near the eviscerating incision; prior to that it was placed on the chest. Frequently there was more than one example of any specific amulet on the body, and they would be scattered over the chest.

Old Kingdom and First Intermediate Period Amulets

In the Old Kingdom the number and variety of amulets found with the mummy are limited. They increased somewhat in the Middle and New Kingdoms, but it was from the Third Intermediate Period onward that amulets became very important and their number proliferated. The few Old Kingdom mummies examined and unwrapped contained merely 10 to 15 amulets, in stark contrast to Tutankhamun's 143, and the 53 or 54 commonly found on noble burials of the Late Period.

The Old Kingdom burials all tend to include the *wadjet* eye, but they have virtually none of the other amulets found in later periods. Most of the Fifth Dynasty mummies

153 Some of the most common amulets: clockwise from top left: *tjet* knot; *djed* pillar; *wadj*; *djed* pillar; *wadj*; Anubis; Horus; serpent-head; Thoth. From KV 62; CM JE 61834; 61778; 61860; 61779; 61861; 61865; 61864; 61848; 61863.

from the cemetery of Deshasheh examined by Petrie had the *wadjet* eye, a bee amulet, leopard and jackal heads, a frog amulet and a double lion amulet. The precise function, other than protection, of most of these is unclear. The bee might mean protection by the pharaoh of the deceased as it was part of the royal titulary. The jackal head signifies Anubis, the dog/jackal god of the Necropolis, the god of embalming who was responsible for the first mummy ever, that of Osiris. Several Sixth Dynasty mummies sported a recumbent Anubis amulet, though oddly enough it is infrequently seen in the Middle and New Kingdoms. The frog probably referred to Heket, a frog goddess associated with magic; this rarely appears in later periods. The only other amulet that occurs in the Old Kingdom and on down through Egyptian history is the *djed* pillar. Said to represent a column of vertebrae or a tree trunk, it is the symbol of

Osiris and signifies endurance and stability. It was popular for both the living and the dead. Chapter 155 of the Book of the Dead refers to it, and it was generally found on the mummy's throat, as well as on the chest. Several *djed* pillars may be found on a single mummy; most are made of faience or lapis lazuli. Some amulets representing different parts of the body are found on late Old Kingdom and First Intermediate Period mummies. No doubt these were to serve as replacements should the actual body be destroyed.

The First Intermediate Period mummies whose amulets have been found *in situ* seem to have an abundance of *wadjet* eyes, in addition to diverse other amulets, notably body-parts. In some cases the amulets were spread out over a length of twisted and knotted flaxen thread which was put over the mummy. The earliest *pesesh-kef* amulets with bewigged human heads at the end of the flat blades also

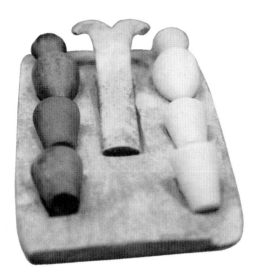

154 This Old Kingdom model *pesesh-kef* set contains the major elements: a knife, with two blades, and two sets of jars for oils.

date to this period and into the early Middle Kingdom. They derive from the *pesesh-kef* knife set that was involved in the ritual of Opening of the Mouth, a procedure that had its origins in the cutting of the umbilical cord and clearing the newborn infant's mouth of mucus so that it could breathe and eat. The New Kingdom *pesesh-kef* amulets lack the human head, and are made of obsidian, basalt, steatite and serpentine. It is possible that they evolved into or are confused with the two feather amulets (symbolizing Amun) found in the Late Period. The *pesesh-kef* amulet guaranteed the use of all facilities in the Afterlife. The two fingers amulets, generally made out of a dark stone, are also probably related to the *pesesh-kef* set, the fingers being those used to clear the newborn's mouth. This amulet tends to be found on the left side of the pelvis, near the embalming incision. Another interpretation is that it represents the fingers of the embalmer who made the visceral incision.

Middle Kingdom Amulets

Funerary amulets became more numerous in the Middle Kingdom. It was during this period that the heart scarab, the classic mummy amulet, was introduced. It comprised a large scarab placed over the heart, its base inscribed with texts from the Book of the Dead, notably Spell 30:

O my heart which I had from my mother, O my heart which I had upon earth, do not rise up against me as a witness in the presence of the Lord of Things; do not speak against me concerning what I have done, do not bring up against me anything I have done in the presence of the Great God, Lord of the West.

The heart scarab protected the heart of the deceased, and served as a replacement should the original heart be destroyed. The heart was the most important organ for the Egyptians since they believed that it was the seat of one's spirit and very being. When the deceased went to the Hall of Judgment and was judged by Osiris, the heart would be weighed against the feather of truth or *Maat*. If the heart was heavier, the deceased would be eaten by Ammit the Devourer (the hideous crocodile-hippopotamus-lion hybrid that lurks near the scales of justice in vignettes from the Book of the Dead) and disappear forever; if the heart was in balance, he could proceed safely to the Afterworld. Thus, a stand-in for the heart was necessary in case anything ever happened to the original. Heart scarabs continued to be used well into the Roman Period.

Scarabs of any sort were also popular amulets and derived from the beetle, *Scarabaeus sacer*. Such amulets symbolized resurrection, probably because the scarab beetle lays its eggs and wraps them in a dung ball which provides the larvae with nourishment. To the Egyptians the ball of dung from which new life sprang was miraculous. They associated it with the sun-disc that travels across the sky,

155 The heart scarab was the most important amulet placed on the deceased as it replaced the real heart should it be damaged. This one (both sides shown) once adorned the mummy of King Shabaka. Twenty-fifth Dynasty, from El-Kurru; MFA 21.301.

156 The winged scarab was often placed over the chest of the mummy. It invoked the protection of solar deities for the mummy. From KV 62; CM JE 6194.

being re-born each day, and identified it with the new-born sun-god, Khepri. Scholars have also suggested that scarabs are so closely identified with mummies because the beetle pupae resemble wrapped-up mummies. Furthermore, the egg-bearing dung ball is created in an underground chamber reached by a vertical shaft and horizontal passage, much like a tomb. Whether this was something that the ancient Egyptians were conscious of and incorporated into their symbolism is unclear, although possible. Scarabs began appearing as amulets in the Sixth Dynasty, although at this early time with no primarily funerary association. An interesting scarab dating to the Middle Kingdom and found in the tomb of Wah at Thebes was made of solid silver, and had

its eyes and mouths hammered and roughened before being set on the mummy so that the beetle could not harm it.

Scarabs were not always in the form of beetles. Human- and animal-headed examples have been found, with one of the most striking being the human-headed heart scarab of Sobkemsaf I or II of the Seventeenth Dynasty (ill. 150). From the Late Period on, some were pierced by holes around the edge so that they could be stitched on to the mummy wrappings or incorporated into the bead nets that decorated the wrapped body. From the late New Kingdom onwards pectoral scarabs with outstretched wings became popular additions to the amulet repertoire. These were generally placed over the chest and neck.

Other amulets that started appearing on the body in the Middle Kingdom were snake-headed ones symbolizing the uraeus (serpent-image of kingship) and its protective powers. The name bead or *swrt/swit* amulet is also particularly typical of the Middle Kingdom, and continues being a part of the mummy's adornments thereafter. It takes the form of a barrel-shaped bead worn on a necklace on the throat, generally inscribed with the name of the deceased so he/she would not lose his/her identity in the hereafter. It is even represented on mummy-masks and anthropoid coffins as well as in the object friezes of the Middle Kingdom rectangular coffins. The beads are often made of carnelian or similarly coloured materials.

New Kingdom Amulets

The New Kingdom saw an increase in the variety and number of amulets. The most notable addition to the repertoire was the embalming-wound cover. This was a wax or metal plate placed over the incision made to extract the viscera. These thin, generally oval, plates sometimes had the *wadjet* eye inscribed on them, to provide extra protection for the wound. The richest burials had gold plates. They seem to have ceased being used some time before the Twenty-sixth Dynasty, from then on being either totally abandoned or often replaced by the two-finger amulet. The *tjet* amulet also made its appearance in the New Kingdom. It symbolizes protection by the blood of Isis and supposedly represented a piece of cloth, looped and knotted, indicating either the buckle or girdle of Isis. It could also represent a cloth worn between the legs of a pregnant woman to prevent bleeding and to protect the child in her womb, or be associated with menstruation and the potential fertility of a woman. *Tjets* are mentioned in Chapter 156 of the Book of the Dead. They were worn by both men and women, the early examples dating to the late Eighteenth Dynasty. They tend to be made of red jasper, carnelian and glass, and are located on the neck and chest of the mummy.

The *ka* amulet, symbol of the soul, is found exclusively on mummies of the Eighteenth Dynasty. The *ba* amulet, the human-headed bird aspect of the soul, is found after the reign of Tutankhamun, and was placed on the chest of the mummy should the deceased's own *ba* refuse to return. *Ankh* signs, the symbol of life, as well as *ib* or heart jars, were placed on mummies of the New Kingdom and later.

157 Clockwise from top: the heart, *wadj* and *tjet* amulets. Reign of Ramesses II from the Serapeum at Saqqara; Louvre Museum.

158 The *ankh*, the sign of life, one of the most ubiquitous amuletic hieroglyphs, in origin the representation of a sandal-strap, the Egyptian word for which has the same consonants as that for 'life'.

They protected the mummy and provided it with extra hearts, and are mentioned in Chapters 26 to 29 of the Book of the Dead. They are made of lapis, feldspar and carnelian as well as faience. *Wadj* amulets in the shape of a papyrus stalk symbolizing fertility and regeneration were also common from this period onwards, reaching a peak of popularity in the Twenty-sixth to Thirtieth Dynasties. They tend to be made of faience or any green stone, the colour most closely associated with rebirth and regeneration. The *wrs* or head-rest amulet also started being used in the Eighteenth Dynasty. Frequently made of haematite, it

was placed under the head of the deceased and was supposed to stop the head from falling off or being stolen. A spell that was often found inscribed on it appears in the Coffin Texts Spell 232 and in the Book of the Dead Chapter 166. These amulets became increasingly popular in the Late Period. The spell on them reads as follows:

> O N, may they awaken your head at the horizon. Raise yourself, so that you may be triumphant against what is done against you, for Ptah has felled your enemies, and it is commanded that action be taken against those who would harm you.... Your head shall not be taken from you afterwards, your head shall not be taken from you forever.

Most amulets were placed on the neck and chest, with specific ones, such as the head-rest, under the neck and a *wadjet* amulet on the embalming wound. Some mummies, such as that of Sethos II, had a string of amulets wound spirally around the legs from ankle to knee. Sethos' string comprised *wadjet* eyes, scarabs and small sphinxes. Why they were placed on the legs is unclear and quite unusual.

Third Intermediate and Late Period Amulets

In the Third Intermediate and Late Periods amulets proliferated. They appeared in the shape of the goddess Maat or her feather of truth; *nefer* amulets, signifying good or beautiful, became common; and various snake amulets to save the mummy from snakebite in the Netherworld were placed on the mummy's throat. The *shen* or symbol for eternity as well as the *sa* amulet, symbolizing protection, and an amulet in the shape of stairs to reach the sky also became common, and the Four Sons of Horus were each wrapped with the viscera that they protect. An amulet in the shape of a trussed ox, perhaps signifying endless offerings of meat, and the rather obscure architectural measure also appeared. Amulets in the shape of deities also became the norm from the Twenty-sixth Dynasty onwards. Nephthys, Amun, Thoth, Horus and other gods frequently figured as part of the funerary paraphernalia on the

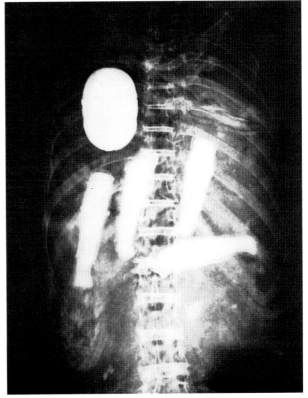

160 The heart scarab and amulets of the Four Sons of Horus can be seen in this X-ray of Queen Nodjmet's torso. Twenty-first Dynasty; CM.

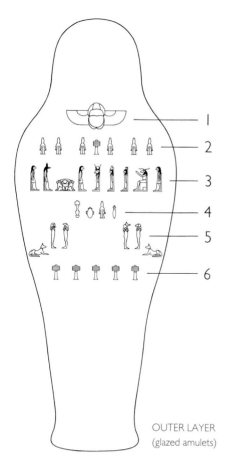

OUTER LAYER
(glazed amulets)

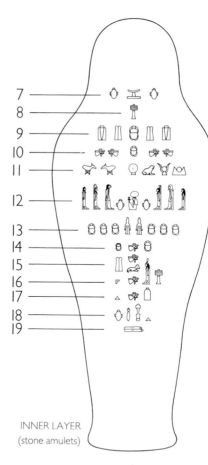

INNER LAYER
(stone amulets)

KEY
....

OUTER LAYER
1 Winged scarab
2 Three *tjet*, *djed* pillar, *tjet* of Isis
3 Horus, Anubis, double lions
4 Lungs, heart, *tjet*, papyrus column
5 Jackal, Four Sons of Horus, jackal
6 Five *djed* pillars

INNER LAYER
7 Heart, headrest, heart
8 *Djed* pillar
9 (Unknown), two feathers, heart scarab, two feathers, (unknown)
10 Two *wadjet* eyes, scarab, two *wadjet* eyes
11 Two bound gazelles, sun disc, frog, sun disc between horns of Hathor, horizon
12 Goddess, Isis, Horus, heart, Re seated, heart, Nephthys, god, goddess
13 Three scarabs, two *tjet*, three scarabs
14 Scarab, *wadjet* eye, scarab
15 Two feathers, *wadjet* eye over recumbent animal
16 Carpenter's square, *wadjet* eye, Maat, *djed* pillar
17 Carpenter's or mason's level, *wadjet* eye, necklace counterpoise
18 Heart, papyrus column, lungs, carpenter's or mason's level
19 Two fingers

mummy. Surprisingly, Osiris amulets are quite rare. Osiris, god of the dead, only appeared in amuletic form in the Late Period, with notable early examples coming from the Twenty-second Dynasty burial of Prince Hornakhte at Tanis. Isis amulets are known from the New Kingdom onward, but were not common until the Late Period. These generally appeared as a pair on the upper chest, with Isis by herself, and also suckling Horus. There is a list of important funerary amulets from ancient Egypt in the MacGregor Papyrus, which specifically mentions the importance of including an Isis suckling Horus on the mummy to ensure life everlasting.

The hypocephalus, an amulet appearing briefly in the Middle Kingdom, became a prominent and important part of the burial in the Late and Ptolemaic Periods, when it was placed beneath the head of the mummy. A hypocephalus was circular and was inscribed with Spell 162 of the Book of the Dead: a spell to cause a flame beneath the head of a spirit. Figures of various deities adorned it, including Amun-Re, Isis, Nephthys, Thoth, Re, Horus and his Four Sons. This curious charm has an interesting and compli-

161 Late Period arrangement of amulets.

162 The hypocephalus protected the head of the deceased and was similar in function to the headrest. Solar symbols were commonly shown on the hypocephalus.

cated history. In a few tombs of the Middle Kingdom, notably that of the courtier Wah, buried at Thebes, and Senebtisi, buried at Lisht, a decorated resinous cake inscribed with spells was found beneath the head of the mummy. In the Eighteenth Dynasty, pads of linen substituted for the resin cake and were often placed under the deceased's head, occasionally being inscribed with spells. It was only after the Twenty-first Dynasty that they appeared more often. These amulets are made of stuccoed linen, papyrus and bronze, and are a favourite in the burials of priestly families (of Amun-Re and Min) of Upper Egypt.

Another piece of mummy decoration that began to appear in the Twenty-second Dynasty was the bead net, which forms part of the external decoration discussed in Chapter 6. Bead net dresses were made of long faience beads threaded into a lozenge pattern with faience amulets in the shape of winged scarabs and the Four Sons of Horus incorporated into the decoration. They were especially popular in the Twenty-fifth and Twenty-sixth Dynasties and later.

The origin of the coverings made in this technique go back a long way, however. Bead net dresses have been depicted on statues and paintings of women, and referred to in Egyptian stories. In the Fourth Dynasty tomb G 7440Z at Giza, Reisner found a mummified body with the remains of a bead net dress laid over her, and Brunton excavated a similar dress from Qau. Probably, at this time, the net dress was something that the living individual would have worn, equivalent to the kilt found on the intact

163 The belt and tail found around the Twelfth-Dynasty mummy of Senebtisi. From Lisht; MMA 08.200.29.

164 The Roman Period saw the advent of the amulet-frame, a contraption that permitted amulets to be suspended together on a frame, and placed over the wrapped body. BM EA 6714.

The Roman Period saw the continuation of the popularity of amulets, with one or two additions. Tongue plates, rough rectangular or oval plates of gold, were placed in the mouth or over the lips of the deceased so they could speak in the Afterworld. A few examples of these have been found in Twenty-sixth Dynasty burials, but most date to the Roman Period. Gold ovals were also placed over the eye, a mixture of Classical and Egyptian tradition, with pieces of gold being the equivalent of the coins placed on the eyes of the deceased so that Charon, the boatman of the river Styx, could be paid. Frequently, in the Roman Period, an amulet frame was placed over the mummy. It consisted of a U-shape frame made of palm fibre, with horizontal pieces filling in the U. Upon these horizontal bars were strung a series of amulets, giving the effect of an abacus.

Hand and Feet Covers

In addition to strictly amuletic items, other categories of object are found on some high-status mummies. First, there are the finger- and toe-stalls, often made of gold, that were placed on the bandaged fingers and toes of wealthy individuals. The stalls helped to keep the extremities from breaking off and being lost. Examples come from the burial of Tutankhamun, and from the royal necropolis of Tanis.

Secondly, a number of these mummies also wore 'clothing' in precious metals. Tutankhamun and Shoshenq II wore sandals of solid gold. Tiny silver gloves were found in KV 56, and seem once to have protected the hands of an infant princess. Such gloves have been found on other

mummy of Nefer/Waty from the Fifth Dynasty. However, by the Third Intermediate Period it had acquired some funerary importance as well, and by adding certain amulets to it, became a funerary garment, found almost exclusively on female corpses. Some ornate examples have elaborate beaded designs such as faces worked into the garment itself.

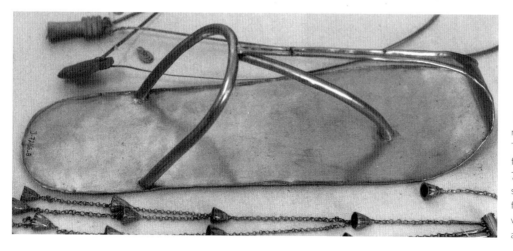

165 Gold sandal from the mummy of Shoshenq II. Twenty-second Dynasty, from Tanis NRT III; CM JE 72166B. These flimsy gold sandals are an example of funerary jewellery since they would have been useless and impractical in life.

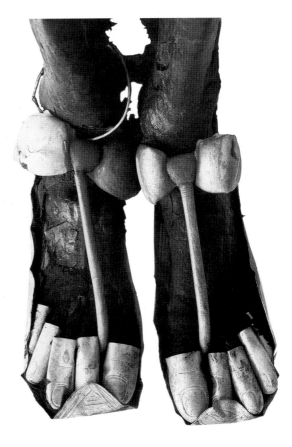

166 Finger stalls of Amenemopet. From NRT III; CM JE 86048; 86050.

167 Toe stalls and gold sandals upon the feet of Tutankhamun; CM JE 60680-3.

mummies, for example one unwrapped by Samuel Birch, belonging to Lord Londesbrough. On some poorer ones, such as the early Third Intermediate Period Lyons mummy, the hands were bound in linen so as to imitate gloves.

Jewellery

Adorning the body with jewellery, ranging from shells and beads to gold and semi-precious stones, was a very important part of Egyptian burial practice. From the Predynastic Period onward mummified corpses wore some sort of jewellery, and it formed a significant part of the burial equipment. Two categories have been found on mummies. The first comprises items made specifically for the burial, and the second, jewellery used during the lifetime of the deceased.

Burial jewellery (eg. ill. 157) is distinguished from real jewellery by its flimsy construction, for example being stamped from thin sheet-gold, and its partially amuletic function. The most common types of such ornaments are collars of hammered and incised or stamped gold in the shape of protective vulture goddesses or serpents or other amuletic shapes. Gold bands for wrists or ankles were also produced. Good examples come from the tomb of Tutankhamun. These were placed on the mummy where real jewellery would have been worn, but were significantly cheaper, and provided an economical alternative for the deceased and his family. Perhaps this cheaper type of jewellery was thought to lessen the chances of a robber violating the body, if not the tomb. Other examples of burial jewellery, such as were found in the tomb of the Lady Sitwerut at Dahshur, were made of wood covered with a thin layer of gold leaf.

'Real' jewellery, actually worn during the lifetime of the deceased, is solidly made and elaborate, using different technologies and materials. It includes earrings, diadems, a variety of neck-ornaments, armlets, bracelets and rings. Amongst the most spectacular are the diadems found on relatively intact royal mummies, such as those of Tutankhamun, Inyotef VI and Khnemet. Khnemet's tiny

169 A few of the layers of jewellery and other items that lay within the
wrappings of Tutankhamun's mummy.

circlet of golden wires, interspersed with minute inlaid
flowers, is one of the triumphs of Egyptian jewellery. Other
spectacular items are the Twelfth Dynasty pectorals from
Dahshur and Lahun, the bracelets found round the possible
arm of the Horus Djer at Umm el-Qaab, and the rare silver
inlaid bracelets from Queen Hetepheres' tomb. These limited examples of real jewellery that have been recovered
provide a hint of the boundless wealth of the ancient
Egyptians.

COLOUR PLATES

XII, XIII The crown and floral circlet, found in the coffin of Princess
Khnemet; the latter is one of the most exquisite pieces of jewellery
known from Egypt. Twelfth Dynasty, from Dahshur, enclosure of
Ammenemes II; CM CG 52859-60.

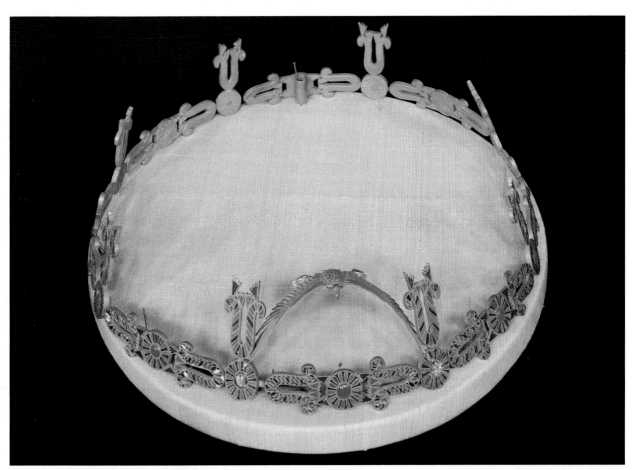

XII

XIII

XIV Amulets (clockwise from top left): Horpakhered; *ba*; two crouched female sphinxes; Bastet; *tjet*; *sa*; *ankh* and *was* combined; cowrie; cat; plummet; head-rest; ram's head on column; human-headed *pesesh-kef*; monkey with baby; harpoon; twin fingers. First Intermediate to Late Periods; BM EA 57866; 3361; 57793; 14754; 65533; 7499; 65332; 65539; 14586; 59859; 8338; 8315; 64604; 30848; 71029; 64629; 59500.

XV Selection of *wadjet*-eye amulets, which represented the eye lost by Horus in battle with Seth, healed and transfigured into a symbol of protection and nutrition. New Kingdom to Late Period; BM EA 29222; 14846; 12752; 13430; 90112; 16966; 15609; 7321; 29040; 15836.

XVI (*overleaf*) Pectoral found in a casket in the 'Treasury' of KV 62, comprising an elaborate rebus on the prenomen (throne name) of Tutankhamun, together with the symbolic representation of the birth of the sun and moon; CM JE 61884.

Wrappings

Chapter 5

Mummy bandages and wrappings provide information not only about patterns of bandaging for dating purposes, but also about the quality and type of cloth and clothing produced and worn in ancient Egypt. The Egyptian word for mummy wrappings was *wyt*, a word that sounded similar to the words meaning 'embalm', 'place of embalming', 'embalmer' and 'bandager'. Another word meaning 'mummy cloth' was *wenkhyt*.

The wrapping of the dead body held great symbolism, since covering or hiding holy objects was a significant part of Egyptian religion in defining sacredness. Thus, through the embalming process, the body became a holy image. As each limb was bandaged the priest read specific spells to protect and reanimate it in the Hereafter. The bandaging ritual was one of the most magically powerful moments in the process of mummification. Most bandages were actually re-used clothes or linen sheets, often bearing laundry marks giving the name or titles of the deceased. A nice description of this and how it fits into funeral ritual comes from the walls of New Kingdom tombs in some of the last words of relatives before the mummy was sealed in its tomb: 'Woe, woe,...Alas this loss! the good shepherd has gone to the land of Eternity; he who willingly opened his feet to going is now enclosed, bound and confined. He who had so much fine linen, and so gladly put it on, sleeps now in the cast-off garments of yesterday' (Erman 1907: 137). Wrappings specially produced for mummies only began to appear from the late Eighteenth Dynasty onwards.

Summary of the Development of Mummy Wrappings

The earliest form of wrapping was a goat skin into which the flexed body was placed prior to burial. Strips of linen sheeting were soon substituted, particularly with the advent of artificial mummification. Linen strips of varying thickness and quality continued to be wrapped around the body thereafter.

Middle Kingdom burials saw an increase in the amount of linen used; large folded sheets were included in the wrappings to give the mummy some bulk and to protect the body from being damaged when it was placed in the coffin. The process was elaborated in the New Kingdom when close overlapping spiral bandaging of individual limbs became common. The Nineteenth Dynasty saw the introduction of polychrome textiles used as shrouds. In the Third Intermediate Period, notably in the Twenty-first Dynasty, shrouds (*tayet* or *suhet* in Egyptian) decorated with black or red ink drawings of Osiris with accompanying protective texts, became a standard part of the wrappings. In the Twenty-sixth Dynasty, wrapping patterns grew more elaborate, with bodies wrapped in narrow bandages wound cunningly in complex patterns. Bandaging in geometric patterns reached its acme in the Graeco-Roman Period (ill. 190).

170 (*above*) The fully-wrapped mummy of Wah. Eleventh Dynasty, from Thebes (see ills. 176-81).

In the Christian Period, towards the end of the practice of mummification in Egypt, bodies ceased to be wrapped in bandages; instead they were dressed in their best clothes.

THE PREDYNASTIC AND ARCHAIC PERIODS

Although Predynastic burials were not mummified, they provided the template for preserved bodies and were the inspiration for mummification. At first, bodies were buried directly in the sand without any wrappings at all. Shortly thereafter, by 4000 BC, they began to be wrapped in animal skins, generally those of goats, and occasionally gazelle. Animal-skin wrappings are unique to the Predynastic Period with one exception: a very peculiar mummy, Unknown Man E, was found in the Deir el-Bahari cache, and must have dated to at least the Eighteenth Dynasty if not later. He lay in an uninscribed white-painted coffin. The plain box contained a large bundle sewn into a shrivelled sheep-skin, a material not at all favoured by the ancient Egyptians as it was considered ritually impure. The skin was cut open in 1886, revealing the unmummified, sour-smelling, naturally desiccated corpse of a young man whose leathery face was contorted into a terrible grimace, and who had all his internal organs intact. His hands and feet were tied together with leather thongs, his arms lying so that the hands covered his genitalia. The evidence seems to indicate that he had been sewn into the sheepskin while still alive. Asphyxiation in this woolly shroud would have been a slow and horrible death. A small amount of natron was packed around the bundle in the coffin. If thus executed, why was he placed among the royal mummies? Perhaps he was a prince who had erred heinously, but owing to his royal blood could not be executed like a common criminal. Alternatively, it is possible that at a later date the priests, for some unknown reason, decided to inter the offender in this secret place. Some scholars, however, prefer other, less dramatic, explanations for this curious interment. They have suggested that post-mortem trauma can produce similar outward features – an arguable fact, depending to some extent on the position of the body prior to *rigor mortis.*

171 Unknown Man E. This body, found in TT 320, had been sewn up in a sheepskin, a material that was usually not used by the ancient Egyptians. It appears that he may have been buried alive. CM CG 61098.

The skin wrappings of the Predynastic were followed by mat wrappings. These merged typologically with coffins of the same material, and, like them, isolated the body from the hot, desiccating sand, thereby contributing to the failure of 'natural mummification' as burials became more elaborate. Mat wrapping continued to be used for poor burials throughout pharaonic history. The end of the Predynastic probably saw the introduction of linen in burials, as can be seen by the Naqada II wrapped burials from Hierakonpolis. Certainly, it was used by the First Dynasty when bodies would be bundled up in it and placed either on beds or in very simple coffins. The arm from the tomb of King Djer, from Umm el-Qaab, was wrapped in strips of fine linen. The Second Dynasty body of a woman found at Saqqara was wrapped in at least sixteen layers of bandages, each limb being separately wrapped. The bandages were unusually broad, giving the impression of sheets. Strangely enough, the six layers of cloth closest to the body were of coarser material than the ten outer layers, reversing the usual priority. Perhaps the bandages closest to the body were more prone to decay, so the embalmers used better-quality cloth on the outside where it would be visible and display the wealth and prosperity of the deceased.

172 The bandaged and jewelled arm of King Djer was the earliest wrapped royal mummy ever found.

173 The earliest external ornamentation of mummies took the form of the moulding of the body-contours into plaster-soaked linen-wrappings. From Giza. G2037bX; MFA 39.828.

THE OLD KINGDOM

Linen bandages of varying length and thickness used for wrapping the bodies of Old Kingdom date tended to be wider, 8 cm or more, than those of later periods. They were particularly important during this period as the emphasis

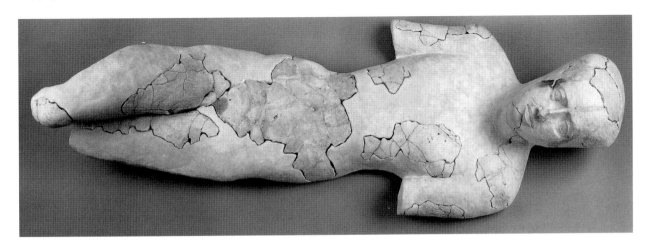

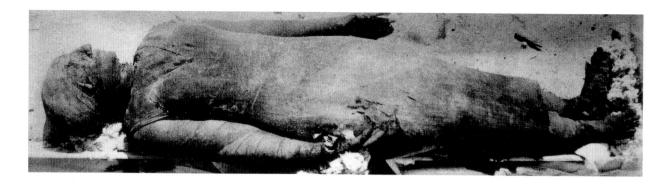

174 This Fourth Dynasty mummy was dressed in a linen dress similar to the one she would have worn in life. From Giza G 2220 B.

was on the appearance of the wrapped body rather than on the preservation of the corpse itself. The bandaged body could be covered with a layer of stucco-plaster over a layer of very fine linen, or dressed in clothes that had been worn in life, especially in the Fifth and Sixth Dynasties. Details of the development of the exterior forms have been dealt with in the previous section.

The bandages, often impregnated with natron, and kept in place with resin, were wrapped around each limb and extremity to form a 'fleshed' out image of the deceased which was painted to look more life-like. The mouth was frequently filled with a twisted-up pad of linen, the lower jaw first wrapped separately. The poor were generally wrapped in mats, or casually enfolded in large pieces of cloth.

The major change that occurred at the end of the Old Kingdom was that after individual wrapping of the limbs, they were put into further layers of all-enveloping bandages, producing the 'classical' quasi-cylindrical mummy-form, enveloped in a large shroud. With a few exceptions, this remained basic practice until the end of mummification in Egypt.

THE FIRST INTERMEDIATE PERIOD AND MIDDLE KINGDOM

There is little information available concerning the wrapping patterns of First Intermediate Period burials. There is, however, much more known about those of the Middle Kingdom. The intact Eleventh Dynasty mummy of Wah was unwrapped in 1935 in the Metropolitan Museum

of Art. The body lay in its coffin wearing a linen shawl as a kilt. It had been wrapped in about 375 square metres of linen. The bandages had been bound spirally around the corpse, with those nearest to the body being covered by a dark resin, which had also been applied to the flesh. The spiral bandages were kept in place by further dabs of resin. A mouse, a cricket and a lizard had accidentally become entangled with the wet resin and wrappings. The arms had been individually wrapped, with sheets placed over the body for protection and padding (ills. 176–81). Some of the sheets, shredded to make wrappings, bore the deceased's name, while fragments were inscribed with the names of others. Perhaps the family provided as many sheets as possible from their own stock, and friends or the embalmers provided the remainder, as necessary.

Many of the bandages wrapping the sixty so called 'soldiers of Mentuhotep II' bore the same linen mark, indicating a common source, perhaps the royal household or the army store. Many Middle Kingdom bandages bear dates and/or texts identifying the owner. Nakhtankh's mummy, from Rifeh, has a date of 'Year 4' on several fragments; however, the name of the ruler is not preserved. Linen from a royal household tended to have its quality marked on it: 'good' or 'very good'. Sometimes it was merely noted as coming from 'the store of fine linen'.

The mummies of Karenen and Nefersemdent, found at Saqqara by Quibell in 1906–7, were also thickly wrapped in linen. The burials are unusual in their use of large pieces of cloth in addition to bandages, some of it resembling towelling, with tufty bits of linen woven as part of the pattern. Like the mummy of Wah, these also had separately wrapped arms and legs. But, unlike Wah's spiral binding, they each had a long sheet in contact with the skin. This was followed by another sheet, then by long thin bandages, covered by pads of folded cloth, laid upon the front and sides of the body. The cloth was held in place by a series of bandages that had been knotted together. They were then covered by broad bands of cloth laid along the body, with more knotted bandages and large pads of folded cloth placed on the front. These, in turn, were held in place by oblique bandages from the shoulder to the feet (the closest these wrappings get to the spiral format used for Wah), covered by cloth pads on the sides, and a folded towel on the front. This last was held in place with a long sheet of cloth wrapped around the body. The mummy of Senebtisi was similarly wrapped with alternating sheets of fine linen and bandages, the bandages notably coarser than the sheets. The space between her body and her coffin lid was filled out by twelve fringed shawls.

THE SECOND INTERMEDIATE PERIOD AND NEW KINGDOM

The few surviving burials dating from the Second Intermediate Period show that the final sheets enfolding the mummy were held in place by horizontal bands of linen, sometimes eight, and sometimes six. Rolls of coarse linen were placed at the feet to fill up the space between feet and coffin. Arms and legs continued to be separately bandaged, as were fingers. Spiral bindings for the extremities were favoured.

Given the number of royal mummies found of New Kingdom date, one would have assumed that a great deal can be determined from their wrappings. However this is not so, since virtually all the cache mummies were rewrapped in the Twenty-first Dynasty, and thus any information they provide is for this later era. One must turn to the non-cached burials for information about New Kingdom royal bandaging. The only non-cache royal burial from this period is that of Tutankhamun. Unfortunately his wrappings had become carbonized through the reaction of the oils and resins that had saturated them, and little could be discerned of the patterns of wrappings, though the quality of linen used was clearly very fine. The soaking of the bandages with oils and resin is typical of rich New Kingdom burials.

Private mummies of the period have individually wrapped limbs, and usually independently wrapped extremities,

175 Linen marks from the burial of Queen Ashayet. Sometimes the writing on the linen identifies it as having belonged to someone other than the deceased. This would indicate that either friends would donate their old clothes/sheets to the deceased's family, or that such supplies were given to the embalmers to use at their discretion. Reign of Mentuhotep II, from Deir el-Bahari DBXI.17; CM JE 47352.

including the penis. The bandages tend to be 4–6 cm in width, and wrapped around each portion of the body in a tight spiral. The bandaged body was often wrapped in a shroud held in place with a long vertical bandage extending from head to foot and horizontal bandages, five or six, holding it in place at the head near the ears, and at the chest, wrists, knees and ankles, all of which are mimicked in the coffin decoration. Large amounts of linen were used, the richer the burial, the larger the quantity of linen. The mummy of Senenmut's mother, Hatnofret, was wrapped with 14 sheets, 80 bandages, 12 cloth pads and 4 sets of trussing tapes, and took over 4 days to unwrap. Nakht the weaver (now in Toronto, dating to the Twentieth Dynasty) was wrapped in bandages and pads, and two tunic-like robes, no doubt garments belonging to the dead man.

An unusual and unique type of mummy wrapping appears from the early Eighteenth Dynasty in the burial of Meryetamun, wife of Amenophis I. Along with the regular bandages interspersed with some layers of cloth, two human-shaped sheets were placed on the mummy. Thus far these are unknown from any other burial of any era. The late Eighteenth Dynasty saw the first appearance of a decorated shroud-type from Thebes. One found in the tomb of

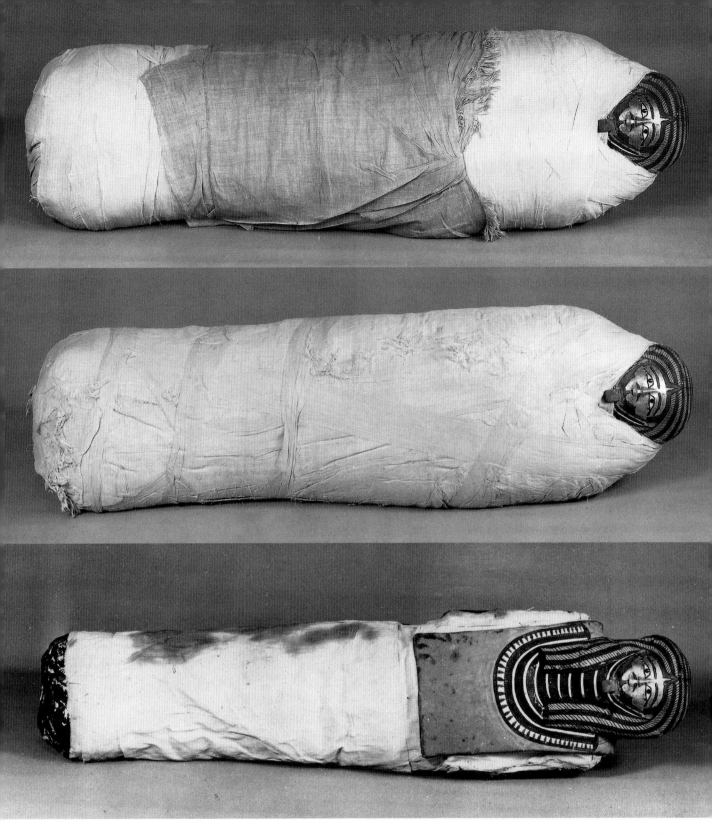

176–181 The Middle Kingdom mummy of Wah was found at Thebes by Winlock. It was unwrapped in New York, revealing the body of a middle-aged man with his hands crossed over his chest. Some 375 square metres of linen were used in wrapping the body. MMA 20.3.203.

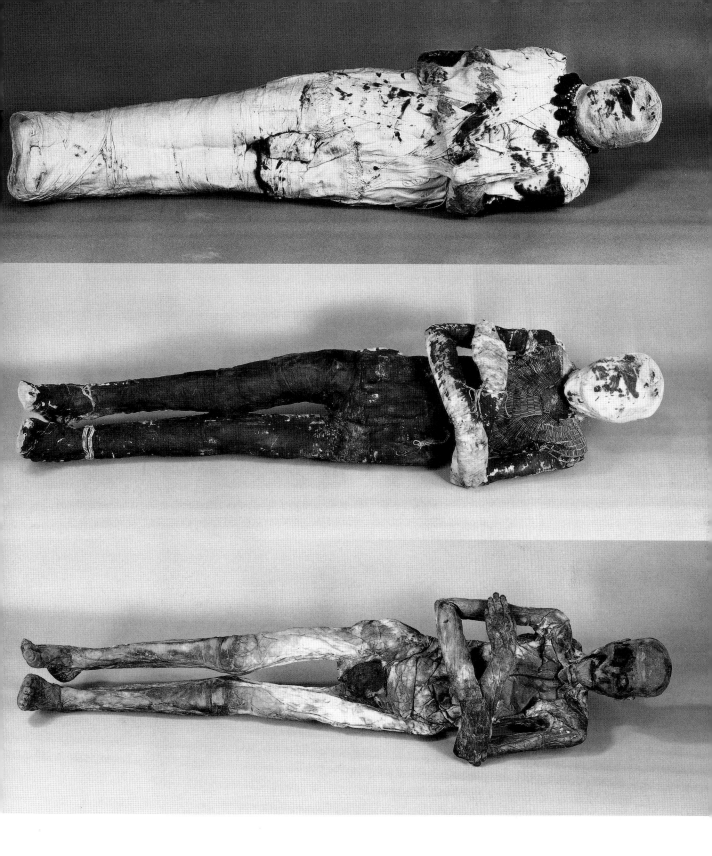

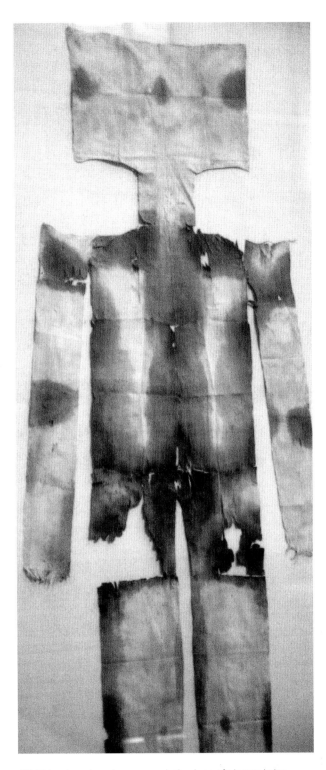

182 This unique shroud was woven in the shape of a human being. Eighteenth Dynasty, from the tomb of Meryetamun, Deir el-Bahari; CM.

Sennefer at Deir el-Medina (1159: CM JE 54885) covered the chest of the coffin and showed a man seated in front of an offering table piled high with a vast variety of foods. Other similar pieces have been found in a few other tombs from Deir el-Medina, as well as from Deir el-Bahari. Some of the Deir el-Bahari pieces show offerings being made to a cow goddess by the deceased, or the deceased in front of a tomb with a cow emerging from the tomb itself. These might have been votive offerings to the goddess Hathor, associated with the Theban necropolis, and not mummy cloths at all. Some outer sheets or shrouds from the Eighteenth Dynasty onward are frequently covered with texts selected from the popular funerary books of the time, such as the Book of the Dead. These seem to start being popular during the reigns of Hatshepsut and Tuthmosis III, although an earlier Seventeenth Dynasty example comes from the bandages of Inyotef VI.

The shroud of Hatnofret, Senenmut's mother, had texts from the Book of the Dead inscribed on it, with Chapters 1, 2 and 3 being the most often quoted on bandages. These spells concentrate on the spirit's reawakening and successful transit and movement in the realm of the dead. Hatnefer also had similar texts buried with her on a leather roll and two papyri. Approximately nine shrouds bearing inscriptions from funerary books survive. The text was written in black and the chapter headings in red, just as they were on papyri. Small vignettes accompanying the text are highly coloured and are beautiful examples of early polychrome textile decoration.

THE THIRD INTERMEDIATE PERIOD AND THE LATE PERIOD

Bandaging techniques changed radically in the Twenty-first Dynasty, keeping pace with the more complicated mummification style. As in the New Kingdom, the arms, legs and extremities were first wrapped separately using very tight spirals that look almost horizontal, enveloping the body. Then the legs were bound spirally together from ankles to hips. Following this, long bandages were used to form a

183,184 These early Third Intermediate Period mummies were beautifully wrapped with vertical and horizontal bandages. From KV 34; CM CG 61099/100.

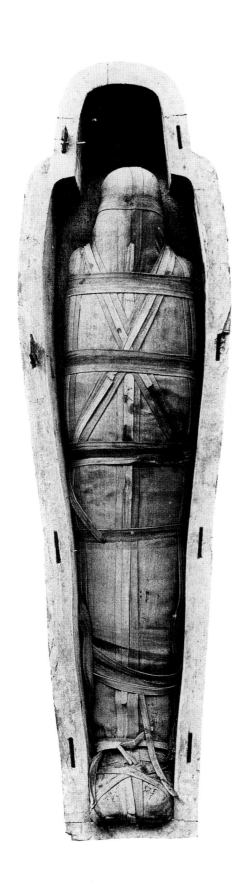

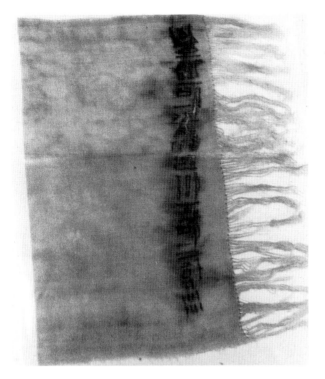

figure '8' shape of bandaging from ankles to hips. The figure '8' was an innovation in the Twenty-first Dynasty and was used on the legs, torso and sometimes also the head. Interspersed with occasional pads of linen to plump out the body, especially at the neck, and to ease the wrapping procedure, this method was more secure, with less chance that the bandages would unravel. Bandagers of the period were very generous with their wrappings; up to twenty-five kilograms of bandages have been recovered from many of these mummies. Generally, they were the usual re-used strips of plain white linen, often fringed. Occasionally, they were made of old coloured clothes; some red bandages have been found on the body of a middle-aged woman, and one mummy was elaborately wrapped in alternating pink and yellow. The lengths used for padding were sometimes old shirts or tunics, which provide us with an insight into Egyptian fashions for the living. It is noticeable that generally in this period the best-quality linen bandage was placed closest to the body, with the coarser linen away from it; the final and visible covering for the body was a shroud of fine linen.

The bodies were covered by a sheet held in position by strips of linen at the neck, hips, thighs and ankles. Many of the sheets were made of unusual pieces of linen and in some instances were decorated with red and blue borders. If these sheets covered male bodies which had not been painted red, as was common in this era, the sheet would be coloured red. This was especially true of the bodies of priests found in Thebes. A mummy that was unwrapped in Lyons had a shroud that seems to have been made out of a sail. This may have been an economical re-use of the cloth, or perhaps the body was that of a sailor. The sail might have some symbolic meaning alluding to the sacred boat that conducts the deceased to Amenti – The West, abode of the dead. Frequently the mummy would have another two sheets over it. The outer one was of plain linen that

185 Fringed linen used for rewrapping the mummy of Queen Meryetamun, bearing the name of the Twenty-first Dynasty High Priest Masaharta, and the date 'Year 8' [of King Smendes]. From TT 358; CM JE 55182.

186 Detail of the inscribed shroud from the mummy of Tayuheret, wife of the High Priest Masaharta. Like other Twenty-first Dynasty examples, it bears an image of Osiris, together with the lady's name and title. From TT 320; CM JE 46951.

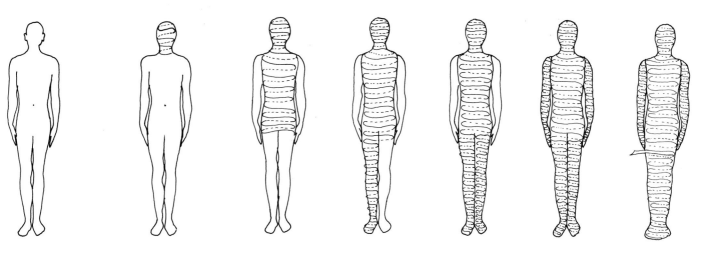

187 (*above* and *below*) Diagram of wrapping a mummy. There were several variations in how mummies were wrapped. First the head was wrapped, then the arms, legs and torso. Linen pads were then placed on the legs before they were bound together from the ankle to the hips. More pads were placed on the legs as well as on the rest of the body. Then the entire body was bound spirally. A shroud was wrapped around the body and secured, followed by another shroud that was neatly bandaged in place.

was larger than the body, fringed at the bottom, and sewn up the back. The inner one was a decorated shroud, a significant feature of the Third Intermediate Period.

These shrouds, or *suhet* in ancient Egyptian, had cords woven into the back so that they could be tied into place. Three types of decoration are generally found on them. The first is a standing figure of Osiris wearing his *atef* crown, the second shows the deceased standing before Osiris, and the third consists merely of a vertical line of text. The shrouds, unlike the outer sheets, were made of coarse thick linen with the decoration in black or red. The text on them usually contained some of the titles of Osiris, offerings or religious formulae, as well as the name and

titles of the deceased. The outer plain sheets were kept in place by precisely tied transverse and longitudinal (and in some instances, diagonal) bandages.

In the Late Period, especially in the Saite Period, the amount of cloth used in bandaging and padding decreased, although the figure-'8' method of wrapping had been retained. Often, lines of text from funerary books appeared on the bandages. Less attention was paid to wrapping each limb individually. By the end of the Late Period the arms were not bandaged separately, although, for some time, the legs were. Fingers and toes were wrapped together as a whole hand or foot. The bandages were kept in place by strips of white or pink linen tied about each wrist, elbow,

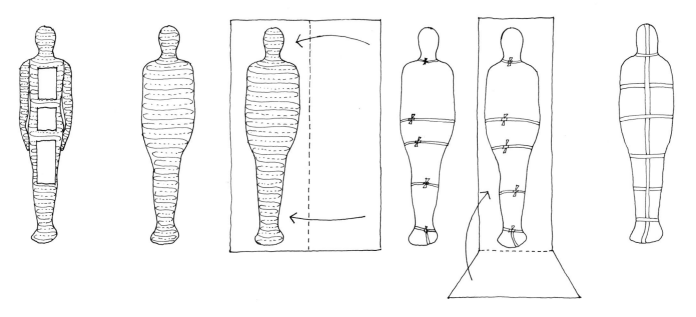

ankle and knee. Facial bandaging became more elaborate: the faces of a few mummies of the period have overlapping bands of pink and white bandages in almost a herringbone pattern. This patterning, whether bichrome or monochrome, was a prelude to the elaborate patterns popular in the Graeco-Roman Period. The outer shroud was generally undecorated, although it was often dyed reddish brown and kept in place by an intricate series of diagonal and horizontal white linen bandages. Some examples of decorated shrouds with images of Osiris, Nephthys and Isis, accompanied by passages of text, are known from this period.

THE GRAECO-ROMAN PERIOD

In the Ptolemaic and Roman Periods the wrapping of the mummy became more important than the preservation of the body itself. Some late Ptolemaic/early Roman mummies were wrapped in almost horizontally wound bandages and were covered with elaborate polychrome shrouds decorated with images of Isis and Nephthys, texts, figures of the deceased, or vignettes from one of the Underworld books surrounding a large mummy-figure making up the centre of the composition. These decorations are of the same type as would have been found in tomb-chapels of the period.

The Roman Period continued this pattern, as well as producing mummies with the most elaborate external bandaging of all. These mummies, dating from the first and second centuries AD, are known for their distinctive rhomboid coffers. The coffer would be held in place by a gold or gilded stud, or the bandages wrapped over a small piece of gold foil, leaving it exposed at the bottom of the coffering. Sometimes different coloured bandages were used to make two sides of each coffer coloured and two plain; red or pink and white were the most favoured combinations. When coloured bandages were used the gold foil was abandoned in favour of a button or boss as the centrepiece of the coffer. This rhomboid patterning was popularly used with mummies that had wooden portrait-panels wrapped into the bandages, occurring between the first and third centuries AD (see Chapter 6). The bandaging closest to the

188 A male mummy of the Roman Period, bandaged to leave all limbs separate, with features painted on the surface of the wrappings. The surface treatment harks back to Old Kingdom practice. BM EA 6704.

body is remarkable in its paucity. An unusual element of the inner bandaging is a linen belt marking the waist, and a set of bandages lying in an 'x' across the torso, somewhat reminiscent of the leather braces placed on Third Intermediate Period mummies (see Chapter 6).

Another type of shroud, known as the 'red-shrouded' type, began to occur towards the end of the first century AD, and lasted through the second century. This shroud-type, which resembles cartonnage in that it is stiffened to some degree, is painted red. It often has the face, limbs and clothing of the deceased, as well as funerary vignettes, painted – sometimes in gold – on the cloth.

One shroud, noted by Birch in 1872 at a mummy unwrapping in Florence, was painted in imitation of a panther-skin. The mummy was tentatively dated to the Graeco-Roman Period. So far this treatment is unique, though real panther-skin garments were worn by *sem* priests (mortuary priests) as they performed the funerary rites. Such skins are also pictured stretched out on the canopies

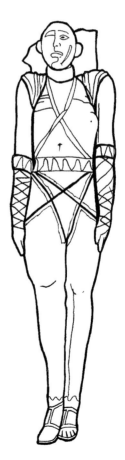

found on the Middle Kingdom model-boats that were meant to transport mummies.

Yet another type of Roman Period mummy-dressing was to paint the deceased's features on the shroud itself, rather than on a separate mask or panel (see Chapter 6). The body portion of the shroud varied: sometimes the deceased was shown wearing the clothing worn in life, at other times the traditional mummiform body covered by funerary vignettes was shown.

By the end of the fourth century AD the tradition of elaborate wrappings and shrouds had almost died out, as most burials were of Christians. Christians prior to this time, however, were wrapped, and Christian mummies can be differentiated from pagan ones by a cross in ink placed on the neck or head of the bandaged body. Copts or Egyptian Christians were generally not bandaged. Occasional examples of facial padding and bandaging secured by palm ropes are known from the site of Lisht and from Nubia, but otherwise the dead were buried in their own clothes, generally a mixture of linen and wool, or plain linen, chitons.

189 During the Roman Period, external wrappings were often arranged in a criss-cross pattern. This example is unusual in that a Christian cross has been inscribed on the neck. Graeco-Roman Museum, Alexandria.

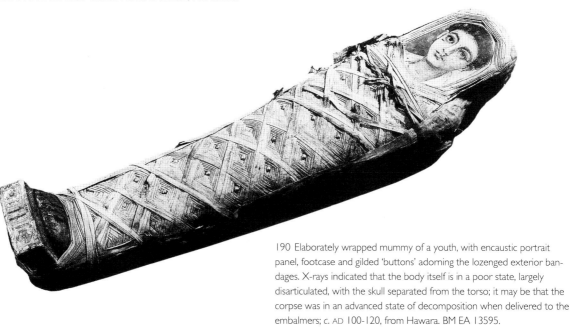

190 Elaborately wrapped mummy of a youth, with encaustic portrait panel, footcase and gilded 'buttons' adorning the lozenged exterior bandages. X-rays indicated that the body itself is in a poor state, largely disarticulated, with the skull separated from the torso; it may be that the corpse was in an advanced state of decomposition when delivered to the embalmers; c. AD 100-120, from Hawara. BM EA 13595.

Chapter 6 Masks and External Ornamentation

The external ornamentation of the body covers a variety of elements, ranging from simple outer bandaging to rigid, elaborately decorated, full-body casings. In between, one finds jewellery, inscribed shrouds, and masks covering the head and shoulders of the body. The masks range from crude plaster images, to the staggeringly beautiful mask of Tutankhamun, beaten from solid gold. Many of these constituents are closely tied to the development of anthropoid coffins, discussed in Chapter 7.

Summary of the Development of External Ornamentation

In the Archaic Period and Old Kingdom, the body was wrapped so as to display the facial features and the separate limbs of the deceased, often modelled in a layer of plaster spread over bandages, with sometimes the addition of clothing; until the Fourth Dynasty, many bodies were placed in a flexed posture, on their left sides. Later, in the Old Kingdom and until the Second Intermediate Period, mummies were universally buried outstretched, but still on their sides. They were also soon wholly enveloped in wrap-

191 (*above*) The gilded cartonnage mask of Tjuiu, which has reverted to the close-fitting design of earlier times. It is equipped with inlaid eyes of crystalline limestone and obsidian, framed in blue glass. Glass is also used for the decoration of the collar. The dark covering is the remains of a linen shroud, which still adhered when this photograph was taken. Reign of Amenophis III, from KV 46; CM CG 51009.

pings, with features limited to those depicted on a cartonnage helmet-mask, which remained the fundamental item of mummy adornment down to Roman times.

Masks were in some cases superseded by anthropoid coffins in later Middle Kingdom/Seventeenth Dynasty times, but resurrected early in the Eighteenth Dynasty. In the second half of that era, open-work cartonnage cages or covers appear below the chest, with both masks and covers replaced by full-length wooden mummy-boards from the Nineteenth to the early Twenty-second Dynasties. Some early examples of mummy-boards show the deceased clothed as in life; later ones were decorated in the same manner as contemporary coffins.

After the reign of Osorkon I, mummy-boards disappeared in favour of all-enveloping cartonnage cases, sealed and extensively painted with funerary motifs on a different pattern. These remained the norm for perhaps two centuries, after which a net of beads over the mummy-shroud became the most common form of adornment, to which a small mask of cartonnage, wood or beads, was often added.

In the middle of the Ptolemaic Period, helmet-masks reappeared, with the addition of a number of painted cartonnage elements fixed to the shroud. At the dawn of the Roman Period, full-body cartonnages reappeared, a wide variety of surface treatments being current during the following centuries. Included amongst these was the use of a painted portrait of the dead in lieu of a mask, let into the upper part of the wrappings.

192 The earliest external ornamentation of mummies took the form of the moulding of the body-contours into plaster-soaked linen-wrappings. The photograph here shows such a 'mask' still overlying a skull, from Giza. CM JE 67568.

THE OLD KINGDOM

The earliest wrappings of Predynastic bodies were animal skins, generally goat, followed by mat-wrappings, and then later simple linen swathing. During the Archaic Period, however, a clear system becomes apparent, when wrappings were carefully applied to retain the full outline of the body, with limbs, fingers and toes separately covered.

By the early Old Kingdom, as described in Chapters 1 and 3, bodies had a layer of plaster added to the outer covering of bandages, to enable more detailed modelling of the features. Thus we find facial features rendered realistically, even down to moustaches, highlighted by the use of colour. Female breasts, and the penis, were carefully rendered, as well as arms and legs. The body was usually represented nude, but several examples show a woman's complete dress placed over her reconstructed form (ills. 173-4).

These 'rebuilt' bodies span the transition from the crouched bodies of Archaic times, to the fully outstretched mummies of the second half of the Old Kingdom. In between, corpses are found in all kinds of postures, although slight flexing became normal by the beginning of the Fourth Dynasty. Whatever their posture, all bodies continued the Predynastic practice of being laid on their left sides, often facing about 30 degrees up from horizontal. This arrangement remained standard well into the Middle Kingdom.

During the very end of the Old Kingdom, the 'moulding' of the outer wrappings of the body was superseded by a technique in which individual limbs were no longer discernible in the finished article, thus creating the classic mummy form. However, the concept of representing the features of the deceased was continued by the adoption of helmet-masks, normally over the entire head, and sometimes incorporated into the upper body wrappings. Widely used from at least the Eighth Dynasty, such masks were made of cartonnage (plaster-soaked linen) and painted, reinforcing the link with the earlier decorative technique.

THE MIDDLE KINGDOM

Masks of this kind remained in use for over a thousand years, although their style varied with time, and other materials were also employed. Additionally, by the Middle Kingdom, the form itself exhibited certain developments which would lead to the evolution of an entirely new item of funerary equipment.

The fronts of some masks were lengthened downwards, to provide a covering for the front of the torso and the legs; on this, protective texts might be inscribed (ills. 193-5). Such 'extended masks' are not particularly common, but by adding a shell that covered the back of the mummy, an anthropoid coffin was created (ill. 254). This later became the classic form of Egyptian funerary container; its further development will be followed in Chapter 7. The remains of a partly gilded plaster-and-resin covering were found encasing the mummies of the daughters of Ammenemes II at Dahshur (ill. 26). However, the decayed condition of the deposits makes it difficult to know whether an extended mask, coffin or something akin to later cartonnage cases (see below) was involved.

The Middle Kingdom also saw a shift in the posture of the body, away from the time-honoured left-side placement, towards straightforward laying out on the back. As with the shift from flexion, no specific time can be identified for the move; it may have been spread over a considerable period, depending on the conservatism of individual undertakers. For example, the Lady Senebtisi, now dated to the reign of Ammenemes III, lay on her side, but Ammenemes II's daughter, Ita, lay on her back fifty or more years earlier, albeit with her head apparently turned slightly to the left. One suspects that the change may have first occurred with royalty, and was then adopted more slowly by commoners.

193 *(far left)* A variant form of mask was extended below the chest to cover the whole front of the mummy, thus providing a prototype for the mummiform coffin. This example bears a standard offering formula, but omits the name of its owner. Twelfth Dynasty, from Beni Hasan 140; present location unknown.

194 Cartonnage mummy-mask, one of the finest examples known. The beard shown on it was fashionable for a fairly limited period in the Middle Kingdom. Twelfth Dynasty, provenance unknown; CM TR 24.4.26.1.

195 The front panel of this mask, of Iyni, is extended to allow for the inclusion of an extensive text. Twelfth Dynasty, from Meir; CM CG 28073.

The supine pose seems to have become fairly usual by the middle of the Thirteenth Dynasty.

While most Middle Kingdom masks are broadly similar, wearing the archaic tripartite wig, many stylistic variants are found, some of which appear to be regional, others chronological. For example, early masks had rather 'flat' faces that were often only summarily modelled. As time passed, however, much better modelled faces and ears became common. Some benefited from gilding and/or inlay, but most were painted, faces being frequently yellow-ochre, both for males and females. Ladies' masks sometimes incorporated breasts, while all normally showed a broad collar around the neck of the deceased. Various other ornaments were occasionally represented, including the regular false beard; real beards also appear on earlier masks, reflecting what seems to have been a practice restricted to the first part of the Middle Kingdom: apart from a Fourth Dynasty fashion for moustaches, Egyptians were usually clean-shaven.

THE LATE MIDDLE KINGDOM TO THE EARLY NEW KINGDOM

During the latter part of the Middle Kingdom, the mummy-mask was, at least in high-status burials, eclipsed by the development of the anthropoid coffin. On the other hand, the interment of King Hor of the Thirteenth Dynasty included what seems to have been a separate mask. It is of very thinly-carved wood, overlaid with plaster and gold foil, rather than cartonnage, and wears the royal nemes-headdress as the prototype for all such later royal examples.

As will be seen, the dominant feature of coffins of the Seventeenth Dynasty was their feathered decoration. Some

196 During the Seventeenth Dynasty, feathering became the dominant motif on anthropoid coffins. Mummy-masks of the same general period, and perhaps somewhat earlier, also adopt a decorative scheme that depicts the mummy as avian-plumed, with a human face. Of the rare surviving examples, at least three display particularly small faces, perhaps attempting to reduce its proportions to that of the bird's beak, or perhaps visualizing the whole head as a *ba*-bird. From Pit 3 in the Asasif; CM JE 45629.

of the rare masks of the Thirteenth to early Eighteenth Dynasties also incorporate avian plumage, early ones having headdresses that are entirely feathered. These pieces have minuscule faces compared to the size of the rest of the mask, possibly intended to reflect the proportions of the bird's beak. On the other hand, the disposition of wing feathers down the sides of the face may indicate that the entire mask was meant to be a complete *ba* – a human-headed bird.

This extreme conception does not seem to have lasted far beyond the start of the Eighteenth Dynasty, although residual wings appear over the head-covering of the elegant

198 The mask from the mummy of Maihirpri. Its lack of cut-aways for the shoulders is in keeping with other mid-dynasty examples. End of the reign of Amenophis II or slightly later, from KV 36; CM CG 24096.

197 Masks such as that in ill. 184 gave rise to early Eighteenth Dynasty examples, one of the finest (c. the reign of Tuthmosis I) being that of the Lady Sitdjehuty, with a gilded face, collar and feathering around the front part of the head. The tab at the bottom has been broken off. Probably from Thebes, BM EA 29770.

mask of the Lady Sitdjehuty in the British Museum. And, as with the earlier examples, there is a 'tab' protruding from the front of the mask, on which was written a text. Wings are, however, absent from subsequent masks, typified by the large entirely-gilded piece of Hatnofret. This is a much 'heavier' work, reflecting the bulk of the underlying wrappings.

Similar proportions are seen on the mask of Maihirpri, dating to the end of the reign of Amenophis II or the beginning of that of Tuthmosis IV. However, this one's colour scheme mirrors the gold and black seen on Maihirpri's outer coffins, the headdress and collar being striped in black resin and gold foil.

Proportions became more elegant again with masks from the reign of Amenophis III. While those down to the time of Tuthmosis I had been cut away to allow them to fit over the shoulders, the 'heavy' pieces (as Hatnofret's mask described above) completely enclosed the shoulders. A reversion to earlier practice allowed proportions to become

more natural, well illustrated by the fine mask of Tjuiu (col. pl. XVIII). As with most New Kingdom examples, it follows coffin ornamentation closely, being covered in gold foil with stone and glass inlay.

An important innovation seen at the same time is the addition of rigid cartonnage bands to the outer ornamentation of the body. The transverse and longitudinal bands of linen that usually held the shroud in place had long been represented on anthropoid coffins, and served as a vehicle for various funerary texts. Gilded imitations of these were now placed over the actual mummy-bands, and bore the same kind of texts as found outside. An elaboration of this was to place open-work deity figures in the rectangular spaces between the bands, thus introducing a new element of funerary adornment, the mummy-board.

A more costly version of banding was found on the mummy of Tutankhamun. The head was enclosed in a mask of the form seen much earlier in the tomb of Hor, but in this case made of beaten gold, inlaid with stone and glass (col. pl. XVII). Sewn to the outer shroud were inscribed bands made of gold, inlaid with coloured glass, with the addition of a pair of gold hands and sceptres, and a gold inlaid *ba*-bird. The mummy was thus a simulacrum of a contemporary anthropoid coffin.

The open-work cartonnage banding continued into the late Eighteenth Dynasty, becoming steadily more elaborate to match contemporary coffins. The spaces between the crossed bands became increasingly filled with divine vignettes and a figure of Nut is to be found above them; in addition, bare feet were represented. At the same time, the front of the mask began to extend downwards, to include crossed arms and a pair of hands; women's masks were further equipped with the elaborate hair-dos of the period. A two-piece mummy-cover was thus formed.

The next step was to abandon the separate elements, and produce a full-length wooden mummy-board, resembling a coffin lid, but very shallow and lacking a trough. In the early Nineteenth Dynasty, the boards often show the dead in everyday dress; women were depicted wearing full-length dresses, males either kilts alone, or with an upper

199 Tjuiu, Amenophis III's mother-in-law, had an elaborate cartonnage 'cage', incorporating figures of the mortuary deities overlying her shroud. This clearly provided the prototype for the mummy-covers of the end of the Eighteenth Dynasty and later. CM CG 51011.

200 The mask and mummy-trappings of Tutankhamun, which attempt to transform the mummy into a replica of an anthropoid coffin, complete with hands, sceptres and inscribed bands CM JE 60672, 60673, 61902a, 61903.

201 Mummy from the coffin of Katebet (col. pl. XXX). While the arrangement of a *shabti* at the legs and the originality of the other ornaments of the lower part of the mummy might lead one to question whether the body as it stands is a nineteenth-century conflation of items of different sources, the cartonnage mask is clearly of late Eighteenth/early Nineteenth Dynasty date. It has a gilded face and, unusually, bears the deceased's crossed arms. Still more unusually, the fingers are separated and wear real rings. This expansion beyond earlier mask-designs probably prototypes the soon-to-be introduced full-length mummy-covers. From Thebes; BM EA 6665.

202 (*above*) During the Nineteenth Dynasty, one finds a number of mummies with a reed layer outside the shroud. In this case, the mummy of Iset has a 'daily life' coffin (see pp. 216, 225), a mask, as well as the matting. From TT1; CM JE 27309.

203 Late Ramesside middle-class mummy, much smaller than its container, and ornamented solely with floral tributes. From an intrusive deposit in TT 97.

204 Gold mask from the anthropoid 'mummy' of an Apis bull buried by Prince Khaemwaset under Ramesses II. Somewhat crude, the mask formerly had inlaid eyes and brows. This 'mummy' has been mistakenly attributed in the past to the prince himself. The bull-burials were made in such a way as to make them difficult to distinguish externally from those of humans. From Saqqara Serapeum chamber K; Louvre N2291.

body covering as well. Masks were not abandoned altogether, being found on bodies that lacked mummy-boards. Some of these, however, were influenced by the boards; they were no longer designed as helmets, but merely to be placed on top of the mummy's face.

A further external feature of certain early Nineteenth Dynasty mummies is their envelopment in reed mats, extending from the head to the foot. Although found with full sets of coffins, mats are also found as the sole coverings of other corpses, laid to rest in simple graves, as indeed they had been since the very earliest times.

THE THIRD INTERMEDIATE AND SAITE PERIODS

Twenty-first to early Twenty-second Dynasties

The 'daily-life' mummy-boards do not appear to extend beyond the middle of the Nineteenth Dynasty, although the lack of datable material makes judgment difficult. Nevertheless, boards continued frequently to cover mummies down to the first part of the Twenty-second Dynasty; their design, however, precisely followed that of contemporary coffins, with few features specific to them. An exception is the so-called 'rhomboid' patterning, perhaps imitating a bead netting, that is found over much of the surface of some mid/late Twenty-first Dynasty mummy-boards. Reverses were usually plain black or red, but some

205 Mummy-cover of a Ramesside/early Twenty-first Dynasty lady. Although the upper part marks the elaboration seen on coffins of this era, the lower part's white ground recalls earlier types. A twin sash descends from below the kneeling figure of Nut. From intrusive burial in TT 97; present location unknown.

206 Profile of the gold mask of Amenemopet. Compared with that of Psusennes I (col. pl. XX), this object is made from far thinner gold sheet, with a tiny uraeus on its brow. From Tanis NRT III; CM JE 86063.

207 The mummy-cover of Pinudjem I, local king of Thebes in the early Twenty-first Dynasty. It follows the same YIIa decorative pattern as his coffin (ill. 301), also suffering from the theft of much of its gilding. From TT 320; CM CG 61025.

208 The mummy-cover of the High Priest of Amun, Pinudjem II. It conforms to the coffin-type YIIIa, as do his coffins (ills. 303-4). From TT 320; CG 61029C.

were decorated, displaying a number of different motifs, ranging from a large polychrome figure of Neith, through a series of smaller divine figures (e.g. Osiris), to vignettes applied in light outline only. While the vast majority of boards were solid, a few early/mid Twenty-first Dynasty examples display the old open-work technique of early Ramesside times.

The exception to the rule of one-piece boards is evident in royal burials, where separate masks and body-covers are still to be found. In keeping with the royal conservatism to be discussed in the next chapter, neither element resembled contemporary private patterns. In the intact ensemble of Psusennes I, the mask once again perpetuates the form of that of Hor (col. pl. XX), while the cover, which stretches from the upper chest to the feet, incorporates the crossed arms, sceptres and winged deity of Tutankhamun, together with inscribed longitudinal and transverse bands. Apart from figures of Nephthys and Isis on top of the feet, the rest of the sheet-gold cover is plain, in strong contrast to the *horror vacui* exhibited by private examples.

In addition to the mummy-boards, the outer shrouds of Twenty-first Dynasty mummies were often very well presented, with neatly arranged, dark, longitudinal and transverse bands such as on that of Isetemkheb D. The shrouds themselves were plain, but immediately below them a further cloth bore an ink image of Osiris, together with amuletic inscriptions (see Chapter 5).

Leather braces were introduced in this period. Several mummies of Priestesses of Amun (amongst others) have them crossing over the body, as have coffins of the late Twenty-first/early Twenty-second Dynasties. Generally made of red leather, they averaged approximately 52 cm in length and 4 cm in width, widening at the ends. In one case a scrap of papyrus was wrapped up and placed inside the brace; it bore the name of the reigning High Priest and a picture of him facing the ithyphallic fertility god, Min. The purpose of braces is obscure; perhaps they served some ritual function as they do not seem to be necessary to hold the shroud in place.

The Twenty-second Dynasty

Mummy-boards continued to be used into the reign of Osorkon I, as always closely resembling contemporary coffin lids. At this point, however, radical changes occurred in funerary assemblages, most strikingly in the adornment of the wrapped mummy. The body was henceforth entirely enveloped in a rigid cartonnage casing, richly decorated with mythological vignettes. Since the surviving earliest examples, from Thebes, show no 'prehistory', it has been suggested that the type might have originated in the north of Egypt, where preservation of such material is poor.

The casing seems to have been built up initially out of plaster and gummed linen over an armature of mud and straw, leaving a gap at the rear and under the feet. The armature having been removed, the mummy was inserted into the sheathing, laced up at the back, and closed with a board under the feet. The surface was then covered with a fine layer of gesso and painted. Compared with the preceding mummy-boards, the decorative patterns were far less crowded, and were dominated by winged deities. Ram- and

209 Decoration of the cartonnage of Nakhtefmut, dating to the reign of Osorkon I and the earliest datable example of such an object. It reverts to the 'vertical' arrangement of decoration seen in Ramesside/earlier Twenty-first Dynasty coffins, but uses a white background rather than the yellow aspect. From the Ramesseum; Fitzwilliam E.64.1896.

falcon-headed figures spread their wings over the chest and lower thorax, winged tutelary goddesses stood lower down, on either side of the median line. Against the lower legs, the goddesses were sometimes replaced by falcons. The Four Sons of Horus often occupied parts of the area directly under the chest. All these motifs were usually painted in bright polychrome on a white ground, clearly distinguish-able from the 'yellow' aspect of most mummy-boards. Yellow varnish is, however, sometimes found over the actual vignettes, and occasionally more generally.

While the vast majority of cartonnages are of straight-forward mummiform shape, a few hark back to the early Nineteenth Dynasty in depicting the arms unwrapped and separate from the body. Examples exist in Cairo and London that show the classical woman's pose of the right arm straight down the side, and the left against the breast. One, that of Tentqerel, has its torso and legs painted a uniform white, with exposed feet, and is thus particularly close to the prototypes (col. pls. XXI, XXVIII). The other, in London, is decorated with the usual winged deities.

212 Twenty-second Dynasty painted cartonnage of a woman. It is a stock piece, with the area intended to hold the lady's name blank. The first register shows Ptah-Sokar-Osiris in a shrine, flanked by the Four Sons of Horus; the second contains Isis and Nephthys in the form of winged cobras, with the lowest depicting *ba*s. From Thebes, BM EA 6686.

210, 211 The rears of the cartonnages were laced up; the open foot end was closed with a piece of wood. In some cases, these were pegged in position. In others, it was laced in place. BM EA 20744 and 30720, respectively.

COLOUR PLATES

XVII Beaten gold mummy-mask of Tutankhamun, inlaid with coloured glass. Eighteenth Dynasty, from KV 62; CM JE 60672.

XVIII The gilded cartonnage mask of Tjuiu. Reign of Amenophis III, from KV 46; CM CG 51009.

XIX Gilded cartonnage mask of Yuya. In contrast to that of his wife, Tjuiu, it is minimally inlaid. The chubby features, with narrow up-angled eyes, date the piece to the latter part of the reign of Amenophis III. Badly damaged by robbers, it was skilfully restored in 1996. From KV 46; CM CG 51008.

XVIII

XX The beaten gold mask of Psusennes I. It is much simpler than the earlier example of Tutankhamun, being made of thinner gold, and lacking much of the earlier mask's inlay. It was combined with a gold mummy-board, covering the body from the base of the mask to the foot. From Tanis NRT III; CM JE 85913.

XXI Upper part of the mummy-cartonnage of the Lady Tentqerel, dated to the reign of Osorkon I by the body's equipment with leather straps giving that king's name. From KV 44; CM JE 35055.

XXII (*overleaf*) One of the very finest of all encaustic mummy portraits, adorned with gold leaf. From el-Rubayyat, *c.* 160–70; BM EA 65346.

XXIII (*overleaf*) Gilded cartonnage mask of Mareis, with inlaid eyes and a series of funerary vignettes. It is wholly Egyptian in concept and execution, although dating to Roman times, around AD 20–40. From Hawara; BM EA 21807.

88
8·6
5
21807

213 Although the vast majority of Twenty-second Dynasty-type cartonnages are polychrome, some employ a much more restricted pallet. This example is predominantly green, with figures delineated in red. It should be noted that Duamutef and Qebehsenuef have swapped heads, as sometimes occurs during this period. From Thebes, Alexandria Museum.

214, 215 Cartonnage of Shoshenq II. The broad concepts of the decoration of the body follow contemporary private examples. The major difference is the use of a falcon's face, found on kingly coffins and cartonnages of the early Twenty-second Dynasty. From Tanis NRT III; CM JE 72196A.

Royal burials also adopted cartonnages, with the same basic divine images, but sometimes in gold foil, rather than paint, and with the striking difference of a falcon's head in place of a human one. This may reflect the king's identification with Horus and/or the funerary god, Sokar, but produces a strangely disturbing effect. A decayed but complete example came from the intact burial of Shoshenq II, with a partial one perhaps from that of Osorkon III, and debris from the tomb of Osorkon II. The Shoshenq II ensemble had something never found in private burials: a standard mummy-mask with a solid gold face was placed over the mummy's head, within the cartonnage casing.

Some deviations from the 'standard' polychrome pattern are known, both in composition and colour. The former may include vignettes of assorted deities in lieu of some of the more usual winged images, recalling aspects of Twenty-first Dynasty practice. In the matter of colour, a few cartonnages adopted a blue/green-backed monochrome scheme, the figures themselves being plain white, with a few ink details. The majority of these deviant pieces seem to date to the early part of the series, one of the 'monochrome' examples to Osorkon I's time. Some of the latest cartonnages, however, had the forms of coffin decoration current later in the Twenty-third Dynasty.

Another oddity is the covering of a number of decorated cartonnages with a layer of black material; this is also found on some late Twenty-first/early Twenty-second Dynasty coffins, and must reflect a form of anointment.

COLOUR PLATE

XXIV Gilded cartonnage panels from a Ptolemaic mummy. The sandals were placed below the feet, with the remainder on the lower torso and legs of the body. The upper pair of plaques depict the genii Qebehsenuef and Duamutef, the lower two, Isis and Nephthys. Copenhagen, Nationalmuseet.

216 Bead face. Late Period; CM TR 12.11.2.14.

THE TWENTY-THIRD DYNASTY TO THE LATE PERIOD

Cartonnages continued in use into the Twenty-third Dynasty, but then fall out of the record as a new type of inner coffin came into use. The external adornment of the enshrouded mummy became a network of beads arranged in diamond shapes. A restricted network of this type was found within the cartonnage of Shoshenq II, but full-size ones, covering the body from the neck to the ankles, are typical of the end of the Third Intermediate Period and the Saite Period. Often attached to, or woven into these, were winged pectoral scarabs and figures of the Four Sons of Horus; other images were also sometimes included, particularly kneeling winged goddesses. Many examples extended upwards to include a bead-work face over that of the corpse.

These bead-work faces were sometimes distinctly out of proportion with the size of the mummy. Mummy-masks, which were also usually small, were reintroduced during the Saite Period, and were in essence two-dimensional, designed to be sewn onto the shroud over the front of the skull, linking up with the bead net that then continued down to the feet. These masks were of wood or precious metal, elements of the net sometimes including gold or silver. At least one Saite example, however, shows a full-size, three-dimensional mask, incorporated into a resinous

217 Late Period bead-nets continue to be important elements of the surface decoration of Late Period mummies, this example displaying a face, pectoral scarab and Nut-figure, together with the Four Sons of Horus. From Beni Hasan; present location unknown.

carapace enclosing the mummy's head; this could reflect the archaism that was a major motif of the Twenty-fifth/sixth Dynasties.

From the end of the Saite Period to the end of the Late Period, there is little well-dated funerary material, making it difficult to follow any particular chain of development. The basic conception of adorning the body with a bead net, and sometimes a form of facial representation, seems to have continued, before new elements appeared around the beginning of the Ptolemaic Period.

THE PTOLEMAIC AND ROMAN PERIODS

The era of Greek rule started with the development of a series of cartonnage adornments of the mummy. First, the helmet-mask returned to favour, painted in polychrome and often equipped with a gilded face. Then, collars, pectorals, 'aprons' and 'shin pads' of painted/gilded cartonnage were fixed to the front of the shroud.

The overall ensemble was generally made up of a mask, a pectoral, frequently in the shape of a *wesekh* collar, an apron over the legs, boots covering the feet and ankles, and sometimes additional pieces covering the rib-cage and stomach. The motifs borne by these varied widely: scenes of the Four Sons of Horus, Anubis and the mummy, winged goddesses and bead netting are amongst the elements represented. Quality also varied from fine modelling to crude painting. In addition to the usual painted examples, certain individuals possessed elaborately gilded pieces, spread over a large part of the mummy's surface. Occasionally, pieces of cartonnage were fashioned into winged scarabs, *ba* birds and other amulets, and sewn onto the bandages.

As the Ptolemaic Period progressed, these separate cartonnage pieces had a tendency to join together, producing a single sheet over the front of the mummy. The elaboration of the motifs increased, and whole-body cartonnage cases nearly akin to those of the Twenty-second Dynasty were to be found in some burials.

These are a reflection of a trend for the mummy to become free-standing, perhaps housed in a rectangular wooden sarcophagus, but without an intervening anthropoid coffin. This development came to fruition during the succeeding Roman Period which saw a range of outer treatments, some broadly maintaining earlier principles, while

218 Gilded cartonnage mummy-mask, with painted vignettes of Osiris and the Four Sons of Horus, depicted in an archaic manner with uniformly human heads. Late Ptolemaic/early Roman Period; CUMAA Z.44754.

219 Painted cartonnage panels, as affixed to the shrouds of many Ptolemaic mummies; the sandals were placed under the feet. CM TR 9.12.25.17.

220, 221 Gilded cartonnage mask, still according with Egyptian tradition, with the jackal of Anubis on the lappets of the head-dress, with Horus below, flanking the Four Sons of Horus; compared with ill. 218, the head is shown as though resting on a pillow. On either side of the head, a vulture-bodied goddess is shown above an image of Osiris, attended in this case by the god Shu, and the goddess Nephthys. AD 25-50, from Meir; CM JE 28440.

others diverged widely, although remaining true to basic concepts. The fundamental division is between mummies that conformed to a traditionally-derived 'Egyptian Group', and a 'Roman Group', which incorporated elements grounded in Classical art. There are, however, numerous examples which blur the distinction.

The former category continued with the use of separate cartonnage helmet-masks, together with other foot and body adornments in the same material. Distinctive points, however, are the head which was somewhat raised and angled forward, and the feet which were greatly extended. The mass of the mummy was also sometimes heightened to make it more closely resemble the proportions of a coffin. As time passed, masks took on a less 'Egyptian' look. A Hellenistic style prevailed in the area of the head and shoulders, while traditional Egyptian vignettes and ornamentation remained around the sides and crown of the head.

Another Roman mummy-form, common from the end of the first century, and through the second, was the 'red shrouded' type – the shroud was usually stiffened to a

222 The foot-end of many Roman mummies have exaggeratedly tall feet, with extensions to the top; in this case, it bears a figure of Anubis. AD 25-50, from Meir; CM JE 42952.

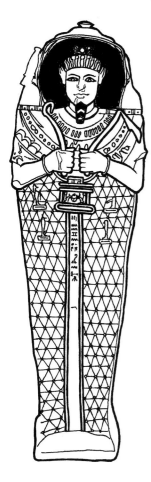

223 Extremely elaborate early Roman cartonnage of a young early-Roman child. The body is painted as though covered in a bead net, with amulets of the Four Sons of Horus, as well as a pectoral, modelled. The gilded face is flanked by *atef*-crowned rams' heads. From Akhmim; BM EA 29588.

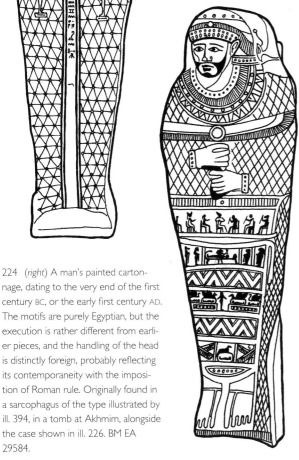

224 (*right*) A man's painted cartonnage, dating to the very end of the first century BC, or the early first century AD. The motifs are purely Egyptian, but the execution is rather different from earlier pieces, and the handling of the head is distinctly foreign, probably reflecting its contemporaneity with the imposition of Roman rule. Originally found in a sarcophagus of the type illustrated by ill. 394, in a tomb at Akhmim, alongside the case shown in ill. 226. BM EA 29584.

greater or lesser degree, and had various features painted or modelled on the cloth (see Chapter 5). A cartonnage footcase was sometimes added.

Most striking about these 'Roman' mummies, however, are the portraits that lay over the faces of the corpses. In marked contrast to the 'Egyptian' three-dimensional representations that had been employed since the Old Kingdom, we now find the famous 'mummy portraits': panels on which images representing the dead person were painted, often in the wax encaustic technique, which produced an extremely life-like effect. Often regarded as unique to Fayoum sites, such as Hawara and El-Rubayyat, whence the majority of known examples have been recovered, mummy portraits have also been found from Aswan in the south to Marina el-Alamein in the far north-west. However, it is clear that the tradition originated in the Fayum, which was the great centre of Greek settlement in Roman Egypt. Other types of mummy-adornments of the period also have definite geographical distinctions.

The portraits, including those painted directly upon shrouds, provide important dating criteria in the form of clothing, jewellery, hairstyles and beards, virtually all of which conform to Roman fashions of the time. Not much can be determined about the status of most of the females, other than that they were fairly wealthy. However, the men's clothing can be significant. A seven-pointed gold star worn as a diadem denotes a priest of the sun-god; a blue cloak and a leather belt over the shoulder indicates a soldier; and undraped men were probably athletes or active men who died in the prime of life.

225 (*below*) Gilded stucco mummy, with glass-inlaid details such as a collar, ram-deity, adoring figures, a winged goddess on the legs and a crowned uraeus down the side of the case. The gilt face-piece has been lost. Early second century AD, from Siwa Oasis; Alexandria, Graeco-Roman Museum, 27808.

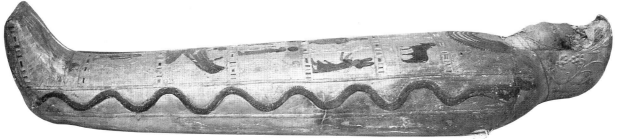

Mummy portraits are also found on more elaborate cartonnage casings that show such details as the arms, clothing, sometimes feet, and mythological vignettes in relief; the surfaces may be gilded, although later ones were mainly painted. While earlier examples of these 'stucco mummies' incorporated the old images of Nut, Anubis, etc., the later ones were usually adorned with geometric motifs, interspersed with small figures of birds and animals, giving what one might term a 'Byzantine' effect.

227 This mummy combines gilt cartonnage with a painted portrait. Circa AD 130, from Hawara; CM CG 33216.

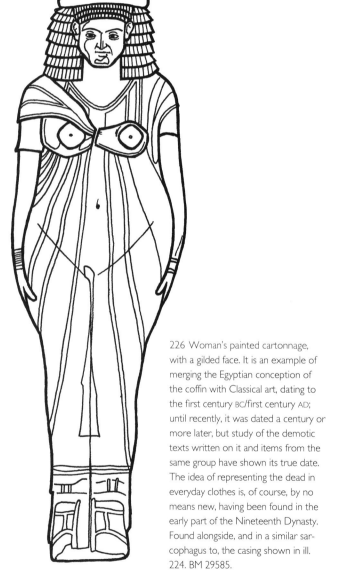

226 Woman's painted cartonnage, with a gilded face. It is an example of merging the Egyptian conception of the coffin with Classical art, dating to the first century BC/first century AD; until recently, it was dated a century or more later, but study of the demotic texts written on it and items from the same group have shown its true date. The idea of representing the dead in everyday clothes is, of course, by no means new, having been found in the early part of the Nineteenth Dynasty. Found alongside, and in a similar sarcophagus to, the casing shown in ill. 224. BM 29585.

From the second to the fourth centuries AD, mummy portraits are found on mummies with elaborate surface decoration moulded in stucco (hence 'stucco mummies'), but from Augustan times until the appearance of portrait-panels, these casings are also found with a more conventional three-dimensional face piece. The masks, often gilded, are incorporated into the casing in an Egyptian manner, but are wholly Hellenistic in aspect. As well as forming complete cases, some coverings extended to just below the hands, the remainder of the body often being wrapped in the rhomboid manner.

Although involving two distinctly different traditions of portraiture, the Roman treatments thus far described all have a firm footing in Egyptian iconographic practice. Others, however, are well-removed from this, with only the concept of mummification and provision of external portraiture linking them with the others, aside from a few debased vignettes in Egyptian style.

Some unusual cartonnage cases from Akhmim in Middle Egypt, gaudily painted and gilded, date to the very beginning of the Roman Period. Those belonging to

228 Cartonnage mummy-mask, showing the deceased with his head raised upon a cushion, whose vertical surfaces are decorated with Egyptian funerary deities. The dead person is, however, depicted in a wholly Graeco-Roman manner. Second century AD, from Meir (Nazali Ganoub); CM CG 33130-1.

229 Far more Classical in its form is this example in the Cairo Museum.

women show the deceased clothed, as though alive; the men present a more-usual 'wrapped mummy' appearance, but deviate widely from traditional patterns. They do not fit easily into the other contemporary series of mummies, and reflect a particular local trend. Related kinds of covering are found at Thebes in later centuries, illustrating the clear division between northern and southern practice.

A further apparently restricted style is a reversion to the Old Kingdom conception of leaving the limbs free of all-enveloping wrappings, and covering the bandages in plaster to allow the features to be modelled and painted on the surface (see also Chapter 5 e.g. ill. 188).

Other portrayals of a whole-body 'daily life' mode are also to be found later in the Roman Period. The most important late-Roman form, from the first to the mid-third centuries AD, comprised a three-dimensional plaster head. It usually formed part of a unit extending from a pair of hands to the head, raised up as though on a pillow. These

elements are wholly Classical in their aspect, although Egyptian motifs are found on casing around the top and sides of the mummy's head.

The features of the deceased painted on the shroud itself was yet another variant in the Roman Period (ill. 231). The treatment of the face was usually akin to that seen on the mummy portraits, with which these are broadly contemporary. That of the body was much more variable: at one extreme, the dead person was clothed as in life; at the other, an Osirian mummified body could be shown, covered with the usual funerary vignettes; various intermediate options also existed.

Towards the end of the Roman Period, during the late third/fourth centuries AD, painted shrouds are to be found with the actual face modelled in three dimensions in stucco and painted to blend with the two-dimensional body. Based on what seems to be a Theban decorative tradition, they are garishly coloured, with dark rings around their eyes and sometimes rouged cheeks; while not without charm, they stand in stark contrast to the dignified visages seen on masks and portraits of earlier times (ill. 232).

230 Gilded face of a bearded man, from a gilded cartonnage mummy. CM.

231 Another approach was to paint the image of the dead person on the shroud, as is the case on the mummy of the 11-year-old Kleopatra Kandake; her sarcophagus is shown in ill. 395. Circa AD 120, from Sheikh Abd el-Qurna; BM EA 6707.

232 Very late Roman Period shroud, equipped with gilded plaster mask. From Thebes, CM.

Conclusion

Looking back over the history of Egyptian mummy adornment, the recurring theme is the attempt to portray the features of the underlying person on the exterior. From the outset, the depiction of the all-important face was common, but the treatment of the remainder of the body varied considerably. For most of the time, the approach was to use the surface of the shroud (or a representation of it) as a ground for funerary texts and vignettes. In doing so, the mummy and the anthropoid coffin converged in both form and adornment. At various times a desire to show the deceased as alive was evident, particularly in the Old Kingdom, the early Nineteenth Dynasty and in Roman times, with odd appearances in between. These various manifestations illustrate the common Egyptian approach to esoteric matters: 'the one and the many'.

Coffins

Chapter 7

A 'coffin' is usually defined as a 'chest in which a corpse is buried'. For the purposes of this book, this is refined as meaning the container(s) nearest the fully-adorned body, to be distinguished from the 'sarcophagus' dealt with in the next chapter.

The Egyptian origins of the coffin are rooted in the myth of Osiris, central to the ancient Egyptian belief of the hereafter. The story goes that Seth had made an elaborately carved and decorated box that would only fit his brother, Osiris. He then planned a banquet to which he invited Osiris, among others. At the end of the banquet the chest was produced and offered to whoever fitted it perfectly. Naturally, this was Osiris. Once Osiris was safely in the box, Seth slammed down the lid, and with the help of his henchmen, tossed it into the Nile. This was thus the first coffin ever made, and subsequent ones could be regarded as owing their design to it.

Ancient Egyptian coffins can take two basic forms: rectangular and anthropoid, largely depending on date. The former are almost universally of wood; the latter, while usually composed of wood, can also be of stone and, occasionally, cartonnage – to be distinguished from 'cartonnages', the cases described in the previous chapter, by having separate lids and troughs, rather than being a sealed sheath. The Egyptians had two words for coffin: an inner/anthropoid coffin was a *suhet* (the same word was also used for shrouds); a rectangular coffin was called *qersu* (*qerset* is used generically for 'burial').

Summary of Coffin Development

The first wooden coffins were rectangular, sized to hold a contracted burial, the more elaborate examples being panelled and topped by a rounded lid, with rectangular end-pieces (the *per-nu* form). Plain, full-length troughs, with flat lids, replaced them during the Old Kingdom, and continued until the end of the Middle Kingdom. In the course of the latter, painted decoration became increasingly elaborate, with the general reappearance of the *per-nu* lid towards the end of the period. During the Thirteenth Dynasty, coffins were often painted black, with new forms of text.

Anthropoid inner coffins appeared sporadically during the Middle Kingdom, but became dominant during the Seventeenth Dynasty, when they were decorated to show the deceased as a human-headed bird (the *rishi* style). This type was henceforth used by kings until the Twenty-first Dynasty, but for private individuals it was replaced by a predominantly white anthropoid design early in the Eighteenth Dynasty, and then by a black one in the middle of the dynasty. A yellow form, with increasing numbers of polychrome vignettes and texts, then began to come into general use before the beginning of the Nineteenth Dynasty, and remained the standard type until the first part of the Twenty-second Dynasty. Stone versions of these are

233 (*above*) The coffin of the Lady Naneferheriset, a good example of a coffin of the Saite Period. CM TR 21.11.16.10.

COFFINS 193

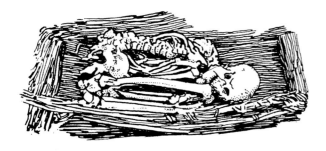

234 First Dynasty coffin of basket-work, containing a contracted skeleton. From a grave cut in the superstructure of the mastaba at Tarkhan; BM EA 52887.

quite common from the latter part of the Eighteenth Dynasty into the Ramesside Period.

Changes in themes and arrangements, together with the use of a greater variety of colours, came in from fairly early in this dynasty, until more standardization returned in the Twenty-fifth/sixth Dynasties. Quantities of text greatly increased *vis à vis* vignettes, together with the general adoption of a pedestal below the feet of the coffin.

The Late Period saw a revival of stone coffins, which continued into Ptolemaic times. Wooden coffin proportions in general changed to become more top-heavy, particularly where outer cases were concerned; decoration was simplified, with very prominent collars dominating it. Finally, in the Roman Period, traditional anthropoid coffins seem to have disappeared, although some examples are known, bodies usually being given a cartonnage covering and a wooden sarcophagus.

FROM THE EARLIEST TIMES TO THE OLD KINGDOM

The very earliest Egyptian burials had no coffins; bodies were simply laid in a pit scooped into the sand, with the natural mummification resulting as already discussed. Gradually some kind of covering was provided, the body being laid on a reed mat, and sometimes covered by an animal skin and/or linen sheet. An example of this, from Gebelein, is in the British Museum.

235 Another very early coffin-type is the oval pottery container, shown here with its partly-wrapped skeleton. From Beni Hasan.

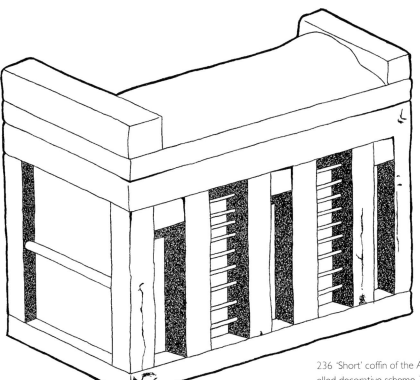

236 'Short' coffin of the Archaic Period, showing a fairly elaborate panelled decorative scheme. This form is current throughout this period, and down to the Fourth Dynasty. From Tarkhan; CM JE 43794.

Complete lidded baskets were also used as funerary containers, as well as large storage jars, sometimes with an inverted second jar as a lid, before proper coffins appear in the record. One type was an extension of the earlier 'pot-burials' – an oval pottery coffin to hold the contracted body. The other type was composed of wood, and formed the prototype for all succeeding coffins and sarcophagi.

Since all early burials were in a contracted pose, such early coffins were relatively short. Many were simple boxes, without ornament, but early in the Archaic Period examples are found with sides constructed to show the so-called 'palace-façade' motif – a representation of the panelled exterior of a dwelling, reflecting the coffin's status as the house of the deceased. Lids were sometimes flat, but generally they had a vaulted central section, with raised rectangular sections at either end. This seems to have signified the roof of an archaic shrine (▥), which was to become characterized as the *per-nu*, the national sanctuary of Lower Egypt at Buto. Such a lid is to be seen on coffins and sarcophagi down beyond the New Kingdom, forming the hieroglyphic sign for them, although other types appeared during and after the latter epoch, and a plain flat cover remained an option throughout.

THE OLD KINGDOM AND FIRST INTERMEDIATE PERIOD

For as long as contracted burials continued to occur, such 'short' coffins continued in use – well into the Fourth Dynasty – but full-length ones began to be used during the Third Dynasty, if not earlier. An interesting fragmentary coffin from a subsidiary tomb under the Step Pyramid was made from six layers of plywood, the outer having a carved ribbed pattern that had been adorned with sheet-gold.

A few fragments of wood from the pyramid at Meidum seem to have come from a panelled coffin, and may represent that of the monarch interred in the pyramid, perhaps King Huni. However, indications are that wooden coffins were not employed *within royal sarcophagi* until the Fifth Dynasty, since the latters' internal dimensions seem too small. The coffer (lower half of the sarcophagus) of the Fifth Dynasty king Unas, and those of subsequent kings, had vertical grooves cut inside the long sides, clearly intended to accommodate the ropes needed to lower a close-fitting coffin into the interior.

Little survives of full-length private coffins, but a considerable number have come from tombs of the Fifth and

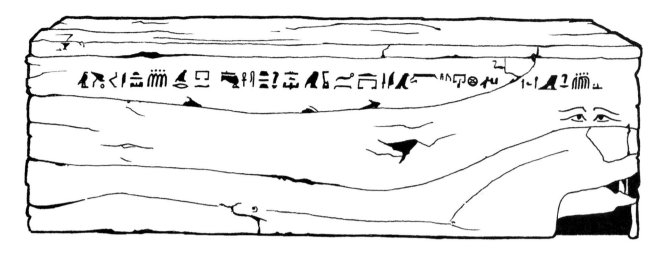

237 Late Old Kingdom type RI wooden coffin of Nebhotpe. Unlike most later examples, the decoration is carved. The coffin has been constructed out of a pegged-together patchwork of native woods, which rarely produce planks ideally suitable for coffin-manufacture. From Asyut; BM EA 46629.

Sixth Dynasties. Externally they were plain, with flat lids. The decoration consisted of a single incised line of offering-text running round the upper part of the box, to which a pair of eyes were added on later examples (type RI). The mummy's face lay behind the pair of eyes, making it possible to 'see' out, reflecting the fact that, until late in the Middle Kingdom, the body lay on its left side.

Late in the Old Kingdom, around the beginning of the Sixth Dynasty, the interiors of rectangular coffins, formerly plain, started to acquire ornamental texts, with lists and representations of various offerings and objects, plus a false door. Similar elements are also found on the walls of contemporary burial chambers, the objects depicted (clothing, jewellery, weapons, furniture, etc.) relating to funerary rituals.

THE MIDDLE KINGDOM

The Eleventh and Twelfth Dynasties: the perfection of the rectangular coffin

Interior decoration has been found on probably the majority of surviving coffins from the end of the Old Kingdom until the latter part of the Middle Kingdom, although there are many exceptions which are plain inside. By the end of the First Intermediate Period the decoration is accompanied by the magical inscriptions that are referred to collectively as the Coffin Texts. These have their basis in the Pyramid Texts, inscribed inside the tombs of the kings of the late Old Kingdom, but contain much additional matter. They are intended as a prophylactic against the dangers of the next world, to bring about an afterlife approximating that of the king – joining the gods in the sky – and ensuring proper nourishment and fellowship in the Beyond. Often written in cursive hieroglyphs (hieratic), the Coffin Texts may cover much of the interior surface, including that of the lid, and are interwoven with the other more ancient decorative elements. Vignettes illustrating parts of the Coffin Texts are sometimes found inside Middle Kingdom coffins, also maps of parts of the Underworld and, on certain lids, so-called 'star-clocks'. Dating to the Eleventh/early Twelfth Dynasties, star-clocks were matrices showing the periods when certain stars are visible: they have been (wrongly) assumed by some to represent the conjunction of the stars at the coffin-owner's birth (ill. 252).

While the earliest rectangular coffins had a simple, single row of incised text, comprising the *hetep-di-nesu* formula that ensured the supply of food and drink to the deceased, exterior decoration showed wide variation during the Middle Kingdom, although within the same basic framework. The most fundamental variation was in the presence and number of vertical text columns that supplemented the horizontal inscription. The fourteen basic types show various combinations, most of which are chronologically restricted. The vertical texts usually proclaim the deceased's honour (*imakh*) before various deities, although some have less familiar formulations based on the Pyramid Texts.

A further strip of text usually extended along the lid. This invoked the goddess Nut, the sky-deity whose body spanned the heavens, and who swallowed the sun at evening, giving birth to it again at dawn. It was significant for the conceptual interpretation of the coffin, which came to be regarded as a microcosm of the world, its lid symbolizing the heavens. The star-clocks mentioned above were an aspect of this belief. The role of the lid became even more explicit in later times, when a complete figure of Nut might be found inside it, arched over the body of the deceased.

Another point of variation was the presence or absence of the 'palace-façade' motif, surrounding the now-invariable eye-panel (apparently first so-adorned at Akhmim), and/or between the text-columns. The latter type (RVI) was widespread in the later Middle Kingdom, and sometimes substitutes for the motif at the head and foot figures of the goddesses Isis and Nephthys, both of whom previously invariably figured in the texts at these locations. This physical representation of the invoked deities is something which was continued, and then extended, into the Second Intermediate Period and New Kingdom.

There are a number of regional variations within the coffin types, and the tutored eye is often able to assign a particular coffin to a site, even without other information. This is a result of the high degree of political independence enjoyed by the regions during the First Intermediate

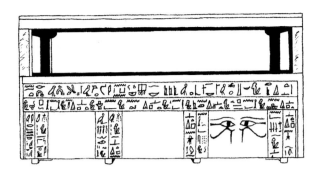

238 A coffin of Asyuti I type, belonging to Nakhti, showing the distinctive multiple rows and columns of text. From Asyut 7; Louvre E 11936.

Period, continuing in modified form into the Middle Kingdom. It is particularly evident in the case of the 'Asyuti' coffin-types, from the major Middle Egyptian city of Asyut. Here, they employed double/triple rows/columns of text in place of the singles found elsewhere in Egypt; they often also applied pictures and lists of offerings on the *outsides* of their boxes – in contrast to coffins of all other localities, with the exception of a few from Akhmim.

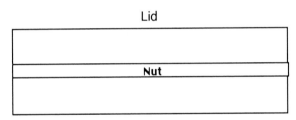

239 The layout of the deities invoked on a typical type RIV Middle Kingdom coffin. There are, however, variations seen on this basic arrangement, particularly in certain geographical localities.

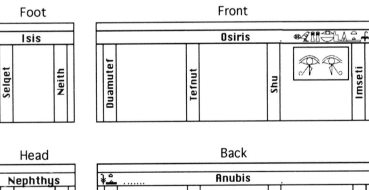

Other less obvious local particularities include the possibility that, at Beni Hasan only, type RIV coffins were preferred for women and type RVI for men, prior to all adopting the RVI around the end of the Twelfth Dynasty. At Meir one finds various spellings that do not seem common elsewhere; at Rifeh combinations of Asyuti and RIV/RVI features may be seen; while at Saqqara, most of the known coffins are of the very rare types RXII, XIV and XV.

Coffins that clearly diverge from the patterns described above are those belonging to members of the royal family, and others, buried in the Middle Kingdom royal cemeteries at Lisht and Dahshur. Known as 'Court' type, they have simpler, but richer decoration. The earliest examples, belonging to four princesses buried in the pyramid enclosure of their father, Ammenemes II at Dahshur, had no texts on the outside. Instead, on the inside, two rows of

hieroglyphs were painted under the lid and on each of the long sides, plus four or five rows at the ends. The plain wood exterior was adorned by ribbed gold foil around the edges and an inlaid eye panel. These coffins had arched lids, without the end-pieces that are usually *de rigueur*. One of the few parallels is seen on a stone sarcophagus from Lisht (see below, p. 251).

Other coffins of 'Court' type did have external texts, inscribed on gilded bands, but of a rather different formulation from that seen on 'ordinary' coffins. Extreme simplicity still remained the keynote. Apart from the lid type seen on those of the Dahshur princesses, some coffins were topped with flat covers, but more usual were variants of the *per-nu* pattern, with a narrow flat area added on either side of the vaulted section of the lid. This is also found on contemporary sarcophagi and canopic chests.

Type XII

Type XIII

Type XIV

Asyuti I

Asyuti II

Type VII

Type VIII

Type IX

Type X

Type XI

242 Rectangular coffins: types RVII to RXI.

243 Rectangular coffins: types RXII to RXIV and Asyuti I and II.

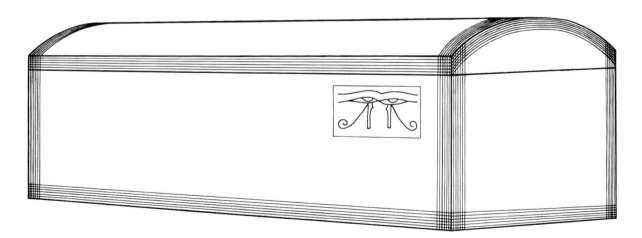

244 The coffin of the Princess Ita, one of the earliest of the 'Court'-type. It is notable for its lack of external texts, gilded edge decoration and curved lid *without* the usual end-pieces (cf. ill. 345). Twelfth Dynasty, from Dahshur, pyramid complex of Ammenemes II.

245 The coffin of Nefwa, nominally of type RI, but with an unusual multi-coloured bordering on the box and lid, which is covered by a wide variety of tomb-models. It would seem to date to the reign of Sesostris III or even later. Beni Hasan 186; CM JE 37564.

246 The outer coffin of Amenemhat is of type RIII, but has incised texts and inlaid eyes. The lack of paint is doubtless due to a desire to show off the costly imported wood employed. From El-Bersha 21; CM CG 28092.

247 (above) The nested type RI coffins of Nefri, showing the outer coffin's decorated interior, including Coffin Texts under the lid, and the plain inner surface of the latter. As usual, the cartonnage-masked mummy lies on its side inside, its face behind the eye-panel. From Beni Hasan 116; CM JE 37563a-b.

248 The typical type RIVb coffin of Waretankh, with a fairly elaborate eye panel. From BH 39; present location unknown.

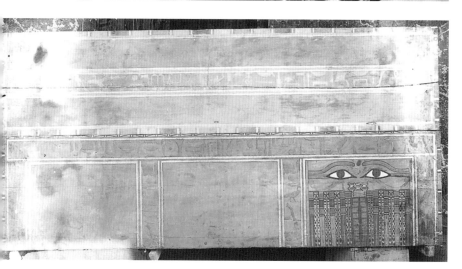

249 Of RVI-pattern is the coffin of Maa. The horizontal inscription is a standard offering formula; the vertical ones state that the deceased is revered before Imseti, Geb, Ptah-Sokar and Duamutef. From BH 500; Brussels E5037.

250 (right) Outer coffin of Mesehti, an Asyuti I coffin dating to the Eleventh Dynasty. Notable are the lack of paint, incised texts, and inlaid eyes (cf. ill. 246). From Asyut; CM CG 28119.

251 (above) Head-end of an Asyuti I coffin, belonging to Heni, with texts invoking Nephthys. Twelfth Dynasty, from Asyut; BM EA 29576.

252 Interior of the lid and a side of the coffin of Nakhte. The former shows depictions of an offering table and other items, directly behind the place occupied by the eye-panel on the other side. The lid contains a so-called star-map, the side standard offering lists and Coffin Texts. Provenance uncertain; Pelizaeus-Museum, Hildesheim 5999.

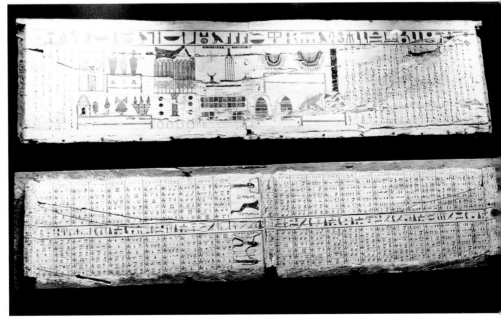

The canopic chest featured in the next major development, which was a great increase in the height of the vault and end-boards, and is an important development for dating items made in the latter part of the Middle Kingdom and early Second Intermediate Period.

The Genesis of the Anthropoid Coffin

As we have seen in the previous chapter, most mummies were equipped with masks by the beginning of the Middle Kingdom, and continued to have them throughout the period. However, for certain high-status individuals, a significant innovation occurred early in the reign of Mentuhotep II. The earliest example was found in the coffin of Queen Ashayet. The mummy was not wearing a mask, but was wholly enveloped in a cartonnage anthropoid coffin, in effect an imitation of the wrapped mummy wearing a mask. Many of the early examples follow this pattern, with the bodies painted white, occasionally bearing a brief inscription, and/or depicting the longitudinal and transverse bands that sometimes held the shroud in place.

However, as time passed, anthropoid coffins began to progress from merely copying the mummy to take on a character of their own. Some acquired a black aspect, the colour of rebirth, but others became polychrome, perhaps imitating an (otherwise unattested) elaborately-woven shroud-type. Even richer decoration is seen on some

254 The anthropoid coffin of Userhet, one of the earliest private examples of its kind; dating to the time of Sesostris III, it is the exact simulacrum of a wrapped, masked, mummy. From Beni Hasan 132; Fitzwilliam E.88.1903.

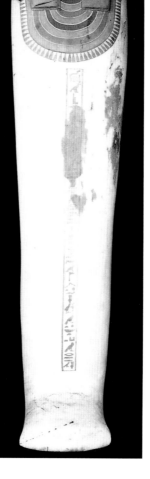

253 Even when enclosed in an anthropoid casing, the mummy and its container both still lay on their right sides inside the type RVI rectangular coffin, of the variant that placed goddesses' figures at head and foot. LUSACOS E.512. For the anthropoid coffin, see ill. 254.

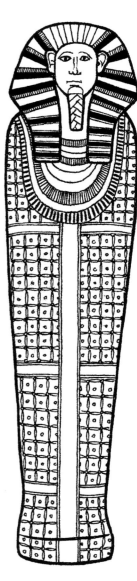

255 (*right*) A more elaborate version, with polychrome patterning on the 'shroud' area, is exemplified by the coffin of Khnumnakhte. Twelfth Dynasty, from Deir Rifeh IIa; Manchester 4740.

associated with the 'Court'-type rectangular coffins of the later Twelfth Dynasty.

Amongst the most gorgeous Middle Kingdom anthropoid coffins are those of the Lady Senebtisi and Princess Neferuptah, which were covered in gold foil, applied on a base of coarse linen and plaster, and inlaid with semi-precious stones, highlighting the ladies' headdresses and collars. An interesting feature of these (and other) coffins is the locking mechanism that ensured that once closed, the lid could not be opened other than by force. While of little help against the determined tomb-robber, it would protect against dishonest undertakers – whom we have seen were common in ancient Egypt.

The Thirteenth Dynasty: Continuity and Change

The 'Court' types of rectangular coffin continued for royalty into the Thirteenth Dynasty. King Hor was interred in a very simple one, essentially of type RIV, with gilded textbands and subtle faience ornamentation. It had a flat lid which would have been unfashionable by this time: *per-nu* lids had been current for such high-status burials since the Twelfth Dynasty. The king's daughter (or sister?), Nubheteptikhered, buried in the adjacent tomb at Dahshur, also had a lid of this kind on her 'Court'-type coffin.

The distinctive Thirteenth Dynasty form, particularly at Thebes, was type RXX. These not only had the 'exaggerated' *per-nu* lids, but changed their whole aspect by adopting a black-varnished ground, and by an increased number of inscription-columns containing a completely new set of texts that seem specific to the Thirteenth Dynasty. Some examples (RXXb/c) incorporate a system of panelling into the lower part of their boxes: this is clearly a borrowing from late-Twelfth Dynasty sarcophagi.

The distinctly archaic appearance of Hor's coffin when set beside such innovative monuments might occasion some surprise, since royal sarcophagi were usually at the forefront of developments in design, as were Middle Kingdom royal tombs. However, as will be seen later, a similar situation existed in the New Kingdom and early Third Intermediate Period, when an otherwise obsolete coffin design was retained solely for royal burials. In that instance, it is possible that a conscious decision to place the divine body in a 'primeval' container was involved: one could invoke the same reasoning to explain the coffin of King Hor.

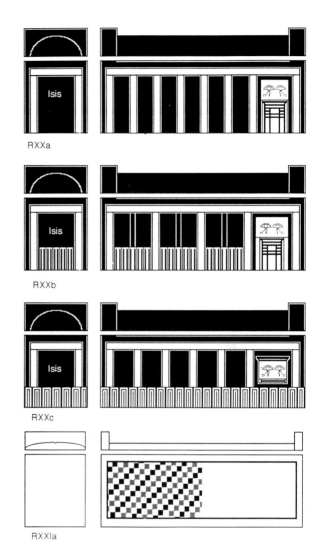

RXXa

RXXb

RXXc

RXXIa

256 Rectangular coffins: types RXX and XXI.

257 Hor's coffin. Thirteenth Dynasty, from Dahshur. Gilding and eye-panel CM CG 28100/28106.

One similarity between Hor's coffin and the private examples is the use of 'mutilated' hieroglyphs. As they represented real beings, bird- or animal-signs were thought to be able to come to life and endanger the body according to Egyptian magical belief. Thus, during the Thirteenth to Seventeenth Dynasties we find birds deprived of their legs, snakes cut in half, and wherever possible, inanimate signs substituted for those representing creatures.

THE SECOND INTERMEDIATE PERIOD: THE TRIUMPH OF THE ANTHROPOID COFFIN

In the face of the Hyksos occupation of Lower Egypt, the end of the Thirteenth Dynasty saw the transfer of the Egyptian royal seat to Thebes. Although the earliest coffins of the new regime closely followed the patterns established by the end of the Thirteenth Dynasty, new developments are soon seen in the archaeological record of the new, Seventeenth, Dynasty.

The continuing existence of rectangular coffins is attested by various fragments, including that of a Prince Herunefer (in the British Museum), as well as a series of fairly crude private pieces broadly reminiscent of Twelfth Dynasty archetypes. A coffin from Beni Hasan, for example, had bands of polychrome rectangles along the edges in the place occupied by texts on 'classic' rectangular coffins, and only a single vertical column of text in the middle of the side.

However, far more fundamental developments were afoot at Thebes, focusing on anthropoid coffins. As we have seen, these had first appeared back in the Eleventh Dynasty, but were little more than downward extensions of the ubiquitous mummy-mask, a status made clear by their relatively rare appearance in the record. During the Seventeenth Dynasty, however, anthropoid coffins attained a status all their own, and rapidly displaced the long-serving rectangular coffin as the container of choice.

This transformation came about through a total revision in their surface decoration and, to a lesser degree, their mode of construction. Earlier coffins had been painted to resemble the mummy, but the new conception visualized the body as a human-headed bird. Exactly what was being represented has been much debated, the most likely interpretation being a concrete expression of the *ba* – the

human-headed bird that was the form in which the dead could travel abroad.

Sprouting from the shoulders of the deceased were wings folded down the front of the torso and legs, reaching to the feet. Further feathering covered the headdress, the whole coffin lid thus being enveloped in plumage, with the exception of the exposed face, the soles of the feet and a painted collar below the throat. The decoration is the origin of the Arabic name by which this kind of case is now universally known: *rishi* or 'feathered'. It is important to distinguish the true *rishi*, representing the body as a winged being, from later designs that simply superimposed protective winged deities over the coffin surface. The feathered decoration was usually indicated in polychrome paint on a plastered surface. The trough of the coffin was not, however, included in the scheme, normally being painted a uniform dark colour, generally black or blue.

The underlying wooden core represents another departure from earlier practice. Rather than being made from separate pieces of wood, the coffins were often hollowed out of trunks of sycamore trees, with patches provided where necessary. The cedar wood which had formerly been used for high-status individuals was no longer available as an option, since access to such foreign materials was hampered by the occupation of the north of Egypt by the Hyksos regime, and probably the relative poverty of the Theban monarchy.

In spite of this, sufficient gold was available to enable kings of the Seventeenth Dynasty to gild their coffins. The earliest of these date to the reign of Inyotef VI, probably the eleventh king of the line. Two were made then, one at the beginning of the reign for his elder brother and predecessor, Inyotef V, and another for Inyotef VI himself. The lids were carved from single pieces of wood, overlaid with plaster. Into this were engraved the feathered elements; the details of the traditional royal headdress; a column of text down the front of the legs and between the wings; and, under the feet, kneeling figures of Isis and Nephthys. Thin gold leaf was applied to the plaster surface.

The sides of the troughs were, like private examples, painted black, but the backs received a coating of yellow paint, presumably to correspond to the gilding on the lids. Posteriors were fairly well moulded, with the pigtails of the headdresses and the buttocks indicated in moderately high relief.

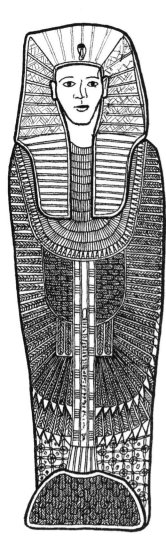
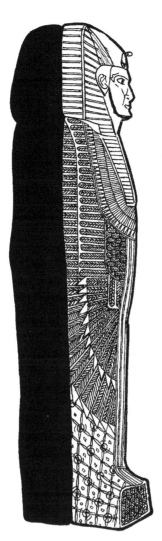
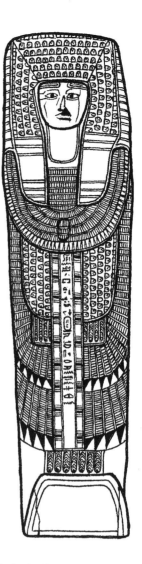

258, 259 The gilded *rishi* coffin of Inyotef VI. Its decoration (partly restored here) has been incised into the layer of gilded gesso that overlies the plain wooden carcass. The king had earlier made a very similar coffin for his brother, Inyotef V. The decoration is restricted to feather-patterning, with the exception of kneeling goddesses under the feet. The sides of the trough are painted blue, with the very back yellow. From Dira Abu'l-Naga; BM EA 6652.

260 The coffin used for the burial of King Inyotef VII; it had been made as a 'stock' coffin, with a polychrome feathered design. On the king's premature death, one cartouche was inserted into the requisite space in the text, with the other daubed on the lower part of the collar. Seventeenth Dynasty, from Dira Abu'l-Naga; Louvre E3020.

Private examples of *rishi* coffins are quite numerous, and vary considerably in quality, particularly in the handling of the faces. Almost all the non-royal examples wear the otherwise-royal nemes headdress. Although this appears on some Middle Kingdom pieces, in the Seventeenth Dynasty the feature seems all but universal. Most cover the surface of the headdress with feathering, but others show in whole or part the stripes that are otherwise specific to kings.

Within a short period, the simple conception of the winged mummy had additional items of decoration added to the basic feathered scheme; also, the fairly close moulding of the trough to the contours of the mummy was gradually superseded by a deeper box. As part of these developments, figures of Anubis began to appear on the feet of the lid, and later longitudinal and lateral bands were superimposed over the feathers. This was a subversion of the *rishi* idea, since the bands were integral to the original conception of the anthropoid coffin as a mere simulation of

261 The upper part of the lid of the coffin of Taa II, penultimate king of the Seventeenth Dynasty. It continues the 'massive' proprtions of the earlier royal coffins of the dynasty. It originally carried the same kind of incised gilded decoration, but this was removed during the Twenty-first Dynasty. From TT 320; CM CG 61001.

a mummy, the bands being the linen straps that held the shroud in place around the body: now they prevented the *ba* from spreading its wings! *Wadjet*-eyes appear on the sides of the trough: initially there was one on each side (in spite of perfectly adequate eyes being available on the coffin-face), but eventually both appeared on the left-hand side of the trough as had been usual on rectangular coffins. Such a position was without practical basis, since the body had ceased to lie on its side at some point during the Thirteenth Dynasty, if not earlier, making the eyes' role as a means to 'see out' wholly obsolete. However, as we shall observe on numerous other occasions in Egyptian funerary practice, a feature will lose its original *raison d'être* but be retained, or even reintroduced, simply because it had been sanctified by long use. This retention of contradictory elements is seen throughout religious and ritual practice. As one writer has put it, the Egyptians had a whole ring of keys that might fit the lock of eternity, and they were loath to discard any of them for fear of throwing away the one that actually might work.

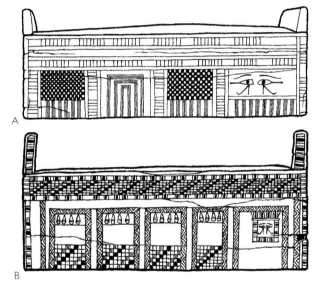

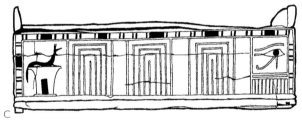

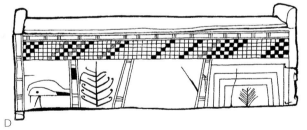

262 Although *rishi* anthropoid coffins were becoming standard by the end of the Seventeenth Dynasty, rectangular coffins are still found. These examples, from Asasif tomb 37, show the variety found, many of which depend on geometrical patterns:

A The decoration is a debased form of Middle Kingdom schemes, with parts of the panelling replaced by chequer-patterns. CM JE 43645.

B Closer to Thirteenth Dynasty 'black' coffins in its number of panels is

this example. CM JE 43644.

C The dissolution of the eye panel is shown on this piece, which has an eye on each side. The appearance of Anubis on a shrine recalls contemporary canopic chests (see ill. 410). CM JE43642.

D Further divorced still is this coffin, with its pictures of trees, and wholly nominal panelling. CM JE 43643.7.

THE NEW KINGDOM

The Eighteenth Dynasty

At the time when Egypt was reunified under the rule of
King Amosis, the *rishi* coffin largely reigned supreme at
Thebes, most private individuals being buried in the
slightly debased versions just described. A further development seen on some was the white painting of the trough
and its use as the background for scenes of funerary ceremonies. Such scenes are also found on the rectangular
coffins that continued in use infrequently down beyond the
end of the Second Intermediate Period. Their overall shape
was that of the *per-nu*, but decoration was now polychrome, and often deviated from earlier norms.

The reunification of Egypt once again made the skills
and products of the north available to the monarchy. The
fruits of this can be seen on the inner coffins of King
Amosis himself, and of his son, Siamun. Rather than simply scoring the feathered patterning and other elements
into plaster overlying relatively poor local wood, as had
been the case with the coffins of Amosis' parents, Taa II
and Ahhotpe, cedar was again available. The royal crafts-
men made use of this finer medium to carve the pattern
into the wood itself, the feathers being modelled, rather
than simply outlined. The whole surface was then gilded
over a fine layer of whiting intended to allow the gold leaf
to adhere. In addition, a further technique was introduced
to highlight certain elements of the decoration – in particular the stripes of the headdress and the collar – by inlaying
them with coloured glass or possibly semi-precious stones.

Cartonnage had been the medium for many of the
mummy-masks of the Middle Kingdom and some of the
earliest anthropoid coffins; in the years around the time of
the reunification, it was now used for a series of colossal
outer coffins that seem for a while to have been limited to
queens of Egypt. Complete examples survive of those of

263 The inner coffin of Prince Siamun. The case is closely modelled to the body, and although covered with a fine *rishi*-pattern, it is closer in form to the Middle Kingdom early anthropoid cases (e.g. ill. 254) than Seventeenth Dynasty anthropoids. From TT 320; CM CG 61008.

264 The *rishi* coffin of Queen Ahmose-Nefertiry. This piece has a number of unusual features: firstly it is colossal, approaching 4 metres long; secondly, it lacks a conventional lid, only the part down to the waist being removable, very much as is the case with pottery 'slipper' coffins (ills. 292-3). This is probably due to the mode of construction, which is cartonnage over a wooden frame. From TT 320; CM CG 61003.

Ahhotpe and Ahmose-Nefertiry, mother and wife of Amosis, together with fragments of that of his daughter, Meryetamun. Well over 3 metres long, they had wooden frameworks over which cartonnage forms were built up. Probably as a result of their mode of construction, conventional lids were replaced by ones with only the part from the waist upwards removable. The decoration followed that of Amosis, though the surface was largely plaster. Inner coffins were of wood.

Such nests of coffins do not seem to have been used for private individuals, who were given a single anthropoid coffin, perhaps within a wooden sarcophagus. It is, however, difficult to be certain, given the curiously small number of such coffins which have survived from the period. It has been suggested that many private coffins of the early New Kingdom were re-used in later times, with their surface decoration removed and new surfaces applied to the wooden carcasses, thus concealing their origin. While there are a few known examples where this probably occurred, there is insufficient evidence to prove that it was common practice.

The surface decoration initiated by Amosis was further refined under his successor, Amenophis I. The colossal cartonnage case of Meryetamun (sister-wife of King Amenophis) contained a further giant coffin of superbly jointed cedar. Perhaps the finest coffin ever made in Egypt, the feathers of its *rishi* design are exquisitely carved, even to the level of individual filaments. Great care would have been required to ensure that the gilding of the surface did not obscure the detail, and it is clear that the manufacture of such coffins must have been extremely time-consuming. Indeed, it was abandoned within a few reigns in favour of less labour-intensive methods.

265 Although *rishi* details were usually modelled or inscribed into the gesso of coffin-gilding, under Amosis and Amenophis I it was scribed into the surface of the wood itself. This very finely-detailed example is of the 'body-feathers' from the inner coffin of Queen Meryetamun. The bands derive from the Twenty-first Dynasty re-decoration of the coffin. From TT 358; CM JE 53141.

It is during the reign of the first Tuthmosids that we begin to find the same divergence between private and royal practice as we saw when comparing the coffin of King Hor with those of his contemporaries (p. 203). Early on, a new form of anthropoid coffin appeared in parallel with the old *rishi* design. It seems to look back to those of the Middle Kingdom in again resembling the wrapped mummy, with its external accoutrements. Predominantly white (hence its generic name the 'white coffin'), it had longitudinal and transverse bands in yellow. The wig was usually black or dark green and the face in the conventional male/female colours. This colour scheme embraced both lid and trough, the sides of the trough sometimes bearing painted scenes

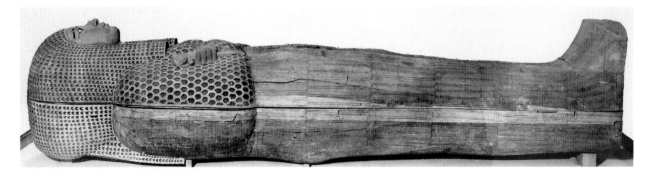

266 The giant middle coffin of Queen Meryetamun, wife of Amenophis I. Unlike that of Ahmose-Nefertiry (ill. 264), it is made of solid cedar. Perhaps one of the finest coffins ever made, it was originally gilded and inlaid. From TT 358; CM JE 53140.

267 Early 'white' coffin of Ahmose, son of Nakhte. Like many of its date, the beginning of the Eighteenth Dynasty, it incorporates mourning and offering scenes, the deceased's wife and children being shown on the side of the trough, and an offering-bearer on the foot. These are soon replaced by figures of funerary deities. The lid, on the other hand, bears a 'funerary' vulture-pectoral, recumbent figures of Anubis and, on the foot, the goddesses Isis and Nephthys. The eye on the shoulder harks back to the eye-panel of Middle Kingdom coffins, although the dead man is quite able to 'see' through the face of the lid. From Asasif tomb 37; MMA 14.10.2.

between the transverse bands – scenes which included the deceased receiving offerings, depictions of mourning and the posthumous voyage to Abydos.

An apparently unique example in the British Museum (EA 39) is of limestone, although painted in the same way as those in wood, with polychrome figures of the funerary deities on the sides, head and foot. The name of its owner is unreadable, but his high status is assured by the coffin's provenance – a pit-tomb in the Valley of the Kings, where only those most closely in the king's favour were interred.

Rishi and 'white' coffins appeared together in a Theban tomb datable to the early years of Tuthmosis III. The *rishi*

example was one of the latest known variants, and the very latest datable private *rishi* coffin. For kings, the type was to remain in use for another five centuries.

A sadly battered example of one of Tuthmosis III's coffins survives to show the new way in which the decoration was applied. In contrast to practice since the time of Amosis, nothing was inscribed or inlaid into the wooden surface. Instead, layers of plaster-soaked linen were applied, then a fairly thick covering of fine white plaster. Feathers, jewellery and details of the headdress were carved into the plaster in low relief, before being covered in gold foil. Inlay was used extremely sparingly, essentially limited to the eyes

268 Detail of the coffin of Nebseny, showing the polychrome deity-figures that are found on the later 'white' coffins. As with most Eighteenth Dynasty private coffins, figures of Thoth bracket the other mortuary deities on the trough-sides. Here, as usual, Hapy takes first place on the left-hand side. The transverse bands that continue from the lid are tinted yellow, in imitation of the gilding seen on some later 'black' coffins. From TT 320; CM CG 61016.

and eyebrows. A complete example of precisely this decorative technique is to be seen in the outermost coffin of Tutankhamun, and seems to have been used as the basis for most future royal coffin decorations.

With the disappearance of *rishi* from all but royal coffins, a new type was added to the private repertoire. This was the 'black' coffin, soon to become ubiquitous, and the standard form until the end of the dynasty. As its appellation implies, the dominant colour was a lustrous black, deriving from the thick resinous varnish that was applied to the wood. There has been much debate over whether this black coating ever incorporated bitumen, or was merely tree-resin darkened by heat. However, recent research has shown that both materials were in use during the Eighteenth Dynasty, if not earlier; further work is thus needed on the composition of the varnish.

The elements excluded from this black treatment were the face, headdress and bands; also the figures of funerary deities that were placed between the bands on the sides of the trough and on the soles of the feet. All these were painted in yellow (or flesh colour in the case of the face) or gilded, depending on the status of the owner. The choice of black was probably, as in earlier times, due to its association with the concept of fertility and rebirth. Some 'black' coffins also had a top layer of yellow varnish applied, particularly over areas of text; this may also have had ritual significance, the varnish having the same Egyptian name as incense – often derived from the same natural resins. Thus, 'to varnish' (*senetjer*) could also mean 'to make divine'. Another variation was to be seen around the edges of the lid and trough, which were frequently painted red. This colour is known to have had a protective significance, and its use would have been regarded as reinforcing the weakest point of the coffin, where the two halves came together. Red colouring is also found on some Middle Kingdom coffins, and the idea of a 'ring of protection' is seen in various forms on later coffins as well.

The earliest datable 'black' coffin is that of Hatnofret, mother of Hatshepsut's architect, Senenmut; as befitted her son's exalted status, the features and other details were covered with thin gold leaf. She was buried in a chamber in front of her son's tomb-chapel probably around the seventh year of the reign of Tuthmosis III – the date of Hatshepsut's assumption of the co-regency. Reburied there with her was the body of her husband, Ramose, who had

269 The 'white' coffin of Ramose, the father of Senenmut, confidante of Queen Hatshepsut. Of fine workmanship, with a gilded face and wig-stripes, it would appear to have been made for Ramose' reburial in the first decade of Tuthmosis III's reign. It is accordingly one of the latest coffins of the type, his wife's similarly-dated coffin being of the incoming 'black' type. From near TT 71; CM JE 66196.

died earlier. He had been interred in a 'white' coffin, in contrast to his wife's. Other members of Senenmut's household had also been buried in the area, all of whom had 'white' coffins, which seem to have remained in use, alongside the new type, until at least the end of Tuthmosis III's fifty-four-year reign.

Where a single coffin was used in a burial, it was a 'black' one. However, where a nest was involved, at this period only in the case of the very rich, they would be of separate types. Such high-status burials are exemplified by three tombs dating to the reigns of Tuthmosis IV and Amenophis III – those of Maihirpri; Kha and Meryet; and

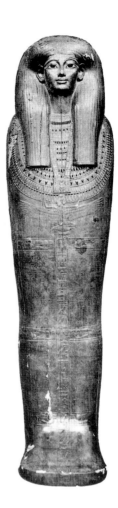

270, 271 The middle and inner coffins of Maihirpri. The former is interesting in being unifinished. It was intended to be a standard high-status 'black' coffin, with gilded details. However, black resining never took place, allowing the study of the decorative technique of the bands. First, a single layer of linen was glued onto the bare surface of the wood, cut to the approximate dimensions of the band or divine figure in question. Next was applied a layer of fine plaster, which overlapped the edge of the band or image; this was cut back to the correct outline, the discarded edges leaving 'wet' marks on the wooden surface that are still visible. The texts and other details were then incised into the surface of the plaster, which was then gilded.

The reason for its non-resining is to be seen in the fact that, owing to some manufacturing error, the coffin turned out marginally *smaller* than the inner case! This is of the wholly-gilded type that is usually found at the core of a high-status (i.e. gilded banded) nest of 'black' coffins. It appears that the application of black resin took place in the tomb, the discovery of the discrepancy in coffin sizes thus apparently being found out during the funeral.

In contrast to most other coffins of the type, the decoration is incised into the surface of the gilded plaster, rather than being moulded in raised relief. From KV 36; CM CG 24003-4.

272, 273 The coffins of Tjuiu, mother-in-law of Amenophis III. Unlike all other known examples of the period, the outer case is not 'black', but entirely gilded like other high-status *inner* coffins. The layout of the decoration is, however, wholly conventional, with a kneeling figure of Nut appearing above the usual texts. The inner coffin, like that of Tjuiu's husband Yuya (ill. 276), dispenses with hands, although accompanied by conventionally-arranged texts. From KV 46; CM CG 51006-7.

Yuya and Tjuiu. Each of the men had three coffins within the sarcophagus, their spouses two. The outer and middle coffins of Maihirpri and Kha were (or were intended to be) conventional 'black' cases, with gilded details. The black varnish had been applied after the gilding, a process which seems to have occurred in the tomb. In many places the gold leaf is disfigured by surplus resin.

The middle coffin of Yuya is also of conventional 'black' design, but here the blackening effect was achieved in a more sumptuous way, the bulk of the coffin being covered in silver leaf. Yuya's outer case was treated in the usual way.

The innermost coffins of all five of these people abandoned black in favour of an all-gold aspect. The manufacturing technique was just the same as that found on kingly coffins, although the decoration corresponded to the elements found on 'black' ones. The finest, that of Yuya, differed from its fellows in depicting the body without hands, and in the sparing use of inlay to enhance the pectoral vulture.

While the vast majority of Eighteenth Dynasty coffins are of wood, the reign of Amenophis III saw an upsurge in the use of stone. Rather than the limestone of the early 'white' examples, these were usually of harder stones, in particular basalt and granite. Most of their owners were distinguished individuals, for instance Amunhotpe-son-of-Hapu, Amenophis III's most important counsellor, and Merymose, his Viceroy of Nubia. Their form exactly mirrored contemporary wooden pieces; in some cases they replaced only the outer wooden coffin, but Merymose possessed a full nest of three, all in stone. The two inner cases were of granodiorite, the outer of red granite, with an integral sledge. Such sledges are seen supporting coffins and sacrophagi on numerous tomb walls; in this case it was

275, 276 The middle and inner coffins of Yuya. Although of 'black' type, the middle coffin is unusual in employing silver-leaf instead of resin as the contrasting element. Both coffins are also unusual in having their vertical text columns separated by a full-length figure of Nut, her usual position on the chest being taken by a spread vulture. From KV 46; CM CG 51003-4 = JE 95227-8.

277 The contemporary inner coffins of Merymose are of essentially the same design as those of Yuya and Tjuiu, but made in stone, amongst the prototypes of a genre that would become common in the next dynasty. This is the innermost coffin. From TT 383; BM EA 1001.

clearly intended to aid the movement of the heavy coffin-nest to its last resting place, on the Qurnet Murai hill at Thebes.

The Later Eighteenth Dynasty

The upheavals of the so-called Amarna Period, starting with the reign of Amenophis IV (when the king, changing his name to Akhenaten, abandoned polytheism in favour of the worship of the Aten or solar disc), certainly left their mark on Egyptian coffin design. Regrettably only a small amount

of material is available from which to judge. A pair of wholly traditional 'black' private coffins date to the very beginning of Akhenaten's reign, but they have all the customary mortuary deities, and do little to give us a real idea of what may have occurred after the full switch to monotheism.

We do, however, have one royal coffin. It was found in 1907 in the Valley of the Kings, and had originally been made for Akhenaten's junior wife, Kiya. She had, however, fallen from favour, and the coffin was ultimately altered to take the mummy of the king's elder son and short-lived co-regent, Smenkhkare/Neferneferuaten. It shows that, in

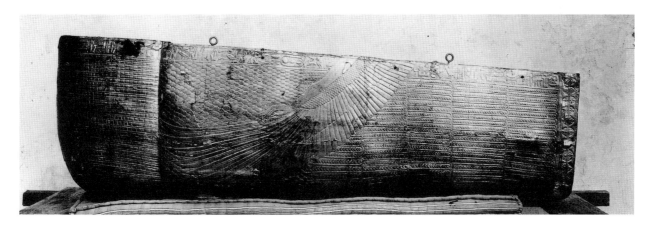

278 The trough of the outer coffin of Tutankhamun, showing clearly the *rishi* decorative scheme that was by now a kingly prerogative. One may distinguish the short 'body' feathers of the upper torso from the 'wing' feathers over the legs. The latter are now far more stylized than back in the Seventeenth Dynasty, and no longer mark out the outlines of the wings themselves. The wings half-way along belong to one of the goddess' figures that adorn the lid. In KV 62.

spite of the change in religion, *rishi* was still current for royalty, though it is of a more stylized pattern than earlier, and is depicted in brightly-coloured glass.

This inlaid *rishi* is first seen on fragments from the tomb of Amenophis III, but is otherwise not known outside the Amarna Period. It should perhaps be compared with the almost unique wide use of composite statuary during the following reign of Akhenaten. Such statues were made of numerous pieces of material, selected to correspond with the colours of the body – thus yellow jasper was used to depict the skin of royal ladies. The most dramatic change on the coffin, however, was in the texts. Rather than the usual speeches by, and invocations of, the traditional gods of burial, we find only an address to the king, the sole permitted intermediary between this world and that of the god.

Smenkhkare/Neferneferuaten had not, in spite of his parentage, apparently been a devoted Atenist and had, during his short joint occupation of the throne, begun the manufacture of funerary equipment that corresponded to traditional religious norms. At least one of the planned coffins did, however, incorporate the colourful inlay of Atenist confections, although accompanied by eminently old-fashioned texts. Smenkhkare's intention to have a traditional funeral was, however, apparently frustrated by his death before Akhenaten. His un-used original coffin was taken over for the burial outfit of his younger brother Tutankhamun, who was the figurehead for the restorationist régime that followed Akhenaten's death. It then formed the middle of a nest of three coffins. All of these were *rishi*, but in contrast with the preceding inlaid examples, the inner and outer ones carried a simple incised feathered pattern, only the inner one bearing any extensive inlay, and then essentially restricted to images of avian tutelary deities added secondarily. This inner coffin is remarkable in being hammered from solid gold; it remains uncertain how many, if any, other royal coffins were similarly wrought. Otherwise it reflects a simple development of the evolution begun by the Inyotefs (Dynasty 17).

Private coffins of the end of the Eighteenth Dynasty are uncommon. A number date to the early years of Amenophis IV, and show that the standard 'black' type remained in use, although a new 'yellow' type had been developed late in the reign of Amenophis III. Extensive inlay is seen on some of the inner cases from the Saqqara

279 The middle coffin of Tutankhamun, of wood decorated with gold foil and glass. This kind of extensive inlay is only found on royal coffins made under Amenophis III and Akhenaten. The coffin had been made for Smenkhkare/Neferneferuaten, but had not been used for that king; the cartouches were later replaced when the coffin was appropriated for Tutankhamun's burial. CM JE 60670.

280 Inner coffin of Tutankhamun. It is of solid gold, with minimal inlay. In this it more closely resembles the outer coffin than the usurped middle one. CM JE 60671.

281 (right) The nested mummy and coffins of Tutankhamun. The mummy is shown after the removal of its external ornaments, shown in ill. 200.

tomb of the vizier Aperel, which may reflect a similar phenomenon to that seen on royal examples. The pattern of a gilded inner coffin, coupled with 'black' outer coffin(s), is seen in the burials of the two still-born daughters of Tutankhamun; they were interred with their father in miniature coffins and masks that paralleled adult examples.

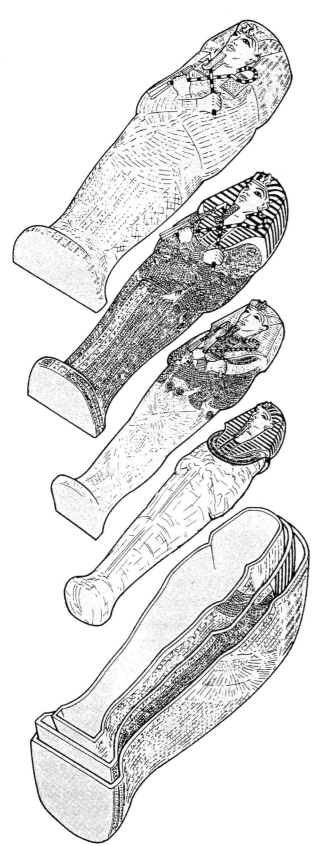

They represent the latest certain examples of the 'high-status' version of the 'black' coffin, although the version with painted inscriptions and no inner case survived a few more decades. One pair, those of Sennefer and Neferiyt, from Deir el-Medina, can be dated to the time of Tutankhamun by the 'Amarna-esque' form of the *shabtis* from their burial. The last securely-dated examples of the genre date to the reign of Ramesses II, from a tomb at Gurob, although the style may have lingered a little while longer into the Nineteenth Dynasty.

In addition to 'real' coffins, the second half of the Eighteenth Dynasty saw *shabti* figures frequently placed in miniature coffins. These usually imitate closely the form and decoration of full-size examples. They also occur in faience, particularly in the Nineteenth Dynasty, and occasionally in glass.

THE RAMESSIDE PERIOD

At the end of the reign of Amenophis III, a new type of coffin (and sarcophagus) had appeared on the scene in the workmen's community at Deir el-Medina. Contrasting with the heavy application of black resin on the former type, the new pattern used the natural colour of the wood, or a similarly-coloured layer of gesso, as a backdrop. Polychrome figures and texts were applied to this, then

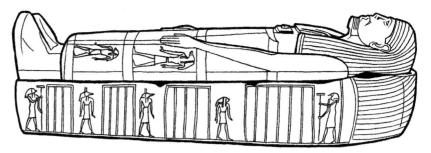

284 (*above*) The inner coffin of vizier Paramesse (later King Ramesses I), made of granite and depicting him wearing everyday dress. The trough decoration, and the addition of the figures of the Four Sons of Horus to the front of his clothing, however, follow conventional coffin design of the time. The piece was later partly reinscribed for Prince Ramesses-Nebweben, a son of Ramesses II. Reign of Horemheb, from Medinet Habu; CM JE 72203.

283 (*left*) More developed is the outer coffin of the Lady Henutmehyt, displaying its figures and texts inscribed into the surface of the wood. Late Eighteenth/early Nineteenth Dynasty, from Thebes; BM EA 48001.

finished off with a coat of yellow varnish. The number and extent of these decorative motifs were rapidly multiplied as the type developed, the few early, simple, examples including the coffin of Katebet, in the British Museum and the very earliest example of all, that of Teti in the Brooklyn Museum. The use of a gilded interior coffin, with the same motifs moulded in the underlying gesso, was continued for high-status burials, but surviving examples are very rare, the best-known being that of Henutmehyt, also in London.

Early in the Nineteenth Dynasty, however, a wholly novel type of inner coffin appeared – intended to represent the dead person in daily dress. This approach is also found amongst the mummy-covers that appeared at about the same time (see previous chapter), but a number of actual coffins dating from the reigns of Horemheb to Ramesses II are of this type (type YIb in the scheme published by Andrej Niwinski).

In wood, and fully painted to show the lady in her linen finery, we have the excellent example of the coffin of the Lady Iset, from TT1. Interestingly, it was the *mummy-covers* of her father- and mother-in-law, Sennedjem and Iyneferti, from the same tomb that were of the daily-life type (ills. 37, 201, 286). Others have been found in stone, in particular one that is possibly the earliest datable example of the type. This two-coffin set had an interesting history. It seems to have been made as part of the funerary equipment of Paramesse, the vizier of Horemheb, who was later to become his successor as Ramesses I. The vizier was shown with the slightly archaic 'apron' which seems to have gone with the office, his arms extended with hands over thighs.

XXVI

XXVII

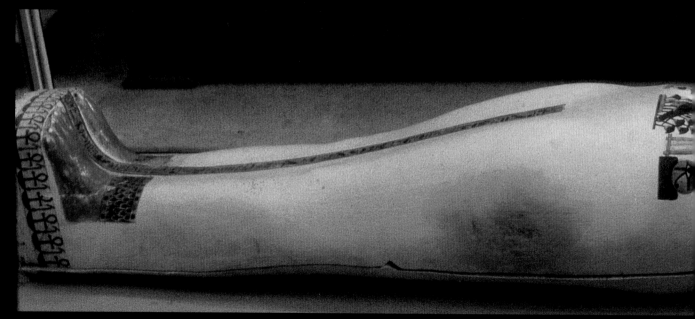

XXVIII

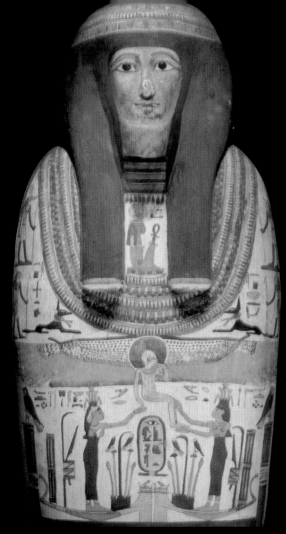

XXIX

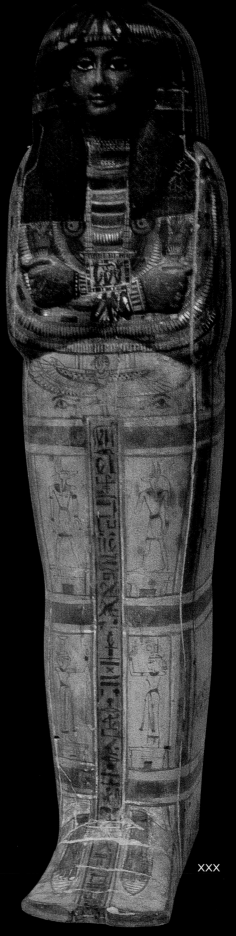

XXX

XXXI The coffins and sarcophagus of the Prophet of Montju, Djeddjhutiufankh, a typical assemblage of the end of the Twenty-fifth Dynasty. Notable are the hawks on the corner posts of the sarcophagus, and 'archaic' hawk and recumbent jackal on its lid. Found in an intact tomb at Deir el-Bahari, under the Shrine of Hathor in the temple of Hatshepsut; Ashmolean 1895.153-6.

(*Overleaf*)
XXXII Stopper from one of the compartments of the canopic chest of Tutankhamun. Calcite, from KV 62; CM JE 60687.

XXXIII Canopic jar of Tjuiu, bearing an invocation to the genius Hapy. Eighteenth Dynasty, from KV 46; CM CG 51019.

XXXIV Canopic jar of Tjuiu, bearing an invocation to the genius Qebehsenuef. The lid has been removed to show the small gilded cartonnage mask that decorates the contained bundle of embalmed viscera. Eighteenth Dynasty, from KV 46; CM CG 51021.

XXXV Set of canopic jars of the Lady Nesnetjeret. Unusually, the Hapy and Duamutef jars have swapped heads, with the former with the canine head, and the latter with that of an ape. Twenty-second Dynasty, from the Ramesseum (Thebes); Philadelphia, Pennsylvania University Museum, E.1869-72.

XXXVI Calcite canopic chest of Tutankhamun, mounted on a gilded wooden sledge. Each corner bears a figure of one of the four protective goddesses. Eighteenth Dynasty, from KV 62; JE 60687.

XXXI

XXXII

XXXIII

XXXIV

XXXV

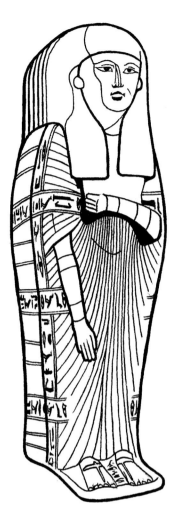

286 (*above*) The coffin of Sennedjem, dating to the reign of Sethos I. It is one of the earliest firmly dated examples of 'yellow' coffins, belonging to a workman at Deir el-Medina. It bears polychrome figures of deities on a yellow ground, the hands holding *tjet*-amulets. The side of the trough shows two figures of Thoth, plus the genii, Hapy and Duamutef; the opposite side substitutes Imseti and Qebehsenuef for the latter pair. The lid has a winged figure of Nut below the crossed arms, then a recumbent figure of Anubis, the tutelary goddesses Isis and Nephthys, and then the deceased receiving the libation of the sycamore-goddess, whose tree occupies the sides of the feet. From TT 1; CM JE 27308.

285 (*left*) The wooden 'daily-life' coffin of a young girl, Tairsekheru, a design apparently restricted to the very end of the Eighteenth Dynasty and the first part of the Nineteenth. From Thebes; RMS 1887.597.

Both of Paramesse's coffins were abandoned when their owner became a king with a royal sarcophagus and coffins. As spares, they lay unused until the reign of Ramesses II, when they were adopted for the burial of Prince Ramesses-meryamun-Nebweben. The hunch-backed young man was interred in the partly re-inscribed outer coffin in a tomb at Gurob, but the inner case, although prepared for him, was found in a shaft at Medinet Habu (ill. 284).

The wooden coffins of the period (type YIa) are best exemplified by the large group found in the tomb of Sennedjem at Deir el-Medina (TT1). They show the basic pattern of arms crossed at the breast, but largely concealed by a collar. The body of the lid is divided into sectors by the usual vertical and lateral inscribed bands, the former

287 The 'daily life' form is also found in stone, this particular example being made for the Steward Nia. From Saqqara; Louvre D.2 = N.338.

XXXVII The painted quartzite sarcophagus of Tuthmosis IV, the largest of the Eighteenth Dynasty examples; this shows the rounded head end with the goddess Nephthys.

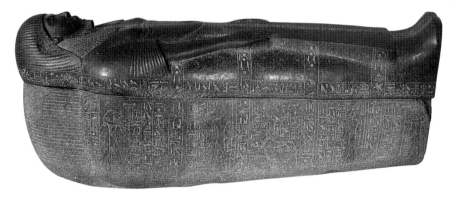

288 The unfinished coffin ultimately used for the reburial of Ramesses II. It was clearly intended to be gessoed, *rishi*-decorated and gilded after the manner of Tutankhamun's outer coffin, but was instead brought to completion early. The most likely original owner was Ramesses I, whose tomb was also cut short on his premature death. The coffin is, however, extremely finely carved, and its features clearly recall post-Amarna art. From TT 320; CM CG 61020.

Owing to the fragility of the calcite of which most were made, only one example, the trough of Sethos I's coffin, survives intact; however, fragments have now been identified from those of most of the kings of the period. The latest of the type, that of Ramesses VI, differs from earlier examples in being made of the much harder greywacke; nevertheless, only its broken remains survive today.

There is unfortunately a dearth of dated examples of private coffins from the later Nineteenth and earlier

containing figures of funerary deities and/or the deceased. These small 'filling' items around the main compositional elements contrast with the general absence of such figures on the previous 'black' coffins; nevertheless the overall scheme retained a feeling of space – something lost in the later development of such coffins.

While private coffins kept evolving, the style of the royal nested coffins remained essentially static, as it had since the demise of the *rishi* coffin as a private container, back in the reign of Tuthmosis III. The royal inner coffins that have survived, belonging to Ramesses I, Sethnakhte, Ramesses III and Ramesses VI (a fragment only), show that *rishi* remained their standard, although with the addition of divine figures along the side of the trough by the end of the Nineteenth Dynasty. Innermost containers were only of wood, except for that of Sethnakhte, which was of cartonnage. Ramesses III's trough is notable for having been carved out of a single piece of cedar wood, with very thin walls.

Outermost coffins, on the other hand, changed fundamentally under Sethos I, being stone-carved for most of the remainder of the New Kingdom. Their decoration also changed, mirroring royal sarcophagi of the Ramesside Period in featuring the various 'Books of the Underworld'.

289 Basalt coffin of an unknown man, reused for Psusennes I. The piece dates to the late Eighteenth or very early Nineteenth Dynasty, with a simple decorative scheme. From Tanis NRT III; CM JE 85911.

290 A particularly crude piece, whose status as anthropoid is somewhat marginal. Probably of late Ramesside date, but with rather odd decoration. CM.

291 (*below*) Lid of the stone coffin of Amunhotpe, dating to the end of the Nineteenth or beginning of the Twentieth Dynasty, and later reused to bury the Twenty-first Dynasty General Wendjebaendjed. Compared to earlier examples, the coffin is more bulky, and less finely made. From NRT III; displayed at Tanis.

Twentieth Dynasties (ills. 294–5). It is not until the closing stages of the Twentieth Dynasty that we can once again pick up the thread of wooden coffin development at Thebes (ill. 296). The majority of our coffin evidence in the New Kingdom and later periods comes from this area.

Private *stone* coffins, on the other hand, although not common, are extant and usually datable through into the early Twentieth Dynasty, although not beyond. The majority of such pieces are of standard form and decoration: straightforward mummiform anthropoid shapes, with 'YI' decorative motifs, contrasting with the 'Underworld Books' of the royal examples.

An interesting variation at the end of the Nineteenth Dynasty is an apparent merging of the stone coffin and sarcophagus in certain very high-status burials. A notable example is the granite case made for Tawosret as queen,

292 (*above*) Crude 'slipper' coffins were common during the New Kingdom, and also appeared in Levantine contexts. The corpse was introduced via the removal of the front of the head and shoulders. This was made necessary by the material, a similar solution being seen on the wood/cartonnage coffin of Ahmose-Nefertiry (ill. 264).

293 Pottery 'slipper' coffin of a child. Dating to the Nineteenth Dynasty, the decoration precisely follows that of contemporary wooden coffins. From Amada; MFA 1985.808.

294 A late Ramesside lady's coffin, belonging to Taysetmuttaweret. Although in poor condition, the coffin shows polychrome figures of Osiris in the upper quadrants of the legs, and the mortuary genii in the lower ones. From an intrusive deposit in TT 97.

and re-used by a Prince Amenhirkopshef. The outline of the lid and trough was broadly anthropoid, but the actual mummiform figure was much narrower, lying on the domed lid in a similar manner to those seen on the sarcophagi of Merenptah and succeeding kings (see below, p. 262). The decoration was fundamentally that of contemporary 'YI' coffins. Other examples of the type, belonging to Ramesside princes, lacked this decoration and, taking other features into account, are better classified with sarcophagi (see below, pp. 262-3).

THE THIRD INTERMEDIATE PERIOD

The Twenty-first Dynasty

From the Twentieth Dynasty through to the early years of the Twenty-second, the basic 'yellow' type of coffin ('Y') continued in use, but with considerable elaboration as time passed. In type YIIa, current up to, and including, the Theban pontificate of Pinudjem II, the distinction from types YI was fairly subtle. The arms and hands were now

295 This example is rather simpler, with most of the figures merely outlined, with a small amount of colour on some only. These two coffins show the variety exhibited on late-Ramesside private coffins of persons of middling-status. From an intrusive deposit in TT 97; present location unknown.

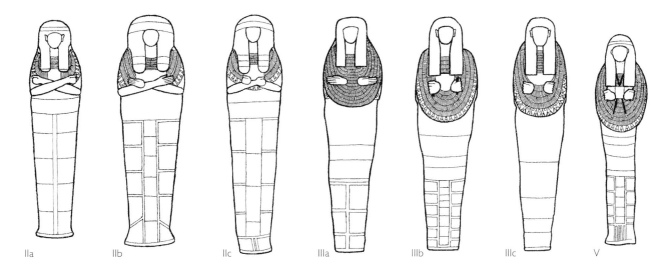

| IIa | IIb | IIc | IIIa | IIIb | IIIc | V |

296 The development of the 'yellow' coffin types.

depicted *over* the collar, while the vertical text bands down the front of the legs multiplied, and the vignettes of the gods and the deceased became more extensive, but still with a feeling of space.

In contrast to this continuing development of the Ramesside private coffin type, kingly burials continued to cling to the archaic *rishi* design. This is best exemplified by the silver coffin of Psusennes I from Tanis, with an all-over *rishi* scheme that closely follows that seen on Tutankhamun's gold coffin. The main differences are to be seen in the arrangement of the avian deities superimposed on the basic scheme; otherwise the whole appearance of the coffin would have been consistent with a New Kingdom date. It was enclosed within a usurped stone coffin of

Eighteenth/Nineteenth Dynasty date, in keeping with the re-used nature of much of the material at Tanis.

The condition of later Twenty-first Dynasty royal coffins is too poor to be able to provide much information. All were of gilded wood, with no surviving evidence to show whether or not they continued the *rishi* patterning. Also badly damaged is the only original private coffin known from Tanis, a silver confection belonging to the General Wendjebaendjed. It would be interesting to know whether it followed the pattern of contemporary southern coffins, or differed from them in any major way.

A feature of the Twenty-first Dynasty was the existence at Thebes of a quasi-royal High-Priestly/military line which occasionally claimed kingly attributes. None employed

297 Coffin of Psusennes I, the last known example of a *rishi* coffin. Silver, from Tanis NRT III; CM JE 85912.

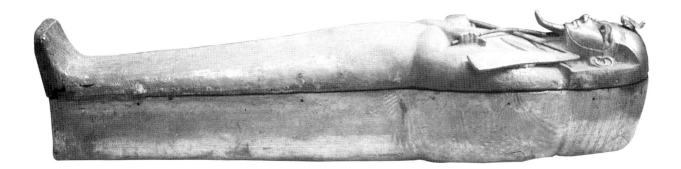

298 (*left*) Khonsuhotpe was a priest of the late King Horemheb. His type YIIc coffin was made in the middle of the Twenty-first Dynasty. From Thebes; RMO AM.26.

299, 300 The type YIIa coffins of the God's Wife of Amun, Maetkare, of the early Twenty-first Dynasty. Important features are the continued division of the decoration into sections by vertical and transverse bands, and its 'vertical' arrangement. They represent the 'luxury' variant of the type, with gilded faces and hands – both elements having fallen victim to thieves in the case of the inner coffin. From TT 320; CM CG 61028.

rishi-style coffins, but for a number of individuals 'luxury' forms were made. Based on the standard yellow types, they employed gilding for hands and faces or, in three cases, complete gilding and inlaying. The latter cases were those of the local king, Pinudjem I; his wife, Henttawy; and Nodjmet, the slightly earlier wife of the local king, Hrihor. The coffin of Pinudjem I is fascinating in that it was made from the battered shell of the ancient coffin of Tuthmosis I of the Eighteenth Dynasty, being completely regilded and adorned for its new occupant, with the addition of a purpose-made mummy-board. Such inner covers were

301 The coffin of Pinudjem I. Although conforming to a richly gilded and inlaid version of the contemporary YIIa type, under the Twenty-first Dynasty gesso lay an early Eighteenth Dynasty *rishi* coffin made for Tuthmosis I. It may have been taken over for antiquarian reasons, Pinudjem I being much attached to the Tuthmoside pharaohs, naming two of his children after the prenomina of two of these ancient rulers – Menkheperre (Tuthmosis III) and Maetkare (Hatshepsut). From TT 320; CM CG 61024.

302 (*left*) The type YIIIa coffin of the priest Amunhotpe. Mid/late Twenty-first Dynasty, from Thebes; RMO AMM.16.

303, 304 The type YIIIa coffins of Pinudjem II (late Twenty-first Dynasty). Apart from their use of gilding on their hands and faces, and the front-texts of the inner case, they typify their sub-type, with the vignettes disposed more horizontally across the body than is the case with earlier 'yellow' coffins. From TT 320; CM CG 61029A-B.

particularly popular later in the dynasty, many being known under Pinudjem II.

It was under Menkheperre that further changes began, producing variants that soon replaced the old type YIIa. Slight variations on this were followed by an increase in the density of the vignettes – a trend that continued throughout the remaining life of the 'yellow' coffin, culminating at the end of Menkheperre's pontificate in type YIId, which left just the hands carved in the round, and the forearms indicated in paint only.

Under the last High Priesthoods of the Twenty-first Dynasty, those of Pinudjem II and Psusennes II, a major revision of coffin decoration took place. Most notably, the collar was enlarged to cover the whole front of the torso. Only the hands could be seen, fixed unnaturally on the surface of the collar, as if projecting through holes. The density of vignettes increased once more, although they retained the 'vertical' position seen since the Nineteenth Dynasty.

This distribution of decorative elements changed as Pinudjem II's high-priesthood progressed, and vignettes began to be spread horizontally across the width of the coffin. Some, such as that of Isetemkheb D, wife of Pinudjem, had the old vertical system on the leg area, with a horizontal one above (type YIIIb), both showing a high density of figures – almost exhibiting a *horror vacui*. Fully horizontal layouts are to be found on type YIIIc lids, which lasted until the disappearance of the yellow type, late in the reign of Osorkon I (Dynasty 22). Elbows were no longer shown, and the collar reached its ultimate stage of enlargement, down almost to the waist, with type YV, current from the very end of the Twenty-first Dynasty. An additional item, a pair of crossed 'mummy-braces' overlying the collar, make type YV particularly distinctive.

Typological developments such as these are largely to be seen on coffin lids and mummy-covers; coffin-troughs are generally less distinctive from this point of view. In general, troughs always had a frieze along the top edge, either

305 The interiors of 'yellow' coffin-troughs often contain extensive polychrome decoration. The principal vignette in this case shows the owner, Ankhefenkhonsu, offering to Osiris. Early Twenty-second Dynasty, from Thebes; CM TR 23.11.16.3.

schemes are found on coffins and mummy-covers of the highest-status individuals, with polychrome figures of Osiris and the other funerary deities.

Trough interiors had ground colours which were either dark (black or dark red) or light (yellow varnished). From Ramesside times to the early Twenty-first Dynasty, and again in the middle of the dynasty, no decoration, or a simple monochrome scheme was favoured, in some cases extended to the exterior by a coat of black resin *overlying* the varnished painted decoration. However, in the early/mid Twenty-first Dynasty, polychrome vertical compositions were to be found. Figures painted on the side-walls would face towards the bottom of the trough. This then changed so that the figures, now on an exclusively dark background, began to face the other way, out of the coffin, together with a movement toward a more horizontal arrangement of figures, just as on contemporary exteriors. Late in the dynasty, the movement to the horizontal was completed, here accompanied by a change to an invariably yellow ground. A feature of the earlier troughs, with vertical compositions, was a large figure painted on the bottom, either Nut or Osiris, the latter often in the guise of a *djed*-pillar. With the change to horizontal designs, the figure disappeared to allow vignettes to span the trough from one side wall to the other.

Although the yellow coffin dominated the period from the early Nineteenth to early Twenty-second Dynasty, a number of anomalous examples (dubbed 'type YIV') are known, many of which recall the earlier forms of mummy-case. They are mainly to be found in the mid/late Twenty-first Dynasty (late Psusennes I to Psusennes II), in parallel with type YIII examples. Type YIVa is notable for having a white ground, rather than the generally yellow hue of the other types; the figures are, however, conventionally varnished and it has been suggested that all surviving examples came from the same workshop. The density of figures is low, a small increase being seen on the rare type YIVb, with a strange collar and upper part that is reminiscent of early Ramesside work.

Also clearly modelled on Ramesside prototypes are coffin-lids of type YIVc, a very rare (four known examples) design that resembles the daily-life dress of type YIa, but with the lower part covered with figures (mid/high density). The solitary type YIVd dates to the very end of the dynasty; the usual yellow coffin colours were used but the arms were

containing text, or geometrical elements, or both. The frieze was separated from the rest of the decoration by a thick, dark green line. Striped headdresses sometimes covered the area surrounding the mummy's head – but were not usually found on lids of the Twenty-first Dynasty, exceptions being those of the coffins of Pinudjem I and II.

As with the lids, the vignettes painted on the troughs became more densely-packed as time passed, moving towards the more horizontal layout, achieved around the end of the dynasty and matching the type YIIIc lids. Backs of coffin-troughs were very rarely decorated; the same was true of the insides of earlier lids and mummy-covers, which were usually resined or painted dark red. A few had outlined figures, although later in the dynasty more elaborate in very high relief, with raised elbows. Whereas the inner-most shelter for the body was usually a mummy-cover, in this case a third coffin was provided, but a plain trough betrayed its origins: as such it may have been a precursor of the cartonnage cases that appeared in the next dynasty.

A few of these gorgeously decorated coffins, and a number from subsequent periods, survive today covered in a black coating, which often wholly obscures their ornamentation. This blackening must surely be associated with the black resin that was used in high-status funerals in the Eighteenth Dynasty, and was believed to endow the coffins with the power of the black-fleshed King of the Dead, Osiris.

Pottery Coffins

While most individuals aspired to elaborately decorated wooden coffins, much simpler boxes sufficed for some of the poor, and others made do with mortuary containers of pottery. At the lowest end of the scale, two large vessels, placed mouth to mouth, would enclose the summarily wrapped body. Above this, however, lay purpose-made pottery coffins; simple examples go back to Predynastic times. By the New Kingdom, pottery anthropoid cases were being made (ills. 292–3).

They are usually referred to as 'slipper' coffins, since they were usually made as one piece, with a removable face and chest to allow for insertion of the body. Some are quite fine, painted in the contemporary wooden coffin scheme. The vast majority, however, are rougher, with only summary facial features. They have been found in Palestine as well as in Egypt, some suggesting a direct Egyptian control of sites, but most were probably simple cultural borrowings.

The Twenty-second Dynasty

The first part of the Twenty-second Dynasty saw a continuation of the coffin-types of the previous dynasty, lasting until at least the latter part of the reign of Osorkon I.

By this time, a wholly new assemblage enclosed the mummy. As discussed in the previous chapter, the key factor of this development was the 'white' cartonnage, which replaced the mummy-boards of the previous dynasties, and the masks of earlier times. Additionally, the coffins that enclosed the cartonnage-clad mummies were given a

306 Face of the silver coffin of Pediset, a late Twenty-second Dynasty High Priest of Ptah. It is a rather crude piece, and is devoid of decoration. From Memphis, CM.

rather different treatment from the elaborate decoration of the old yellow type.

Apart from the loss of the overall yellow aspect so common until then, there was a general simplification of the intricate motifs and texts that had typified the YIII-type coffins, together with a much greater variety of decorative approaches. In general, there were more solar allusions and, rather than specific extracts from the funerary books, 'generalized' vignettes, with assorted mortuary deities. Only certain themes continued in use from the former Y-types of coffin. Indeed, some coffins appear to refer back to Eighteenth Dynasty prototypes, both in their arrangement of texts and figures, and sometimes in the use of yellow motifs on a black ground. Others have an austere aspect, sparse texts and vignettes on a plain wooden (or wood-coloured) ground, and frequently lack arms. The

307 Rather than being integral with the lid decoration, the troughs of later Third Intermediate Period coffins usually have some form of single horizontal composition. This may take the form of vignettes of divinities or the deceased, or a text in large hieroglyphs; the latter is seen on this coffin, of Pasherihorawesheb. From Thebes; BM EA 6666A.

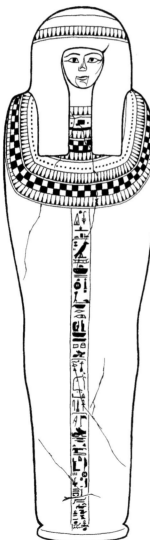

decoration of the outermost coffin was often considerably less elaborate than that of the inner case(s). External trough decoration usually took the form of a single row of large hieroglyphs or protective divine figures occupying almost the whole height of the side.

Where more than one coffin was employed, each case thus tended to differ in its decorative approach; where only one was used, however, it might display elements from a range of sources. An unusual grey background occurs on certain examples: it has been suggested that this may be an attempt to imitate the silver now being used for royalty.

At almost the same time as the new ensemble was adopted by commoners, royal practice appears to suddenly spring back into essential synchronization with that of private individuals – much as seems to have occurred during the Seventeenth Dynasty.

The key illustration of this is the silver coffin of Shoshenq II, generally believed to have been the prematurely defunct co-regent of Osorkon I. The body of the

308 Coffin of Nesyperennub, son of Ankhefenkhonsu, a good example of the much simpler forms of coffin that replaced the elaborate 'yellow' types during the Twenty-second Dynasty. The mummy found within was encased in the usual type of cartonnage case. From Deir el-Bahari; BM EA 30720.

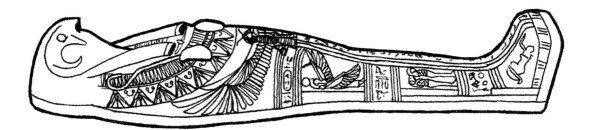

309 Lid of the Twenty-second Dynasty silver coffin of King Shoshenq II. Apart from the hawk-head, specific to kingly burials, the basic scheme of decoration follows standard contemporary practice on cartonnages (cf. ill. 212). A ram-headed, vulture-bodied image of the sun-god is followed by winged figures of Isis and Nephthys and then the Four Sons of Horus. The two feet bear the protective kneeling forms of Selqet and Neith. From Tanis NRT III; CM JE 72154.

coffin was decorated in a manner that recalls a contemporary private cartonnage, with quadrants containing the principal mortuary deities. Nowhere was there any sign of the ancient *rishi* pattern that had remained the underlying feature of royal coffin decoration, despite the various auxiliary changes seen over the previous centuries.

However, the *rishi* motif was replaced by a new royal feature, one which is particularly startling: the face of Shoshenq's coffin became that of a falcon, as did the face of the cartonnage that lay within. The disappearance of one avian feature coinciding so closely with the appearance of a new one, makes it likely that what we see is a redefinition of the king's posthumous aerial rôle in a more explicit manner than had been represented by the by now wholly stylized *rishi*.

While the ensemble of Shoshenq II was the only one recovered essentially intact from the royal necropolis of Tanis, parts of those of other kings came to light, showing that the convention of an avian head for the coffins/cartonnages was continued. Another example, in granite, comes from the tomb of a local king of Thebes, Harsiese. He had lain in a granite coffin closed with a hawk-headed lid. The granite coffin trough, however, was a re-used piece, in this case from the lost Queens' Valley tomb of Henutmire, sister of Ramesses II. No effort had seemingly been made to change the names and inscriptions on it, presumably because the case was to be sunk into the floor of the burial

310 Of similar hawk-headed design is the granite coffin lid of the slightly later Theban king, Harsiese. The missing beak was probably in metal. Twenty-second Dynasty, from Medinet Habu, tomb 1; CM JE 60137.

311 Coffin of Paiwayenhor. Twenty-second Dynasty, its form and coloration reminiscent of cartonnages of the time; CM TR 21.11.16.9.

chamber, out of sight. By the latter part of the Twenty-second Dynasty the royal avian-headed approach was abandoned, to judge from the presence of inlaid human eyes on the king's coffins and cartonnage in the tomb of Pimay.

The Twenty-third Dynasty

During the Twenty-second Dynasty, images of Nut became very common inside coffins, sometimes shown full-face, on either the trough or the lid. Under the Twenty-third Dynasty, which ruled Thebes in parallel with the latter part of the Twenty-second, falcon-headed figures of Sokar, supported by Isis and Nephthys, are also found inside coffin troughs.

The same dynasty shows major morphological changes in coffin structures. Progressively, troughs became shallower and, most noticeably, a 'pedestal' appeared under the feet, with a shallow pillar under the back of the trough. This clearly copied the pattern normally seen on statues. At the same time, the lid and trough decorations became reintegrated, with columns of text extending round to the back pillar.

Curiously these features, first seen during the Twenty-third Dynasty, are initially restricted to inner coffins, which less regularly held cartonnage casings. They may have derived from a need to stand the inner coffin upright during the funerary ceremonies.

The Twenty-fifth and Twenty-sixth Dynasties

The adoption of 'pedestal' coffins was followed by other changes in decoration during the Twenty-fifth Dynasty.

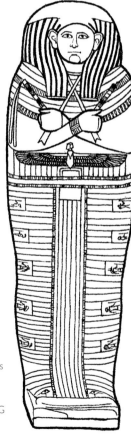

312 (*left*) The coffin of Kephaese. Although its coloration and form are closely modelled on Twenty-second Dynasty cartonnages, it is mounted on a discrete pedestal, and is a proper wooden coffin. It is thus a 'missing link' between these cartonnages and the new inner coffins that became current during the later Twenty-third Dynasty. Copenhagen, Ny Carlsberg ÆIN 298.

313 Coffin of Besenmut ii, a good example of the text-heavy decorative arrangements of later Twenty-third/fifth Dynasty coffins. The presence of sceptres and braces is less usual, however. Late Twenty-third Dynasty, from Deir el-Bahari, under Hatshepsut temple; CM CG 41047.

314 The coffin of Harsiese M; it is of the same date, and from the same grouping of burials, belonging to the priestly families of the Mentu-cult. The texts on the exterior and interior are predominantly from the Book of the Dead; Berlin 8237.

Kushite artistic and mortuary practice, these Nubian kings having also adopted pyrmids for their burial places.

By the start of the Twenty-sixth Dynasty, a winged figure of Nut had returned to the pectoral position she had occupied in the New Kingdom. Below might be vignettes from the Book of the Dead, with the thorax, legs and feet covered with vertical and horizontal texts, which extended on to the sides and back of the trough. Standing figures of deities might be found among the texts, and *wadjet*-eyes on top of the feet.

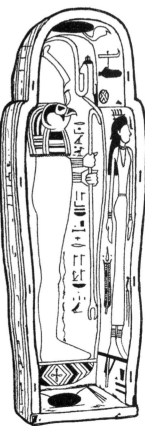

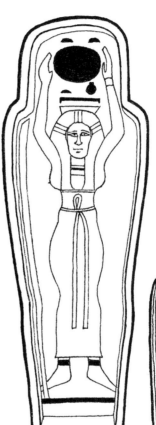

315 Interior of the lid of the coffin of Inamunnefnebu, showing the sky-goddess, Nut, stretched out over the body of the deceased. Twenty-fifth/sixth Dynasty, from Thebes(?); RMO AMM.1.

Motifs of the previous dynasties were retained but, as time passed, the size and variety of vignettes diminished, accompanied by an increase in the quantity of texts, usually taken from the Book of the Dead. Reflecting the same kind of increasing density of decoration seen on the late yellow coffins, texts started to be placed on bands of various colours, in particular orange, yellow and green. Another change was that, in certain cases, the coffin lid was varnished but the trough left matt.

Fragments have been found of royal coffins from the end of the Twenty-fifth Dynasty. The outer cases were very large. It is clear from numerous pieces of inlay recovered that avian plumage played an important part in their decoration; whether this took the form of winged/bird deities, or some kind of revived *rishi* is uncertain. If the latter, it would be yet another example of the archaism to be seen in

316 Interior of the trough of the coffin of Neskhonsupakhered, showing Ptah-Sokar-Osiris on the floor, with Isis on the side-wall. An epithet of Horus, 'the Behdite', is written above her. Twenty-fifth/sixth Dynasty, from Thebes; BM EA 47975.

317 The latest extant royal coffin is also the oddest, for by the time it was made, the mummy it was to contain was some two thousand years old. It was made during the Twenty-fifth/sixth Dynasty for the reburial of the desecrated remains of the Fourth Dynasty king, Mykerinos. Now badly damaged, it followed an archaizing design, and is very small, reflecting the dimensions of the royal sarcophagus and the partial human remains. From the Third Pyramid, Giza; BM EA 6647.

Aside from the mainstream of Twenty-fifth/sixth Dynasty coffin development, the archaism of the time also led to the production of near-replicas of ancient coffin designs, in particular the Twelfth Dynasty 'white' anthropoid type typified by that of Userhet from Beni Hasan (see p. 202). Their true date is usually revealed by over-large collars and the inclusion of a pedestal under the feet, together with more subtle stylistic elements, but are often creditable attempts at copying an old artifact.

Some wooden coffins of the Twenty-sixth Dynasty reveal a considerable increase in the size of outer cases. A good dated example is that of Ameniryiret (BM EA 6667), a functionary of the Divine Adorer, Amenirdis II, in the early Twenty-sixth Dynasty. It was massive in all directions, with very thick walls and squat proportions. Similarly sized outer coffins became common in Saite/Late times, although at first the favoured material seems to have been stone.

SAITE PERIOD

Stone Coffins of the Saite Period

At the end of the New Kingdom, the stone coffin appears to have become extinct, those used in Third Intermediate Period burials being second-hand. During the Twenty-first to -fifth Dynasties, all known new coffins were of wood; the dislocation of the country may have made it difficult for private individuals to obtain suitable stone. However, with the reunification under Psammetikhos I, the material reappeared for anthropoid cases.

The earliest of them seems to have been that of Pabasa from Thebes. Of granite, it shared many similarities with New Kingdom examples, and lacked the pedestal of most contemporary coffins. Illustrating the period's conscious archaism, the sides of the trough bore the same series of genii and Anubis-forms, bracketed by figures of Thoth, as New Kingdom coffins. The lid decoration was simple, with longitudinal and transverse bands, contrasting with later Twenty-sixth Dynasty developments.

The same overall form is seen on the coffin-lid of Sisobk (BM EA 17), but here the overall 'feel' of the piece was changed by the employment of a fine-grained schist as material. The lid decoration remained simple, with merely a Nut-figure and double text column. Other coffins datable to Psammetikhos I's reign had more ornamentation and inscriptions including the various funerary deities. They also display a plinth below the feet. The early years of the Twenty-sixth Dynasty thus showed a rapid evolution from a type reflecting old practices to one more in keeping with current wooden custom.

Rapid further development led to stone coffins taking on a form essentially of their own, manifested in a greatly reduced length:breadth ratio; some wooden examples had similar proportions (e.g. the aforementioned BM EA 6667), but it is unclear which material had priority. Coffins of this type appear extremely corpulent, with the height of the feet and face above the surface of the lid distinctly reduced. In most cases decoration of the lid was restricted to numerous columns of text on the front of the body, supplemented in some cases by a winged figure of Nut below the collar and/or lines of text on the top of the foot.

The latest definite attestation of this particular type of stone coffin comes in early Persian times, in that of

318 Basalt coffin of Pedismatowy showing the procession of funerary deities along the side of the trough, and Nephthys at the left shoulder. The squat proportions of the piece are very clear, while on the the trough, on the side of the head may be seen two eyes – the persistance of the old eye-panel, over one and a half millennia after the change in mummy-posture had made it obsolete. From Kom Abu Yasin; CM JE 31566.

319 A similar basalt coffin belonging to Pakhap, also called Wahibreemakhet. This Twenty-sixth Dynasty piece is typical of its time, in being extremely broad relative to height. From 'Campbell's Tomb' at Giza (LG 84); BM EA 1384.

320 Some such coffins were exported to Syria, at least three being used for royal burials at Sidon; this one bears a Phoenician inscription indicating its new role as the burial place of King Ashmunazar II. Another found at the same site had formerly belonged to an Egyptian general before usurpation. Fifth century BC, from Saïda; Louvre AO.4806.

Udjahorresnet, whose career spanned the end of the Twenty-sixth Dynasty and the initial part of the Persian domination. No other such cases can be dated to Persian times, stone coffins apparently re-appearing only during the Thirtieth Dynasty.

LATE PTOLEMAIC AND ROMAN PERIODS

Wooden Coffins of the Late Ptolemaic and Roman Periods

The Persians dominated Egypt for a large proportion of the Late Period, which seems to have had an effect on the material available for coffin production; certainly, no stone anthropoid cases seem to be datable to the epoch.

321, 322 Wooden coffin of Hedbastiru, its proportions reminiscent of Saite stone examples, and its decoration of painted pieces. The coffin's decoration is partly unfinished (see detail): while the figures of Hapy and Qebehsenuef are complete, the opposite ones, to be Imseti and Duamutef, are only outlined, with a large block of wood left for the label-texts. Leipzig 494.

Wooden cases continued to exhibit the patterns of the Saite Period, with the pedestal retained under the feet, together with a dorsal pillar. Precise dating is often difficult, but later examples have a noticeably 'heavier' feel, the head being positioned further down into the body, ears sometimes being almost level with the shoulders. In this they betray the influence of stone coffins.

Decoratively, the coffins show a wide variety of motifs, although the volume of texts is noticeable. A significant piece is the coffin of Petosiris, from Tuna el-Gebel (very early Ptolemaic), which had its texts inlaid with polychrome glass. Proceeding further into the Ptolemaic Period, notable features are the widespread use of gilding on coffin-faces (perhaps paralleling its use on the faces of a number of mummies – see Chapter 3), together with very large collars. These were depicted as though laid upon the chest, rather than actually worn; they usually began some way below the shoulders, and could stretch down to the bottom of the abdomen.

Many coffins have survived from the Ptolemaic Period, but their quality diminishes as the period progresses, the

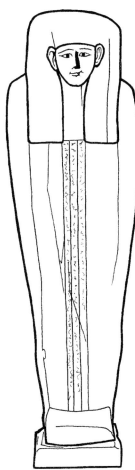

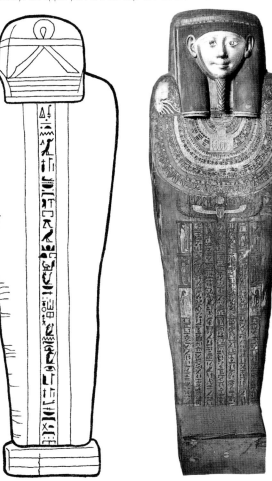

324 Thirtieth Dynasty/early Ptolemaic coffins continue the fundamental form begun in the Twenty-third Dynasty, but with distinctive aspects that include a broad collar slung around the lower torso, rather than, more realistically, the upper part of the body. CM TR 21.11.16.11.

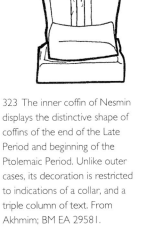

323 The inner coffin of Nesmin displays the distinctive shape of coffins of the end of the Late Period and beginning of the Ptolemaic Period. Unlike outer cases, its decoration is restricted to indications of a collar, and a triple column of text. From Akhmim; BM EA 29581.

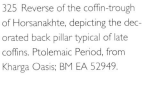

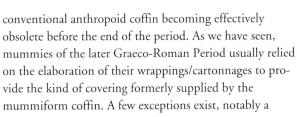

325 Reverse of the coffin-trough of Horsanakhte, depicting the dec-orated back pillar typical of late coffins. Ptolemaic Period, from Kharga Oasis; BM EA 52949.

conventional anthropoid coffin becoming effectively obsolete before the end of the period. As we have seen, mummies of the later Graeco-Roman Period usually relied on the elaboration of their wrappings/cartonnages to pro-vide the kind of covering formerly supplied by the mummiform coffin. A few exceptions exist, notably a

326, 327 Gilded faces are to be found on a considerable number of Ptolemaic coffins. The flat-topped lid of this piece, belonging to Hamedjyotef, is also a distinctive feature of Late/Ptolemaic coffins. Its interior shows a rather inelegant figure of Nut, surrounded by portions of the Book of the Dead and astronomical representations. From Thebes; BM EA 6678.

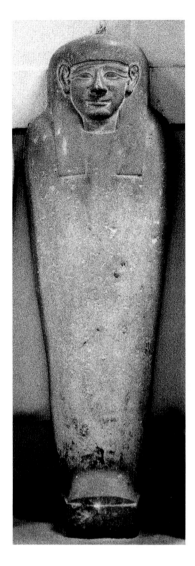

of stone coffins, although the material continued in use for sarcophagi. It has been suggested that this derives from a loss of status by Egyptians under foreign rule, but other explanations might be possible. However, under Nektanebo I stone coffins once again appear in the archaeological record.

They were less massive than the Saite examples, and were generally made of limestone. Spanning the period from the Thirtieth Dynasty down into the reign of Ptolemy I, they were usually decorated simply with a number of vertical columns of text. No hands were shown, the top of the head was round, and the face low-set; the coffin's foot stood upon a shallow podium.

There then appears to be another gap in the record of stone coffins until the second half of the third century BC, although the similarity between some examples normally so-dated and others to be placed in the reign of Ptolemy I (310–282 BC) may suggest that the former should be dated somewhat earlier. The basic shape remained the same, although faces became rather fatter. Decoration ranged from the simple columns of text seen on earlier coffins to far more intricate compositions, including numerous figures of deities. Amongst the most elaborate is that of Desqerdes, in the Louvre, where almost every square centimetre of the lid, including the wig, was covered with texts or vignettes. Curiously, the back of the trough also bore columns of text, though it would have been in contact with the ground.

THE MANUFACTURE OF WOODEN ANTHROPOID COFFINS

The highest-status coffins were usually made of expensive, imported, cedar and juniper. This was certainly the case for most of the royal coffins of the New Kingdom, and quasi-royalty of the Twenty-first Dynasty High-Priestly family (Masaharta, Maetkare, Pinudjem II, Nesikhonsu, Isetemkheb and Djedptahiufankh). However, as usual, the majority were made of native woods, in particular sycamore and fig, and occasionally acacia and tamarisk.

Due to the paucity of good-quality wood in Egypt, coffins were often made from several small pieces of timber dowelled together. In particular, some Middle Kingdom rectangular examples show an amazing patchwork of tiny pieces of planking. The joins would then be obscured with plaster.

328 A limestone coffin of typical Thirtieth Dynasty/early-Ptolemaic type. Perhaps from Abydos; CM TR 24.2.21.1.

wooden example in the British Museum (EA 55022) which takes the form of the full-length figure of a man wearing a Greek cloak, standing on a pedestal. Thus reminiscent of the daily-life coffins of the early Nineteenth Dynasty, it at the same time marks the end of an element of Egyptian burial tradition going back to the Middle Kingdom.

The Last Stone Coffins

With the exception of specimens carried over from the preceding Saite Period (e.g. that of Udjahorresnet), the term of Persian occupation and immediately following native dynasties seems to have seen a cessation of the manufacture

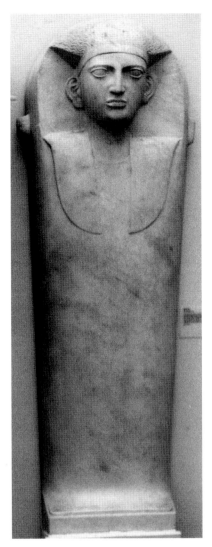

329 The Egyptian concept of a stone anthropoid coffin spread far: this example comes from Syria. BM.

Essentially, anthropoid coffins were made of ten basic wooden components, five for the lid, five for the trough although these might be made up of further smaller pieces. Those of the lid were a flat top-board, two low side-walls, a low head-board and a foot-board. The face, front of skull, hands, feet, ears and other elements were made from separate pieces, and glued or pegged in place. The trough usually consisted of a bottom (normally made up of two planks), two long sides, a foot-board and a head-board. This was, of course, only possible with access to large planks; other anthropoid coffins were made from larger numbers of elements, although still skilfully formed into the same range of basic components.

Decoration: 'Black' Coffins with Gilding

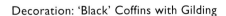

First, a single layer of linen was glued on to the bare surface of the wood, cut to the approximate dimensions of the band or divine figure in question. Next was applied a layer of fine plaster, which overlapped the edge of the band or image. This was cut back to the correct outline, the discarded edges leaving 'wet' marks on the wooden surface that are still visible. The texts and other details were incised into the surface of the plaster, which was then gilded.

Later (in the tomb, in some cases) the bare wooden surfaces were coated with thick black resin. This was frequently done with little care, the resin intruding upon the carefully tooled and gilded areas.

Decoration: 'Yellow' Coffins

The basis of the decorative scheme was a white gesso covering all surfaces to be painted. The remainder was left bare, or painted red, grey or black.

After gessoing, the surface was divided into panels with red lines. Red was also used to outline the vignettes, which were filled in with red, pale blue and dark blue. (Dark blue was obtained by overlaying a thin coat of black with blue.) The background was painted yellow (brownish-red on the interior of the coffin), the whole then being varnished. Certain coffins had their vignettes modelled in the gesso before painting, thus following some Eighteenth Dynasty gilded examples, such as those of Yuya and Tjuiu.

There has been a debate over whether the heavy yellow hue was intentional, or a by-product of the varnish ageing. On certain deviant coffins which display areas of white, varnish had clearly been avoided on purpose, but there are also a number of un-varnished examples with yellow-painted grounds.

Paint was supplemented by gilding on some high-status coffins, and by inlays of coloured pastes. Inlaid eyes were rare, in contrast with the practice during the New Kingdom. Some coffins of the Twenty-first Dynasty seem to have been re-made from earlier pieces, although the evidence is fairly scarce.

Sarcophagi

Chapter 8

The word 'sarcophagus' derives from the Greek for 'flesh-eater', apparently from an Hellenic belief that some stone used for body-containers actually consumed its contents. The *Concise Oxford Dictionary* defines the term as meaning a stone coffin, the usage which is probably the most common in Egyptology, although a number of writers call all body-containers 'sarcophagi', regardless of their material or form. However, definition by material is not particularly helpful, as was noted in the chapter on coffins. More important is a container's role in the funerary ensemble, and thus here a 'sarcophagus' is defined as a container for coffins, specifically an *outer* case. Of wood or stone, it is essentially rectangular, and clearly distinguishable from the rectangular or anthropoid *coffins* that lay within. The Egyptians themselves called the sarcophagus *neb ankh*, the 'lord of life'.

Some of the stone sarcophagi produced by the Egyptians are amongst the most accomplished stone works of man. Quartzite, used for the coffers of a select few, was the hardest stone worked by ancient people; in this intractable material, as well as others, superb works of art were produced that formed fitting shelters for their royal and noble sponsors.

Summary of Sarcophagus Development

Sarcophagi first appeared in the Third Dynasty, the earliest examples providing a basic form that continued to be found throughout their history: a plain coffer (the 'box' of the sarcophagus), topped by a rounded lid, with rectangular end-pieces (the *per-nu* form). During the Old Kingdom, some coffers acquired panelling, with a number of additional lid forms. The Middle Kingdom included some sarcophagi built from separate slabs of stone, and at the end of the Twelfth Dynasty examples were made which had a band of panelling around the bottom margin of the coffer only.

During the New Kingdom, contrary to earlier practice, stone sarcophagi became largely the prerogative of kings, most private individuals being restricted to wood. These followed the old *per-nu* design, although the *per-wer* style, with a sloping lid, also appeared during the dynasty. Royal sarcophagi were initially rectangular, but soon adopted an oval, cartouche-form, plan, which continued into the Twentieth Dynasty, with the exception of the Amarna Period.

The Third Intermediate Period largely did without sarcophagi, with the exception of its kings, who first used usurped earlier pieces, and then adopted a rounded-head

330 (*above*) The sarcophagus of Amenophis II, a less elegant enlargement of that of Tuthmosis III. The coffer bears a series of divine figures, from the left, Qebehsenuef, Anubis-Imywet and Hapy. The eye-panel was retained from Middle Kingdom examples, in which the mummy had lain on its left side. By the New Kingdom, the body lay supine, rendering panel an anachronism. The king's mummy is to be seen inside the sarcophagus; it was removed to Cairo in 1932. In KV 35.

plan. A modified rectangular *per-nu* design in wood was used by private individuals from the Twenty-third Dynasty onwards. Stone once again became widespread in the Saite, Late and Ptolemaic Periods. The coffer by then had a rounded head, a taper towards the foot, and a new lid shape. In Roman times, modified versions of the wooden *per-nu* sarcophagus remained in use, but stone examples became wholly Classical in their form.

THE OLD KINGDOM

Although stone had begun to be used for the paving of burial chambers back in the middle of the First Dynasty, the material's use for a container for the body only appeared at the beginning of the Third Dynasty. It can hardly be chance that this coincided with the construction of the first major building to be composed of hewn stone – Djoser's Step Pyramid at Saqqara.

We have already looked at the remains of the apparent mummy of Djoser. Its burial chamber could not easily have accepted a usable rectangular wooden coffin: built of massive granite blocks, entered via a hole, stopped like a bottle, the chamber could, however, be looked upon as a gigantic built-in sarcophagus – something which we shall see in a number of later pyramids.

Nevertheless, the Step Pyramid elsewhere housed the earliest known stone sarcophagi. Under the east side of the pyramid lay eleven galleries, at least five of which formed the tombs of members of the royal family. All of these contained the remains of calcite sarcophagi, or their bases. Two complete examples showed that they were rectangular, following wooden practice, with arched lids with raised end-pieces. This lid-form imitated the ancient *per-nu* sanctuary, later symbolic of Lower Egypt. A raised lip around the inner edge of the coffer aided the accurate seating of the lid, and a U-shaped boring at each end of the lid enabled the use of a rope to lower it into place.

Both of these Step Pyramid sarcophagi were relatively small, together with another pair which were seemingly removed from the galleries during the Twelfth Dynasty, and were found in the complex of Sesostris III at Dahshur. They could not have held the coffined body of an adult, though one contained the body of a child, within the plywood coffin described in the previous chapter (p. 195).

The next known stone sarcophagus is one of the most interesting – and mysterious. It was found below the unfinished pyramid of the King Horus Sekhemkhet at Saqqara (ills. 89, 332–3). Like the Step Pyramid examples, it was of calcite, but in place of a conventional lid, had a sliding panel at one end. The size of the aperture again implies that

331 An alabaster type Se sarcophagus found at Dahshur, in the enclosure of the pyramid of Sesostris III of the Twelfth Dynasty. The piece is, however, of Third Dynasty date and one of the earliest stone sarcophagi known. It appears to have formed part of the burial of a member of the family of King Djoser, under the east side of his Step Pyramid at Saqqara. CM CG 28103.

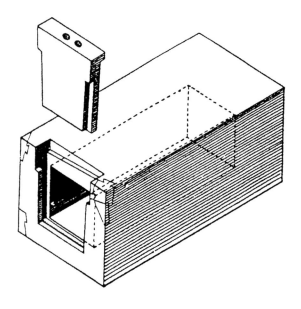

332, 333 The sarcophagus from the pyramid of Horus Sekhemkhet. Unlike all other sarcophagi it was closed by a sliding panel at one end; in spite of being apparently sealed shut when found, it proved to be empty, and seems never to have been used. Saqqara.

it was not intended to include a wooden coffin, but the panel was found sealed in place, suggesting to the excavator that a Third Dynasty royal mummy might lie within. Inexplicably, the sarcophagus proved to be empty.

A similar situation existed at the Unfinished Pyramid at Zawiyet el-Aryan, where an odd *oval* sarcophagus was found, carved out of one of the granite flooring blocks. Its form is unique amongst surviving complete sarcophagi, and in spite of the lid being sealed in place by clay, its cavity proved to be empty. The pyramid's date has been much debated, with many scholars arguing for either a mid-Fourth or late-Third Dynasty attribution. Certain architectural features favour the later dating, as does the possibility that an oval sarcophagus was used in the undoubtedly Fourth Dynasty pyramid at Abu Rowash.

However, the majority of sarcophagi of the Fourth Dynasty conformed to a number of standard, rectangular, forms. The most common of these was employed for the Step Pyramid sarcophagi described above, although calcite seems generally abandoned in favour of harder stones early in the Fourth Dynasty. One calcite piece is the flat-lidded sarcophagus of Hetepheres, wife of Seneferu and probably

mother of Kheops, found closed but empty in a shaft at Giza in what appears to have been a reburial.

The earliest of the hard-stone examples is from Mastaba 17 at Meidum, perhaps belonging to the heir of the owner of the pyramid there. Made of red granite, it was completely plain, apart from the *per-nu* shape of the lid, and is the prototype for the majority of Old Kingdom sarcophagi (type Se).

The coffers of Kings Kheops and Khephren, within the two largest pyramids at Giza, continued to be plain. Khephren's was sunk into the floor of the burial chamber, with a flat lid (type Sd). However, the middle years of the Fourth Dynasty saw the appearance in stone of the panelled decorative motif found on many coffins of the preceding period (types Sd(p) and Se(p), depending on the lid-form), together with the periodic inscription of the deceased's names and titles.

The panelling varied from the simple to the extremely elaborate, with the best examples being amongst the earliest. Perhaps the finest of all sarcophagi with this decorative scheme was that of King Mykerinos; regrettably, we can only appreciate its quality from nineteenth-century

334 The type Sd(p) granite sarcophagus of Queen Meresankh II, daughter
of Kheops, with a single 'palace-façade'
false door in the middle of the side.
Lugs for the manoeuvring of the lid
remain in place. From Giza G7410;
MFA 27.441.

335 The type Sd sarcophagus of King
Khephren. It was sunk in the floor of
his burial chamber in the Second
Pyramid at Giza. Its present appearance is owing to the removal of most
of the chamber floor by Vyse and
Perring in 1837.

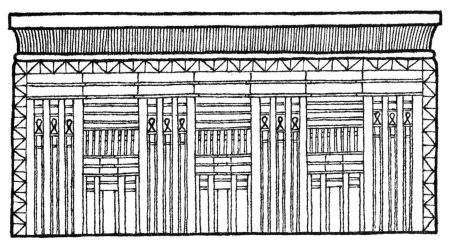

336 The panelled sarcophagus of King
Mykerinos, from the Third Pyramid at
Giza, its form paralleled only by two
others of its time (type Sf(p)).

engravings, for it was removed from the burial chamber under the Third Pyramid at Giza in 1837 and lost at sea off the Spanish coast.

This sarcophagus is one of at least three that deviated from the lid forms already referred to. Rather than the simple slab or *per-nu* form, their flat-topped covers had flared edges, with narrow vertical ribs. It imitated the 'cavetto cornice' which was later an almost universal architectural ornament on Egyptian buildings, and is featured on many sarcophagi and canopic chests of the New Kingdom, defining sarcophagus type Sf. Mykerinos' panelling assigns his monument to sub-type Sf(p).

The other two sarcophagi belonging to this shrine-like group are those of Mykerinos' successor, Shepseskaf, and one later re-used for the burial of the very late Old

337 The later Fifth Dynasty limestone sarcophagus of Ptahdjefa, showing the most elaborate version of the 'palace-façade' decorative scheme. From Giza; CM JE 66681.

338 (*above left*) The late Fourth Dynasty type Sf sarcophagus re-used for the burial of Prince Ptahshepses at the very end of the Old Kingdom. It is one of a small group, including those of Mykerinos and Shepseskaf, to have a cornice-edged lid, plus elaborate corner-mouldings. From Valley Building of Unas, Saqqara; CM JE 87077.

339 (*above*) The late Old Kingdom limestone type Sg sarcophagus of Weta, exhibiting by contrast a very simple design, with a plain box and flat lid, ornamented only by the large-sized texts, giving the deceased's name and titles. The lugs used to aid in the positioning of the lid have not been removed. From Giza; CM CG 1787.

340 An intermediate between these two extremes is shown by the simplified panelling on the Fifth Dynasty granite sarcophagus of Werirni. Found between Giza G7810 and 7820; CM JE 48078.

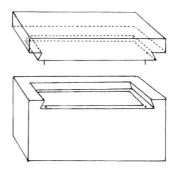

Kingdom prince, Ptahshepses, whose mummy has already been mentioned (p. 112). The first had a completely plain coffer, and the second a zig-zag moulding around the coffer-edges. Since all three date from the end of the Fourth Dynasty, the appearance or non-appearance of the panelling is seen as having no chronological significance.

The block quarried for a sarcophagus often comprised the material for both the coffer and the lid, the latter being sawn from the bottom of the block, while the burial cavity was carved from the larger part. Many sarcophagus lids were simply laid on top of their coffers, being kept in place only by their own weight, but a considerable number had rather more ingenious methods of attachment. The most elaborate is shown in ill. 341. When this system was used, robbers were still able to break in, but only after expending considerable effort in forcing the lid out of its grooves – or destroying it completely.

To aid workmen in manoeuvring a sarcophagus lid, the lid was often equipped with one or two projecting lugs at each end. These were intended to be broken off after the funeral, and some have been found on the floor of the burial chamber where they had been dropped. Others, however, were frequently left in place through either oversight or laziness. As an additional support, walls were sometimes constructed between the coffer and the wall behind it, to hold up the lid until after the funeral, when it could easily be slid into place. A more elaborate example of this was found in the tomb of Mereruka at Saqqara, where

a ramp had been built from the floor of the sepulchral chamber, up which the lid could be manoeuvred into place.

By the beginning of the Fifth Dynasty, private sarcophagi with *per–nu* lid types, Se and Se(p), had become the most common, particularly at Giza. However, Saqqara tombs of the latter part of the Old Kingdom often employed the less refined type Sg/Sg(p), distinguished by a heavy lid of an ill-defined, round-edged shape.

While many of the earliest sarcophagi are too short to have contained more than a simple mummy, royal coffers of the late Fifth and Sixth Dynasties had vertical grooves cut inside the long sides, intended to accommodate the ropes needed to lower a close-fitting coffin into the interior. Little is known of the sarcophagi of kings between Shepseskaf and Unas, most of them being either lost in the destruction of the interiors of the pyramids of Abusir by medieval stone-robbers, smashed or insufficiently recorded.

The sarcophagus of Unas, last king of the Fifth Dynasty, was uninscribed, but those of Sixth Dynasty

343 The sarcophagus of the late-Sixth Dynasty queen, Ankhnespepy. Its coffer was manufactured from a block that had previously been inscribed for use in a building of Pepy I. The over-sized lid also came from a previously quarried slab, in this case of the greatest historical importance, since it has recently been seen to contain part of the Royal Chronicle of the Sixth Dynasty. Reuse of material for sarcophagi seems to have been not uncommon in this period (cf. ill. 338). From the mortuary temple of Queen Iput II, South Saqqara; CM JE 65908.

Few sarcophagi are identifiable from the obscure First Intermediate Period. The tomb of King Inyotef I at El-Tarif may have contained one, now totally lost. Sandstone and limestone fragments deriving from the sarcophagi of wives of Inyotef III came from his mortuary complex.

Meaningful remains begin, however, with the resurrection of the kingdom under Mentuhotep II, comprising examples known from the tombs that were built in and around the king's funerary complex at Deir el-Bahari. Amongst the most interesting are a series of limestone sarcophagi belonging to the king's women-folk.

They were made of a number of separate slabs rather than carved from a single block, and the scope of the carved and painted decoration of those of Ashayet, Kawit and Kemsit, was unusual. This principally included domestic scenes, rather than the ritual and 'other-worldly' motifs generally seen on Middle Kingdom coffins. The exteriors of the sarcophagi were carved; the interiors were only painted. More conventional, and reflecting coffin practice, was the painted interior decoration of the sarcophagi of the vizier Dagy and the Treasurer, Harhotpe, although the latter incorporated a cavetto-cornice which was unusual for the period.

Another novelty was the burial chamber of Mentuhotep II himself which, instead of a sarcophagus, contained a shrine constructed from calcite blocks. This was of *per-wer* shape, that of the traditional Upper Egyptian sanctuary (⬠), contrasting with the *per-nu* (⬚) hitherto standard for funerary containers. This reflects the southern origins of the royal line; the *per-wer* did not otherwise become current for sarcophagi until the late Eighteenth Dynasty. The sepulchral shrine at Deir el-Bahari had a row of holes around its interior, perhaps intended to support a pall over the royal coffin.

The sarcophagus of the last king of the Eleventh Dynasty, Mentuhotep IV, is known only from a text left in the Wadi Hammamat by the expedition responsible for quarrying the greywacke block from which its lid would be manufactured. His place of burial remains unknown, but was presumably somewhere in Western Thebes.

In the Twelfth Dynasty, our knowledge of the sarcophagi of the earliest kings is hindered by the fact that the sepulchral chambers of the two pyramids of Lisht are

royalty all bore texts. Teti's had long speeches by the goddess Nut on the interior; the Pepys' had brief versions of their names on the east side; and Nemtyemsaf I's had long versions of his names and titles down the centre of the lid and around the sides of the coffer. Private inscribed cases became less common as the Sixth Dynasty progressed.

A feature of the late Old Kingdom was a series of small, highly decorated, stone-built private burial chambers that were often little larger than the coffins they contained. Examples have been found at such Delta sites at Tell Basta, as well as in the Memphite necropoleis. Their decoration closely resembled that found inside coffins of the Sixth Dynasty and later, and illustrates the degree of artificiality sometimes present in distinguishing the various types of funerary container. Similar decoration has also been found inside full-size burial chambers; a good example is under the mastaba of the early Sixth Dynasty vizier, Mereruka, at Saqqara.

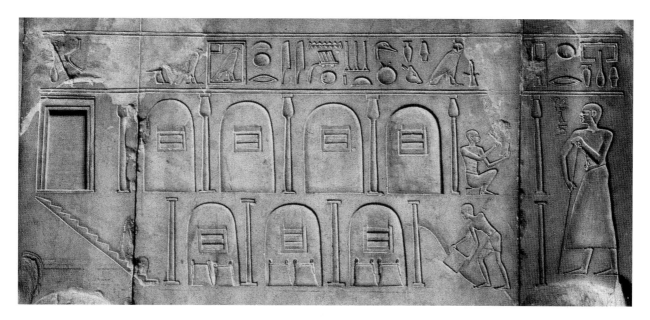

344 The limestone sarcophagi from the tombs of the womenfolk of Mentuhotep II are interesting both for their construction and decoration. They were constructed from a series of slabs of stone, held together by rope passed through borings in the components, and then hidden by plaster. The exteriors show various so-called 'daily life' scenes. Here, the foot of Ashayet's coffer shows a set of seven granaries and their overseer. Eleventh Dynasty, from DBXI.17; CM JE 47267.

345 An early Twelfth Dynasty granite sarcophagus, showing cross battens borrowed from wooden examples, and an odd lid, lacking end-boards. From the North Mastaba, near Sesostris I's pyramid at Lisht; MMA 09.180.528a.

flooded by ground water, and have thus not been visited in modern times. However, sarcophagi have been found in some of their subsidiary tombs, notably an anonymous grey granite example from the North Mastaba at the site, whose curved lid lacks the traditional end-pieces. As we have seen, this was also a feature of certain later royal coffins of the dynasty. The relationship between this sarcophagus and contemporary coffins can again be seen in the cross-battens that are depicted under the trough: meaningless in a work of stone, but part of the basic construction of one in wood.

More material is available from the time of Ammenemes II. The king himself was laid to rest in a quartzite coffer, built from six separate slabs, and covered by three more,

embedded in limestone blocks below the floor of his burial chamber. This is the first known manifestation of the security-imperative that becomes so clear in subsequent Middle Kingdom royal tombs. Conventional *per-nu* sarcophagi were employed in the burials of the king's family, in his enclosure at Dahshur, although also essentially embedded in stone.

Under Sesostris II and III some real innovations appear in the sarcophagus record. Sesostris II's own coffer had a curious deep lip around its upper part; combined with an irregular bottom, it may once have been intended for insertion into a chamber floor. That of his wife(?) adopted Old Kingdom-style panelling, also seen on the contemporary sarcophagus of Ibu from Qau, although the latter is more closely influenced by coffins of the time (type RVI).

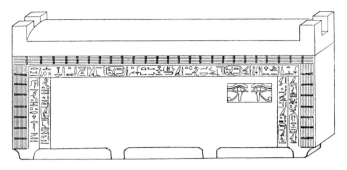

346 A sarcophagus made at the command of Sesostris II was that of Amenemhatsonbe. Of red granite, it introduces a common mid/late Twelfth Dynasty decorative motif, the adornment of the edges by 'bundles of reeds', and incorporates the cross-battens borrowed from wooden coffins. Its particularly unusual feature is that instead of complete end-boards, the lid has a square post at each corner. This kind of arrangement is found very occasionally in the New Kingdom, and generally in the Third Intermediate Period and later, but then only on *wooden* sarcophagi; Amenemhatsonbe's thus appears to be unique. Provenance unknown; Florence 2181.

The sarcophagi produced under Sesostris III had a replica of the Third Dynasty enclosure wall of Djoser's Step Pyramid carved around their lower parts. This motif appeared on the king's own sarcophagus, and became ubiquitous amongst late-dynasty high-status sarcophagus owners. Half a millennium later it was resurrected for the princely sarcophagus of Merenptah, heir, and ultimately successor, of Ramesses II. The type continued in use under Ammenemes III, and, though little evidence survives, perhaps into the early years of the Thirteenth Dynasty.

A major innovation in royal usage is seen some half-a-dozen reigns into the new dynasty, in the substructure of the pyramid of Ameny-Qemau at South Dahshur. This embodied what is typologically the earliest of a new kind of combined sarcophagus/canopic chest, carved out of a single quartzite block. It formed the floor of the burial chamber, and was sealed by a lid which was slid into position from an antechamber area directly north of the sarcophagus. The

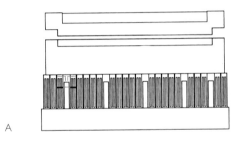

A

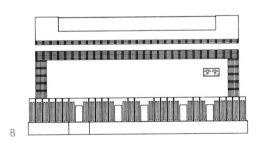

B

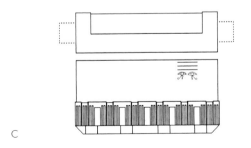

C

347 Royal sarcophagi of the late Twelfth Dynasty.

A Sesostris III, in his pyramid at Dahshur. The sarcophagus introduces this style of panelling around its lower portion, imitating the enclosure-wall of the Third Dynasty pyramid of Djoser at Saqqara, including the clear distinction of that structure's real entrance from a number of dummies. Sesostris III modelled his whole pyramid-complex after this ancient monument, burying within it a pair of sarcophagi salvaged from under the Step Pyramid (see ill. 331). The lid follows the standard *per-nu* type, made so that it slid onto the coffer and then locked in position in the same manner as Old Kingdom examples (ill. 341).

B Ammenemes III, in his first pyramid at Dahshur. This develops the design instituted by his father, refining the overall shape, and adding an eye-panel and a ribbed edge-decoration, apparently imitating bundles of reeds. This feature is also found on some royal coffins (ill. 245).

C Princess Neferuptah's. Originally to be buried inside her father's second pyramid nearby, she was ultimately interred in her own tomb. Most members of the royal household of the late Twelfth Dynasty followed Sesostris III's pattern of sarcophagus-design; in Neferuptah's case, the proportions have changed to make the whole monument 'deeper'. It additionally harks back to wooden containers in the re-presentation of cross-beams below the panelling, as found on some other stone sarcophagi (e.g. ills. 345-6). Manoeuvring of the huge lid was aided by massive lugs at either end, removed after the burial. From her pyramid at Hawara; CM.

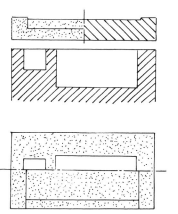

348 Section and plan of a combined sarcophagus/ canopic chest of Ameny-Qemau from his pyramid at Dahshur. The lid, of *per-nu* form and entirely filling the area of the burial chamber, was slid into place from the pyramid's antechamber and locked in place by a sliding portcullis-block.

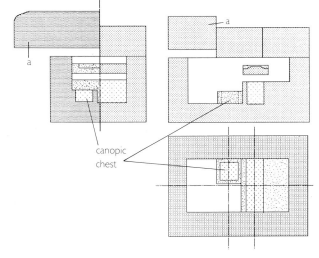

349 Like other sarcophagi of the period, this one follows Sesostris III's example in bearing a panelled lower margin. A removed manoeuvring lug may be seen on the lid, which has the modified *per-nu* form, with a narrow flat band along the edge of the upper surface. From Lahun; CM.

lid was locked into place by a sideways-sliding portcullis slab.

In the somewhat later South Pyramid at Mazghuna, the coffer had been considerably deepened, leaving a void above the coffin- and canopic-cavities, while a conventional lid was replaced by two more massive blocks. One was intended as a fixture, cut away below to give additional headroom for the burial party, the other was supported by a pair of quartzite props, via which the block was lowered by 'sand hydraulics', a technology first introduced to close the burial chamber of Ammenemes III at Hawara.

This design was also used in the pyramid of Khendjer, and then, further enhanced, in the Unfinished Pyramid at South Saqqara. There, the principal burial chamber was carved out of a single block of quartzite, with a *per-nu* sarcophagus and canopic chest within – but carved as one with the chamber.

351 Plan and sections of the quartzite burial chamber of the Thirteenth Dynasty Unfinished Pyramid at southern South Saqqara, with a sarcophagus and canopic chest of conventional form cut as one with the chamber. The room was entered via a movable roof-block (a) and represents one of the great mechanical achievements of the ancient Egyptians, quartzite being the hardest stone worked by an early civilization.

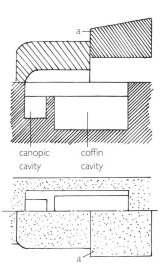

350 Section and plan of a combined quartzite burial chamber/sarcophagus/canopic chest from the South pyramid at Mazghuna. The entrance block (a) was lowered by means of a 'hydraulic' system filled with sand.

canopic cavity   coffin cavity

canopic chest

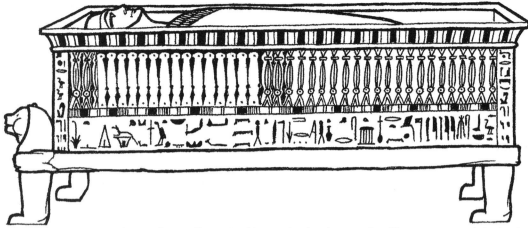

352 A rather unusual housing for a coffin is this funerary bed of Ity, containing his anthropoid coffin. It may represent a particularly Theban practice. Late Twelfth Dynasty, from Sheikh Abd el-Quma; CM TR 19.11.27.4.

Conventional sarcophagi still remained in use: in the pit tomb of King Hor, and the sepulchres of the wives of Khendjer, there were ordinary *per-nu* sarcophagi. The arrangement of King Hor's burial chamber, however, reflected the practice exhibited in the pyramid of Ameny-Qemau, with the coffer and canopic chest sunk into the ground, their rims level with the antechamber floor, from which the lids were slid into place.

THE SECOND INTERMEDIATE PERIOD AND THE NEW KINGDOM

The Seventeenth and Eighteenth Dynasties

The Thirteenth Dynasty royal sarcophagi are the last known stone examples of Middle Kingdom date; indeed, the *genre* seems to disappear for a period of over two cen-

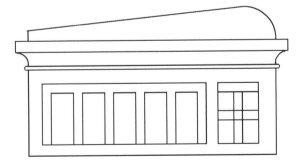

353 The sarcophagus of Queen Mentuhotep, wife of King Djehuty of the early Seventeenth Dynasty. It is the earliest coffin known with the sloping lid of the *per-wer* sanctuary of Upper Egypt. This shape is perpetuated in sarcophagi and canopic chests of the New Kingdom.

turies. However, around the beginning of the Seventeenth Dynasty at Thebes, properly differentiated examples started to appear in wood.

The first of these belonged to Queen Mentuhotep, wife of Djehuty, one of the earliest kings of the new dynasty. Now lost, but seen and sketched by the Egyptologist Wilkinson before 1834, the lower part of the box conformed to usual later Thirteenth Dynasty coffin practice, with an elaborate panel, and six columns of text on the long sides. The upper part, departing from all earlier examples, had the complete set of a cavetto cornice, torus moulding, and sloping lid with rounded front. These features imitate the so-called *per-wer* sanctuary, seen in Mentuhotep II's burial (p. 250). They contrast with the rounded lid-form with raised end-boards derived from the Lower Egyptian *per-nu* shrine.

It can be no coincidence that this sudden appearance of the *Upper* Egyptian sanctuary form in the sarcophagus record corresponds almost exactly with the native monarchy's temporary relegation to the *south* only. From this point onwards, the *per-wer* form became increasingly prominent, the two lid-forms becoming essentially interchangeable towards the end of the Eighteenth Dynasty.

The interior of Queen Mentuhotep's sarcophagus was covered with hand-written hieratic texts, giving perhaps the earliest known collection of Book of the Dead spells. Similar ones are found on a fragment of the box of another member of the early Seventeenth Dynasty royal family, the Prince Herunefer, now in the British Museum.

Virtually nothing is known of sarcophagi, wooden or stone, for most of the later Seventeenth Dynasty, the only exception being a rock-cut coffer that is said to have held the coffin of King Inyotef VI when found by local plunder-

354 Three of the earliest stone sarcophagi of the New Kingdom. On the left is the small box of Hatshepsut, not much larger than a Middle Kingdom wooden coffin and made while she served as Regent. To its right is her ultimate sarcophagus, as king, and on the far right that of Tuthmosis I (see ill. 359). In between the last two is the canopic chest of Hatshepsut; all these objects are of quartzite. From Wadi Siqqat Taqa el-Zeide, KV 20 and KV 38; CM JE 47032, 37678, 38072 and 52344 (l to r).

355 The burial chamber of KV 42, showing the unfinished sarcophagus of Tuthmosis II, undecorated and still bearing lifting-lugs on the lid. It appears to be the earliest of all New Kingdom stone sarcophagi and the proto-type for later examples. In situ in KV 42.

ers in the 1830s. It is assumed that wooden cases were used in some instances, but the evidence suggests that most *rishi* coffins of the period went unsheltered.

A few fragments may derive from the wooden original sarcophagus of Tuthmosis I, but the earliest identifiable Eighteenth Dynasty sarcophagus is a stone one made for Tuthmosis II. Although unfinished, it was lying in his tomb in the Valley of the Kings (KV42). Similar, but more complete, is that made for his widow, Hatshepsut, while she was serving as regent for the young Tuthmosis III. They are made of the same amazingly hard quartzite as the royal sarcophagi of the Thirteenth Dynasty, but, curiously, are closer to the simply designed royal coffins of that dynasty (see Chapter 7) than the often-elaborate stone sarcophagi of the Middle Kingdom. Indeed, they are in all essentials stone replicas of the former, down to the very arrangement of texts. They may be seen as a new starting-point, perhaps connected with the aura surrounding the 'primeval' rectangular coffin that seems to have been provided for Hor and, presumably, other kings. This perhaps

went along with the definitive abandonment at this time of the rectangular coffin in favour of the anthropoid form.

The simplicity of a rectangular box, flat lid and minimal textual adornment was, however, soon subverted. Shortly after becoming her ward's co-regent, Hatshepsut commissioned a new sarcophagus, similar in basic form to her earlier one, but larger, and with a much more elaborate decorative scheme, both inside and out. Whereas the first sarcophagus had merely quoted the speeches of the various protective deities, the second one actually depicted these deities. Also, on the lid was inscribed a great cartouche, the sacred oval enclosure of a royal name.

The royal oval was to become the dominant motif of most later royal sarcophagi. The third sarcophagus made for Hatshepsut, still larger than the second, adopted the

356 The second sarcophagus of Hatshepsut, made on her assumption of royal titles, and replaced by that in the centre of the next figure. It was then partially re-cut for the first reburial of her father, Tuthmosis I. Prominent is the eye-panel, taken over from the Middle Kingdom, but now displaced from its position beside the head of the mummy by the desire for a balanced placement of mortuary deities – from the left, Qebehsenuef, Anubis-Imywet and Hapy. From KV 20; MFA 04.278.

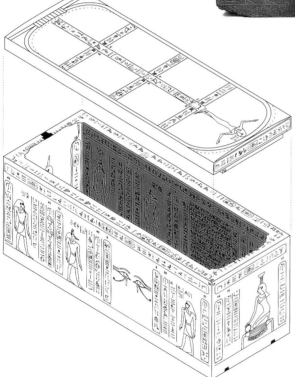

357 The second sarcophagus of Hatshepsut.

358 The painted quartzite sarcophagus of Tuthmosis III, shown lying in the burial chamber of his tomb; the walls of the latter display the characteristic 'imitation papyrus' decorative scheme of the earlier part of the Eighteenth Dynasty, drawn on the walls in pen and ink after the interment had taken place. The sarcophagus, pulled off its broken base-block by plunderers, is of yellow quartzite, painted red and varnished. Generally recognized as the finest of its kind, its decoration was copied a thousand years later in the manufacture of the coffer of Hapymen (see ill. 386). In situ in KV 34.

359 The sarcophagus made for Tuthmosis I by his grandson, Tuthmosis III. In design, it almost exactly follows that of the younger king's. Of cartouche-form, we see the foot-end, bearing the image of Isis. On the long-side, the nearest figure is that of the genius Qebehsenuef. In front of him is Anubis-Khentysehnetjer, with Hapy nearest the head-end, separated from them by the eye-panel which is inherited from Middle Kingdom coffins. From KV 38; CM JE 52344.

360 Detail of the sarcophagus of Tuthmosis IV, the ultimate development of the type initiated by Tuthmosis II and Hatshepsut. Of quartzite, the figures of the goddesses at the head and foot, together with the deities on the sides, are painted in polychrome. In contrast to earlier sarcophagi, all male deities face towards the head of the coffer. In situ in KV 43.

plan of a cartouche. Decoratively, it maintained the pattern established by her previous monument: at the head, both inside and out, knelt Nephthys, her sister, Isis, protecting the foot. Three male deities stood along each side of the trough. Nearest the head were Imseti on the right, Hapy on the left; both faced towards the foot. After a panel on the left-hand side that held the pair of *wadjet* eyes that had been a feature of almost all coffins and some sarcophagi

since time immemorial, the remaining deities faced towards the head end of the case. First came Anubis Khentysehnetjer (right) and Imywet (left), and then Duamutef (right) and Qebehenuef (left). The goddess Nut appeared on the floor of the trough, under the lid, and on a smaller scale on the upper part of the lid. Hatshepsut was thus protected by divinities on all sides on her journey to the Afterworld.

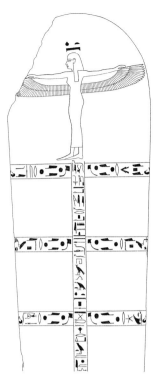

361 Upper part of the sarcophagus lid of Amunhotpe-son-of-Hapu. Stone sarcophagi are very rare in private burials of the New Kingdom, while the form of this particular piece, gently tapering from the shoulders to the ankles, is essentially unique. From Qurnet Murai; Louvre D.4.

The same basic form of sarcophagus and decoration was maintained by all kings down to Amenophis III. The main developments were in the increased size of the sarcophagus and slight rearrangements of the texts and other decorative motifs. Most interesting was the appearance of a pair of *wadjet* eyes on the underside of the lid of Amenophis III: although the body had turned on to its back during the Middle Kingdom, eye panels had remained on the left-hand side of the sarcophagus and coffin trough. At last the supine corpse had been provided with a means to see out directly! The growth in the size of royal sarcophagi was significant. Tuthmosis II's trough had a volume of about 10 cubic metres; that of Tuthmosis IV was no less than 52 cubic metres. The reason for this cannot be attributed to the size of royal coffins, which do not seem to vary appreciably during the dynasty.

In the Old and Middle Kingdoms, stone sarcophagi were to be found in almost all high-status burials. However, their reintroduction during the Eighteenth Dynasty was far more limited. While universal for kings from Tuthmosis II onwards, the use of a rectangular, or quasi-rectangular,

stone outer case seems to have been greatly restricted amongst even the grandees of New Kingdom society. Though some may remain concealed in un-cleared burial chambers on the Sheikh Abd el-Qurna hill at Thebes, extant examples are extremely rare.

The earliest New Kingdom sarcophagus from a private burial is the wholly anomalous one belonging to Senenmut, the close associate of Hatshepsut, who had had it clearly modelled on that of his royal mistress, and of oval plan, aping the royal cartouche. Rather more conventional is that of Nehi, Viceroy of Nubia under Tuthmosis III. Rectangular in shape, its decoration has Isis kneeling at the foot, Nephthys standing at the head, and the standard male deities along the sides.

Both of these monuments belonged to exalted individuals, as did that of Amunhotpe-son-of-Hapu, a major figure of the reign of Amenophis III, and later a god. Like that of Senenmut, its form is anomalous, with a smoothly curved lid-surface, and a plan that displays a rounded head, and a contour that tapers from the shoulders to the flat foot-end. Though the shape is found on Third Intermediate and Late Period sarcophagi, it is otherwise unknown in the New Kingdom. The lid and trough decoration remained purely traditional.

In contrast to the monuments of these great men is a stone sarcophagus from Soleb in the Sudan, dating to the time of Amenophis III. Wabset was a necropolis employee, with a sandstone sarcophagus of the end-boarded-lid (*pernu*) type. The trough sides carried the conventional deities, plus Thoth and another, with one eye on each of the front-left and front-right panels. On the top of the lid, a shallow image of the deceased's face peered out from one end of the flat lid-surface. As with a number of coffins of lowly individuals, this would seem to be a sarcophagus made by its owner, who by using the stone he worked for a living had ignored the niceties of status.

Wooden sarcophagi are known from a number of high-status tombs in the Valley of the Kings and at Deir el-Medina, all belonging to close associates of the king. Their decorative technique was essentially identical to that seen on the associated 'black' coffins. The earliest is that of Maihirpri, a plain rectangular box, with a pitched and end-boarded lid. The usual deities guarded the sides and ends, with eyes on both the coffer and the lid. The coffer had a plain base, with the exception of the cross-battens found on

362 The sarcophagus of Maihirpri (mid Eighteenth Dynasty). Private wooden sarcophagi of the New Kingdom employed the same surface technique as contemporary 'black' coffins. This example is one of the earliest and of very simple design, with a simple rectangular coffer, and *per-nu* lid. The canine-form Anubis and genii may be seen, together with the usual Isis on the foot-end, outlined in gold foil. Eyes were inscribed on the upper surface of the lid, one on each side of the centre-line. From KV 36; CM CG 24001.

363 Black-varnished wooden sarcophagus of Yuya; Isis and Nephthys adorn the head and foot, with Thoth (twice), Imseti, Duamutef and Anubis along the side. All figures and text-bands are gilded. The sarcophagus, although fitted with runners, was assembled around the coffins when actually in the tomb. Reign of Amenophis III, from KV 46; CM CG 51001 = JE 95226.

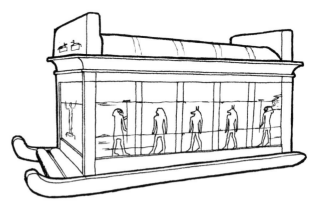

most such boxes. The somewhat later sarcophagi of Yuya and Tjuiu, however, had bases in the form of sledges. In Tjuiu's case, battens below showed it to have been purely ornamental; in Yuya's, there was no floor to the coffer, the contained coffins resting on the ground. It is clear that these sarcophagi were assembled and black-varnished inside the tomb, the varnish sometimes clumsily smeared on the previously applied gilded decoration. They also differed from Maihirpri's monument in that coffers were topped with the classic Egyptian motif of a cavetto cornice and torus moulding.

Yuya's lid-shape was similar to that of Maihirpri, but Tjuiu's sarcophagus had the sloping lid of the *per-wer*, with the cornice and torus moulding assembled as part of the lid. This arrangement was also found on the stone sarcophagus of King Akhenaten, found in fragments in his tomb at Amarna (ill. 366A). The overall form of the latter abandoned the cartouche-shape of his royal predecessors', adopting a design closer to the rectangular private form. Its decoration was far divorced from the usual assemblage of

364 The sarcophagus of Tjuiu, constructionally very much like that of Yuya, but with the artificiality of the runners made explicit by the cross-pieces under each end. Apart from less textual area and differently arranged deities, the most striking difference is the *per-wer* lid replacing the old-style *per-nu* of Yuya. Note that the cornice of the sarcophagus forms part of the lid, as it does in Eighteenth Dynasty canopic chests. Reign of Amenophis III, from KV 46; CM CG 51005.

365 Not only human beings possessed sarcophagi; this limestone example belonged to the pet cat of Crown Prince Djhutmose, heir of Amenophis III. From Memphis; CM CG 5003.

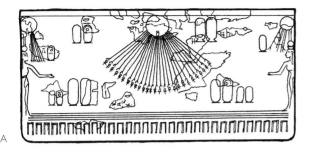

A

B

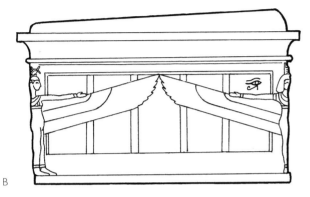

C

D

366 The sarcophagi of the kings of the late Eighteenth Dynasty.

A The granite coffer of Akhenaten, restored on the basis of fragments. The decoration is dominated by Aten's sun-disc; at the corners stands Queen Nefertiti, with her own depiction of the sun-disc. The sarcophagus was being carved in Year 9 of the king's reign, when the writing of the god's name was changed: the old version appears on one of the long sides. The cornice of the sarcophagus was incorporated into the totally-wrecked lid, following wooden precedents. From Amarna TA 26; CM TR 3.3.70.1.

B The sarcophagus of Tutankhamun. Made of quartzite, with a granite lid, it has the goddesses Isis, Nephthys, Neith and Selqet at the corners. They were originally carved without wings, which were added to the arms during an extensive re-carving of the piece, probably after the king's name-change from Tutankhaten to -amun. The cornice has now been transferred to the coffer, far more practically in a stone context. In situ in KV 62.

C The granite sarcophagus of Ay. The coffer was badly broken by a treasure-hunter in the nineteenth century, but has been restored. The winged sun-disc is a unique feature for a royal sarcophagus. The goddesses' figures are carved on the sides of the sarcophagus, rather than bent around the corners, as was the case on the two earlier boxes. The lid is of the rare simple arched form, otherwise seen mainly in the Middle Kingdom (e.g. ill. 345). In situ in Valley of the Kings WV 23, after a period as CM JE 72131.

D The sarcophagus of Horemheb, like that of Ay made of granite. Compared to the latter, it reverts to the pre-Amarna practice of showing the genii and two forms of Anubis on the sides of the coffer, as well as resurrecting the *per-nu* lid. In situ in KV 57.

gods and goddesses: the sides were dominated by the many-armed sun-disc of his god, the Aten, while the deities' tutelary role was taken by Akhenaten's wife, Nefertiti. Her image is found at each corner, her arms enfolding the coffer. This motif seems to have been borrowed from royal canopic chests, where the usual four mortuary goddesses take the same pose. Akhenaten's sarcophagus form was retained by three of his orthodox successors who, however, substituted the four traditional deities for the queen.

The first of these succeeding royal sarcophagi was made for Tutankhamun; initially the goddesses were shown bare-armed, but later acquired wings. The quartzite coffer was topped with a *per-wer*-shaped lid, whose cornice and moulding had now been incorporated into the coffer itself, probably for technical reasons. The lid was of granite, a material used for the sarcophagi of Amenophis III and Akhenaten and many later ones, but not for any other royal pieces of the early Eighteenth Dynasty.

367 Miniature sarcophagus of Re, of the late Eighteenth Dynasty, decorated in the same manner as full-size examples. This limestone box contained a small black figure of a mummy, lying on a bed, its *ba* at its side. CM Ex 3382.

The remaining two sarcophagi of this 'corner-goddess' type (those belonging to Ay and Horemheb) incorporated further changes, the goddesses having their wings angled downwards; for Horemheb the genii and Anubis-forms were resurrected on the sides. Curiously, the two sarcophagi displayed different lid-forms, that of Ay having a simple arched shape, as occasionally found in the Middle Kingdom, and Horemheb the old *per-nu* pattern.

Much as miniature coffins were used to hold *shabti* figures from the middle of the Eighteenth Dynasty, small replicas of sarcophagi have also been discovered, usually holding an image showing the mummy on a bier. They are found in both royal and private contexts.

The Nineteenth Dynasty

The transition between the Eighteenth and Nineteenth Dynasties marked the same kind of changes in sarcophagus design as we have already seen in coffins, and will later see in canopics. Private wooden examples continued the sledged, *per-wer*, shape seen with the sarcophagus of Tjuiu, but with a totally different surface decoration. Like contemporary coffins, a yellow background and sealing varnish were prominent. In place of the simple figures of single goddesses at the head and foot and the male deities on the sides, a combination of motifs appeared, together with extensive texts, along the trough sides. These included funeral scenes and those of adoration, as well as sets of deities. Two goddesses were depicted at each end, Isis and Nephthys at the head, Neith and Selqet at the foot.

While stone rectangular cases still seemed to be the preserve of royalty, occasional private ones are known, for example the limestone coffer of Menena, found in the provincial cemetery of Sedment.

The granite sarcophagus of Amunhotpe-Huy was a curious specimen. It dates to the reign of Ramesses II and is most unusually found in a re-used context at Memphis. The lid is most unusually deeper than the coffer, with the usual coffer-side decoration moved up to the side of the lid; the coffer merely bears a single row of text.

At the beginning of the Nineteenth Dynasty, royal practice abandoned the 'corner-goddess' type of sarcophagus in favour of the old cartouche form, with a gently curved lid. Such a monument, albeit unfinished, was found in the burial chamber of Ramesses I in the Valley of the Kings. Strangely, no stone sarcophagus, or trace of one, is known from the succeeding tombs of Sethos I and Ramesses II. In neither case can such a sarcophagus not have been ready for the burial. However Sethos I (and probably Ramesses II as well) possessed a new type of stone outer coffin (see p. 226). Perhaps in the belief that only one stone covering was required, the rectangular or quasi-rectangular outermost covering was supplied in wood. Given the weight of the coffin inside, this would probably have been the bottomless type seen in the burial of Yuya.

Although the king at this point seemingly rejected the stone sarcophagus (or perhaps as a result of it having been given up by the pharaoh), a number of his family possessed such monuments. The lids survive of those of two of Ramesses II's consorts, Nefertari and Meryetamun. They were of simple form, with slightly raised end-pieces and a shallow-vaulted upper surface. Their lost coffers would have been rectangular, as was that of the ultimate Crown Prince, Merenptah. Uniquely, Merenptah's sarcophagus adopted the panelled lower part that had been popular in the late Twelfth Dynasty: this was almost certainly an instance of conscious archaism. Likewise the friezes on the interior recalled the object friezes of Middle Kingdom coffins, various items of regalia being shown inside. However, the divine figures who formed the remainder of the decoration were of New Kingdom type.

The probable reversion to wood for the sarcophagi of Sethos I and Ramesses II was ostentatiously dropped in the

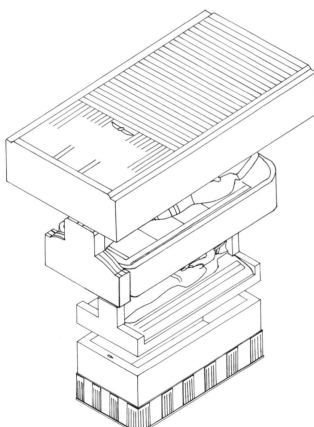

368 (top) The inner sarcophagus of Merenptah. The coffer, made for him as a prince and still bearing traces of his titles as such, carries Middle Kingdom-style panelling, but also various beings from the chapters 144 and 147 of the Book of the Dead. One end of the coffer is cut at an oblique angle to the rest of the box; the reason for this is obscure. The lid has a three-dimensional figure of the goddess Nut underneath, a feature also found under the middle lid and the slightly later example of Sethos II. From Tanis NRT III; CM JE 87297.

369 (left) The nested sarcophagi of Merenptah. The innermost was removed for use in the burial of Psusennes I at Tanis, necessitating the destruction of the coffers of the outer two sarcophagi. The lids, and some fragments, of the latter remain in the Valley of the Kings KV 8.

370 (above) Detail of part of the decoration of the inner coffer of Merenptah, showing the clearly-secondary cartouches of Psusennes I.

371, 372 The coffer and lid of the sarcophagus of Ramesses III. The design of its decoration, its dimensions, and the form of the figure on its lid, suggest that it was made soon after the sarcophagi of Merenptah, and may thus be in origin the intended outer sarcophagus of Sethos II. From KV 11: Louvre Museum D.1; Fitzwilliam Museum E.1.1823.

actual burial of Merenptah, by now king. To the core of his princely coffer he added a new lid, and two further complete sarcophagi. The first of these was of the cartouche form revived by Ramesses I, but with a wholly different decoration replacing the simple texts and figures of the principal mortuary deities with extensive inscriptions and vignettes from the Book of Gates, one of the 'Books of the Underworld' found in royal tombs of the period. This had been adopted for the earlier coffin of Sethos I – the first time the text had appeared on a coffin – and was also employed on Merenptah's calcite outer coffin.

The lids of both these inner sarcophagi introduced the motif of the recumbent figure of the dead king carved in the round upon the upper surface. Perhaps influenced by the contemporary vogue for stone anthropoid coffins, this concept was to be widespread among royal sarcophagi for half a century. The outermost sarcophagus, on the other hand, was of huge dimensions and plain rectangular form, with the simple type lid seen on the monuments of Ramesses II's wives. The decoration, as on the middle sarcophagus, included parts of the 'Books of the Underworld'. The lid of the inner sarcophagus had a rounded surface, with raised end-pieces and also a recumbent mummiform figure. Nut kneels in protection at its head, and appeared

again underneath the lid, carved in the round, stretching out her body above the mummy.

The nest of sarcophagi rested on a calcite base; such supports are known since the earlier Eighteenth Dynasty, but while those were plain, Merenptah's had the outline of a bier carved on its side, recalling the coffins of Tutankhamun which were supported by just such a lion-footed bed within his sarcophagus.

Sethos II clearly intended to have a similar nest of sarcophagi. However, his reign seems to have been interrupted by the usurpation of his son(?) Amenmesse, and his tomb and equipment were unfinished at his death. Only the lid of the innermost sarcophagus is present in the tomb, and closely resembles that made for Merenptah. The king is represented wearing the divine 'tripartite' wig (in contrast to the *nemes* on Merenptah's middle lid and most royal coffins), while on the underside there is again a three-dimensional figure of the sky-goddess Nut. Stretched out across the roof of the burial cavity she is depicted in the pose in which she spanned the heavens, and nose-to-nose with the coffin which lay within.

It is possible that an outer sarcophagus was begun for Sethos II but only partly completed at his death, and then finally used some forty years later for the burial of Ramesses

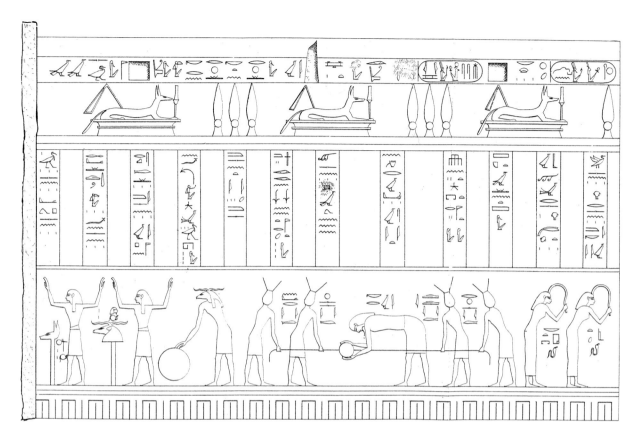

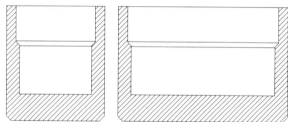

373 The sarcophagus of Ramesses IV, in situ in KV 2.

374 Sections through the coffer of Ramesses IV, showing the coffin-receptacle within. This contained an alabaster coffin, now almost totally destroyed.

III. In the interim, a pair of sarcophagi had been made for Siptah and Tawosret (the latter usurped by Sethnakhte), both of similar design, featuring on the exterior a frieze of Anubis-jackals and *khekher* decorative motifs, together with extracts from the somewhat unusual Book of the Earth. Cartouche-form, their lids differed from earlier examples, placing the *atef* crown above the kings' heads and flanking them with shallow-cut images of Isis and Nephthys.

With the exception of that occupied by Ramesses III, whose dimensions suggest earlier inception, royal sarcophagi from Siptah to Ramesses VI continually increased in size, in particular in height, the latest examples having coffers whose rims stood over 2 metres above the floor of

the burial chamber. None showed indications of having contained, or been contained in, additional sarcophagi: those of Merenptah remained unique in that respect, but, as we have seen in the previous chapter, all held stone outer coffins, whose size also increased with time. The coffer of Ramesses IV perhaps contained the last manifestation of the inner sarcophagus, in that the lower part of the coffer had restricted internal dimensions, reminiscent of the evolution of the 'built-in sarcophagi' of the Thirteenth Dynasty. This would have contained his coffins.

In contrast to an almost complete set of known royal sarcophagi, private ones remain an enigma. Examples from the reign of Merenptah show that the pattern seen earlier in the dynasty was maintained up until then, but after this things are largely blank. A fragmentary granite sarcophagus

375 The sarcophagus-cover of Ramesses VII, in situ in KV 1.

of Prince Khaemwaset, son of Ramesses III, bears a recumbent figure on its lid. In his case, the figure lies on a flat base; in others, such as that made for Tawosret while Regent, it lies on the curved surface of a quasi-anthropoid shaped container. These pieces could arguably be regarded as coffins (cf. above, p. 228), but since the concept of the recumbent figure is based on the royal sarcophagi of the time, they may perhaps be considered as such. Another similar example is that of Prince Montjuhirkopshef, discovered by Altenmüller in KV 13, Valley of the Kings, in 1994.

These pieces are, of course, somewhat special in that they belong to royalty, many aspects of whose interments differed from those of ordinary private individuals. Such dignitaries' stone coffins certainly lacked the shelter of a stone sarcophagus, although they may have had wooden outer coverings, destroyed in plundering: there are no intact higher-status burials datable to the later Ramesside Period.

By late in the Twentieth Dynasty the entire sarcophagus genre had probably gone out of use for private interments, since when intact burials reappear in the record, early in the Twenty-first Dynasty, none have a sarcophagus. This may reflect kingly usage, for after Ramesses VI's death conventional sarcophagi are no longer known from the Valley of the Kings.

In Ramesses VII's tomb we find a rather curious arrangement: a cutting in the bedrock to receive the king's coffins, covered by a deep lid. The decoration of this departed completely from the 'Underworld' schemes seen in earlier reigns. The prominence of the four tutelary goddesses, each in winged form near the ends of the long sides, their wings protecting representations of the funerary genii, is a concept reminiscent of the late Eighteenth Dynasty.

After Ramesses VII, with one exception, the royal tombs of the New Kingdom are lost, blocked or unfinished. The exception, that of Ramesses IX, had a cutting in the floor of the burial chamber, but its area far exceeded the dimensions of even the gigantic outer sarcophagus lid of Merenptah: a lid to cover the cutting would have been the most gargantuan known, but no trace of it has ever come to light.

THE THIRD INTERMEDIATE PERIOD

By the beginning of the Twenty-first Dynasty, private individuals had abandoned sarcophagi; the large number of known burials from Thebes contained only simple nests of coffins. The closest thing to a sarcophagus that has been found is the leather funerary tent of Isetemkheb D, wife of the High Priest Pinudjem II. Sarcophagi were found, however, in the royal burials at the new capital, Tanis, where most, if not all, comprised usurped material, in some cases millennia old.

The earliest of these usurpations is by Psusennes I, who took over the inner sarcophagus of Merenptah, removing it from the Valley of the Kings, and largely demolished the associated outer coffers in the process. Their thick bottoms were probably used as building material. It would be interesting to know whether the initial assault on the sarcophagi of Merenptah was prompted by a desire to extract the inner case for re-use, or whether the notion of its salvage arose only while demolition was underway.

Psusennes' successor, Amenemopet, installed a fine quartzite sarcophagus in his small tomb (ill. 356). Clearly a usurped Middle Kingdom piece, to which new texts had been added, it was of a somewhat archaic design with

376 The quartzite sarcophagus prepared for Amenemope. The coffer had been made in the earlier part of the Twelfth Dynasty, and has the wood-imitating cross-beams seen on other sarcophagi of that period. The lid, of granite, was manufactured from an inscribed Old Kingdom slab. From NRT IV; displayed at Tanis (EAO-1, 2).

(wooden) cross batons represented underneath. Though made to fit the coffer, the lid too had ancient connections: it was cut from an Old Kingdom sculptured granite block, a large recumbent jackal dominating the surface, together with elements of an offering formula belonging to one Djededka.

Yet more sarcophagi deriving from antique sources have been found in the Twenty-second Dynasty royal tombs at Tanis. Four lay within the tomb now numbered as NRT I, probably first constructed by Smendes of the Twenty-first Dynasty, but rebuilt by Osorkon II. It provided a burial chamber for Takelot I, laid to rest in a gold coffin, sheltered by a fine late-Twelfth Dynasty sarcophagus, which had once belonged to one Ameny. With its panelled lower section, it represents the original of the design perpetuated in the coffer within the Merenptah/Psusennes I sarcophagus found in the adjacent tomb.

Osorkon II himself was buried in a gigantic granite sarcophagus within his granite-lined burial chamber. It was rounded at the head end, and while the coffer shows no indication of any earlier use, the lid, with its upper surface

377 The sarcophagus lid of Prince Harnakhte, son of Osorkon II. Like a number of royal sarcophagi of the period, it has a fairly low-cut recumbent figure of the deceased upon its upper surface, with protective figures of Isis, Nephthys, Anubis-Imywet and Anubis-Khentysehnetjer. From NRT I; displayed at Tanis.

adorned by a mummiform figure in very low relief, was carved from what had once been a group statue of the Ramesside Period.

A similarly shaped, but much smaller, coffer had been cut out of an architrave of Ramesses II for Osorkon's son Harnakhte. The lid had been made originally for another individual of the Twenty-second Dynasty, but had the same plan. The figure on the top had its wig-margins corresponding to the edge of the coffer, as on an anthropoid coffin, but the remainder of the body was lying as on a flat lid, corresponding to some of the princely containers of the Twentieth Dynasty.

The round-headed sarcophagus plan was maintained for the remaining known kingly examples from the Third Intermediate Period, the very low relief recumbent figure also being found on that of Shoshenq III from tomb NRT V. Many of the coffers were of considerable size, that of Shoshenq V (from NRT I) being 3.5 metres long, a metre longer than that of the slightly earlier sarcophagus of Shoshenq IV (from NRT V).

Outside the Tanite royal necropolis, Third Intermediate Period stone sarcophagi are scarce, Theban private tombs

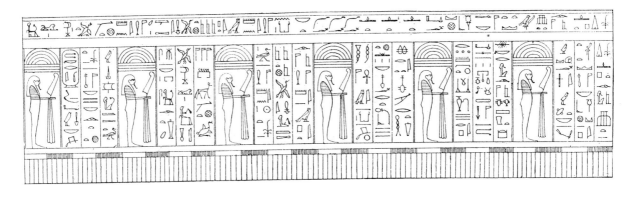

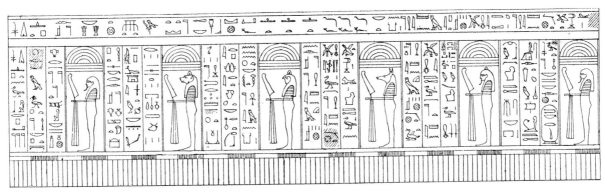

378 Detail of the side-decoration of the sarcophagus of Pamiu, a Priest of Montju, and grandson of King Takelot III. The scheme is dominated by a series of deities inside shrines, the texts by offering formulae with the owner's genealogy. Late Twenty-third Dynasty, from Deir el-Bahari; CM CG 41036.

379 The sarcophagus of Shoshenq III, carved from a Thirteenth Dynasty granite lintel. Its lid, carved from a Ramesside sculpture, bore the king's recumbent image in very low relief. In situ at Tanis in NRT V.

having none. Wooden examples reappear sporadically around the time of Osorkon I, and by the latter part of the period many are known. They are rectangular cases of *per-nu* form, with arched tops, no end-boards, but instead posts at the corners. Similar containers had been used back in the Eighteenth/Nineteenth Dynasties for the burials of Apis bulls. Usually, they were extensively decorated with texts and vignettes, with later examples having three-dimensional figures of hawks perched atop their corner posts and their lids, together with a recumbent jackal. This basic form lasted into Roman times (ill. 394), although the latest examples had most of the structure incorporated into the lid, the 'coffer' being reduced to no more than a simple base-board. In this they followed certain Saite examples.

380 In the Sudan, normal practice was for the coffin to be placed on a bed or a bench, without a sarcophagus. Exceptions were the sarcophagi of two kings contemporary with the Twenty-sixth Dynasty. That of Aspleta broadly follows contemporary wooden practice. c. 593-68 BC, from Nuri Nu.8; MFA 23.729 (Model).

An exception to normal Egyptian practice is evident in the pyramids of the Kushite kings who made up the Twenty-fifth Dynasty. Their burial chambers were each centred on a raised bench, at the corners of which were cuttings to receive the legs of beds that rested on them. Bed burials had long been customary in Nubia, the adoption of the bench being intended to allow the bedsteads to support the weight of the very large coffins that came into use at this time. After the Kushite departure from Egypt, two kings, Anlemani and Aspelta, had large sarcophagi of broadly contemporary Egyptian design made, but their successors reverted to coffin benches. Late examples of these became elaborately decorated.

THE SAITE AND LATE PERIODS

Stone sarcophagi were revived in the Twenty-sixth Dynasty, normally of the round-headed type, except for purely rectangular ones found in certain types of tomb. They now had a definite tapering towards the feet, and a high lid in which curves had been largely replaced by bevelling. Usually extensively decorated, some examples had figures of their owners carved on the top of the lid. A good example is that of the God's Wife Ankhnesneferibre, on which she is shown in two dimensions. A full three-dimensional recumbent figure, a form clearly modelled on late New Kingdom royal examples, was on the lid of another God's Wife,

381 A simpler box, recalling those of the New Kingdom, but much shallower is exemplified by this wooden sarcophagus of Nesmin. *Tjet* and *djed* amulets adorn it, along with a cavetto cornice. Late Period, from Akhmim; Copenhagen Nat. 3890.

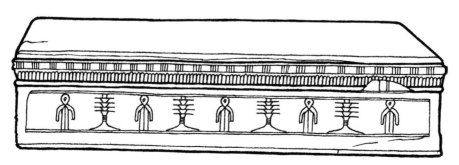

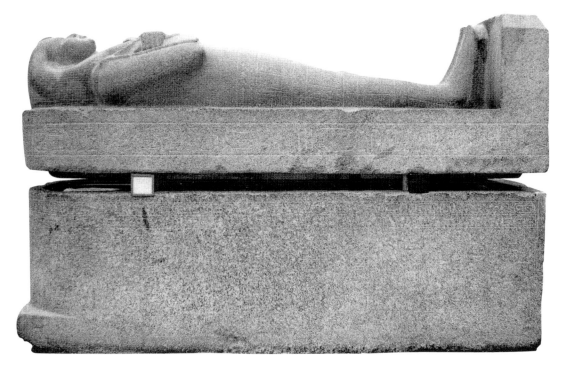

382 Archaism is a feature of many monuments of the Saite Period, and this may be manifested in the sarcophagus here of the God's Wife of Amun, Nitokris. In showing the lady's recumbent body upon the flat lid, it recalls the sarcophagi of the middle Ramesside pharaohs, while the stylized indication of the front of a sledge suggests the occurrences of this feature on New Kingdom coffins and sarcophagi. Originally from Medinet Habu, reused in Deir el-Medina 2005; CM TR 6.2.21.1.

Nitokris. An even more explicit item of Late Period copying is the sarcophagus of the official, Hapymen (ill. 386). Although its shape and the carved figures were contemporary in style, the texts and arrangement of the exterior followed those of the ancient sarcophagus of Tuthmosis III (ill. 358) so closely that direct copying is certain.

Just as in the New Kingdom there was some overlap between anthropoid coffins and sarcophagi with depictions of the owner, so in the Late Period some sarcophagus lids had a face grafted on to them. No trace of body or hands were visible, and the exterior of the coffer was not adjusted to the human shape. But some rectangular coffers had their

383 The sarcophagus of Ankhnesneferibre: the lid bears a raised two-dimensional depiction of the lady. It bears extensive texts, as does the coffer, including its anthropoid interior. Originally from Medinet Habu, usurped by Pimontju in the Ptolemaic Period: Deir el-Medina tomb 2003; BM EA 32.

interiors cut in an anthropoid shape: in certain cases these were only large enough to hold a light inner coffin. In others, there was provision for a large stone container. Some such coffers were very large, completely filling their burial chambers. In them, coffin cuts appear remarkably small against the solid mass of the sarcophagus itself (e.g. ill. 385).

Amongst the large hardstone sarcophagi produced in the Late Period three kingly ones survive, as well as those of a number of queens. The remains of the tomb of Nepherites I with his plain round-headed sarcophagus were found at Tell el-Ruba, fragments of that of Nektanebo I in Cairene buildings; and that of the last pharaoh, Nektanebo II, was found re-used in Alexandria. Their decorations followed New Kingdom practice, respectively of the Eighteenth Dynasty and the Ramesside Period. Certain sarcophagi of queens followed the latter model (ill. 388).

385 During the Late Period, some sarcophagi grew to massive dimensions, with a relatively tiny mummiform cutting to receive the coffin. This limestone example belonged to one Pawenhatef, and came from Batn el-Baqara (Fustat); CM JE 67764.

386 By general consent, the finest of all Eighteenth Dynasty royal sarcophagi (and perhaps of all sarcophagi) is that of Tuthmosis III (ill. 358). That this verdict was shared in antiquity is indicated by the fact that a Late Period official, Hapymen, had its decorative scheme copied in the sarcophagus shown here, although with its figures carved in contemporary style. From Mosque of Ibn Tulun, Cairo; BM EA 23.

387 The sarcophagus-lid of Ptahhotpe, who lived under Darius I. Although bearing a human face, the sarcophagus is not truly anthropoid, and bears Chapter 72 of the Book of the Dead. From 'Campbell's Tomb' at Giza (LG84); Ashmolean Museum 1947.295.

388 One side of the broken sarcophagus of Udjashu, possibly mother of Nektanebo II. Recovered at Masara, its decoration recalls that of the late New Kingdom. For example, the upper frieze follows the sarcophagi of Siptah, Sethnakhte and Ramesses IV, the figures on the lower part also recalling those on these monuments. A similar following of New Kingdom practice may be seen on the fragments of the nearly-contemporary coffer of Nektanebo I; CM JE 40645 = CG 29317.

389 The sarcophagus of Nektanebo II, the last to be made for a native pharaoh. Decorated with the Book of Gates, like many Ramesside pieces, it was never used for a burial, and ended up in use as a ritual bath in a mosque. From Alexandria; BM EA 10.

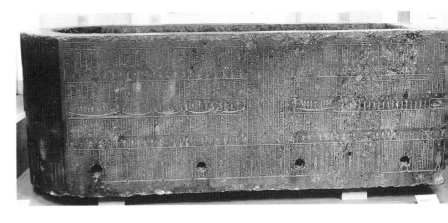

390 A rough limestone sarcophagus, with anthropoid interior, of the Ptolemaic Period at Abydos, containing a coffinless mummy.

391 Typical of Late Period-early Ptolemaic sarcophagi is this basalt example. It is covered with vignettes from the Books of the Underworld; CM.

During the Ptolemaic Period, hardstone sarcophagi continued, but with diminishing quality as the epoch continued,
before disappearing from use well before the Roman take-
over. Also, at many sites crude limestone, tapered, cases
were used as the sole shelter for masked mummies.

We have already noted that the wooden arched-roofed
sarcophagi of the late Third Intermediate Period continued
into Roman times; where a definite coffer continued to be
used, traditional scenes appeared on the sides, although in
the debased art style of the post-pharaonic era. In other
cases, the lower part of the container was simply a board,
over which a highly-arched lid was attached.

At least some sarcophagi were shrines in use as well as
form, according to evidence that mummies remained for
some time accessible to the living before consignment to
the necropolis. A further variant is seen in the wood-
columned 'pavilion' that sheltered the body of Montjuemsaf
in his usurped tomb on Sheikh Abd el-Qurna. This illustrates the variety of approaches current at the beginning of
the Roman Period.

393 (*below*) Painted wooden funerary canopy, closely modelled on a
funerary bed. Isis and Nephthys occupy their customary positions at the
foot and head of the corpse. Ptolemaic Period, from Akhmim; CM
Ex.3263.

392 Another type of rough sarcophagus, this time round-headed, with an
interior that matches the outside contour. Ptolemaic Period, from Beni
Hasan; present location unknown.

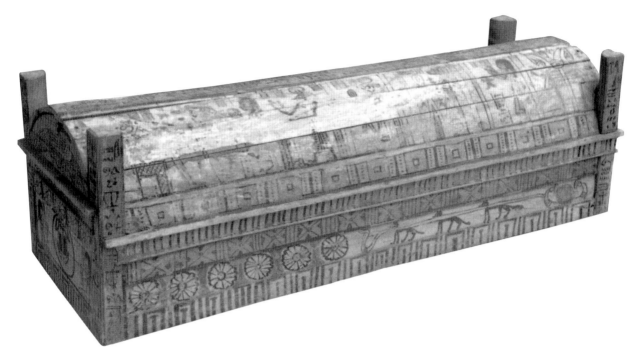

394 The sarcophagus of Tahefat (Tphous), a seven-year-old girl. It has a cavetto cornice, the arched part carrying scenes of the deceased and the gods, with the sun-disc in its boat, here pulled by three jackals, being now found on one side. AD 127, from Sheikh Abd el-Qurna; BM EA 6708.

Stone sarcophagi of Egyptian style seem to have died out by the early years of Roman rule. On the other hand, fully Classical sarcophagi have been found in Alexandria and other hellenized towns; of these, only the stone was Egyptian. In addition to free-standing examples, built-in pieces have been discovered in such sepulchres as the Alexandrine catacombs, sometimes surrounded by ancient Egyptian motifs, painted in a wholly un-Egyptian style.

Conclusion

As with other Egyptian mortuary containers, the development of sarcophagi began with a basically functional form, ritual elements only seen in the choice of lid style. With

395 The interior of another sarcophagus' lid from the same tomb, looking towards the head-end. As is the case on lids going back beyond the New Kingdom, the goddess Nut stretches out above the deceased, in this case the 11-year-old Kleopatra Kandake; her mummy is shown in ill. 231. BM EA 6706.

time, however, additional decorative components were added, and a clear distinction appeared between royal and private monuments, reaching its height with the recumbent-figure examples of the Ramesside Period. It is interesting to note that the last Egyptian-style sarcophagi, the wooden Roman pieces, although heavily decorated, conformed overall to the primeval *per-nu* form.

396 This outer case for a mummy is typical of the Roman Period. It shows how the mummy could be kept in the house in its own shrine, although the mummy-cartonnage here is actually considerably earlier than its shelter, being reminiscent of the Third Intermediate Period, but of Ptolemaic date. If the mummy wished to 'participate' in family life, or receive offerings, the doors would be opened; otherwise it could remain behind closed doors. Berlin 17039/40.

397 An Alexandrine sarcophagus of the late Roman Period, a wholly Classical piece that has nothing to do with Egyptian funerary traditions. Graeco-Roman Museum 25781.

398 Gable-roofed wooden sarcophagus; the end of its lid displays wholly Classical motifs. Roman Period, from Saqqara (Serapeum); CM JE 33101.

Chapter 9

Canopic Equipment

The internal organs removed during the embalming process were usually desiccated, wrapped and placed in close proximity to the body. For most of Egyptian history, they occupied receptacle(s) near its foot, although in certain later periods they were either returned to the body cavity, or placed within the outer envelope of the mummy. These receptacles normally took the form of a cubic chest and/or a set of jars, although on occasion miniature coffins were employed in lieu of the jars. All such items will be referred to as 'Canopic equipment'.

This term actually derives from a mistake by early Egyptologists. Most canopic jars had stoppers in the shape of a human or divine head; by early Roman times, the concept of the human-headed jar was current in a wholly different context. At Abu Kir was worshipped Kanopos, helmsman of Menelaeos, as a form of Osiris. His sacred image was a rotund jar, filled with Nile water, a remembrance of which passed into Arabic literature in the story of El-Zir ('The Jar').

It was from Classical writers' references to Kanopos and his jar that early *savants* made a connection between it and the first visceral jars that were noticed during the

Renaissance. In spite of the subsequent realization that this connection was wholly false, the name has stuck, being further extended to cover all kinds of visceral equipment, allowing us to refer not just to 'canopic' jars, but to chests, coffinettes and even masks.

Summary of the Development of Canopic Equipment

Stone, or rock-cut, canopic chests appeared at the beginning of the Fourth Dynasty, joined by flat-lidded jars at the end of it. Wooden chests may have been in use earlier, but the first surviving examples are of late Old Kingdom date. Such chests might have contained jars, but equally might merely have held the wrapped bundles of viscera.

The first examples of linking the organs with the specific protective deities occurred during the First Intermediate Period. Also, human-headed lids appeared, either as stoppers for jars, or as masks over anthropoid-wrapped visceral bundles. From then onwards, canopic chest design broadly followed that of contemporary coffins and/or sarcophagi.

Standardized texts become normal on canopic jars of the New Kingdom, during which time there was a gradual switch from human-headed stoppers to those depicting the faunal forms of the Four Sons of Horus; this was completed by the Ramesside Period. While private canopic chests continued to be modelled on sarcophagi, special forms developed for kings, featuring goddess's figures at the

399 (*above*) From the middle of the New Kingdom onwards, canopic jars each bore the head of its protective genius, from the left the ape of Hapy, the dog of Duamutef, the human of Imseti and the hawk of Qebehsenuef. Twenty-first Dynasty, from the burial of Nesikhonsu in TT 320; BM EA 59197–200.

corners, with integral jars, and the actual organs placed in miniature coffins. This latter practice was imitated by some private individuals of the Ramesside Period.

During the Twenty-first Dynasty, the internal organs were returned to the body cavity, although some high-status individuals continued to include empty or dummy jars or chests in their funerary assemblage. In the Twenty-sixth Dynasty, some viscera were once again placed in jars, but during the Late Period, and subsequently, the visceral bundles were placed between the legs.

In the Ptolemaic Period, a series of small, tall, canopic chests made their appearance, topped by a figure of a hawk. Some may have contained actual viscera, while others followed the Third Intermediate Period practice by being dummies. A few actual jars also occurred in the Ptolemaic Period, but all canopic items seem to have fallen out of use before the Roman Period.

THE OLD KINGDOM

The earliest occurrence of the preservation of the viscera after their removal from the body remains uncertain. Nothing of definitely canopic nature is known from the tombs of the Archaic Period, nor from the royal pyramid complexes of the Third Dynasty. Unfounded suggestions have frequently been made that the so-called 'South Tomb' at the Step Pyramid might have been intended for the king's viscera. The 'South Tomb' has under it a smaller-scale replica of the substructure of the pyramid itself. The burial chamber, too small to contain a body, has been postulated as the burial place of the king's internal organs. However, the tomb is clearly the prototype of the 'subsidiary pyramids' that accompany nearly all later pyramidal royal tombs: none of these 'subsidiary pyramids' had a canopic purpose.

The earliest tombs to contain elements that can be explained as being intended to contain the viscera were from the beginning of the Fourth Dynasty. Several tombs at Meidum dating to Seneferu's reign contained a series of niches, high up in the wall, whose size and position relative to the body closely corresponded to later indubitably canopic installations.

The first actual examples of mummified viscera also date to this period. They were found in the oldest of the known

400 A second century canopus, a form of Osiris derived from the worship of Kanopos, helmsman of Menelaeos, at Abu Kir. From the Sanctuary of Isis at Ras el-Soda; Alexandria Museum.

canopic chests, in the mysterious burial chamber of Queen Hetepheres, wife of Seneferu, at Giza (G7000X). For an undetermined reason, the body was missing from the sarcophagus. However, the canopic chest, carved from a translucent block of calcite, was found sealed inside a niche at the south end of the west wall of the burial chamber. The chest was divided into four square compartments, each of which contained a mass which almost certainly were the remains of the internal organs. The lid was held in position by a cord passed round the box and secured by a seal.

During the Fourth Dynasty, it became firmly established that the canopic receptacle(s) were placed at the south (foot) end of the corpse, usually slightly offset to the south-east. As may be seen in numerous tombs at Giza, these were normally cubical niches in the chamber wall, or cuttings in the floor, closed by limestone slabs. Nothing is

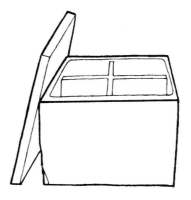

401 The earliest known canopic chest, that of Hetepheres. From Giza G7000X; CM JE 52452.

402 Simple early canopic jar, with a domed lid. From Giza, Leipzig 2362.

very simple in overall form, corresponding to contemporary coffins, although the paucity of surviving examples makes it difficult to conclude much about their variety. In only some cases were canopic jars used; in many others, bundles of wrapped viscera were simply laid in the four quadrants of the canopic chest.

THE MIDDLE KINGDOM

It is from the late First Intermediate Period or the early part of the Middle Kingdom that a concentration of material has first survived to demonstrate the full range of developments that had followed on from this early simplicity. Most importantly, canopic jars started to gain human-headed lids, in place of the former flat or domed specimens. In parallel, jarless canopic bundles were sometimes adorned with cartonnage masks, again with human faces. In both cases, the faces probably represented the dead person, although this would change.

Previously, inscriptions had been restricted to the name and titles of the owner; now, a particular deity associated with the contained viscera was sometimes invoked. The deities were the Four Sons of Horus: the liver was under the protection of Imseti, the lungs under Hapy, with the stomach and intestines the respective responsibilities of Duamutef and Qebehsenuef. Later in Egyptian history they would display respectively human, ape, dog and falcon heads, but at this point they were either uniformly falcon-headed, or uniformly human-headed. The use of human heads became standard for canopic jars from the First Intermediate Period into the New Kingdom, thus allowing an easy transition from a conception of masks and stoppers representing the deceased to their representing the genii. Each genius was under the protection of one of four principal mortuary goddesses, usually in turn Isis, Nephthys, Neith and Selqet. Although these divine ladies appeared in the vast majority of canopic contexts with specific genii, during the Middle Kingdom some odd combinations occurred. Other goddesses occasionally replaced the usual ones, with examples of Renenutet and Sendjet protecting Qebehsenuef and Duamutef.

Aside from masks and stoppers, a number of other novelties appear in the record. For example, the jars of Kuy, from Meir, had lids in the form of masks, placed over the

known of their contents; they may or may not have held wooden boxes.

The first kingly canopic installation is that of Khephren in the Second Pyramid of Giza. It consisted of a pit cut partly into the flooring blocks of the burial chamber, and partly into the underlying rock, south-east of the sarcophagus. It is the only extant example from a pharaoh's tomb until the latter part of the Fifth Dynasty. The apparent absence of others may be attributed to the devastated condition of almost all such tombs of the intervening period.

The first jars to be used as containers for internal organs appeared towards the end of the Fourth Dynasty. The earliest known examples belonged to Queen Meresankh III, and were simple affairs of limestone. Of either stone or pottery, with flat or convex lids, they appeared regularly for the remainder of the Old Kingdom, either in a container or simply standing on the burial chamber floor. The majority are uninscribed, but a few carried the deceased's names and titles, for example those from the mastaba of the vizier, Kagemni, at Saqqara. Also, a fragment of a jar of Isesi, penultimate king of the Fifth Dynasty, bears his name.

This king's jars had been placed in a cubical cutting in the limestone flooring of the royal burial chamber but, by the time of Pepy I, a chest carved out of a block of granite had been installed in the floor, south-east of the king's sarcophagus. This contained a set of canopic jars.

In private tombs, cuttings and/or wooden chests remained usual for private individuals. Wooden chests were

403 Canopic chest of Khnumhotpe. From Beni Hasan BH 107; formerly in the O'Hagan Collection.

404 Canopic chest of Tjau. From BH 186; CM JE 43338.

jar itself as though it were the body; with the chest of Sebeby, there were no jars, but an inner lid had a tiny human head affixed to each quadrant. The treatment of the jar as body is taken further in certain vases which actually adopted human attributes. A few, most importantly those of King Sesostris I, were of conventional form, but had carved arms hanging down their sides; similar were a set from El-Bersha, in Cairo, and others in the Petrie and British Museums. More unusual were cartonnage examples from the tomb of Djehutynakhte at El-Bersha, which were perched upon short legs and feet.

Wooden canopic chests followed the design of contemporary coffins, with text running round the upper part, sometimes accompanied by vertical complements. Usually coffins and canopic chests were of the same basic type classification: this close link between the coffin (or, later, the sarcophagus) and the canopic chest was maintained in most cases down to the New Kingdom. Interiors were usually plain, but sometimes included extracts from the Coffin Texts and, in certain cases from the reigns of Sesostris II and III, small representations of the protective deities.

Chests were usually located near the foot (south) end of the burial, although a number of tombs had the canopic

box in a hole under the place intended for the coffin. It is possible that this reflects the placement of canopic jars under the bier of the deceased in later papyrus and tomb vignettes; or it may simply derive from a desire to save space.

Stone chests also showed parallels with stone body-containers, at their simplest being plain boxes, with *per-nu* lids. During the last part of the Twelfth Dynasty, the 'reed-work edging' seen on certain sarcophagi was adopted, but not apparently the 'Step Pyramid' panelling seen on some of them. A chest from the North Mastaba at Lisht was unique, with a lid of much greater depth than the box; the box was equipped with circular cuttings to contain the bases of the jars (ill. 405). From the reigns of Sesostris III and Ammenemes III come a pair of chests with jar-equivalents carved as one with the box. One of them belonged to a wife of Ammenemes III; the other came from the burial of an embalmer, Khentkhetyemsaf (ill. 408): perhaps this man had taken a professional experiment to his grave.

While a large amount of Middle Kingdom canopic material has survived, only a small proportion of it was made for the kings. From the beginning of the period, we have the wooden lids of two of the jars of Mentuhotep II, together with a few pieces from one of the very fine calcite jars. Although damaged, the heads are finely modelled, but are insignificant when compared with the magnificent calcite lids recovered from the pyramid of Sesostris I at Lisht. The undamaged example is amongst the finest of its genre

405 Unusual canopic chest from the North Mastaba at Lisht, with a lid of far greater depth than the box. The latter also has recesses for each jar. MMA 09.180.528b.

known; regrettably it, and its rather battered mates, are consigned to a dark case in Cairo, where they are seldom, if ever, noticed.

Nothing is known about the location of Sesostris' canopics in his burial chamber, since the chamber has long been flooded by ground water, and efforts at draining it have been unsuccessful. However, the pyramid of his successor, Ammenemes II, at Dahshur, had a chest uniquely located in a position north-east of the corpse. Since the sarcophagus had been constructed under the floor, and the chest's cover was a floor slab, this odd orientation must have arisen from a consideration for security. Initially, the texts on canopic jars and chests had much in common with those of coffins, with basic offering formulae, albeit often invoking the Sons of Horus, or simply stating that the dead person is 'revered' before the genii. Later in the Twelfth Dynasty, however, a more elaborate formula evolved, becoming the basis for most canopic texts down to the Late

406 (above) Granite canopic chest from the reign of Sesostris III. From tomb III in the Upper Gallery in the royal funerary complex; CM CG 4047.

407 (left) It contained two unusual canopic jars of this form, along with two of normal shape. Their very odd 'rectangular' form appears to be unique; the other two had conventional form. CM CG 4026.

408 (right) Another unusual canopic item is this limestone chest of the embalmer Khentkhetyemsaf, with four 'jars' cut integrally with the box. Made under Sesostris III, this design was resurrected centuries later in the chest of Amenophis II (ill. 411). From Dahshur; CM CG 4049=JE 30958.

Period. These called on each tutelary goddess to wrap her protective arms about her genius, and proclaimed the deceased's honour before her and the genius.

A variety of high-status canopic material came from the royal necropolis at Dahshur. An excellent example of a complete canopic set was found in the partly intact tomb of King Hor, with both wooden and stone canopic chests, and fully inscribed jars. Extremely fine, and occasionally unusual, items came from the tombs of the womenfolk of Sesostris III, one particular set including two jars of a unique round-ended rectangular plan.

THE SECOND INTERMEDIATE PERIOD

During the latter part of the Thirteenth Dynasty, coffins had changed their colouration from earlier norms to a largely black aspect, and they had adopted an exaggerated arched lid; canopic chests followed suit. Apart from their overall form, the texts found on them were highly unusual, with almost nothing in common with canopic formulae of earlier or later times. A pair in Moscow can be dated to the reign of Senebmiu, one of the last kings of the Thirteenth Dynasty. Their texts link them with the chest of Djehuty, one of the earliest kings of the Seventeenth Dynasty, though it differs from them in being coloured yellow. It is unclear whether the colour identifies the piece as royal, or whether the black coffins and chests were by then being

phased out of use. Certainly, by the middle of the Seventeenth Dynasty, the overall aspect of canopic chests was white or yellowish gesso, with texts on a yellow-painted ground. The texts reverted to late Twelfth/early Thirteenth Dynasty formulations, although they are badly garbled on most of the preserved boxes.

Leaving aside their colour and texts, all Thirteenth/Seventeenth Dynasty canopic chests had the same basic decorative scheme, which featured a recumbent jackal on each side, lying upon the superimposed hieroglyphs for 'cloth' and 'vegetation' (ill. 410). The design referred to the bandages and herbs of mummification, of which the jackal-god, Anubis, was the patron. Each of the canines was labelled as a different aspect of the god: Nebtadjeser ('Lord of the Sacred Land'), Tepdjeref ('He who is on his Mountain'), Khentysehnetjer ('He who is before the Divine Booth') and Imywet ('He of the Embalming Tent').

The latest of the series belonged to Sobkemsaf II, and had an interesting inner lid bearing paintings of four canopic jars. The chest was too small to have contained such vases, but these representations were each inscribed incursive hieroglyphs with their correct texts. It is an early example of the importance of an element of the funerary

409 Canopic chest of Hor. It was of plain wood, ornamented with faience and gold foil, and the lid held in place by a sealed cord. Its simplicity follows the design of the king's coffin. From Dahshur; CM CG 51266.

410 Wooden canopic chest of Sobkemsaf II. Covered in yellowish gesso, it bears texts on golden-yellow bands, upon which red guidelines may be seen. It is very similar to other chests of the dynasty. From Dira Abu'l-Naga; Leiden AH 216.

outfit, even though it was not physically present or being used for a practical purpose.

THE NEW KINGDOM

The focus on Anubis did not continue into the New Kingdom. Instead, attention shifted to the tutelary goddesses and the genii. We have noticed their occasional depiction on chests of the Middle Kingdom; now, the goddesses were paired on the front and rear of chests, the genii (with human heads) on the sides. The simple boxes were superseded by the form of square *per-wer* shrines – with a flaring cavetto cornice, and sloping, round-fronted, lid – mounted on sledges. This move to shrine forms mirrored developments among private sarcophagi.

The same basic shape is also seen in royal funerary equipment, in quartzite during the reigns of Tuthmosis III and Hatshepsut. Since royal sarcophagi had moved to cartouche plans, this was the first real departure of canopic boxes from the sarcophagi that had formerly closely matched them. It was taken a step further by Amenophis

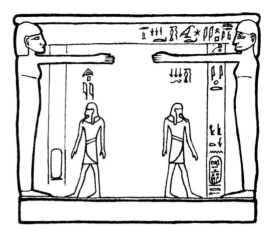

411 Calcite canopic chest of Amenophis II. This piece marks a major change in royal canopic practice, and its divergence from that found in private burials. Externally, the tutelary goddesses are now carved in the round on the corners, while inside the canopic jars are carved as one with the stone of the chest. From KV 35; CM CG 5029.

II, whose chest was of calcite, rather than the quartzite of his sarcophagus. In addition, rather than containing the usual four separate canopic jars, these were carved as one with the box, incapable of removal. Another innovation was the placement of figures of the four goddesses in raised relief around the corners of the chest, their arms thus holding the whole box in their protective embrace. This form of canopic chest would remain in use, unique to kings, down to the end of the Nineteenth Dynasty, when separate jars made their comeback.

412 The Imseti canopic jar of Queen Ahmose-Nefertiry, wife of Amosis. The proportions of the piece are typical of the early Eighteenth Dynasty. From TT 320; CM JE 26255C .

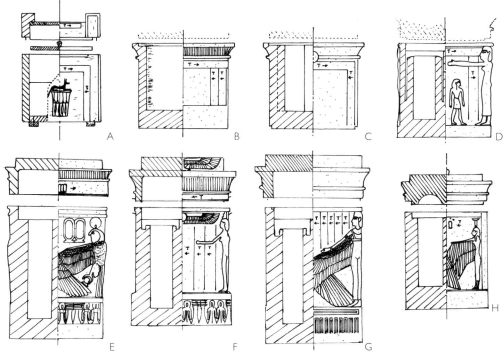

413 The royal canopic chest. From the Second Intermediate Period
onwards.

A   Sobkemsaf II.
B   Hatshepsut.
C   Tuthmosis I.

D   Amenophis II.
E   Akhenaten.
F   Tutankhamun.
G   Horemheb.
H   Shoshenq I.

414 Quartzite canopic chest of Hatshepsut. Its fairly squat proportions mark the end of a trend which may be seen since the Seventeenth Dynasty, while its interior is 'open', formerly divided by wooden boards. Later royal canopic chests are both proportionately taller and have more elaborate internal designs. From KV 20; CM JE 38072.

415 Made under Tuthmosis III and presumably sharing its design with his (lost) chest, the canopic box of Tuthmosis I is interesting for a number of reasons. Firstly, its proportions move back towards the 'tall' form seen in the early Seventeenth Dynasty; secondly, it copies wooden forms in including a fastening knob in its quartzite mass, and thirdly its interior is shaped to accommodate the perimeters of the canopic jars. This is taken a step further in the chest of Amenophis II (ill. 411). From KV 38; CM JE 36416.

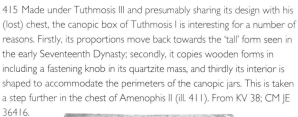

416 The canopic chest of Maihirpri, with the exception of its use of real gold, is typical of private canopics of the Eighteenth Dynasty: most have their decoration in yellow paint. Isis and Nephthys are to be seen on the front of the box, Duamutef and Qebehsenuef on the side. As is the case until the end of the dynasty, all genii are human headed. From KV 36; CM CG 24005.

The canopic jars of the earlier part of the Eighteenth Dynasty were a slightly different shape from those of the Middle Kingdom, but bore broadly the same texts. They retained human-headed stoppers, except in a very few cases, where Hapy's jar acquired the head of an ape, Duamutef's that of a canid, and Qebehsenuef's that of a falcon. This became universal in the Ramesside Period, but throughout the Eighteenth Dynasty human heads were found in all significant tombs. In one case, that of Hatnofret, mother of Senenmut, architect of Hatshepsut, three heads were human, but the fourth was that of a dog; the reasons behind this are wholly obscure. Another exceptional set was that of Neferkhauet, which omitted the usual texts in favour of a panel showing a faunal-headed genius facing his name.

Up until the mid Eighteenth Dynasty, masks on visceral bundles had been a cheap alternative to jars. However, some rich Eighteenth Dynasty burials had both, a fine example being the canopic material from the burial of Tjuiu, maternal grandmother of Akhenaten. She was equipped with a naos-form chest, black-varnished, with texts and divine images richly gilded (thus precisely matching her sarcophagus). Within lay four human-lidded, calcite jars, with long texts filled with black pigment. Inside, the visceral bundles had been formed into the shape

418 Canopic chest of Tjuiu. Its design closely follows that of her sarcophagus (ill. 364), its 'moulded' gilded decoration contrasting with the technique shown on Maihirpri's. From KV 46; CM CG 51013.

419 The reconstructed canopic chest of Akhenaten. Unlike other Eighteenth Dynasty royal canopic chests, it does not possess goddesses at its corners, rather the falcons that were the earliest incarnations of the Aten. From Amarna TA 26; CM JE 59454.

of mummies, and over the 'head' of each was placed a gilded cartonnage mask.

As with sarcophagi of the New Kingdom, private individuals were seemingly restricted to the use of wood for their canopic chests, with only a few exceptions. Indeed, only one stone chest of a private person has apparently survived from the New Kingdom, belonging to Amunhotpe-Huy, Chief Steward of Memphis under Amenophis III. In design, however, it exactly followed wooden prototypes.

The Amarna interlude is sparsely represented in the canopic record. The most impressive items are the four jars found accompanying the mysterious royal mummy in Tomb 55 in the Valley of the Kings. Their fine human heads seem to have been made for one of Akhenaten's daughters, the jars themselves having once belonged to the king's junior wife, Kiya. Although erased before final use, their texts have been restored as giving the names and titles of the king, the Aten, and the deceased: the traditional gods and goddesses of burial had no place in Akhenaten's religion. The monarch himself had a chest of the general pattern of his royal predecessors since Amenophis II's time, but with the hawk, the earliest embodiment of his god, replacing the protective goddesses at the corners.

The protective goddesses reappeared in the equipment of Tutankhamun, where they not only enfolded the corners of the stone chest, but also, as gilded wooden statuettes, stood guard around the great wooden shrine that enclosed it (ills. 421, 425). The chest was a solid block bored with four cylindrical compartments, topped with carved heads of the king (ills. 421, 423). Inside lay four exquisite solid gold miniature coffins, each holding a package of viscera (ill. 424). As with other parts of the king's funerary equipment, including one of the coffins, they had originally been made for his brother, King Smenkhkare/Neferneferuaten.

420 The canopic chest of Horemheb. It continues the practice of placing deities at the corners, in this case winged goddesses. Although they had gained wings on royal sarcophagi back in the reign of Tutankhamun (see ill. 366), this is the first canopic chest to show the tutelary goddesses with them. From KV 57; CM TR 9.12.22.1-14.

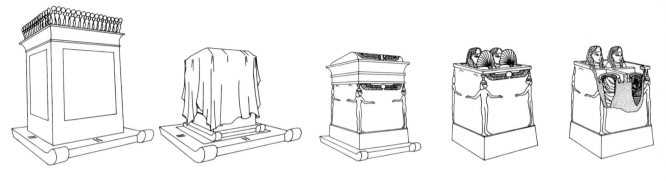

421 The nested canopic equipment of Tutankhamun: the gilded shrine; the calcite chest, covered in a linen pall; the calcite chest, its corners adorned with the tutelary goddesses; with the lid removed to show the stoppers of the internal cavities, in the form of the king's head; section of the interior, with the linen-wrapped gold coffinettes which held the embalmed viscera.

422 The lid of the canopic chest of Tutankhamun, showing a kneeling figure of the sky-goddess, Nut. From KV 62; CM JE 60687.

423 (*below left*) Calcite canopic chest of Tutankhamun, with the lid removed. The chest is of the same type as those of Amenophis II and Horemheb. CM JE 60687.

424 (*below*) Tutankhamun's chest contained four miniature gold coffinettes, which held the actual visceral mummies. They had all originally been made for Smenkhkare/Neferneferuaten. From KV 62; CM JE 60691.

425 (*right*) The canopic shrine of Tutankhamun, of gilded wood. From KV 62; CM JE 60686.

The concept of miniature coffins, rather than jars, to contain viscera was adopted by some individuals in the following Ramesside Period – both at the beginning, in the tomb of Sennedjem at Deir el-Medina, and at the end, with the equipment of Sutymose. Most burials, however, continued the use of traditional jars, although by the end of the reign of Ramesses II, mixed-headed stoppers were usual; the same applied to the later examples of the canopic coffinettes. In addition, usual materials had been supplemented by faience, and decoration was sometimes elaborated with scenes of the dead adoring funerary deities with, on occasion, a sculpture of a recumbent jackal lying upon the lid.

426 Canopic jar lid belonging to an Apis bull buried during Tutankhamun's reign. As with other aspects of its burial (cf. ill. 205), an Apis had precisely the same canopic equipment as a high-status human, only much larger. From Apis tomb C; Louvre E 3942C.

427 Although most Nineteenth Dynasty private burials employed traditional canopic jars, certain individuals used coffinettes of the type more usually associated with kingly interments. This painted limestone example comes from the tomb of Sennedjem (TT 1), reign of Sethos I. CM CG 4252.

The canopic chests of the Ramesside Period, although still of shrine form, with figures of the genii and tutelary goddesses, changed their colour scheme, adopting the same yellow aspect as the private coffins and sarcophagi of the time – and latterly also the canopic coffinettes. The figures were polychrome, sometimes augmented by images of the dead person.

Kings continued to employ calcite integral chests down to the reign of Siptah, although they lost their corner-goddesses under Merenptah. Only fragments survive, however, a testimony to the fragility of the stone – and to the former presence within of golden coffinettes. The fragments from the chest of Ramesses II show its alabaster to have been ornamented with blue glass, rather than the simple pigment used elsewhere.

Early in the Twentieth Dynasty, the 'integral' stone chests seem to have been replaced by separate jars, though much larger than usual – one of Ramesses IV was twice the

428 During the Ramesside Period, traditional canopic texts gave way to a wider range of decorative approaches. This faience example shows the dead man offering to Osiris. Nineteenth Dynasty; MFA 48.1287a.

height of most extant examples. Even larger were those produced for the interment of the sacred Apis bulls from the
reign of Amenophis III onwards (cf. ill. 426). The housing
of the giant royal jars is uncertain, but on the evidence of
the tomb of Ramesses VII they were placed in niches or
pits, two on each side of the sarcophagus. This marked the
first real departure from placing canopics at or beside the
feet of the corpse. It is also found in succeeding periods.

THE THIRD INTERMEDIATE PERIOD

A fundamental change in canopic practice took place
around the beginning of the Twenty-first Dynasty. For
apparently the first time, after separate desiccation and
wrapping, the internal organs were replaced within the
body cavity, often accompanied by small wax figures of the
Four Sons of Horus. Later, some bodies had the wrapped
viscera placed over the legs, or under the feet.

Curiously, this did not result in the demise of canopic
equipment. Although it was not included in the majority of
Third Intermediate Period burials, high-status individuals
continued to possess such items – albeit empty. Many seem
to have been re-used from earlier periods and fitted with
new lids, but kings certainly continued to have them made,
with fine gilded and inlaid lids in some cases.

429 A recumbent figure of Anubis is a feature of the lids of many
canopic chests of late Ramesside and early Third Intermediate Period
times. They also deviate from the patterns seen earlier; this piece, belonging to Queen Nodjmet, lacks almost everything of normal canopic
decoration. From TT 320; CM TR 20.12.25.11.

While most of these jars were empty, at least one king
(Shoshenq II) went so far as to have *dummy* embalmed viscera installed, an excellent example of how an item can gain
an importance far exceeding its function. Here, it may
reflect a belief that the jars were actually manifestations of
the four genii, whose funerary significance certainly went
beyond their canopic role.

A curious exception to the standard royal canopic outfit
of the Third Intermediate Period – jars, plus a simple
wooden chest – was that of Shoshenq I (ill. 431). In contrast

430 The empty canopic jars of the Twenty-first Dynasty seem often to
have been taken from various sources and then inscribed for their new
owners. This 'pair' belonged to Isetemkheb D of the latter part of the
dynasty. The box in the foreground had been made for Hatshepsut, and
was found containing a mummified organ of uncertain origins. From TT
320; CM JE 26254 and 26250.

431 The canopic chest of Shoshenq I. Although Isis and Nephthys are repeated on each side, rather than each tutelary goddess being bent round individual corners, the design is clearly reminiscent of New Kingdom norms. Since there is in excess of a two-century gap between the last New Kingdom chest and this one, it may have been made on the basis of a verbal description of one of them: it is rather suggestive that Shoshenq's reign saw the last reburials of New Kingdom monarchs, who were removed from their own tombs to places of greater safety. Provenance unknown; Berlin 11000.

to his predecessors and successors, he possessed a calcite 'integral' chest reminiscent of those of the New Kingdom. It is, however, distinguishable from them in many details. During Shoshenq's reign many of the Eighteenth Dynasty royal tombs were entered for the last time in antiquity, and it is well known that Shoshenq had ambitions to imitate these kings on the battlefield. Perhaps he wished to reinforce this by possessing item(s) of funerary equipment modelled on theirs.

Also reminiscent of the New Kingdom are the silver coffinettes that held the (dummy) viscera of Shoshenq II; their human faces contrast with the faunal heads of the other royal canopic equipment – jars – that came from the dynastic necropolis at Tanis. These vases were of conventional type but, during the Twenty-second Dynasty, had much-abbreviated texts.

432, 433 The fairly rare chests of the Third Intermediate Period continue the form of New Kingdom types, this early Twenty-third Dynasty box of Pedyimentet showing each of the Four Sons of Horus being libated by his protective goddess on each side. The lid (below) twice shows Anubis, recumbent on a shrine. Reign of Takelot II; Luxor Museum J.75.

Private examples of canopic jars are quite rare, but still rested in shrine-form canopic chests. With solid dummies of jars, equipped with removable lids, their purely symbolic presence is made even clearer. Such jars were initially adopted by the Nubian kings of the Twenty-fifth Dynasty but, towards the end of the dynasty, Taharqa was equipped with hollow jars of a higher quality than had been the case in preceding years, marking the beginning of a renaissance in the use of canopic jars in Egyptian burials.

THE LATE PERIOD

In addition to reviving 'real' jars – in the archaizing atmosphere of the Twenty-sixth Dynasty, some seem to have actually held viscera again – the end of the Twenty-fifth Dynasty also saw a new standard set of canopic texts coming into use. Although the basic themes are those of the Middle and New Kingdom texts, each jar now had its own particular composition, rather than only differing in the names invoked. They tended to include a pun on the name of the genius: for example, that of Qebehsenuef (*lit*: 'He

434 Some late Third Intermediate Period examples lack a cavetto cornice. This piece shows the canopic genii on the sides, and the tutelary goddesses on the front and back. The bolted double-doors on the front should be noted. From Thebes; Leiden RMO.

435 Solid dummy jars were the natural result of replacing the viscera within the body during the Third Intermediate Period. This fairly crude example belongs to King Shabataka of the Twenty-fifth Dynasty. From El-Kurru Ku.18; MFA 21.2813.

436 The Saite Period saw an upswing in the use of canopic jars, some of which were once again used for viscera, their texts also being revised and once more standardized. Durham N.1988 and 1989.

437 The use of canopic jars seems to come to an end around the beginning of the Ptolemaic Period. The latest examples are distinguishable by the flaring lower parts of the lids, these belonging to Djedbastiufankh. From Hawara; Ashmolean Museum 1889.1320-3.

438 The final canopic containers were small, tall, chests, brightly painted and usually topped by an 'archaic' hawk. These fell out of use during the latter part of the Ptolemaic Period; MFA 98.1128.

Who Purifies His Brother by Means of Libation') speaks of 'pouring a libation'.

Large numbers of canopic jars survive from the Twenty-sixth Dynasty, some having been originally placed in niches in the walls of burial chambers, flanking the body. They were usually of calcite with lids that were often crude, their shapes squatter than before. Two kingly examples are known, both belonging to Apries, a king killed after his deposition from the throne. Probably as a result of this, neither of the two jars bearing his name seems to have been used in his burial. One was used about a century later to contain a mummified hawk; the other found its way into an Etruscan tomb in Italy.

The widespread use of canopic jars diminishes again after the Twenty-sixth Dynasty, only isolated examples being datable to the rest of the Late Period and early Ptolemaic Period, when they seem to disappear completely. These late pieces broadly conform to Saite norms, but with some detail changes, such as a considerable flaring of the base of the lids.

Dating of the final canopic equipment is uncertain. During the Ptolemaic Period jars were superseded by small, very tall, brightly painted canopic chests, often mistaken for *shabti* boxes which frequently take the same shrine form. An 'archaic' figure of a hawk perched on the lid, and assorted vignettes on the sides. Most importantly, the side-panels featured the Four Sons of Horus. Occasionally the chests, much smaller than earlier examples, have been reported to contain viscera – or potsherds and bags of natron imitating them. These canopic chests do not seem to have extended beyond the middle of the Ptolemaic era, when the canopic tradition, stretching back to the beginning of the Old Kingdom, finally came to an end.

Part III

Timeline

NAQADA Ⅲ

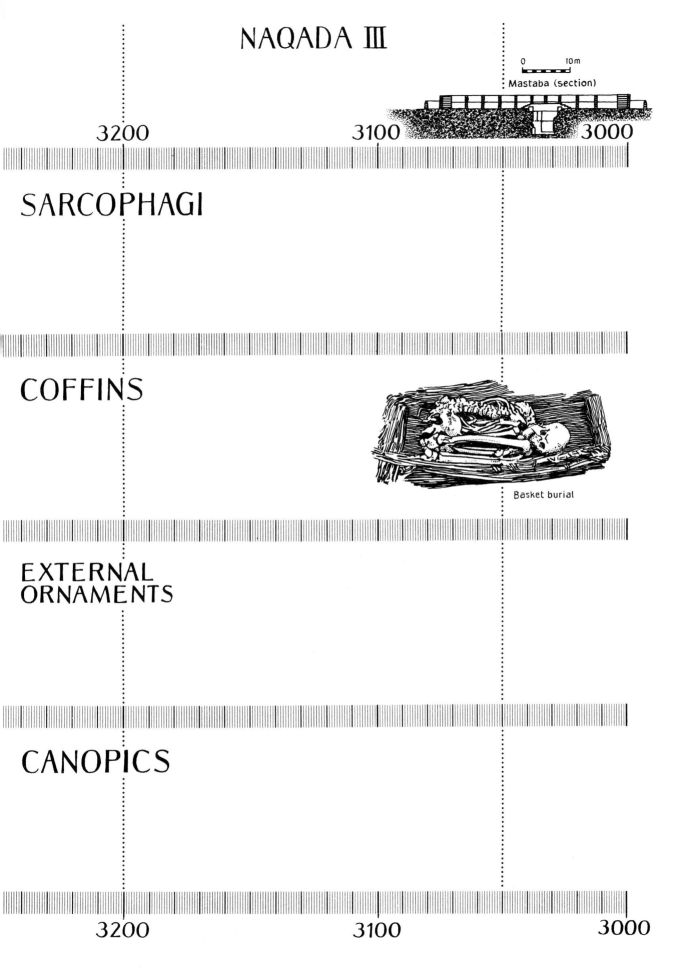

0 ___ 10 m
Mastaba (section)

3200   3100   3000

SARCOPHAGI

COFFINS

Basket burial

EXTERNAL
ORNAMENTS

CANOPICS

3200   3100   3000

ARCHAIC PERIOD

0   10m

Mastaba – Late Dynasty I

3000   2900   2800

SARCOPHAGI

COFFINS

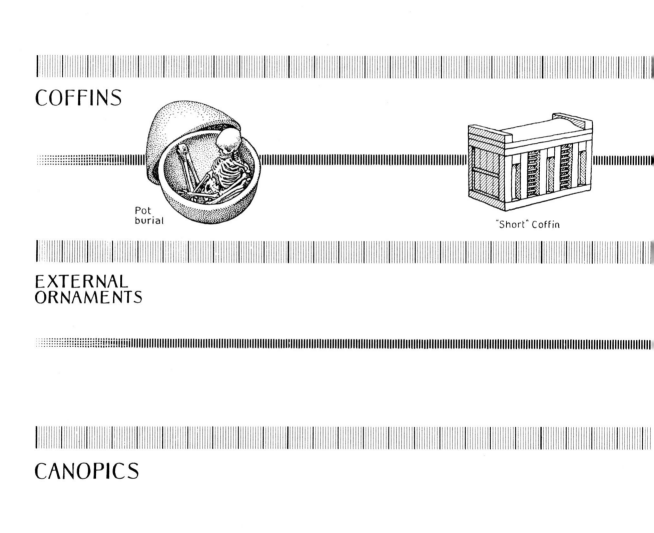

Pot
burial

"Short" Coffin

EXTERNAL
ORNAMENTS

CANOPICS

3000   2900   2800

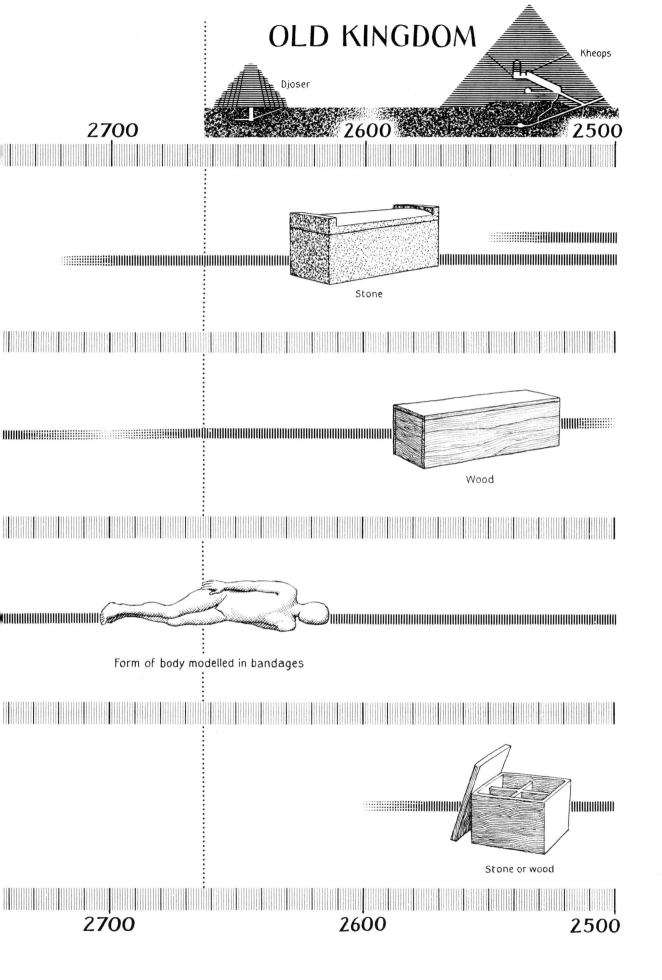

OLD KINGDOM

Djoser

Kheops

2700   2600   2500

Stone

Wood

Form of body modelled in bandages

Stone or wood

2700   2600   2500

OLD KINGDOM

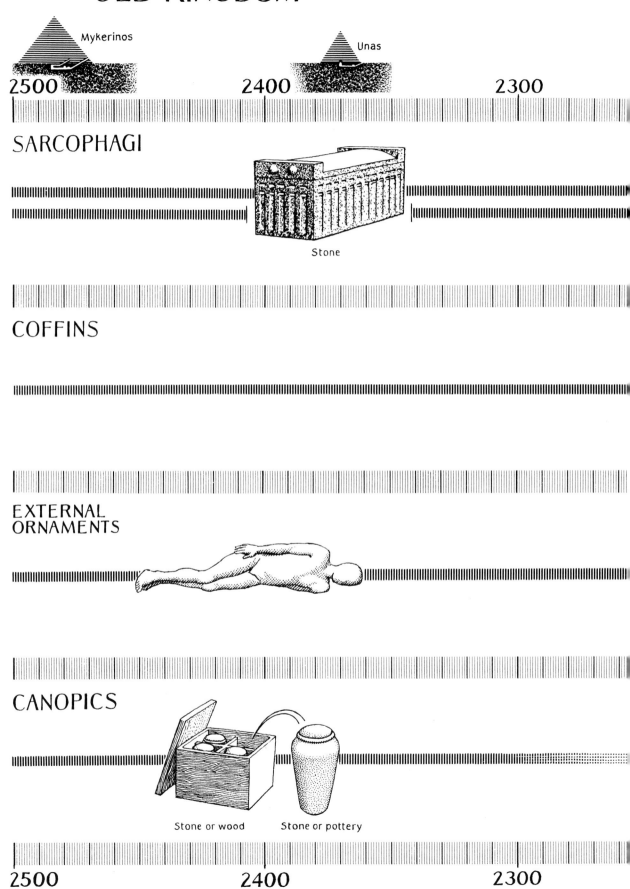

Mykerinos

Unas

2500   2400   2300

SARCOPHAGI

Stone

COFFINS

EXTERNAL
ORNAMENTS

CANOPICS

Stone or wood   Stone or pottery

2500   2400   2300

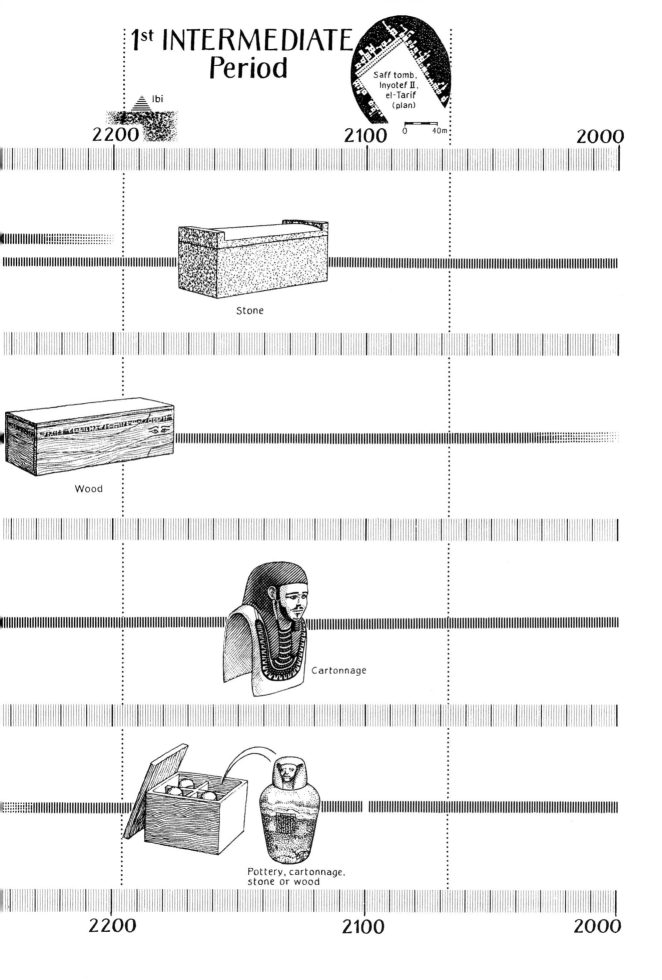

1st INTERMEDIATE Period

Ibi

Saff tomb,
Inyotef II,
el-Tarif
(plan)

0   40m

2200   2100   2000

Stone

Wood

Cartonnage

Pottery, cartonnage,
stone or wood

2200   2100   2000

MIDDLE KINGDOM

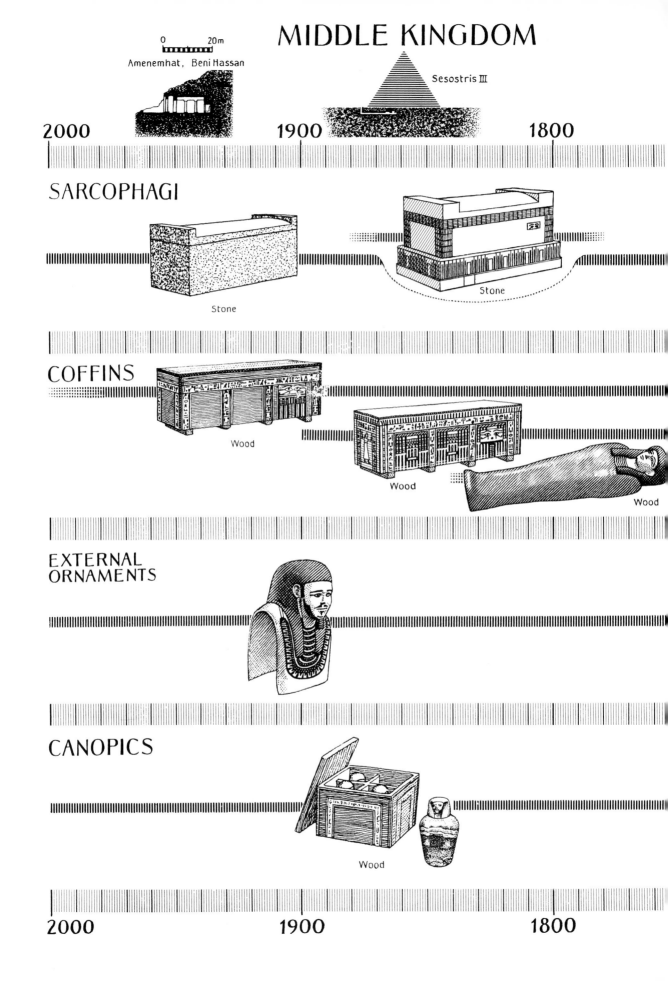

0   20m

Amenemhat, Beni Hassan

Sesostris III

2000   1900   1800

SARCOPHAGI

Stone

Stone

COFFINS

Wood

Wood

Wood

EXTERNAL ORNAMENTS

CANOPICS

Wood

2000   1900   1800

2ⁿᵈ INTERMEDIATE

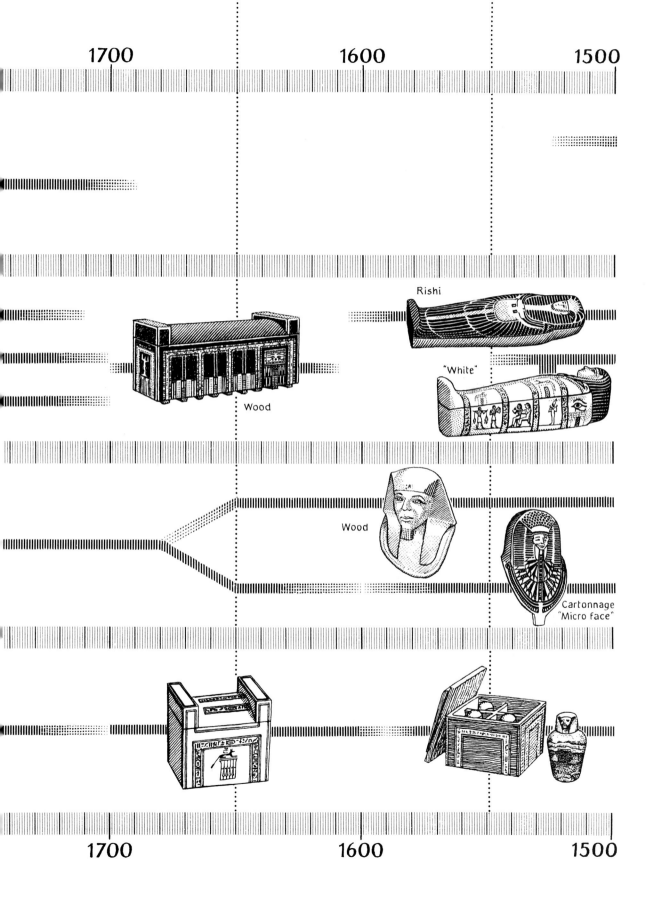

1700   1600   1500

Rishi

"White"

Wood

Wood

Cartonnage "Micro face"

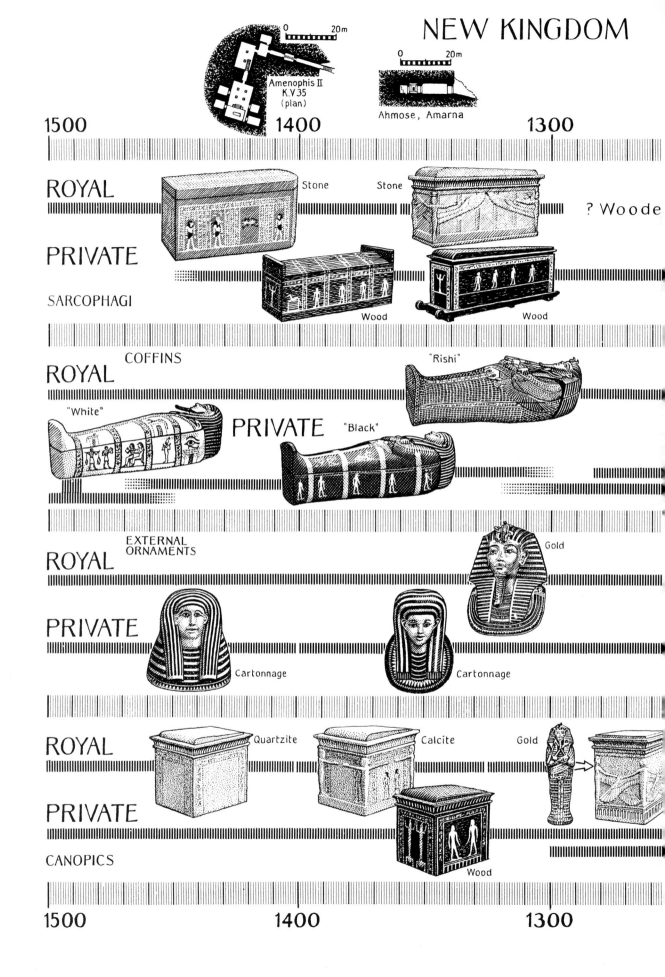

NEW KINGDOM

Amenophis II
K.V 35
(plan)

0   20m

Ahmose, Amarna

0   20m

1500   1400   1300

ROYAL   Stone   Stone   ? Woode

PRIVATE

SARCOPHAGI   Wood   Wood

COFFINS   "Rishi"
ROYAL

"White"   PRIVATE   "Black"

EXTERNAL
ORNAMENTS   Gold
ROYAL

PRIVATE

Cartonnage   Cartonnage

ROYAL   Quartzite   Calcite   Gold

PRIVATE

CANOPICS   Wood

1500   1400   1300

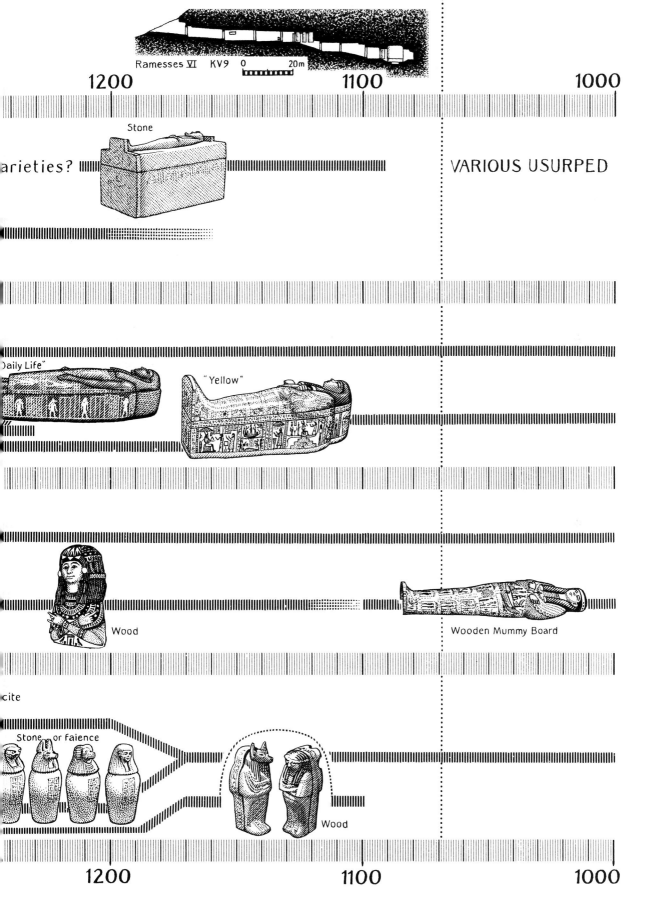

Ramesses VI KV9 0 [____] 20m

1200   1100   1000

Stone

arieties?   VARIOUS USURPED

Daily Life" "Yellow"

Wood   Wooden Mummy Board

cite

Stone or faience   Wood

1200   1100   1000

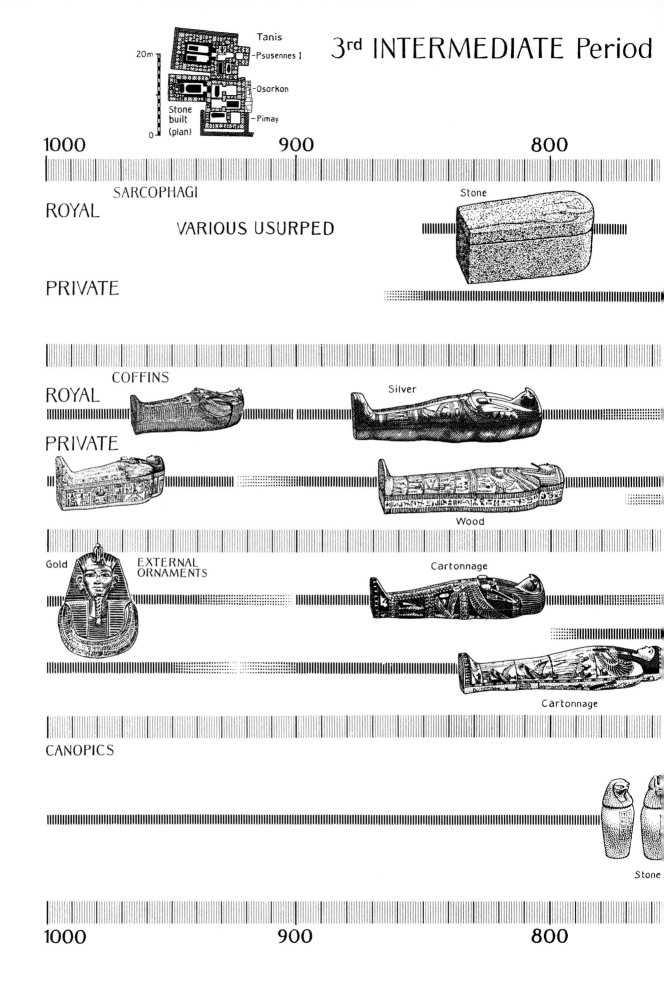

20m

Tanis

Psusennes I

Osorkon

Stone built (plan)

Pimay

0

1000   900   800

SARCOPHAGI

ROYAL

Stone

VARIOUS USURPED

PRIVATE

COFFINS

ROYAL

Silver

PRIVATE

Wood

Gold   EXTERNAL ORNAMENTS

Cartonnage

Cartonnage

CANOPICS

Stone

1000   900   800

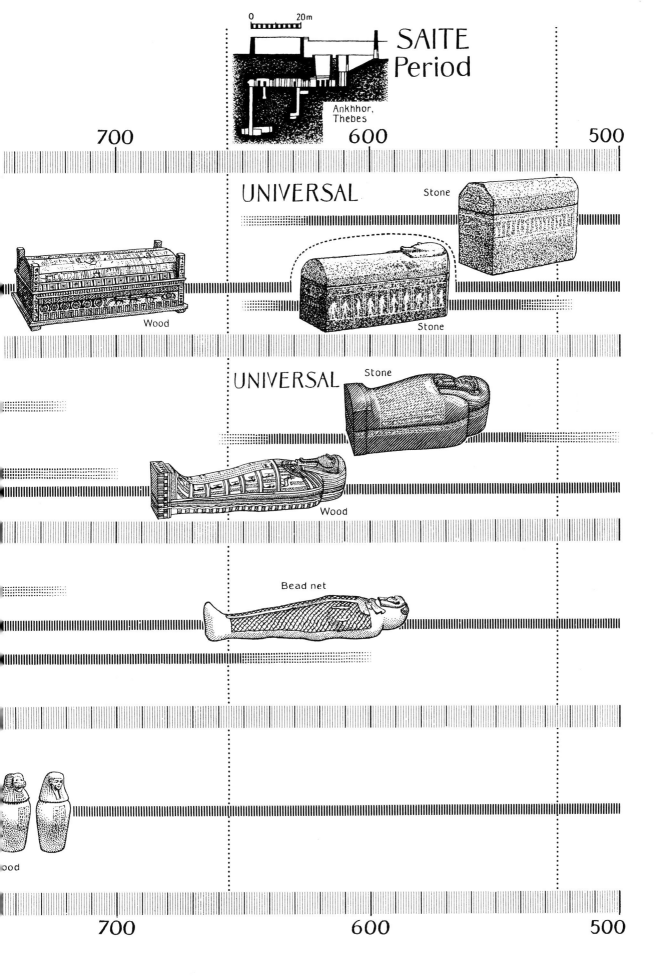

SAITE
Period

Ankhhor,
Thebes

0   20m

700

600

500

UNIVERSAL

Stone

Wood

Stone

UNIVERSAL

Stone

Wood

Bead net

ood

700

600

500

LATE Period

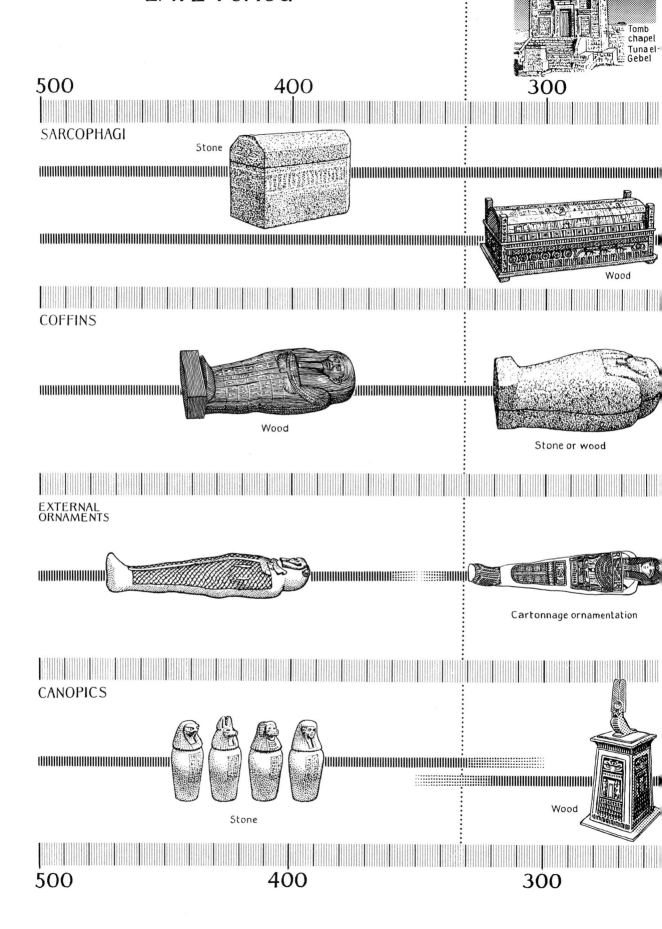

Tomb chapel Tuna el-Gebel

500   400   300

SARCOPHAGI

Stone

Wood

COFFINS

Wood

Stone or wood

EXTERNAL ORNAMENTS

Cartonnage ornamentation

CANOPICS

Stone

Wood

500   400   300

HELLENISTIC Period

ROMAN
Period ➜

200   100   0

VARIOUS TREATMENTS

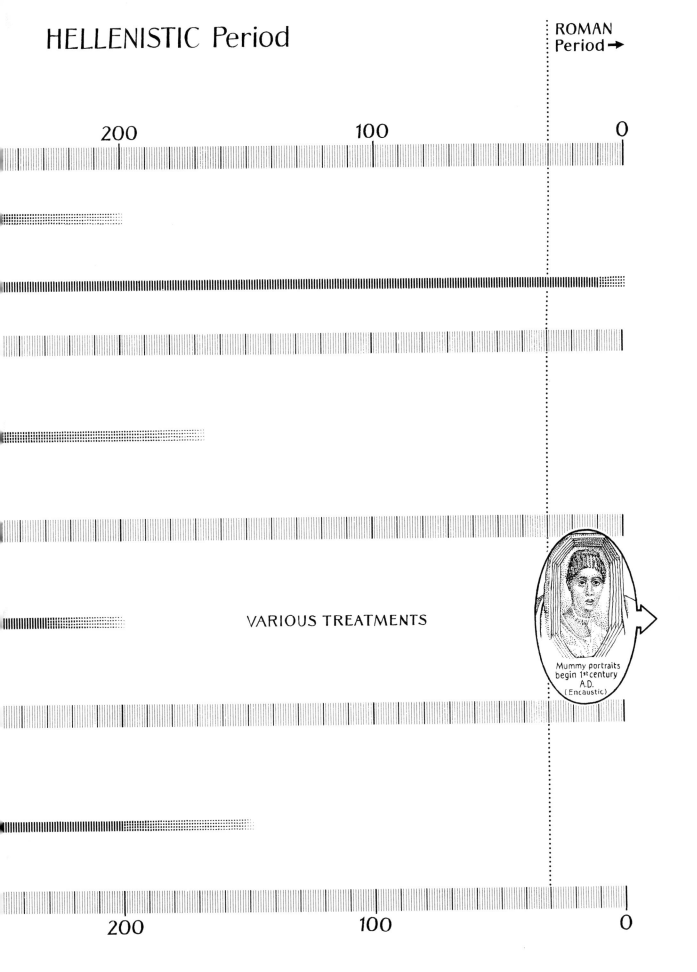

Mummy portraits
begin 1ˢᵗ century
A.D.
(Encaustic)

200   100   0

Glossary

Amenti	'The West', the dwelling place of the Dead.
Ammit	'The Devourer'. The composite crocodile-lion-hippopotamus monster that ate up the parts of the accursed dead in the Judgment Hall of Osiris.
Amun(-Re)	Chief god of Thebes and paramount god of Egypt from the New Kingdom onwards.
Anubis	God of embalming, represented with a jackal's head.
Apis	Sacred bull of Memphis, a form of Ptah.
Apopis	Snake-enemy of the Sun-god.
Aten	The physical sun, or solar disc, worshipped during the late Eighteenth Dynasty and briefly sole god under Akhenaten.
Atum	Human form of Sun-god, Re.
Bitumen	Mineral pitch; any natural hydrocarbon.
Book of the Dead	One of the many funerary books containing spells that would help transport the deceased safely to Amenti. Common from the New Kingdom onwards.
Box	Lower part of a rectangular coffin.
Buchis	Sacred bull whose cult centre was Armant.
Canopic	Of or pertaining to the preservation of the viscera removed from the body in the course of embalming.
Cartonnage	a. Material made from mixture of linen, glue and plaster. b. Painted whole-body casing made from cartonnage.
Coffer	Lower part of a sarcophagus.
Coffin Texts	Texts inscribed on the interior of the coffin to aid the deceased in reaching Amentet.
Coffin	A container for a body of a type usually intended to lie within a sarcophagus. It may be rectangular or anthropoid, of stone or wood, but will always have a separate lid and box/trough.
Duamutef	Mortuary genius and Son of Horus, represented with a jackal head, and associated with the stomach. Under the tutelage of Neith.
Geb	Earth-god; husband of Nut.
Gesso	Mixture of glue and gypsum plaster used to cover coffins, statues, etc.
Hapy	Mortuary genius and Son of Horus, represented with an ape head, and associated with the lungs. Under the tutelage of Nephthys.
Hathor	Goddess, represented in either human or cow form.
Heart scarab	Large scarab placed over the mummies' heart, inscribed with a spell to prevent the organ bearing witness against its Horus. Falcon-god of the sky; son of Osiris and embodiment of Egyptian kingship.
Imseti	Mortuary genius and Son of Horus, represented with a human head, and associated with the liver. Under the tutelage of Isis.
Imywet	Aspect of Anubis, 'Who is in the Embalming House'.
Isis	Goddess; sister-wife of Osiris, mother of Horus and protector of Imseti. Usually found on the foot of a coffin.
Khentyamentiu	Ancient god of Abydos and the dead; represented as a dog, but absorbed by Osiris by the end of the Old Kingdom.
Khentysehnetjer	Aspect of Anubis, 'Who is before the Divine Booth'.
Maat	Goddess of cosmic order.
Mastaba	A tomb-type, common from the Archaic Period onwards. The name, *mastaba*, derives from the Arabic word for mud

Mertesger	brick bench, which they resemble. Goddess of Western Theban necropolis.
Mnevis	Sacred bull of Heliopolis, a manifestation of the Sun-god.
Mummy	Artificially preserved human or animal corpses. The word is derived from the Persian, *mum*, meaning wax or bitumen.
Natron	Combination of sodium carbonate and sodium bicarbonate, used for desiccation and purification purposes in mummification. Occurs naturally in the Wadi Natrun, some 65 km north-west of Cairo, as well as in certain other locations.
Nebtadjeser	Aspect of Anubis, 'Lord of the Necropolis'.
Neith	One of the four tutelary goddesses of the dead; a goddess of warfare and hunting.
Nephthys	Sister of Osiris, Isis and Seth, and wife of Seth. One of the four tutelary goddesses of the dead, always shown at the head of the corpse.
Nut	Sky goddess often pictured on tomb-ceilings and lids of coffins and sarcophagi. Wife of Geb.
Opening of the Mouth	Ceremony which served to reanimate the corpse.
Osiris	God of the Dead and resurrection, brother-husband of Isis, murdered by his brother Seth and who consequently became the first mummy.
Pyramid Texts	Magical texts inscribed in the burial chambers

	of pyramids from the end of the Fifth Dynasty onwards.
Qebehsenuef	Mortuary genius and Son of Horus, represented with a hawk head, and associated with the intestines. Under the tutelage of Selqet.
Renenutet	Snake-goddess of the harvest.
Resin	Adhesive secretion of trees and plants.
Sarcophagus	Rectangular/quasi-rectangular outermost container, intended to hold coffins of a different form or material. It may be composed of stone or wood.
Selqet	One of the four tutelary goddesses; sacred creature was the scorpion.
Sem Priest	Priest who performed funerary rights clad in leopardskin, notably the Opening of the Mouth. Often the deceased's eldest son.
Serekh	Rectangular frame, with panelled lower section, used to enclose the Horus name of a king.
Seth	Brother and murderer of Osiris.
Shabti	Magical servant figure found in tombs from the mid-Middle Kingdom onwards. From the middle of the Eighteenth Dynasty large numbers are to be found in a single burial, ultimately exceeding four hundred in certain interments.
Tepdjeref	Aspect of Anubis, 'Who is Upon his Hill'.
Thoth	Ibis-headed secretary of the gods.
Trough	Lower part of an anthropoid coffin.

The Cemeteries of Egypt

Many sites down the length of the Nile contain cemeteries. The following represents a list of significant Dynastic sites, working from north to south. The widespread prehistoric cemeteries are not listed, with only a selection of Graeco-Roman ones noted. For sites in Nubia, only those down to the Twenty-fifth Dynasty are listed. The range of dates of material is given, together with notes of any particularly important tombs at the site. Numbers represent those on the maps on pages 312–313.

KEY

AP	Archaic Period
FIP	First Intermediate Period
GR	Graeco-Roman Period
LP	Late Period
MK	Middle Kingdom
NK	New Kingdom
OK	Old Kingdom
SIP	Second Intermediate Period
TIP	Third Intermediate Period

1 North Sinai. GR.
2 Tanis (San el-Hagar). TIP. Royal tombs of TIP.
3 Alexandria. GR.
4 Marina el-Alamain. GR.
5 Nabasha. Dyns 19–20; LP.
6 Saft el-Henna. NK-Dyn 26.
7 Mendes (Tell el-Ruba). AP; Dyn 6-MK; LP. Tomb of Nepherites I (Dyn 29).
8 Bubastis (Tell Basta). Dyn 6-GR. Tombs of Dyns 19/20 viceroys of Nubia.
9 Buto (Tell el-Farain). GR.
10 Tell Moqdam. TIP. Tomb of Q. Kama (Dyn 23).
11 Sais (Sa el-Hagar). LP.
12 Tell el-Yahudiya. MK-LP.
13 Tell el-Hisn. AP; Dyn 6-MK.
14 Kom Abu Billu. Dyn 6-NK; LP.
15 Abu Ghaleb. Dyn 6; NK.
16 El-Qatta. AP; Dyns 5–6; NK; LP.
17 Letopolis (Kom Ausim). OK.
18 Athribis. LP. Tomb of Q Takhut (Dyn 26).
19 Heliopolis. AP; OK; NK-LP.
20 Fustat (Batn el-Baqara). LP.
21 Abu Rowash. OK; MK. Pyramid of Djedefre (Dyn 4) and Brick Pyramid of (Dyn 3[?]).
22 Giza. AP-LP. Pyramids of Dyn 4 kings.
23 Zawiyet el-Aryan. AP; OK; NK. Layer Pyramid (Dyn 3) and Unfinished Pyramid (Dyn 4 [?]).
24 Abusir. AP-LP. Pyramids of Dyn 5 kings.
25 Helwan. AP.
26 Mit Rahina (Memphis). MK-TIP. Tombs of High Priests (Dyn 22).
27 North Saqqara. AP-LP. Private tombs of AP-OK; royal tombs and pyramids of Dyns 2–6; private tombs of NK and LP; sacred animal catacombs.
28 South Saqqara. OK. Royal tombs Dyns 4–6.
29 Dahshur. OK-MK; LP. Pyramids of Seneferu (Dyn 4) and MK kings.
30 South Dahshur. Pyramids of Dyn 13 kings.
31 Mazghuna. OK-NK; GR. Pyramids of Dyn 13 kings.
32 Lisht. OK-MK. Pyramids of Dyn 12 kings.
33 Kafr Ammar. OK-FIP; TIP.
34 Gerzeh. FIP-TIP.
35 Tarkhan. AP.
36 Meidum. OK; TIP. Pyramid of Seneferu(?[Dyn 4]).
37 Karanis (Kom Aushim). GR.
38 El-Rubayyat. GR. 'Portrait mummies'.
39 Hawara. MK; LP-GR. Pyramids of Ammenemes III and Princess Neferuptah (Dyn 12); 'portrait mummies' (GR).
40 Abusir el-Meleq. LP-GR.
41 Lahun. MK-GR. Pyramid of Sesostris II (Dyn 12); tomb of Princess Sithathorinunet.
42 Tell Umm el-Breigat (Tebtunis). GR.
43 Harageh. AP; OK-MK.
44 Gurob. AP; Dyns 5–6; NK. Tomb of Prince Ramesses-Nebweben (Dyn 19).
45 Sedment. OK-FIP; NK.
46 Ehnasiya el-Medina (Herakleopolis). FIP-GR.
47 El-Hiba. LP-GR.
48 Zawiyet Barmasha. LP-GR.
49 Deshasheh. Dyn 6.

50 Gebel el-Teir el-Bahari. Dyns 5–6.
51 Tehneh el-Gebel. OK; TIP.
52 Zawiyet el-Amwat/Maitin. OK.
53 Beni Hasan. OK-LP. Tombs of
    nomarchs and court of Dyns 11–12.
54 Tuna el Gebel. Dyn 19-GR.
55 Tell el-Amarna. Dyn 18. Tombs of
    Akhenaten and court.
56 Antinoë (Sheikh Abada). MK.
57 Deir el-Bersha. Dyn 6-MK. Tombs of
    nomarchs.
58 Sheikh Said. Dyn 6-MK. Tombs of
    nomarchs.
59 Quseir el-Amarna. Dyn 6.
60 Meir. Dyn 6-MK; GR. Tombs of
    nomarchs.
61 Dara. Dyn 6-FIP. 'Pyramid' of Khui
    (FIP).
62 Deir el-Gebrawi. Dyn 6. Tombs of
    nomarchs.
63 Asyut. OK-NK. Tombs of nomarchs.
64 Matmar. AP-TIP.
65 Deir Rifeh. Dyn 6-NK. Tombs of
    nomarchs; 'Tomb of Two Brothers'.
66 Mostagedda. Dyns 5–13-XIII.
67 Qau el-Kebir. OK-NK. Tombs of
    nomarchs of MK.
68 Akhmim. GR.
69 Gebel Sheikh el-Haridi. Dyn 6.
70 El-Hawwawish. OK-MK. Tombs of
    nomarchs.
71 El-Hagarsa. OK-FIP.
72 Sheikh Farag. FIP-Dyn 12.
73 Naga el-Deir. AP-MK.
74 Naga el-Meshaikh. AP; NK.
75 Raqaqna. OK.
76 Beit Khallaf. Dyns 3–4. Giant mastabas
    of early Dyn 3.

77 El-Mahasna. Dyn 6-FIP.
78 Abydos. AP-LP. Royal tombs of AP;
    royal cenotaphs of Sesostris III (Dyn
    12) and Amosis (Dyn 18).
79 Balabish. NK.
80 Hu-Abadiyeh. Dyn 6-SIP.
81 Qasr el-Sayed. Dyn 6.
82 Dandara. Dyn 5-MK.
83 Deir el-Ballas. MK.
84 Zaweida, Dyns 5–6.
85 Naqada. AP-OK. Mastaba of Queen
    Neithhotpe (Dyn 1).
86 Western Thebes.
    a El-Tarif. OK-MK. Royal tombs of
      Dyn 11a.
    b Valley of the Kings. NK. Royal
      tombs.
    c Dira Abu'l-Naga. SIP-NK. Royal
      Tombs of Dyn 17; private tombs of
      Dyns 10–20, also Dyn 18.
    d Deir el-Bahari. MK-TIP; GR.
      Mortuary complex of Mentuhotep
      II; tomb of Q. Meryetamun (TT
      352); royal cache (TT 320); tombs of
      TIP.
    e Asasif. MK-GR. Tombs of officials
      of Dyn 26.
    f Khokha. NK-LP. Private tombs of
      NK.
    g Sheikh Abd el-Qurna. Dyn 6-GR.
      Private tombs of NK.
    h Ramesseum. MK; Dyn 22.
    i Qurnet Murrai. NK.
    j Deir el-Medina. NK. Tombs of
      necropolis workmen.
    k Biban el-Harim. Dyns 19–20.
      Tombs of royal family.
    l Medinet Habu. TIP-Dyn 26.

87 El-Rizeiqat. FIP-NK. Tomb of
    Sobkmose.
88 Moalla. FIP; TIP. Tomb of Ankhtify
    (FIP).
89 Gebelein. AP-MK.
90 Esna. FIP-NK.
91 Hierakonpolis. AP-NK. 'Painted
    Tomb' of prehistoric times.
92 El-Kab. OK-NK. Tomb of Paheri
    (Dyn 18).
93 Edfu. Dyn 5-NK.
94 Qubbet el-Hawa. Dyn 6-MK.
95 Bahriya Oasis. NK-GR. Tomb of
    Amunhotpe Huy.
96 Dakhala Oasis. Dyn 5-GR.
97 Kharga Oasis. GR.
98 Awam. GR.
99 Koshtemna. AP.
100 Betekon (Dehmit) NK. Tomb of
    Nakhkmin.
101 Sayala-AP.
102 Aniba. MK-NK. Tomb of Pennut
    (Dyn 20 – now at Amada).
103 Toshka East. NK. Tomb of
    Heqanefer (late Dyn 18).
104 Serra East. NK. SIP-NK.
105 Dibeira East. NK. Tomb of
    Djhathotpe (Dyn 18).
106 Buhen. MK-NK.
107 Mirgissa. MK-NK.
108 Semna West. MK-NK.
109 Soleb. NK.
110 Sesebi. NK.
111 Kerma. SIP.
112 El-Kurru. Dyn 25. Pyramids of Piye,
    Shabaka, Shabataka and
    Tanutamun.
113 Nuri. Dyn 25. Pyramid of Taharqa.

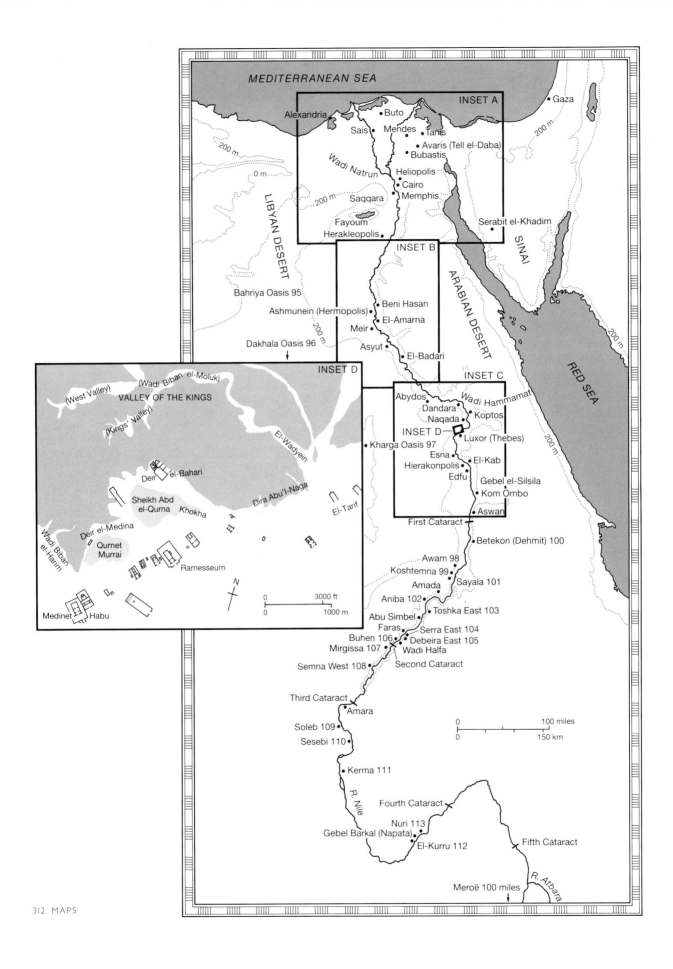

MEDITERRANEAN SEA

INSET A

Gaza

Alexandria

Buto

Sais   Mendes   Tanis

Avaris (Tell el-Daba)

Bubastis

Wadi Natrun

Heliopolis

Cairo

Saqqara   Memphis

SINAI

Serabit el-Khadim

Fayoum

Herakleopolis

LIBYAN DESERT

INSET B

200 m

0 m

200 m

ARABIAN DESERT

RED SEA

200 m

Bahriya Oasis 95

Ashmunein (Hermopolis)   Beni Hasan

El-Amarna

Meir

Dakhala Oasis 96   Asyut

El-Badari

INSET C

Wadi Hammamat

Abydos

Dandara

Naqada   Koptos

INSET D   Luxor (Thebes)

Kharga Oasis 97   Esna

El-Kab

Hierakonpolis

Edfu

Gebel el-Silsila

Kom Ombo

Aswan

First Cataract

Betekon (Dehmit) 100

Awam 98

Koshtemna 99

Sayala 101

Amada

Aniba 102

Toshka East 103

Abu Simbel

Faras

Serra East 104

Buhen 106   Debeira East 105

Mirgissa 107   Wadi Halfa

Semna West 108   Second Cataract

Third Cataract

Amara

Soleb 109

Sesebi 110

Kerma 111

R. Nile

Fourth Cataract

Nuri 113

Gebel Barkal (Napata)

El-Kurru 112   Fifth Cataract

R. Atbara

Meroë 100 miles

0   100 miles

0   150 km

INSET D

(Wadi Biban el-Moluk)

(West Valley)

VALLEY OF THE KINGS

(Kings' Valley)

El-Wadkein

Deir el-Bahari

Sheikh Abd
el-Qurna   Khokha

Dira Abu'l-Naga

El-Tarif

Wadi
Biban
el-Harim

Deir el-Medina

Qurnet
Murrai   Ramesseum

N

Medinet Habu

0   3000 ft

0   1000 m

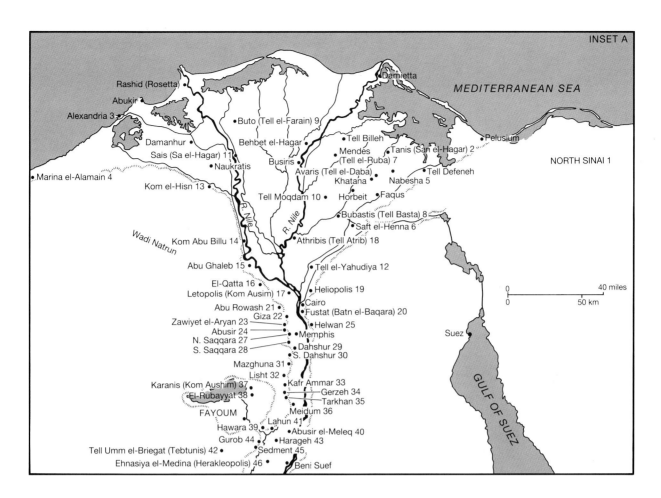
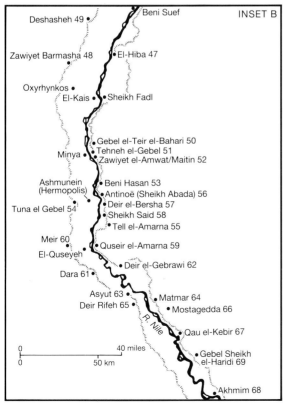
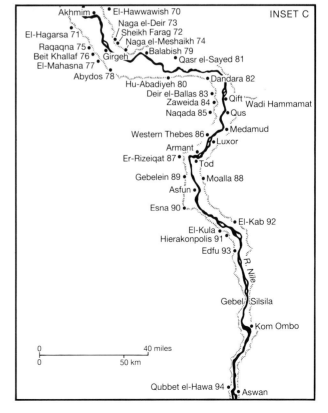

NOTE:

The following list includes all tombs used, or intended to be used, for the burials of rulers of Egypt. The necropoleis in the Nile valley holding the tombs of reigning kings are listed in approximately geographical order, from north to south. Those known only from documentary sources, and as yet undiscovered, are marked with an asterisk; those which have always been known are marked '‡'. A king later reburied either at Deir el-Bahari or in the tomb of Amenophis II (KV 35) is marked '†'. Under 'tomb type', the following codes are used:

KEY

B	Brick tomb chambers sunk in shallow pit	SPB	Step pyramid (brick)
		TPS	True pyramid (stone)
M	Mastaba	TPB	True pyramid (brick)
R	Rock-cut tomb	T	Stone tomb chambers sunk in temple-court yard
SPS	Step pyramid (stone)		

The suffix 'u' indicates unused for burial, either through being incomplete, or some other reason.

1 Probably usurped from Smendes.
2 Reburial?
3 Reburial.
4 'The Great Pyramid'.
5 'The Unfinished Pyramid'.
6 'The Layer Pyramid'.
7 Begun as TPS.

Site	Tomb number	Tomb type	Owner/ occupant(s)	Dynasty	Date of excavation or entry
Alexandria	–	T?	Kleopatra VII	Ptol.	*
Sa el-Hagar (Sais)	–	T	Apries	26	*
	–	T	Amasis	26	*
Tell el-Rub'a (Mendes)	–	T	Nepherites I	29	1992/3
San el-Hagar (Tanis)	NRT I	T	Osorkon II[1]	22	1939
			Takelot I	22	
			Shoshenq V(?)	22	
	NRT II	T	Pimay	22	1939
	NRT III	T	Psusennes I	21	1939/40
			Amenemopet[2]	21	
			Siamun(?)	21	
			Psusennes II(?)	21	
			Shoshenq II[3]	22	
	NRT IV	Tu(?)	Amenemopet	21	1939
	NRT V	T	Shoshenq III	22	1945
			Shoshenq IV	22	
Abu Rowash	L I	SPB	Huni?	3	1986
	L II	TPS	Djedefre	4	‡
Giza	G I[4]	TPS	Kheops	4	‡
	G II	TPS	Khephren	4	1817
	G III	TPS	Mykerinos	4	1837
Zawiyet el-Aryan	L XIII[5]	SPS	Nebkare (?)	4(?)	1900
	L XIV[6]	SPS	Horus Khaba	3	1900
Abusir	L XVIII	TPS	Sahure	5	1902
	L XX	TPS	Niuserre	5	1902
	L XXI	TPS	Neferirkare	5	1902
	L XXVI	M[7]	Neferefre	5	1980s
	–	TPS	Shepseskare(?)	5	–
North Saqqara	L XXIX	TPS	Menkauhor(?)	5	1930
	L XXX	TPS	Teti	6	1881
	L XXXI	TPS	Userkaf	5	1839

Site	Tomb number	Tomb type	Owner/ occupant(s)	Dynasty	Date of excavation or entry
NORTH SAQQARA	L XXXII[8]	SPS	Djoser	3	‡
	L XXXV	TPS	Unas	5	1881
	—	SPSu	H. Sekhemkhet	3	1954
	—[9]	?	?	2	—
	A	M	H. Hotep-sekhemwy	2	1900
	B	M	H. Ninetjer	2	1938
	—	M	Sened	2	*/1930s?
	—	TPS?	Merykare	10	*
SOUTH SAQQARA	L XXXVI	TPS	Pepy I	6	1880
	L XXXVII	TPS	Isesi	5	1945
	L XXXIX	TPS	Nemtyemsaf I	6	1880
	L XL	TPS	Ibi	8	1930
	L XLI	TPS	Pepy II	6	1881
	L XLIII[10]	M	Shepseskaf	4	1870s
	L XLIV	TPB	Khendjer	13	1929
	L XLVI	TPBu	?	13	1929
DAHSHUR	L XLIX[11]	TPS	Seneferu	4	1839
	L LVI[12]	TPSu	Seneferu	4	1839
	L XLVII	TPB	Sesostris III	12	1894
	L LI[13]	TPS	Ammenemes II	12	1894
	L LIV	TPB	Ammenemes V?	13	—
	L LVIII[14]	TPBu	Ammenemes III	12	1894
	L LVIII/1	R	Hor	13	1894
SOUTH DAHSHUR	A	TPB	?	13	—
	B	TPB	?	13	—
	C	TPB	Ameny-Qemau	13	1957
MAZGHUNA	N	TPB	?	13	1911
	S	TPB	?	13	1911
LISHT	L LX	TPS	Ammenemes I	12	1883
	L LXI	TPS	Sesostris I	12	1883
MEIDUM	L LXV	TPS[15]	Huni(?)/Seneferu	3/4	1882
HAWARA	L LXVII	TPB	Ammenemes III	12	1888
LAHUN	L LXVI	TPB	Sesostris II	12	1890
TELL el-AMARNA	TA 26	R	Akhenaten	18	1880s
	TA 27	Ru	Neferneferuaten?	18	1984
	TA 28	R	Neferneferuaten?	18	1984
	TA 29	Ru	Tutankhaten?	18	1984
ABYDOS (UMM el-QAAB)	B10/15/19	B	Horus Aha	1	1896
	O	B	Horus Djer	1	1896
	P	B	Seth Peribsen	2	1898
	Q	B	Horus Qaa	1	1896
	T	B	Horus Den	1	1896
	U	B	Horus Semerkhet	1	1896
	V	B	Horus and Seth Khasekhemwy	2	1897
	X	B	Horus Anedjib	1	1896
	Y	B	Meryetneith	1	1896
	Z	B	Horus Djet	1	1896
WESTERN THEBES: EL-TARIF	—[16]	R	Inyotef III	11a	1970
	—[17]	R	Inyotef II	11a	1970
	—[18]	R	Inyotef I	11a	1970

Site	Tomb number	Tomb type	Owner/ occupant(s)	Dynasty	Date of excavation or entry
DIRA ABU'L-NAGA	—	TPB	Inyotef V	17	*/1860s?
	—	TPB	Inyotef VI	17	*/1860s?
	—	TPB	Sobkemsaf I	17	*
	—	TPB	Kamose	17	*/1912?
	—	TPB	Taa I	17	*
	—	TPB	Taa II†	17	*
	—	R?	Amenophis I†	18	*?
DEIR el-BAHARI	DBXI.14	R	Mentuhotep II	116	1903
MEDINET HABU	MH 1	T	Harsiese	Th.23	1928
	—	T?	Osorkon III	Th.23	*
BIBAN el-MOLUK (V. of KINGS)	KV 1	R	Ramesses VII	20	‡
	KV 2	R	Ramesses IV+	20	‡
	KV 4	R	Ramesses XI	20	‡
	KV 6	R	Ramesses IX†	20	‡
	KV 7	R	Ramesses II†	19	‡
	KV 8	R	Merenptah†	19	‡
	KV 9	R	Ramesses V†/VI†	20	‡
	KV 10	R	Amenmesse	19	‡
	KV 11	R	Ramesses III†[19]	20	‡
	KV 14	R	Tawosret/ Sethnakhte	19/20	‡
	KV 15	R	Sethos II†	19	‡
	KV 16	R	Ramesses I†	19	1817
	KV 17	R	Sethos I†	19	1817
	KV 18	R	Ramesses X	20	‡/-
	KV 20	R	Tuthmosis I? Hatshepsut	18	1903
	WV 22	R	Amenophis III†	18	1799
	WV 23	R	Ay	18	1816
	WV 25	Ru	Amenophis IV/ Neferneferuaten?	18	1816
	KV 34	R	Tuthmosis III†	18	1898
	KV 35	R	Amenophis II	18	1898
	KV 38	R	Tuthmosis I[20]	18	1898
	KV 42	R	Tuthmosis II†	18	1900
	KV 43	R	Tuthmosis IV†	18	1903
	KV 47	R	Siptah†	19	1905
	KV 55	R	Neferneferuaten[21]	18	1907
	KV 57	R	Horemheb	18	1908
	KV 62	R	Tutankhamun	18	1922
EL-KURRU	Ku 15	TPS	Shabaka	25	1919
	Ku 16	TPS	Tanutamun	25	1919
	Ku 17	TPS	Piye	25	1919
	Ku 18	TPS	Shabataka	25	1919
NURI	Nu 1	TPS	Taharqa	25	1916

8 'The Step Pyramid'.
9 The 'Gisr el-Modir'; traces of a similar structure seem to be visible under the sand a little way to the north.
10 'Mastabat Faraoun'.
11 'The Red Pyramid'.
12 'The Bent Pyramid'.
13 'The White Pyramid'.
14 'The Black Pyramid'.
15 Begun as SPS.
16 'Saff el-Baqar'.
17 'Saff el-Qisasiya'.
18 'Saff Dawaba'.
19 Begun for Sethnakhte.
20 Constructed for reburial by Tuthmosis III.
21 Reburial.

Dynasty	Name	Rank
THEBAN TOMB (TT) 320, DEIR EL-BAHARI, discovered 1871		
17	Taa II	King
18.1	Ahmose-Henutemipet	Princess
18.1	Rai	Nurse
18.1	Siamun	Prince
18.1	Sitamun	Princess
18.1	Tetisherit/Unknown Woman B	Queen
18.1	Ahmose-Meryetamun	Princess
18.1	Ahmose-Inhapi	King's Wife
18.1	Amosis	King
18.1	Ahmose-Sipairi (?)	Prince
18.1	Ahmose-Henuttamehu	Princess
18.1	Ahmose-Sitkamose	Princess
18.2	Amenophis I	King
18.2	Ahmose-Nefertiry	Queen
18.2/3	Unknown Man ('Tuthmosis I')	Prince?
18.2	Baket(?)	Princess?
18.4	Tuthmosis II	King
18.5	Tuthmosis III	King
18.5?	Nebseni/Unknown Man C	Steward
19.2	Sethos I	King
19.3	Ramesses II	King
20.2	Ramesses III	King
20.8	Ramesses IX	King
21.1	Nodjmet	Queen/High Priest's Wife
21.3	Masaharta	High Priest of Amun
21.3	Tayuheret	High Priest's Wife
21.3	Henttawy A	Queen

Dynasty	Name	Rank
21.3	Maetkare	God's Wife of Amun
21.3	Pinudjem I	King
21.5	Nesikhonsu	High Priest's Wife
21.5	Isetemkheb D	High Priest's Wife
21.5	Pinudjem II	High Priest of Amun
22.1	Djedptahiufankh	4th Prophet of Amun
22.1	Nesitanebetashru	Wife of 4th Prophet of Amun
?	Five anonymous mummies	
18	Unknown Man E	
TOMB OF AMENOPHIS II, VALLEY OF THE KINGS KV 35, discovered 1898		
18.6	Amenophis II	King
18.8	Amenophis III	King
18.7	Tuthmosis IV	King
18.6	Elder Woman	Queen(?)
19.4	Merenptah	King
19.7	Siptah	King
19.6	Sethos II	King
20.3	Ramesses IV	King
20.4	Ramesses V	King
20.5	Ramesses VI	King
20.1	Unknown Woman D	Queen(?)
18.6	Webensennu	Prince
18.6	Younger Woman	Princess(?)
?	Three anonymous bodies	

The Kings of Egypt: Their Mummies, Coffins and Sarcophagi

King	Tomb	Mummy *=part only	Coffins *=fragments	Sarcophagi *=fragments	Canopics *=fragments
Dyn. 1					
H. Djer	Abydos O	[Cairo]*	–	–	–
Dyn. 3					
Djoser	Saqqara, Step Pyr.	Cairo, Qasr el-Aini*	–	–	–
H. Sekhemkhet	Saqqara	–	–	In situ	–
Huni(?)	Meidum Pyr.	–	Petrie Mus.*	–	–
Dyn. 4					
Seneferu	Dahshur, Red Pyr.	Cairo, Qasr el-Aini*	–	–	–
Kheops	Giza, Great Pyr.	–	–	In situ	–
Nebkare	Zawiyet el-Aryan, Unfinished Pyr.	–	–	In situ	–
Khephren	Giza, Second Pyr.	–	–	In situ	In situ
Mykerinos	Giza, Third Pyr.	? British Mus.*	British Mus.¹	Lost at sea	–
Shepseskaf	Saqqara, Mastabat Faraun	–	–	In situ?*	–
Dyn. 5					
Userkaf	Saqqara, Haram el-Makharbish	–	–	In situ	–
Sahure	Abusir	–	–	?*	–
Menkauhor	Saqqara L. XXIX (?)	–	In situ	–	–
Isesi	Saqqara, Haram el-Shawaf	Cairo, Qasr el-Aini*	–	In situ*	In situ
Unas	Saqqara L. XXXV	Cairo Mus.*	–	In situ	In situ
Dyn. 6					
Teti	Saqqara L. XXX	Cairo Mus.*	–	In situ	In situ
Pepy I	Saqqara L. XXXVI	Cairo Mus.*	?*	In situ	In situ
Nemtyemsaf I	Saqqara L. XXXIX	? Cairo Mus.	–	In situ	In situ
Pepy II	Saqqara L. LXI	–	–	In situ	In situ
Dyn. 11					
Mentuhotep II	Deir el-Bahari	British Mus.*	British Mus.*	In situ	British Mus./ Staten Is. NY

King	Tomb	Mummy *=part only	Coffins *=fragments	Sarcophagi *=fragments	Canopics *=fragments
Dyn. 12					
Sesostris I	Lisht, South Pyr.	–	–	In situ?	Cairo Mus.
Ammenemes II	Dahshur, White Pyr.	–	–	In situ	In situ
Sesostris II	Lahun	Univ. Coll. London?*	–	In situ	–
Sesostris III	Dahshur	–	–	In situ	–
Ammenemes III	Dahshur, Black Pyr.	–	–	In situ	–
Ammenemes III	Hawara	?*	–	In situ	In situ
Dyn. 13					
Ameny-Qemau	South Dahshur C	–	–	In situ	Cairo Mus.*
Hor	Dahshur L. LVIII/1	Cairo Mus.	Cairo Mus.*	In situ	In situ/Cairo Mus.*
Khendjer	Saqqara L. XLIV	–	–	In situ	–
Dyn. 17					
Djehuty	Dira Abu'l-Naga?	–	–	–	Berlin Mus.
Inyotef V	Dira Abu'l-Naga	–	Louvre Mus.	–	Louvre Mus.
Inyotef VI	Dira Abu'l-Naga	–	British Mus.	–	–
Inyotef VII	Dira Abu'l-Naga	–	Louvre Mus.	–	–
Taa II	Dira Abu'l-Naga	Cairo Mus.	Cairo Mus.	–	–
Kamose	Dira Abu'l-Naga	–	Cairo Mus.	–	–
Dyn. 18					
Amosis	Dira Abu'l-Naga?	Cairo Mus.	Cairo Mus.	–	–
Amenophis I	Dira Abu'l-Naga?	Cairo Mus.	–	–	–
Tuthmosis I	V. of Kings KV 20	–	Cairo Mus.	–	–
Tuthmosis II	V. of Kings KV 42	Cairo Mus.	–	In situ	–
Hatshepsut	V. of Kings KV 20	?	?Luxor Mus.*	Cairo Mus.	Cairo Mus.
Tuthmosis III	V. of Kings KV 34	Cairo Mus.	Cairo Mus.	In situ	–
Amenophis II	V. of Kings KV 35	Cairo Mus.	–	In situ	Cairo Mus.
Tuthmosis IV	V. of Kings KV 43	Cairo Mus.	–	In situ	Cairo Mus.
Amenophis III	V. of Kings WV 22	Cairo Mus.	–	In situ*	?*
Akhenaten	Amarna TA 26	–	–	Cairo Mus.*	Cairo Mus.*
Smenkhkare	Amarna TA 28 V. of the Kings KV 55	Cairo Mus.	Cairo Mus.	–	Cairo Mus./ Met. Mus. Art.NY
Tutankhamun	V. of Kings KV 62	In situ	In situ/Cairo Mus.	In situ	Cairo Mus.
Ay	V. of Kings WV 23	?	–	In situ	–
Horemheb	V. of Kings KV 57	?	–	In situ	Cairo Mus.
Dyn. 19					
Ramesses I	V. of Kings KV 16	?	Cairo Mus.	In situ	–
Sethos I	V. of Kings KV 17	Cairo Mus.	Cairo Mus./ Soane Mus.*	–	Soane Mus.*
Ramesses II	V. of Kings KV 7	Cairo Mus.	–	–	British Mus.*/ In situ*
Merenptah	V. of Kings KV 8	Cairo Mus.	–	In situ*	?
Sethos II	V. of Kings KV 15	Cairo Mus.	–	In situ*	–
Siptah	V. of Kings KV 47	Cairo Mus.	Met. Mus. Art.*	In situ	Met. Mus. Art.*
Dyn. 20					
Sethnakhte	V. of Kings KV 14	?	Cairo Mus.	In situ*	–
Ramesses III	V. of Kings KV 11	Cairo Mus.	–	Louvre Mus./ Fitzwilliam Mus.	–
Ramesses IV	V. of Kings KV 2	Cairo Mus.	–	In situ	Berlin Mus.*
Ramesses V	V. of Kings KV 9	Cairo Mus.	–	–	–

King	Tomb	Mummy *=part only	Coffins *=fragments	Sarcophagi *=fragments	Canopics *=fragments
Ramesses VI	V. of Kings KV 9	Cairo Mus.	*In situ**/ British Mus.*/ Cairo Mus.*	*In situ**	–
Ramesses VII	V. of Kings KV 1	–	–	*In situ*	–
Ramesses IX	V. of Kings KV 6	Cairo Mus.	–	–	–
Dyn. 21					
Pinudjem I	?	Cairo?	Cairo Mus.	–	
Psusennes I	Tanis NRT III	Cairo, Qasr el-Aini	Cairo Mus.	Cairo Mus.	Cairo Mus.
Amenemopet	Tanis NRT III	Cairo, Qasr el-Aini	Cairo Mus.*	Tanis	Cairo Mus.
Dyn. 22					
Shoshenq I	?	–	–	–	Berlin Mus.
Shoshenq II	Tanis	Cairo, Qasr el-Aini	Cairo Mus.	–	Cairo Mus.
Takelot I	Tanis NRT I	–	Cairo Mus.*	*In situ*	Stolen 1943
Osorkon II	Tanis NRT I	?*	?*	*In situ*	Stolen 1943
Harsiese	Medinet Habu	Cairo, Qasr el-Aini?	Cairo Mus.	–	Cairo Mus.
Shoshenq III	Tanis NRT V	–	–	*In situ*	Stolen 1943
Shoshenq IV	Tanis NRT V	–	–	*In situ*	–
Pimay	Tanis NRT II	–	?*	*In situ*	Stolen 1943
Shoshenq V	Tanis NRT I?	–	–	*In situ*	–
Dyn. 25					
Piye	Kurru Ku. 18	–	–	–	Mus. Fine Arts
Shabaka	Kurru Ku. 15	–	–	–	Khartoum?
Shabataka	Kurru Ku. 18	–	–	–	Mus. Fine Arts
Taharqa	Nuri Nu. 1	?*	Mus. Fine Arts*	–	Mus. Fine Arts
Tanutamun	Kurru Ku. 16	–	–	–	Mus. Fine Arts
Dyn. 26					
Apries	Sais	–	–	–	Cairo Mus.
Dyn. 29					
Nepherites I	Mendes	?*	–	*In situ*	–
Dyn. 30					
Nektanebo I	?	–	–	Cairo Mus.*	–
Nektanebo II	?	–	–	British Mus.	–

[1] Made in Saite Period.

The Royal Mummies: A Descriptive Catalogue

The royal mummies are listed in their chronological order; all surviving kings are included, with a selection of significant lesser royalties.

NOTE

'JE', 'TR', 'CG' and 'Ex.' numbers refer to the Cairo Museum.

Djer(?) (*c.* 3000 BC)

Djer was buried in a small brick-lined tomb at Abydos, with a much larger pan-elled funerary enclosure a kilometre or so away; from Middle Kingdom times onwards, it was regarded as the tomb of Osiris himself. The tomb was re-excavated by Sir Flinders Petrie in 1900. In a hole in the wall of the burial chamber was found part of the king's arm (or possibly that of the Queen), covered in bandages and bear-ing four gold and turquoise bracelets. The latter are preserved in the Cairo Museum, but the bones were discarded by the then-curator, Emile Brugsch. A skull previously found may have belonged to the same body. It is now lost.

Djoser (*c.* 2654–2635 BC)

In the burial chamber of the Step Pyramid were found a number of pieces of a mum-mified body, most notably the left foot, the upper right arm and shoulder, parts of the chest and elements of the spine. The foot was still partially wrapped in linen includ-ing all of his toes. After removing the upper layers of linen it was found tht the

embalmers had 'sculpted' the tendons and the toes had been modelled so that they overlay the actual toes below. The corpse had been closely wrapped in fine linen, which had then been covered in plaster and moulded to the form of the underlying body. Radiocarbon dates have now led to questions as to this item's identification.

Qasr el-Aini AI. 490

Seneferu (*c.* 2597–2547 BC)

The king first built the Bent Pyramid at Dahshur, but after its internal structural failure replaced it with the Red Pyramid at the same site. Inside the latter, in 1950, were found parts of his mummy, compris-ing parts of the skull, in places still covered with skin, including most of the lower jaw, part of the hip bone, pieces of rib, part of the left foot, the wrappings of the right one, a finger and parts of the vertebrae. The presence of resin on the *inside* of the skull strongly suggests the removal of the brain. The body was that of a man past middle age, but not greatly so, suggesting that the king came to the throne as a young man.

Qasr el-Aini (?)

Meresankh III (*c.* 2500 BC)

The queen, wife of Khafre, was buried at Giza. An inscription tells that she was buried 272 days after her death – far in excess of the usual 70-day period. This may have been due to the need to finish off the tomb before interment – certainly, her tomb and sarcophagus had been prepared

by her mother. The queen's body had been reduced to a skeleton, of a woman around fifty to fifty-five years of age at death. First examined by Dr Douglas Derry on 16 Dec. 1927, the mummy consists largely of broken pieces of skull and vertebrae. She had very worn teeth (several were missing), and she stood about 1.54 m (5 ft 1 inch) in life.

Cairo Museum

Mykerinos (?) (*c.* 2493–2475 BC)

Mykerinos' pyramid was robbed in ancient times, but a new coffin was provided by the priests of the Saite Period (*c.* 650 BC). The body was later disturbed again, the coffin's remains being found under a metre of debris in one of the pyramid chambers. With it were found the legs and lower torso of a human body, together with a foot and some ribs and vertebrae. All were contained within loose and incomplete skin, and had apparently been buried in a slightly flexed position, as were many Old Kingdom bodies. They would at first sight seem to be those of the king, but carbon-14 dating seems to make them at most only 1,650 years old. However, it is possible that contamination since discovery, in 1837, might be responsible for this unexpected date.

British Museum EA 18212

Isesi (*c.* 2413–2385 BC)

Isesi was buried in the Pyramid of the Sentinel at Saqqara. In the burial chamber, amongst the broken remains of his sarcophagus, was found most of the left-hand side of his mummy. These included the side of the face, complete with muscles and skin, parts of the cranium, with skin and hair, the throat, the spine, parts of the chest, elements of the left arm and hand, and parts of the left leg. The king seems to have died in his fifties.

Qasr el-Aini AI. 491

Unas (*c.* 2385–2355 BC)
The royal pyramid was first entered by Maspero in 1880; amongst the debris was found the king's left arm and hand, together with pieces of his skull, well preserved and covered with skin and hair.

TR 2.12.25.1

Teti (*c.* 2355–2343 BC)
Teti's sarcophagus was broken open by ancient robbers; of his body, only a shoulder and arm survived, more poorly embalmed than the remains of Isesi and Unas.

Cairo Museum

Iput I (*c.* 2340 BC) and **Khuit** (ditto)
Only bones remained when the pyramids of Iput and Khuit, both wives of Teti, were excavated. Iput's were of a woman with large eyes and narrow nose, who had died in middle-age.

Qasr el-Aini QA. 108 & QA. 109

Pepy I (*c.* 2343–2297 BC)
When entered in 1880, the king's Saqqara pyramid was found to have been badly destroyed; a single hand seems to have been all that remained of the monarch.

Nemtyemsaf I(?) (*c.* 2297–2290 BC)
The king was buried in his pyramid at South Saqqara, its burial chamber decorated with the Pyramid Texts. It was badly robbed in antiquity, but in the sarcophagus was found a naked mummy. It wore the side-lock of youth, normally worn by those no older than teenagers, and had had its lower jaw destroyed. It was otherwise very well preserved, and has sometimes been regarded as the mummy of the king, which had miraculously survived in its pyramid. It is uncertain, however, whether Nemtyemsaf I was really a child-king, and also the technique of mummification may be far too good to apply to an Old Kingdom mummy.

Ex. 3107

Neith (*c.* 2200 BC)
The headless, broken, remains of the body of Pepy II's wife, to which some soft tissue clung, were recovered from her pyramid at South Saqqara.

Qasr el- Aini AI. 418

Mentuhotep II (*c.* 2066–2014 BC)
The king was buried behind his temple at Deir el-Bahari, Western Thebes, within an alabaster shrine, at the end of a long corridor. The tomb was robbed, and all that survived were some wooden models, two canopic jar lids, a piece of the royal coffin, and some bones. The bones included some pieces of the skull and half the lower jaw.

British Museum EA 49457

Ashayet (*c.* 2050 BC)
The mummy of Ashayet, a wife of Mentuhotep II, was discovered in 1921 by Herbert Winlock, enclosed in what may be the earliest known anthropoid coffin; her beautiful sarcophagus is in the Cairo Museum. The body was in excellent condition, apart from some damage to the left side of the face. The viscera remained within her body cavity, although some resin may have been introduced into the bowel via the anus.

Qasr el-Aini QA 39

Henhenet (*c.* 2050 BC)
The corpse of Henhenet, wife of Mentuhotep II, was discovered by Edouard Naville in 1903–6, and was initially housed in the Metropolitan Museum of Art in New York. It was returned to Egypt in the 1920s, at the request of Professor Derry, at the Qasr el-Aini Medical School. The body was very well preserved, but during its voyage back to Egypt, the left side of the face was broken away. Examination of the body showed that the lady had died in child-birth, at a young age, as a result of having an abnormally small pelvis. No organs had been removed.

Qasr el-Aini AI. 456

Sesostris II (*c.* 1900–1880 BC)
The entrance to the king's pyramid was moved away from its traditional place on the north side to protect it from robbers. They nevertheless came, and all that could be found of the royal body was one of its leg bones, recovered by Sir Flinders Petrie in 1924.

University College London (?)

Hor (*c.* 1730 BC)
Although the tomb at Dahshur had suffered the attentions of robbers, it still contained much of its contents when opened by Jacques de Morgan in 1894. The king's body, reduced to a skeleton, lay inside his decayed coffin, within the sandstone sarcophagus. It was that of a man in his forties. His brain remained in the cranium.

Cairo Museum

Taa II (*c.* 1558–1553 BC)
Taa II was buried in a small pyramid at Dira Abu'l-Naga, at Western Thebes. It was later reburied in the Deir el-Bahari cache in his original coffin which had, however, been stripped of its gold covering. The body of a man about forty years old is poorly preserved, the skeleton largely disarticulated, with only part of the skin surviving, but it is the state of the head which grips one's attention. The skull is covered with horrific wounds: a dagger thrust behind the ear may have felled the king, after which blows rained down upon him. Mace-blows smashed his cheek and nose, while a battle-axe cut through the bone above his forehead. The mummy's mouth still has its lips drawn back in the king's final anguish. Oddly enough, his heart was removed, although his brain remains *in situ*.

JE 26209; CG 61051

Unknown Woman B (Tetisheri?)
(*c.* 1550 BC)
The body is that of an elderly woman, about 1.57 m (5 ft 2 inches) tall, balding, with artificial hair braided into her own white tresses. She had pierced ears. Her face was covered by a black shining resin-like substance. The head and right hand of the mummy had been broken off; X-rays reveal an impacted third molar.

CG 61056

Amosis (*c.* 1549–1524 BC)
The king was probably originally buried at Dira Abu'l-Naga, alongside his ancestors, but his mummy was found at the Deir el-Bahari cache. X-rays revealed that unlike most male Egyptians, Ahmose was uncircumcised; he also suffered from arthritis. The king's brain had been removed in an unusual manner: instead of having been drawn out through the nostrils, it seems that an incision was made on the left side

Amosis

(*above and right*) Unknown Man

of his neck, the atlas vertebra removed, and the brain taken out through the foramen magnum and the empty cranium packed with linen. The arms were extended, with hands inwards at the sides of the thighs.

JE 26210; CG 61056

Ahmose-Nefertiry (*c.* 1505 BC)
Wife and sister of Amosis, Ahmose-Nefertiry was originally buried at Dira Abu'l-Naga. The gigantic coffin of the queen was found at Deir el-Bahari, containing the mummies of Ramesses III and the queen herself. The body's right hand had been ripped off, no doubt to facilitate the removal of bracelets, and then tossed back into the coffin. The queen may have died around the age of seventy. She was going bald when she died and wore false hair braided into her own sparse locks; like a number of other members of the royal family, she had buck teeth.

JE 26208a; CG 61055

Amenophis I (*c.* 1524–1503 BC)
The king apparently died in his late forties. He seems to have been buried on Dira Abu'l-Naga, where a recently discovered tomb has been tentatively ascribed to him. His mummy was moved to the Deir el-Bahari cache in a badly battered state in the Twenty-first Dynasty, with careful new wrappings and equipped with a mask, which still remain in place together with garlands of flowers. It received a 'new' coffin – a mid-Eighteenth Dynasty one, repainted as part of the same batch from which came the replacement coffin of Tuthmosis II. The X-rays of this wrapped mummy (it has never been unwrapped

in modern times) show that his body is actually 1.79 m (5 ft 10 inches) long. It is possible that he was uncircumcised, though this does not show up too clearly in X-rays. Although broken off, the king's arms had been crossed at his breast, the position used for all subsequent New Kingdom monarchs. A wasp was found trapped in the coffin; perhaps it was attracted by the scent of the flower garlands draping the mummy.

JE 26211; CG 61058

Meryetamun (*c.* 1524–1503 BC)
The queen's mummy had been laid in a nest of two cedar-wood coffins, with a cartonnage outer case. The tomb (TT 358 at Deir el Bahari) was robbed in ancient times and the mummy was plundered. Later, in the Twenty-first Dynasty, the tomb was inspected and restored, one of the coffins being painted, and the mummy re-wrapped. The queen, who was arthritic and suffered from scoliosis, died rather young; after examination, the body was re-wrapped, as it now remains.

Cairo Museum

Unknown Man (*c.* 1525 BC?)
The mummy of Tuthmosis I was moved by his daughter to her own burial chamber, but returned to a hall of its own by his grandson, Tuthmosis III. The outer coffin was usurped by the Twenty-first Dynasty priest-king, Pinudjem I, and nothing certain is known of the final fate of Tuthmosis I's body. A mummy often called his was found in Tuthmosis I's usurped coffin but was certainly not that of a king on the basis of the position of its arms, down the side,

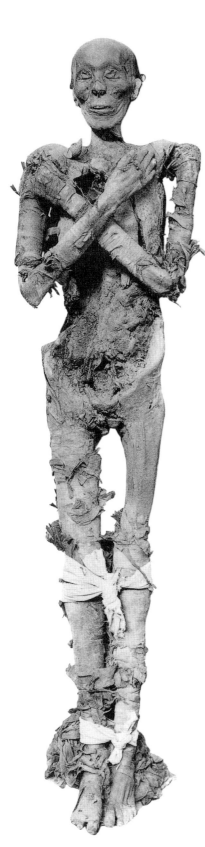

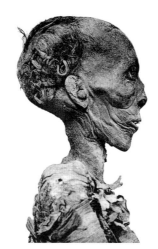

(left and above) Tuthmosis II

with the broken-off hands formerly placed over the genitals. The arms are crossed at the breast on all pharaohs' bodies after Amenophis I. It has recently suggested that, on the basis of its resemblance to other members of the Tuthmoside family, that it might be that of Tuthmosis's putative father, Ahmose-Sipairi.

JE 26217; CG 61065

Tuthmosis II (*c.* 1491–1479 BC)

Buried originally in the Valley of the Kings (probably KV 42), the king's mummy was violated by robbers in its original tomb, leading to its removal for safekeeping to the Deir el-Bahari cache. At some point, the body was restored alongside that of Amenophis I. Tuthmosis II probably died when he was about thirty years old; his skin was covered by scabrous patches, the cause of which is yet to be identified. The embalming agents have darkened the skin considerably. The arms are crossed over the chest, a pose that remained in vogue for kings until the Twenty-first Dynasty when the arms-at-the-side pose became popular again. Tuthmosis's ears and nose were plugged with balls of resin and his penis flattened against one leg, as also found on Tuthmosis III's body. The mummy was unwrapped on 1 July 1886.

JE 26212; CG 61066

Tuthmosis III (*c.* 1479–1424 BC)

Tuthmosis III was originally buried in the Valley of the Kings (KV 34), eventually being moved to the Deir el-Bahari cache in the battered remains of his middle coffin. Like Napoleon I, with whom he is frequently compared, Tuthmosis III was a

Tuthmosis III

short man, measuring just over 1.5 m (5 ft) in height. His hands are crossed on his chest. The mummy was badly damaged by robbers; the restorers of antiquity had to use narrow wooden splints to hold the body together. The visceral incision, which is still in the left side, now takes the shape of a diagonal cut from the hipbone to the pubes. It is only about 10 cm (4 inches) long and is neatly stitched closed. The face is covered with resinous material.

JE 26213; CG 61068

The Elder Woman (*c.* 1400 BC)
In a side-chamber of the tomb of
Amenophis II (KV 35), completely separate
from the cache of kingly mummies elsewhere in the tomb, were found three
mummies. On archaeological grounds,
they certainly belong to the time of
Amenophis II. Two are youngsters, but the
third is an older woman, with long, dark
wavy hair. The left arm is crossed across
her breast, the other straight at her side,
the standard pose for noble women at this
time. Apart from a hole in the chest, the
body is in good condition. A comparison
of the body's hair with a known lock of the
hair of Queen Tiye, wife of Amenophis III,
seemed to show the mummy to be that
lady's, but this has now been seriously
questioned. Her pudenda are covered with
resin. Her left heel seemed to have ulcers
on it; these are filled with linen. Either
these occurred before her death and
became inflamed with the natron, or
occurred during mummification, and
increased in size thereafter.
Valley of the Kings, tomb 35, CG 61070

Amenophis II (*c.* 1424–1398 BC)
His tomb (KV 35) was one of the very few
to have retained its mummy *in situ*.
Although damaged by ancient robbers, the
mummy was replaced in its sarcophagus
when the tomb was converted into a cache
for fugitive royal mummies in the Twenty-
first Dynasty. When the king died, his
brown hair had started greying at the
temples, with a bald spot on the back of his
head. At 1.8 m (6 ft), he was the tallest of
his family.
CG 61069

Tuthmosis IV (*c.* 1398–1388 BC)
Tuthmosis died fairly young and was
buried in the Valley of the Kings (KV 43).
Later his mummy was transferred to the
royal cache in Amenophis II's tomb,
rewrapped in its original bandages, with its
feet broken off. The mummy was very emaciated, perhaps due to a wasting disease that
is yet to be identified. The king was balding,
with pierced ears and manicured fingernails
at death. The embalming incision is crude,
the mummy's hands being crossed over the
chest, the fists clenched to hold the royal
sceptres. The king was unwrapped in modern times on 2 March 1903. The body cavity
was full of linen impregnated with resinous
material. The king's hand positions suggest

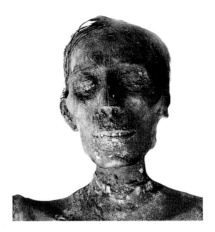
Tuthmosis IV

Amenophis III

he held either sceptres or a crook and a flail
in them.
JE 34559; CG 61073

Yuya (*c.* 1360 BC)
Yuya was the father of Queen Tiye, wife of
Amenophis III, and was buried in KV 46.
The body has flaxen hair, with stubble on
the chin. It is unknown if the hair colour is
natural, or a result of henna and chemicals
mixing over time. There is a gold plate
placed over the embaling incision in the
left side; the arms were crossed under the
chin. The lower part of the body is enclosed
in a 'cage' of gilded cartonnage, adorned
with Yuya's names and titles. He suffered
from arthritis in his knees and back.
CG 51190

Tjuiu (*c.* 1360 BC)
Tjuiu's is one of the best-preserved mummies in the Cairo Museum. Her hair, like
her husband Yuya's, is yellow, the reason
being likewise unclear. Her visceral incision is unusual in that it is almost vertical
and sewn up with string, a practice that
really came into its own only after the
Twentieth Dynasty. Her arms were fully
extended, like other females, and most
non-royal males.
CG 51191

Amenophis III (*c.* 1388–1348 BC)
Amenophis III's body was moved from its
original tomb, in the Western Valley of the
Kings (WV 22), to that of Amenophis II.
This mummy is very badly damaged, with
most of the flesh of the head missing, and
the front of the body damaged, but one
can determine that at the time of his death
Amenophis III was obese, ill, balding, and
in pain, especially from his dental problems.

The method of mummifying this pharaoh
is interesting, as considerable pains had
been taken to restore a life-like appearance
to the body. His skin was packed with resin
and bits of linen and moulded into a life-
like shape; his mouth was also packed so
that the face could be moulded into the
correct form. This method of moulding
the body into a semblance of its living form
became popular in the Twenty-first Dynasty,
but using different materials. The king was
covered with a shroud that was secured with
six bands of linen, and had a vertical line of
hieratic inscription on it showing that it
had been re-wrapped under Pinudjem I.
The body had been mutilated by robbers,
with the head and right leg broken off with
much loss of soft tissue. The limbs had
been replaced in their correct position and
bandages tied around them. The soles of
the feet were protected by linen pads.
Amenophis III's mummy was first
unwrapped on 23 September 1905.
JE 34560; CG 61074

Neferneferuaten/Smenkhkare
(*c.* 1346–1343 BC)
The young king was, against his evident
wishes, probably buried at Amarna in a
second-hand coffin bearing monotheistic
inscriptions. A decade later, on his brother
Tutankhamun's death, the coffin and
corpse were reburied in the Valley of the
Kings (WV 55), deprived of its names as
part of the reaction against the family of
Akhenaten. The tomb was rediscovered in
January 1907 by Theodore M. Davis.
Damp conditions had reduced the body to
a skeleton, with the skull partly smashed by
a rock-fall. It has now been restored. The
body was first thought to have been that of
Queen Tiye, then that of Akhenaten, and

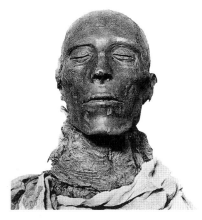

Sethos I

amulet still survives on the king's left arm. The left side of the chest is filled with masses of resin-impregnated linen. His eyes are closed. Bandages saturated with resinous material led to the blackening of the skin. Apparently the skin was brown when the mummy was first uncovered by Maspero in 1886. The heart was found on the right side of the body as it had been displaced during the mummification process.

JE 26213; CG 61077

Ramesses II (*c.* 1279–1212 BC)
The king was originally buried in tomb 7 in the Valley of the Kings, but robbed some time after the interment. The mummy was moved from tomb to tomb in the Valley for safety, eventually finding its way to the Deir el-Bahari cache. Ramesses suffered from abscesses in his teeth and

(below left and right) Ramesses II

then, finally, of Smenkhkare. He died at less than twenty-five years old. The identity of this mummy is still disputed.

CG 61075

Tutankhamun (*c.* 1343–1333 BC)
Found intact in the tomb (KV 62), the mummy has suffered badly from the effects of the decomposition of the sacred oils which were poured over it as it lay in its solid gold inner coffin. These effectively carbonized the flesh and stuck the body to the coffin, meaning that it had to be cut up to remove it. Part of the rib-cage is missing, and there are signs of a head injury, which may have caused the king's death.

Valley of the Kings, tomb 62

Ramesses I (*c.* 1298–1296 BC)
Ramesses was originally buried in the Valley of the Kings (KV 16), and was probably moved later to the Deir el-Bahari cache, where a coffin bearing his name was found; but his body has never been identified. It is possible that it was his mummy that was sold by the nineteenth-century robbers to a pair of ladies who later discarded it in the Nile.

Sethos I (*c.* 1296–1279 BC)
The king was buried in a superb alabaster coffin (now in the Soane Museum, London) in tomb 17 in the Valley of the Kings. His mummy was moved to the Deir el-Bahari cache and, although the skull was separated from the body by plunderers, the head of the mummy is very well preserved. The body itself, however, is badly battered. His arms were crossed, over his chest, with the hands open for the first time; earlier mummies were posed with clenched fists so as to grasp sceptres. X-rays have revealed that an

according to X-ray study, had the worst dentition of all the mummies examined. He suffered from severe arthritis in his hip joint and arteriosclerosis of all the major arteries of the lower extremities, making for difficulty in blood circulation and ambulation. The mummy was unwrapped on 1 June 1886 by Maspero. The event was attended by several important government officials, diplomats, doctors, archaeologists and artists, as well as the Khedive Tewfiq himself. The mummy had silky hair which had been white at the time of death, but had yellowed by the preserving chemicals. His nose and mouth were stuffed with a black resinous paste, and the legs and feet covered with resinous material. His genitals had been broken off by tomb-robbers. The mummy travelled to Paris in 1976 for further study and preservation.

JE 26214; CG 61078

Nefertari (*c.* 1250 BC)
Nefertari, the wife of Ramesses II, was buried in a superbly decorated tomb in the Valley of the Queens, enclosed in a massive granite sarcophagus. The sepulchre was ransacked in antiquity, and all that survives of the queen's body are her knees.

Egyptian Museum, Turin, Supp. 5254

Merenptah (*c.* 1212–1201 BC)
The king was buried in tomb 8 in the Valley of the Kings, his body being later moved to the cache in Amenophis II's tomb. The skin of the mummy was discoloured due to the salt contained in the mummification materials. The presence of salt was once used in the argument that identified Merenptah as the pharaoh of the Exodus who drowned in the Red Sea. Nothing about the mummy would support this claim. Like other pharaohs Merenptah suffered severely from dental problems: most of his molars are missing. He had severe arthritis, arteriosclerosis, and suffered from fractures in his thigh bones. His mummy was badly mutilated by tomb-robbers who split his right clavicle and injured his shoulder by plunging a knife or axe through it. This weapon was also used to hack a hole through his abdomen, and wrench off his right arm. His scrotum is missing and the exposed flesh is covered by resin. Either he was castrated before death, or, more likely, the flesh became over-dried in the embalming process causing the scrotum and testicles to fall off, so the

Merenptah

embalmers disguised the loss by using resin.

JE 34562; CG 61079

Sethos II (*c.* 1201–1195 BC)
Found in Amenophis II's tomb, Sethos's mummy had had its head, arms and portions of genitalia broken off, and his skull pierced by grave-robbers in their quest for plunder. His teeth are in better condition than those of the rest of the family, as are his joints; the king only suffered slightly from arthritis in his hip when he died at a fairly advanced age.

JE 34561; CG 61081

Siptah (*c.* 1195–1189 BC)
The king's body was seriously damaged by plunderers and later moved to the cache in Amenophis II's tomb. Like Merenptah's mummy, that of Siptah is discoloured by salt, the abdominal cavity being filled with dried lichen. His embalming wound is sewn up. The right cheek and front teeth were smashed by robbers, who also broke off the ears and the right arm. There is a painted black line across his forehead to demarcate the hairline. The left leg is shortened, with the foot in a vertical position; this is most probably the result of cerebral palsy.

JE 34563; CG 61080

Unknown Woman D (Tawosret (?))
The trough and lid of the inner coffin of Sethnakhte were found detached in Amenophis II's tomb. The trough contained

Sethos II

the body of Merenptah, while the lid contained a female mummy which might be that of Tawosret, who had originally been buried in the tomb used for Sethnakhte (KV 14); certainly it dates to her period. This mummy, of a very emaciated woman, has the arms stretched out at its sides, and has her own hair which has been styled into closely rolled curls on top of her head. Wrapped parcels of epidermis and viscera were found beneath the soles of her feet. The mummy is undamaged save for a large hole in her chest, which was presumably made by tomb-robbers in search of the heart scarab and other precious ornaments located in and on the chest area. Her body cavity is stuffed with linen bandages. The mummy was unwrapped on 5 July 1905. She wore a headscarf, tied on very much like those worn today.

CG 61082

Ramesses III

The king was buried in tomb 11 in the Valley of the Kings, begun for his father, Sethnakhte, but abandoned on the latter's early death. The mummy was found at Deir el-Bahari, and has been the model for many mummies featured in horror films. The king's arms are folded over his chest with open hands, a common pose for pharaohs of the Ramesside period. It was found well wrapped by restorers in antiquity, the linen carapace over the body still being in place. It has thus been impossible to check the body for any wounds that might derive from his likely murder. X-rays show three figures of the Sons of Horus inside the torso. The eye-sockets are packed with cloth, the pharaoh also sporting pierced ears, fashionable among men from the mid-Eighteenth Dynasty onwards. His hands are not flexed, but fully extended with the palms on the shoulders.

JE 26208b; CG 61083

Ramesses IV (*c.* 1153–1146 BC)

Reburied in the tomb of Amenophis II, after removal from KV 2, Ramesses' mummy was rewrapped clumsily by later priests. Robbers had broken off a foot, and opened a hole in the skull. The visceral incision had been sewn together with a twisted piece of bandage, the abdominal cavity filled with dried lichen, and the anus plugged with a ball of resin, an innovative and unusual feature. The king's own eyes

Ramesses III

Ramesses IV

Ramesses V

had been replaced by artificial ones made of small onions; onions were also placed in his ears, and the nostrils, filled with resin, were covered with the scale of an onion. His penis and scrotum were each bandaged separately.

JE 34597; CG 61084

Ramesses V (*c.* 1146–1141 BC)
It is uncertain where Ramesses V was originally buried, his own tomb being appropriated by his successor. He may either have been placed in its outer part, or a small tomb elsewhere, but after his burial was disturbed, he was moved to the royal cache in the tomb of Amenophis II. The king died in his early thirties, his mummy showing evidence for smallpox: the neck, chest and face being covered with raised nodules. He had an enlarged scrotum which suggests that he suffered from an inguinal hernia. The mummy's thoracic cavity was stuffed with sawdust and portions of internal organs. Such a replacement of the viscera packed with sawdust in the thoracic cavity after embalming became popular during the Twenty-first Dynasty. The king's face was coloured red, and his nostrils blocked with wax. He had an ulcer in his right groin that was smeared with a black resinous paste.

JE 34566; CG 61085

Ramesses VI (*c.* 1141–1133 BC)
Originally the king was interred in KV 9 in the Valley of the Kings, begun by Ramesses V, but completed for his uncle. Ramesses VI's coffins and sarcophagi were shattered by the robbers who broke in a few years after his death. The body suffered severe damage, and was later moved to KV 35. There, it lay within the Eighteenth Dynasty coffin of a priest named Re; under a neat shroud, the disarray became all too apparent. To make the remains look something like a mummy, the ancient restorers had tied the various parts of the body to a piece of the king's original coffin. Only the legs were basically intact, the hips being found where the neck ought to have been, the torso smashed, the arms hacked from the body and the right arm lost. Perhaps to make up for this, two other mummies' hands were found amongst the wrappings, giving the king three in all! The head had been broken from the body, its facial skeleton proving to be totally missing, the face

(*above and right*) Ramesses VI

consisting of no more than a flap of skin, above the still intact lower jaw. Together with that of Amenophis III, Ramesses VI's mummy is perhaps the worst example of tomb-robbers' destruction amongst the royal mummies.

JE 34564; CG 61086

Ramesses IX (*c.* 1123–1104 BC)
Ramesses IX was buried in tomb 6 in the Valley of the Kings. His body was removed during the Twenty-first Dynasty, and was discovered in the Deir el-Bahari cache, lying within one of the coffins of Nesikhonsu, wife of the High Priest of Amun Pinudjem II. The body had suffered considerable damage, its nose being missing and much of the skin badly cracked. Unlike most of the royal mummies, it does not appear ever to have received a full physical examination, but still lies alongside its fellows in the Cairo Museum.

Cairo Museum

Nodjmet (*c.* 1064 BC)
Nodjmet, the wife of the High Priest-King Hrihor, is the earliest mummy found of Twenty-first Dynasty type. The mummy was given artificial eyes made of black and white stones, false eyebrows of real hair, and a wig. Her cheeks and limbs were padded to give a more life-like appearance; she was also coloured with yellow ochre to enhance the effect. Her body was filled with sawdust, and her hands arranged along her hips. In her wrappings lay a heart scarab and statuettes of the Four Sons of Horus. The arms were extended along the length of the body, as was now once again standard. The lady reached an advanced age before death. Her face was very wrinkled and her hair, beneath its wig, was grey. Her embalming wound was plugged by wax, and her eyes, nose, mouth and ears were protected by wax plates.

CG 61087

Pinudjem I (*c.* 1049–1026 BC)
Pinudjem was buried in a coffin originally made for Tuthmosis I, whose body may have been destroyed by robbers. His first tomb seems to have suffered plundering, for his mummy was found in the coffin of the Seventeenth Dynasty queen, Ahhotep, in the Deir el-Bahari hiding place. The body seems to have been undamaged, enclosed in a closely fitting linen carapace;

unfortunately, it does not appear to have been examined since the 1880s.

Cairo Museum (?)

Henttawy A (*c.* 1025 BC)
As with Nedjmet's mummy, the face of this mummy, wife of Pinudjem I, was packed. However, the embalmers were over-zealous, thereby causing the skin to burst. This has recently been repaired, greatly improving the mummy's appearance. Her abdomen was packed with aromatic sawdust; the head was adorned with a wig, made of strands of black string rather than real hair; a painted black line stretches across her forehead. Her embalming incision was covered with a gold plate bearing the *wadjet* eye, the Four Sons of Horus and the queen's name and title. Her body was painted yellow, with the lips and cheeks painted red, and the eyebrows black. She had artificial stone eyes. The visceral packages were replaced in the body, with two of them containing figures of two of the Sons of Horus. The other two are missing, although presumably they were intended to be included.

CG 61090

Maetkare (*c.* 1025 BC)
As with all mummies of her period (Dynasty 21), the body of Maetkare, God's Wife of Amun, had been stuffed to preserve a life-like appearance. Her mummy is a very fine one, the body having been internally packed and moulded into the shape of the living lady, prior to being wrapped in very fine linen. The face was stuffed with mud and painted with yellow ochre. Early examiners believed that she had been prepared as though pregnant, a small mummy found within her coffin possibly being that of a still-born child. Since the God's Wife was supposed to be virgin, this has led to all kinds of speculations. However, X-rays have shown the small mummy to be that of a pet baboon, and it is possible that Maetkare's 'pregnant' appearance may be due to the over-packing seen on a number of other Twenty-first Dynasty mummies.

CG 61088

Masaharta (*c.* 1050–1042 BC)
The original burial place of Masaharta, the High Priest of Amun, is unknown, but his mummy was part of the Deir el-Bahari cache. His coffins were damaged in antiq-

uity, but his body was disturbed in modern times and the accompanying papyrus documents stolen. The face and body were coloured with ochre and both appear grossly corpulent, perhaps due to overstuffing with sawdust, resin and linen. An attempt was made to place the hands over the genitalia, but due to Masaharta's obesity this proved impossible. The embalming incision is higher up than in other contemporary mummies.

Luxor Museum of Mummification
[CG 61092]

Psusennes I (*c.* 1031–981 BC)
Psusennes I was buried in tomb III at Tanis, where his burial was found untouched in 1940. The mummy wore a solid gold mask, and was covered by a gold mummy-board, and lay within a coffin of solid silver, in turn enclosed within a granite coffin, and, finally, a granite sarcophagus, usurped from King Merenptah of the Nineteenth Dynasty. Unfortunately, the wrappings and flesh were totally destroyed by the damp conditions that existed within the tomb; nevertheless, it is clear that embalming of the usual type had taken place. The surviving bones are those of a very old man, who had suffered miserably from dental problems: a number of teeth had been lost through abscesses, one not long before death. He was also afflicted by severe arthritis of the back, and age-related problems with his right foot.

Qasr el-Aini QA. 2

Amenemopet (*c.* 984–974 BC)
Amenemopet does not seem to have been buried in the tomb that bears his name, rather being interred in a chamber of Psusennes I's tomb that had been intended to hold the latter's wife, Mutnodjmet. He was found lying in her sarcophagus, enclosed in a coffin of gilded wood, his face covered by a gold mask. Damp had destroyed the wood of the coffin, together with the mummy's flesh and wrappings. Many of the bones had been broken, but it

was possible to tell that the king had been a big, strongly-built, man, old at death. In contrast to Psusennes, his teeth, although worn, were sound; like him, however, his skeleton showed numerous changes brought about by old age.

Qasr el-Aini QA. 40

Pinudjem II (*c.* 980–958 BC)
Buried in his own adapted tomb (TT 320) at Deir el-Bahari that later provided a refuge for many of the royal mummies, Pinudjem's mummy and coffin are completely intact. The High Priest's mummy was coloured with ochre and his body cavity packed with linen parcels, some containing the embalmed viscera and others with sawdust. His arms were packed with mud.

CG 61094

Isetemkheb D (*c.* 960 BC)
She was interred in her husband's (Pinudjem II) tomb in Deir el-Bahari prior to his burial there. Her coffins were despoiled by the workmen responsible for burying her husband's body in the same tomb some years later. Her body has never been unwrapped, although X-rays show various amulets in the wrapping. She suffered from arthritic knees and from dental decay.

CG 61093

Nesikhonsu (*c.* 970 BC)
Nesikhonsu was a wife of Pinudjem II and predeceased her husband, dying fairly young. Her mummy is one of the best examples of Twenty-first Dynasty embalming. The entire body was packed and moulded without the distention visible in other mummies of the period. She had inlaid stone eyes. The arms were fully extended with the palms turned into the thighs. The heart scarab and a number of other items from her burial were stolen by the Abd el-Rassul family, and appeared on the antiquities market prior to the intervention of the Antiquities Service. Flowers were wrapped around the big toe of each

foot, and a flower lay on the left foot and another around the left ankle.

CG 61095

Shoshenq II (*c.* 895 BC)
Probably buried in a part of Tanis away from the known tombs, the king's mummy seems to have suffered from the flooding of the original tomb, earth and sprouting vegetable material having been carried into the coffin by water. It was accordingly moved to the tomb of Psusennes I in ancient times, where it was found in 1939, and taken to the Qasr el-Aini hospital for examination. The body wore a gold mask, the whole being enclosed in a mummy-shaped casing of cartonnage. This had the head of a hawk, as did the silver coffin that contained it. Damp had destroyed all that was not of bone or metal. The skeleton of the king showed him to have been 1.69 m (5 ft 6 inches) tall, and over fifty at death. The lack had resulted from an injury to the forehead, which had led to a severe infection. An area 8 × 6 cm (3 × 2¼ inches) had been affected, with inflammation spreading under the scalp, and through the bone towards the brain. An area of the interior of the skull was blackened and cracked: death was doubtless through meningitis.

Qasr el-Aini QA. 3

Harsiese (*c.* 867–857 BC)
Harsiese was buried in a stone-lined tomb in the enclosure of the Medinet Habu temple. The trough of his granite coffin had belonged to a sister of Ramesses II, but the hawk-headed lid had been made for him. Only a skull and a piece of arm-bone survived alongside this when the tomb was opened. The skull contains a hole, apparently made through a surgical procedure; the king seems to have survived this ordeal, to judge from the healing shown by the wound.

Qasr el-Aini (?)

Mummies in the Media

Mummies have not only been alluded to in poems and plays, but form the focus of several films, books and comic books. Below are listed a few of the films, books and poems which feature mummies prominently.

FILMS

The prototype for most of the horror-movie mummies is the mummy of Ramesses III, found at Deir el-Bahari.

1909 *The Mummy of the King Ramses*
1911 3 films, one French, one British, one American, all entitled *The Mummy*.
1915 *The Mummy and the Humming Bird*.
1918 *Eyes of the Mummy*. Germany
1926 *Mummy Love*. Germany
1932 *The Mummy* (the best and most famous of its genre, featuring Boris Karloff as the mummy).
1938 *Mummie's Dummies* (starring the Three Stooges).
1940 *The Mummy's Hand* (D. Foran plays the mummy).
1942 *The Mummy's Tomb* (Lon Chaney as the mummy).
1944 *The Mummy's Ghost* (Lon Chaney as the mummy).
1945 *The Mummy's Curse* (Lon Chaney as the mummy).
1954 *Abbott and Costello Meet the Mummy*.
1959 *The Mummy* British. (Hammer Studios version of Karloff in colour, with Christopher Lee and variations in the plot).
1964 *The Curse of the Mummy's Tomb*.
1967 *The Mummy's Shroud*.
1969 *The Night of Counting the Years* or *The Mummy* (based on the Deir el-Bahari cache)

1971 *Blood from the Mummy's Tomb* (an adaptation of Stoker's tale).
1980 *The Awakening* (another adaptation of the Stoker story).
1992 *I was a Teenage Mummy*.
1958 *The Mummy Complex* (a show at the Armstrong Circle Theater, New York).

PROSE

1828 Miss Jane Webb (afterwards J.W. Loudon) *The Mummy! A Tale of the Twenty-second Century*.
1833 W. Bayle Bernard's farce, *The Mummy* or *The Elixir of Life*.
1845 Edgar A. Poe, 'Some Words with a Mummy', in *American Weekly Review*, April.
1858 Theophile Gautier *Le roman de la momie* (about a mummy brought back by Vivant Denon, member of Napoleon's expedition). Translated 1882: *The Romance of a Mummy*.
1902 Isaac Henderson's play, *The Mummy and the Humming Bird*.
1903 Bram Stoker *The Jewel of the Seven Stars*.
1911 R. Austin Freeman *The Vanishing Man*, later called *The Eye of Osiris*.
1925 Mary Gaunt *The Mummy Moves*.
1929 F.M. Pettee *The Palgrave Mummy*.
      Arthur Conan Doyle 'Lot 249'.
      Arthur Conan Doyle 'The Ring of Thoth'.
1932 A. Eadie 'The Nameless Mummy', in *Weird Tales*.
1938 T.P. Kelley 'I Found Cleopatra', in *Weird Tales*.
1979 T.W. Hard *Sum VII*.
1980 A. Madison *Mummies in Fact and Fiction*.
1987 G. Griffith *The Mummy and Miss Nitocris*.
1988 Leslie Halliwell *The Dead that Walk:*

Dracula, Frankenstein, the Mummy and Other Favourite Movie Monsters.
1988 Ambrose Pratt *The Living Mummy*.
1989 Peter Haining *Mummy: Stories of the Living Corpse*.
1989 Anne Rice *The Mummy or Ramses the Damned*.
1990 Pauline Gedge *The Scroll of Saqqara*.
1990 Martin Greenberg (ed.) *Mummy Stories*.
1993 Robert Marrero *Vintage Monster Movies*.
1994 Elizabeth Peters *The Mummy Case*.
1996 Michael Tester *The Mummy Musical*. *The Living Mummy* Marvel Comic book series.
Several of Gary Larson's cartoons feature mummies.

SELECTED CHILDREN'S FICTION

1987 J. Belairs *The Mummy, the Will and the Crypt*.
1987 E. Bunting *I am the Mummy Heb Nefer*.
1987 E.A.M. Jakab *The Mummy Who Wouldn't Die*.
1987 R. Pond *The Mummy Rescue Mission*.
1990 T. Bradman *Sam the Girl Detective: The Case of the Missing Mummy*.
1993 K. Karr *Gideon and the Mummy Professor*.
1994 L. Kent *Norman Thorman and the Mystery of the Missing Mummy*.
1994 S. Kline *Mary Marony, Mummy Girl*.
1994 R. Pond *The Mummy Tomb Hunt*.
1994 R.L. Stine *Return of the Mummy*.
1995 S. Jackson and I. Livingstone *Curse of the Mummy*.
1995 B. Steiner *The Mummy*.
1995 E. Woodruff *The Magnificent Mummy Maker*.
1996 G. Gruesome *The Curse of Cleo Patrick's Mummy*.

Abbreviations and Bibliography

LIST OF ABBREVIATIONS

AL   *Amarna Letters* (San Francisco).

AR   *Amarna Reports* (London).

ASAE   *Annales du Service des Antiquités de l'Egypte* (Cairo).

ATut   *After Tut'ankhamūn* (ed. C.N. Reeves) (London, 1992).

BES   *Bulletin of the Egyptological Seminar* (New York).

BIFAO   *Bulletin de l'Institut Français d'Archéologie Orientale du Caire* (Cairo).

BioAnth   *Biological Anthropology and the Study of Ancient Egypt* (ed. W.V. Davies and R. Walker) (London, 1993).

BiOr   *Bibliotheca Orientalis* (Leiden).

BM   British Museum, London.

BMP   British Museum Press (formerly British Museum Publications).

BMFA   *Bulletin of the Museum of Fine Arts* (Boston).

BMMA   *Bulletin of the Metropolitan Museum of Art* (New York).

BSFE   *Bulletin de la Société Français d'Egyptologie* (Paris).

CAH   *Cambridge Ancient History* (Cambridge).

CdE   *Chronique d'Egypte* (Brussels).

CCG   *Catalogue Général des Antiquités Egyptiennes du Musée du Caire.*

CG   Catalogue Generale (Egyptian Museum, Cairo).

CM   Egyptian Museum, Cairo.

DE   *Discussions in Egyptology* (Oxford).

EEF   Egypt Exploration Fund.

EES   Egypt Exploration Society.

GM   *Göttinger Miszellen* (Göttingen).

JARCE   *Journal of the American Research Center in Egypt* (New York, &c).

JE   Journal d'Entrée (Egyptian Museum, Cairo).

JEA   *Journal of Egyptian Archaeology* (London).

JMFA   *Journal of the Museum of Fine Arts,* (Boston).

JNES   *Journal of Near Eastern Studies* (Chicago).

JSSEA   *Journal of the Society for the Study of Egyptian Antiquities* (Toronto).

LÄ   *Lexikon der Ägyptologie* (Wiesbaden).

MDAIK   *Mitteilungen des Deutschen Archäologischen Instituts, Kairo* (Mainz).

MFA   Museum of Fine Arts, Boston.

MKS   *Middle Kingdom Studies* (ed. S. Quirke) (New Malden, 1991).

MMA   Metropolitan Museum of Art, New York.

MMJ   *Metropolitan Museum Journal* (New York).

NARCE   *Newsletter of the American Research Center in Egypt* (New York).

Obj. no.   Excavators' object number.

OMRO   *Oudheidkundige Mededelingen uit het Rijksmuseum van Oudheden te Leiden* (Leiden).

PM   B. Porter and R.B. Moss, *Topographical Bibliography of Ancient Egyptian Hieroglyphic Texts, Reliefs and Paintings* (Oxford).

P7ICE   *Proceedings of the Seventh International Congress of Egyptologists,* ed. C.J. Eyre (Leuven).

RdE   *Revue d'Egyptologie* (Leuven).

RdT   *Recueil de travauxrelatifs à la philologie et à l'archéologie égyptienes et assyriennes* (Paris).

RMO   Rijksmuseum van Oudheden, Leiden.

SAK   *Studien zur altägyptschen Kultur* (Hamburg).

SJH   *Smithsonian Journal of History* (Washington).

SR   Special Register (Egyptian Museum, Cairo).

Studies... Griffiths   *Studies in Pharaonic Religion and Society for Gwyn Griffiths,* ed. A.B. Lloyd (London: EES, 1992).

TR   Temporary Register (Egyptian Museum, Cairo).

UC   Petrie Museum, University College London.

VA   *Varie Aegyptiaca* (San Antonio, TX).

Wb   A. Erman and H. Grapow, *Wörterbuch der ägyptischen Sprache* (Berlin, Leipzig).

ZÄS   *Zeitschrift für Ägyptische Sprache und Altertumskunde* (Leipzig, Berlin).

Titles given an asterisk (*) are suitable for the general reader.

ABBATE, O.P. 1910. 'Contribution a l'histologie des momies', *BIE* 4: 65-8.

ABDALLA, A. 1988. 'A Group of Osiris-cloths of the Twenty-first Dynasty in the Cairo Museum', *JEA* 74: 155-64.

ABOU SEIF, H. 1924. 'Two granite sarcophagi from Samannûd (Lower Egypt)', *ASAE* 24: 91-6.

— 1928. 'Rapport sur deux sarcophages découverts à Touna el–Gebel', *ASEA* 28: 61-5.

ADAM, S. 1958. 'Recent Discoveries in the Eastern Delta (Dec. 1950-May 1955)', *ASAE* 55: 301-24.

*ADAMS, B. 1984. *Egyptian Mummies* (Princes Risborough: Shire Publications).

ADAMS, C.V.A. 1966. 'The manufacture of ancient Egyptian cartonnage cases', *SJH* 1/3.

— 1990a. 'Shepenmut - Priestess of Thebes. Her Mummification and Autopsy', *DE* 16: 9-17.

— 1990b. 'An Investigation into the Mummies Presented to H.R.H. the Prince of Wales in 1869', *DE* 18: 5-19.

ÄGYPTICHES MUSEUM 1899. *Ausführliches Verzeichniss der aegyptyschen Altertüner und Gysabgüsse* (Berlin: W. Spemann).

ALDRED, C. 1963. 'Valley Tomb no. 56 at Thebes', *JEA* 49: 176-8.

*— 1972. *Jewels of the Pharaohs* (London: Thames and Hudson).

— 1979. 'More light on the Ramesside Tomb Robberies', *Glimpses of Ancient Egypt: Studies on Honour of H.W. Fairman* (ed. J. Ruffle, G.A. Gaballa and K.A. Kitchen) (Warminster: Aris and Phillips): 92-9.

*ALIKI. 1980. *Mummies Made in Egypt* (London: Bodley Head).

ALLEN, J.P. 1976. 'The Funerary Texts of King Wahkare Akhtoy on a Middle Kingdom Coffin', *Studies in Honor of George R. Hughes* (Chicago: University Press): 1-29.

— 1988. 'Two Altered Inscriptions of the Late Amarna Period', *JARCE* 25: 122-3.

ALTENMÜLLER, H. 1994. 'Dritter Vorbericht über die Arbeiten des Archäologischen Instituts Hamburg am Grab des Bay (KV 13) im Tal der Könige von Theben', *SAK* 211–18.

*ANDREWS, C. 1984. *Egyptian Mummies* (London: BMP).

*— 1994. *Amulets of Ancient Egypt* (London: BMP).

ARMITAGE, P. L. and J. CLUTTON-BROCK 1981. 'A Radiological and Histological Investigation into the Mummification of Cats from Ancient Egypt', *Journal of Archaeological Science* 8: 185-96.

ARNOLD, D. 1974, 1981. *Der Tempel des Königs Mentuhotep von Deir el-Bahari*, I, III (Mainz: Phillip von Zabern).

*ASSOCIATION FRANÇAISE D'ACTION ARTISTIQUE 1987. *Tanis: L'or des pharaons* (Paris: Association française d'action artistique).

BADAWI, A. 1957. 'Das Grab des Kronprinzen Scheschonk, sohnes Osorkon's II und Hohenpriesters von Memphis', *ASAE* 54: 153-77.

*BADAWY, A. 1954-68. *A History of Egyptian Architecture,* 3vv. (Cairo; Berkeley: University of California Press).

BADR, M. M. 1963. 'The history of urology in ancient Egypt', *J. Internat. Coll. Surg.* 39: 404ff.

BAGLIONI, S. 1993. 'Sulla conservazione degli organi viscerali di mummie egiziane', *Bolletin e atti accademia medica di roma* 59: 127ff.

BAILET, J. 1900. 'Contribution a l'Histoire des Origines de la Momification', *RT* 22: 180-99.

*BAINES, J. and J. MÁLEK 1980. *Atlas of Ancient Egypt* (New York and Oxford: Facts on File).

BAKRY, H.S.K. 1965. *A Brief Study of Mummies and Mummification* (Cairo: Al-Takaddum).

BALABANOVA, S., F. PARSCHE and W. PERSIG 1992. 'First Identification of Drugs in Egyptian Mummies', *Naturwissenschaften* 79: 358.

BALOUT, L. 1978. 'La momie de Ramses II au Musée de l'Homme.' *Le Courrier du CNRS* 28: 38-42.

BALOUT, L. et al. 1985. *La Momie de Ramses II* (Paris: Musée de l'Homme).

BARRACO, R. A. 1975. 'Preservation of Proteins in Mummified Tissue', *Paleopathology Newsletter* 11: 8.

BARRACO, R. A. et al. 1977. 'Paleobiochemical Analysis of an Egyptian Mummy'. *Journal of Human Evolution* 6: 533-546.

BARTLETT, W.H. 1850. *The Land of Egypt* (London).

BATRAWI, A. 1947. 'The Pyramid Studies: Anatomical Reports', *ASAE* 47: 97-111.

— 1948a. 'The Pyramid Studies: Anatomical Reports 1948. A small Mummy from the Pyramid of Dahshur', *ASAE* 48: 585-98.

— 1948b. 'Report on Anatomical Remains Recovered from the Tombs of Akhet-Hetep and Ptah-Irou-Ka, and a Comment on the Statues of Akhet Hetep', *ASAE* 48: 487-97.

— 1950. 'Remains of the Ka-nefer Family: a Scribe of Ptah's Temple at Memphis during the XXVIth Dynasty', *ASAE* 50: 477-94.

— 1951. 'The Skeleton Remains from the Northern Pyramid of Sneferu', *ASAE* 51: 435-40.

BAUMAN, B. 1960. 'The Botanical Aspects of Ancient Egyptian Embalming and Burial', *Economic Botany* 14: 37-55.

BAUMGARTEL, E. 1960. *The Cultures of Prehistoric Egypt* (Oxford: University Press).

BEINLICH, H. and M. SALEH 1989. *Corpus der Hieroglyphischen Inschriften aus dem Grab des Tutanchamun* (Oxford: Griffith Institute).

BELL, C.F.M. 1888. *From Pharaoh to Fellah* (London).

BELL, M.R. 1985. 'Gurob tomb 605 and Mycenaean Chronology', *Mélanges Gamal Eddin Mokhtar* I (Cairo: IFAO): 61-86.

— 1990. 'An Armchair Excavation of KV 55', *JARCE* 27: 97-137.

*BELZONI, G. 1820. *Narrative of the Operations and Recent Discoveries in Egypt and Nubia* (London: John Murray).

BENNET, M. J. 1981. The Egyptian Mummy as Historical Evidence. Bristol: unpubl paper.

BERKELEY 1979. *The Berkeley Map of the Theban Necropolis: Report of the Second Season, 1979* (Berkeley: University of California).

BERRILL, M. 1989. *Mummies, Masks and Mourners* (London: Hamish Hamilton).

BIERBRIER, M.L. 1988, 'The Lethieullier Family and the British Museum', in J. Baines, T.G.H. James, A. Leahy and A.F. Shore, *Pyramid Studies and Other Essays Presented to I.E.S. Edwards* (London: EES): 220–8.

— (ed.) 1997. *Portraits and Masks: Burial Customs in Roman Egypt.* (London: BMP).

BIETAK, M. and E. STROUHAL. 1974. 'Die Todesumstände des Pharaohs Seqenenre.' *Ann. Naturhistor. Mus. Wien.* 78: 29-52.

BIRCH, S. 1850. 'Notes upon a Mummy of

the Age of the XXVIth Dyn.', *Archaeological Journal* 7: 273-80.

— 1877. 'On a Mummy opened at Stafford House', *Transactions of the Society of Biblical Archaeology*, 5: 122-26.

— 1870. 'Account of Coffins and Mummies discovered in Egypt on the Occasion of the visit of H.R.H. the Prince of Wales in 1868-9', *Trans. Royal Soc. of Literature*, 2nd ser., 10: 185-213.

BLACKMAN, A. M. 1929. 'Sacramental ideas and usages in ancient Egypt', *RdT* 39: 44-78.

— 1924. *The Rock Tombs of Meir*, IV (London: EES).

— and M. APTED 1953. *The Rock Tombs of Meir*, V (London: EES).

BLUMENBACH, J F. 1794. 'Observations on some Egyptian Mummies Opened in London', *Philosophical Transactions of the Royal Society*, 84: 177-95.

BOESER, P.A.A. 1916-20. *Mumiensärge des neuen Reiches* (Hague: M. Nijhoff).

BONOMI, J. and S. SHARPE 1864. *The Alabaster Sarcophagus of Oimenepthah I., King of Egypt* (London: Longman, Green, Longman, Roberts and Green).

BOSSE-GRIFFITHS, K. 1978. 'Some Egyptian Bead-work Faces in the Wellcome Collection at University College, Swansea', *JEA* 74: 99-106.

*BOURRIAU, J.D. 1988. *Pharaohs and Mortals: Egyptian art in the Middle Kingdom* (Cambridge: University Press).

— 1991. 'Patterns of change in burial customs during the Middle Kingdom', *MKS*: 3-20.

*BRIER, B. 1994. *Egyptian Mummies: Unraveling the Secrets of an Ancient Art*. (New York: William Morrow).

BRIER, B. and M.V.L. BENNET. 1977. 'Autopsy of an Egyptian Fish Mummy.' *Post Library Association Report* 5: 8-11.

— 1979. 'Autopsies on Fish Mummies', *JEA* 65: 128-33.

*BROCK, L.P. 1992-3. 'Mummy Business', *KMT* 3/4: 13-17, 84-5.

BROCK, E.C. 1992. 'The Tomb of Merenptah and its Sarcophagi', *ATut* 122-40.

BROTHWELL, D.R. and B.A. CHIARELLI, eds. 1973. *Population Biology of the Ancient Egyptians* (London: Academic Press).

BROTHWELL, D. R. and E.S. HIGGS, eds 1969. *Science in Archaeology* (London: Thames and Hudson).

BROTHWELL, D. and A. T. SANDISON,

eds. 1967. *Diseases in Antiquity* (Springfield: Charles C. Thomas).

BROVARSKI, E. 1977. 'The Doors of Heaven', *Orientalia* 46: 107-15.

— 1978. *Canopic Jars: CAA Museum of Fine Arts, Boston*, Fasc. 1 (Mainz: Philipp von Zabern).

— 1984. 'Sarcophag', *LÄ* V: 471-5.

BRUGSCH, H. 1865. *A. Henry Rhind's Zwei Bilingue Papyri* (Leipzig: J.C. Hinrichs).

— 1883-91. *Thesaurus Inscriptionum Aegypticarum*, 1-5 (Leipzig).

BRUNNER-TRAUT. E. 1980. 'Ichneumon', *LÄ* 3: 122-3.

BRUNTON, G. 1920. *Lahun* I: *The Treasure* (London: BSA).

— 1937. *Mostagedda and Tasian Culture* (London: Bernard Quaritch).

— 1939. 'Some Notes on the Burial of Shashanq Heqa-kheper-Re', *ASAE* 39: 541-7.

— 1941. 'Objects from Fifth Dynasty Burials at Gebelein', *ASAE* 40: 521-27.

— 1943. 'The Bead Network of Shashanq Heqa-kheper-re, Tanis', *ASAE* 42: 187-91.

— 1947. 'The Burial of Pince Ptah-Shepses at Saqqara', *ASAE* 47: 125-37.

BRUNTON, G. and R. ENGELBACH 1927. *Gurob* (London: British School of Archaeology in Egypt).

BRUYERE, B. 1925.*Rapport sur les Fouilles de Deir el Médineh 1923-24* (Cairo: IFAO).

— 1929.*Rapport sur les Fouilles de Deir el Médineh 1928* (Cairo: IFAO).

— 1937a.*Rapport sur les Fouilles de Deir el Médineh 1933-34* (Cairo: IFAO).

— 1937b. *Rapport sur les fouilles de Deir el Médineh (1934-1935)* (Cairo: IFAO).

BUCAILLE, M. et al. 1976. 'Interêt actuel de l'étude radiologique des momies pharaoniques.' *Annales de Radiologie* 19.5: 475-80.

BUDGE, E.A.W. 1885. *The Sarcophagus of Anchnesraneferab, queen of Ahmes II, King of Egypt* (London: Whiting and Co.).

— 1890. *Perefatory Remarks Made on Egyptian Mummies*. (London: Harrison and Sons).

*— 1908. *An Account of the Sarcophagus of Seti I., King of Egypt, B.C. 1370* (London: Sir John Soane's Museum).

— 1910. *Facsimiles of Egyptian Hieratic Papyri in the British Museum* (London: British Museum).

*— 1925. *The Mummy: a Handbook of Egyptian Funerary Archaeology*, 2nd edition (Cambridge: University Press).

BUHL, M.-L. 1959. *The Late Egyptian Anthropoid Sarcophagi* (Copenhagen:

Nationalmuseets Skrifter. Arkaelogisk-historisk raekke, v.6).

CAILLAUD, F. 1823-27. *Voyage a Méroé*. (Paris: Press Royale).

CAMINOS, R.A. 1977. 'Grabräuberprozeß', *LÄ* 2: 862-66.

— 1982. 'The Rendells Mummy Bandages', *JEA* 68: 145-55.

— 1992. 'On Ancient Egyptian Mummy Bandages', *Orientalia* 61: 337-53.

CAMPBELL, C. 1910. *The Sarcophagus of Pabasa in Hamilton Palace, Scotland* (Edinburgh: R. & R. Clark).

CAPART, J. 1935. 'Le cercueil et la momie de Boutehamon', *Bull. mus. roy. d'art et d'histoire*, 3ᵉ ser., 7: 111-13.

— 1943. 'A propos du cercueil d'argent du roi Chechonq', *CdE* 18: 191

CARNARVON, Earl of, and H. CARTER, 1912. *Five Years' Explorations at Thebes* (London: H. Frowde).

CARTER, H. 1901a. 'Report on Tomb-Pit opened on the 26th January 1901', *ASAE* 2: 144-5.

— 1901b. 'Report on the tomb of Mentuhotep Iˢᵗ at Deir el-Bahari, known as the Bab el-Hoçan', *ASAE* 2: 201-5.

— 1902. 'Report on the Robbery of the Tomb of Amenothes II', *ASAE* 3: 115-20.

*— 1927, 1933. *The Tomb of Tut.ankh.amen*, II, III (London: Cassell).

CARTER H. and A.H. GARDINER 1917. 'The Tomb of Ramesses IV and the Turin plan of a Royal Tomb', *JEA* 4: 130-58.

CARTER, H. et al. 1902. 'Procès-Verbal d'Examen du Corps du Pharaon Amenothes II', *ASAE* 3: 120-1.

*CARTER, H. and A.C. MACE 1923. *The Tomb of Tut.ankh.amen*, I (London: Cassell).

CASTEL, G. and D. MEEKS 1980. *Deir el-Médineh 1970* (Cairo: IFAO).

CASTILOS, J.J. 1976. 'A Late Egyptian Mummy at the National Natural History Museum of Montevideo', *RdE* 28: 48-60.

CEJKA, J. et al. 1976. 'Contribution to the Chemical Research on Egyptian Mummies', *ZAS* 103: 128-39.

CERNY, J. 1973. *A Community of Workmen at Thebes in the Ramesside Period* (Cairo: IFAO).

CHAMPOLLION, J.-F. 1845. *Monuments de l'Egypte et de la Nubie* (Paris: Didot).

CHASSINAT, E. 1909. *La seconde trouvaille de Deir el-Bahari (sarcophages)*, I (Cairo: IFAO).

— 1916. 'La mise a mort rituelle d'Apis', *RT* 38: 33-60.

CHRISTENSEN, O. 1969. 'Un examen radi-ologique des momies égyptiennnes des musées Danois.' *La Semaine des Hôpitaux* 45: 1990-8.

CICCARELLO, M. and J. ROMER 1979. *Preliminary Report of the Recent Work in the Tombs of Ramesses X and XI in the Valley of the Kings* (San Francisco).

CLAYTON, P.A. 1994. *Chronicle of the Pharaohs* (London and New York: Thames and Hudson).

COCKBURN, T.A. 1973a. 'Autopsy team seeks a mummy's Medical Secrets.' *Smithsonian* 4.8: 80-89.

— 1973b. 'Death and Disease in Ancient Egypt', *Science* 181: 470.

COCKBURN, T.A. et al. 1975. 'Autopsy of an Egyptian Mummy.' *Science* 187: 1155-60.

COCKBURN, A. and E.(eds) 1980. *Mummies, Disease, and Ancient Cultures* (Cambridge: University Press).

*COMMISSION DES MONUMENTS D'ÉGYPTE 1809-22. *Description de l'É-gypte, ou Recueil des observations et des recherches qui ont été faites en Égypte pen-dent l'expédition de l'armée français: Antiquités (Planches)*, 9 + 10vv (Paris: Imprimerie impériale).

CONNOLLY, R.C et al. 1976. 'Seriological Evidence of the Parentage of Tutankhamun and Smenkhkare.' *JEA* 62: 184-6.

CONNOLLY, R.C. et al. 1980. *Mummification Supplement. MASCA Journal* 1.6. (Philadelphia: University of Pennsylvania).

COOK, N. 1996. 'Burton's Mummy', *Minerva* 7/6: 26-9.

COONEY, J. D. 1969. 'Cleveland's First Egyptian Mummy', *The Historical Society News* 23.7: 2-3.

CORCORAN, L.H. 1995. *Portrait Mummies from Roman Egypt (I-IV Centuries A.D.), with a Catalog of Portrait Mummies in Egyptian Museums* (Chicago: Oriental Institute).

CORCORAN SCHWABE, L. 1985. 'Hawara Portrait Mummy No. 4', *JEA* 71: 190-3.

COUGHLIN, E. A. 1977. 'Analysis of PUM II Mummy Fluid', *Paleopathology Newsletter* 117: 7-8.

COURVILLE, C. B. 1949. 'Injuries to the Skull and Brain in Ancient Egypt,' *Los Angeles Neurological Society* 14: 53-85.

CUENCA, E.L. 1978. *Radiological Examination of the Egyptian Mummies of the Archaeological Museum of Madrid* (Madrid: Museo Arqueológico Nacional).

DARESSY, G. 1898. 'Notes et Remarques', *RdT* 20: 72-86.

— 1900. 'Les Sépultures des Prêtres d'Ammon a Deir el-Bahari', *ASAE* I: 141-8.

— 1902a. *Fouilles de la Vallée des Rois 1898-1899 (CCG)* (Cairo, IFAO).

— 1902b. 'Procès-Verbal d'Ouverture de la Momie No. 29707', *ASAE* 3: 151-4.

— 1903a. 'Observations prises sur la momie de Mahepra', *ASAE* 4: 74-5.

— 1903b. 'Tombe de Hor-Kheb a Saqqareh', *ASAE* 4: 76-83.

— 1903c. 'Notes Sur la Momie de Thoutmosis IV: Procès-Verbal d'Ouverture', *ASAE* 4: 110-2.

— 1907. 'Les cercueils des prêtres d'Ammon (deuxième trouvaille de Deir el-Bahari)' *ASAE* 8: 3-38.

— 1908. 'Le cercueil du roi Kamès', *ASAE* 9: 61-3.

— 1909. *Cercueils des cachettes royales (CCG)* (Cairo: IFAO).

— 1910. 'La Tombe de la Mere de Chéfren', *ASAE* 10: 41-9.

— 1917a. 'Un Sarcophage de Tounah', *ASAE* 16: 115-20.

— 1917b. 'Sarcophage ptolémaïque d'Assiout', *ASAE* 17: 95-6.

— 1917c. 'La Momie du Pharaon Ménephtah', *BIE* 11 5ᵉ série: 39-47.

DARESSY, G. and C. GAILLARD 1905. *La Faune Momifiée de l'Antique Égypte.* (Cairo: IFAO).

DARESSY, G. and G.E SMITH 1903. 'Ouverture des momies provenant de la seconde trouvaille de Deir el-Bahari', *ASAE* 4: 150-60.

D'AURIA, S. et al. 1988. *Mummies & Magic: The Funerary Arts of Ancient Egypt* (Boston: Museum of Fine Arts).

*DAVID, A.R. 1979. *The Manchester Museum Mummy Project* (Manchester: University Press).

DAVID, A.R., ed. 1986. *Science in Egyptology.* (Manchester: University Press).

*DAVID, A.R. and E.TAPP, eds. 1984 *Evidence Embalmed* (Manchester: University Press).

*DAVIES, N. and A.H. GARDINER 1915. *The Tomb of Amenemhat* (London: EEF).

DAVIES, N. de G. 1943. *The Tomb of Rekh-mi-Reʿ at Thebes* (New York: Metropolitan Museum of Art).

DAVIES, W.V. and R. WALKER, eds. 1993. *Biological Anthropology and the Study of Ancient Egypt* (London: BMP).

DAVIS, T.M., et.al. 1908. *The Tomb of Siphtah, the Monkey Tomb and the Gold Tomb* (London: Constable).

— 1910. *The Tomb of Queen Tiyi* (London: Constable).

DAWSON, W.R. 1925. 'A mummy of the Persian Period', *JEA* 11: 76-7.

— 1927a. 'On two Mummies formerly belonging to the Duke of Sutherland', *JEA* 13: 155-61.

— 1927b. 'Making a Mummy', *JEA* 13: 40-9

— 1927c. 'On two Egyptian Mummies pre-served in the Museums of Scotland', *Proceedings of the Society for Anthropology, Scotland* 61: 290-6.

— 1928. 'References to Mummification by Greek and Latin Authors', *Aegyptus* 9: 106-112.

— 1929a. *A Bibliography of works relating to Mummification in Egypt* (Cairo: Institut d'Égypte).

— 1929b. 'A Note on the Egyptian Mummies in the Castle Museum, Norwich', *JEA* 15: 186-90.

— 1929c. *Magician and Leech* (London: Methuen).

— 1934.'Pettigrew's Demonstrations on Mummies. A Chapter in the History of Egyptology', *JEA* 20: 170-82

— 1953. 'Remarks on the Memoir by Dr. Franz Jonckheers entitled "Autour de l'au-topsie d'une Momie". Bruxelles, 1942'. MSS. 11 I.

— 1973b.'Death and Disease in Ancient Egypt', *Science* 181: 470-1.

DAWSON, W.R. and P.H.K. GRAY 1968. *Catalogue of Egyptian Antiquities in the British Museum*, I *Mummies and Human Remains* (London: British Museum).

*DAWSON, W.R., E.P. UPHILL and M.L. BIERBRIER 1995. *Who Was Who in Egyptology* 3rd edition (London: EES).

DEBONO, F. 1952. 'La Nécropole Prédynastique d'Héliopolis', *ASAE* 52: 625-52.

DE BUCK, A. 1935-1961. *The Egyptian Coffin Texts*, 7vv (Chicago: University Press).

DE CALUWE, A. 1993. 'Les Bandelettes de Momie du Musée Vleeshuis d'Anvers', *JEA* 79: 199-214.

DE GOROSTARZU, X. 1901. 'Lettre Sur Deux Tombeaux de Crocodiles', *ASAE* 2: 182-4.

DELORENZI, E. and R. GRILLETTO 1989. *Le Mummie del Museeo Egizio di Torino, N. 13001-26: Indagine antropo-radiologia* (Milan: Istituto Editoriale Cisalpino-La Goliardica).

DE MEULENAERE H., and P. MACKAY 1977. *Mendes*, II (Warminster: Aris and Phillips).

DE MORGAN, J. 1895, 1903. *Fouilles à Dahchour* I, II (Vienna: Adolphe Holzhausen).

DERCHAIN, P. 1965. *Le Papyrus Salt 825 (BM 10051): Rituel Pour la Conservation de la Vie en Egypte*. Brussels.

DERRY, D.E. 1934. 'An X-ray examination of the Mummy of King Amenophis I', *ASAE* 34: 47-8.

— 1935. 'Report on the Human Remains From the Granite Sarcophagus Chamber in the Pyramid of Zoser.' *ASAE* 35: 28-30.

— 1939a. 'The 'Mummy' of Sit-Amun', *ASAE* 39: 411-6.

— 1939b. 'Note on the Remains of Shashanq', *ASAE* 39: 549-51.

— 1940/41. 'An examination of the Bones of King Psusennes I', *ASAE* 40: 969-70.

— 1942a. 'Report on the Skeleton of King Amenemopet', *ASAE* 41: 149.

— 1947. 'The Bones of Prince Ptah-Shepses', *ASAE* 47: 139-43.

*DESROCHES NOBLECOURT, C. 1963. *Tutankhamen: life and death of a pharaoh* (London: Michael Joseph).

*— 1985. *The Great Pharaoh Ramses and his Time* (Montreal: Canada Exim Group).

DIENER, L. 1973.'A Human-masked and Doll-shaped Hawk-mummy'. *CdE* 48/95: 60-5.

DOBSON, J. 1959. 'A Curator's Curiosity.' *Annual of the Royal College of Surgeons* 24: 331-7.

DODSON, A.M. 1986. 'Was the sarcophagus of Ramesses III begun for Sethos II?' *JEA* 72: 196-8.

— 1987. 'The Tombs of the Kings of the Thirteenth Dyansty in the Memphite Necropolis', *ZÄS* 114: 36-45.

— 1988a. 'The Tombs of the Kings of the Early Eighteenth Dynasty at Thebes', *ZÄS* 115: 110-123.

— 1988b. 'The Tombs of the Queens of the Middle Kingdom', *ZÄS* 115: 123-36.

— 1988c. 'Some Notes Concerning the Royal Tombs at Tanis', *CdE* 63/126: 221-3.

— 1988d. 'Egypt's first antiquarians?', *Antiquity* 62/236: 513-7.

*— 1991. *Egyptian Rock-cut Tombs* (Princes Risborough: Shire Publications)

— 1992a. 'KV 55 and the End of the Reign of Akhenaten', *VI Congresso Internazionale di Egittologia* (Turin): 135-9.

— 1992b. 'On the Burial of Prince Ptahshepses', *GM* 129: 49-51.

— 1993a. 'On the Origin, Contents and Fate of Biban el-Moluk Tomb 55', *GM* 132: 21-8.

*— 1993b. 'Something Old, Something New, Something Borrowed, Something ... Granite', *KMT* 4:3: 58-69, 85.

— 1994. *The Canopic Equipment of the Kings of Egypt* (London: Kegan Paul International).

*— 1995a. *Monarchs of the Nile* (London: Rubicon).

*— 1995b. 'Of Bulls and Princes: the Early Years of the Serapeum at Sakkara', *KMT* 6/1: 18-32.

*— 1998a. *After the Pyramids* (London: Rubicon).

— 1998b. 'On the burial of Maihirpri and certain coffins of the Eighteenth Dynasty' *P7ICE*.

— 1998c. 'A Funerary Mask in Durham and mummy adornment in the late Second Intermediate Period and early Eighteenth Dynasty', *JEA* 84.

— forthcoming. *The Coffins and Canopic Equipment from the Tomb of Tutankhamun.*

DONADONI ROVERI, A.M. 1969. *I sarcophagi egizi dalle origini alla fine dell' Antico Regno* (Rome: Università degli Studi di Roma).

DORMAN, P.F. 1988. *The Monuments of Senenmut* (London: Kegan Paul International).

*DOXIADIS, E. 1995. *The Mysterious Fayum Portraits: Faces from Ancient Egypt* (London: Thames and Hudson/New York: Abrams).

DRIOTON, E. 1940. 'Bernhard Grdseloff - *Das ägyptische Reinegungszelt*', *ASAE* 40: 1007-14.

— 1944. 'La Ceinture en Or Recemment Decouverte à Sakkara', *BIFAO* 26: 77-90.

DRIOTON, E. and J.-Ph. LAUER 1951. 'Les tombes jumelées de Neferibrê-sa-Neith et de Ouahibrê-men' *ASAE* 51: 469-90.

DUNAND, F. 1994. *Mummies: a Journey Through Eternty* (London: Thames and Hudson/New York: Abrams).

DUNHAM, D. 1931. 'A Fragment from the Mummy Wrappings of Tuthmosis III', *JEA* 17: 209-210.

— 1950. *Royal Cemeteries of Kush* I, *El-Kurru* (Boston: MFA).

— 1955. *Royal Cemeteries of Kush* II, *Nuri* (Boston: MFA).

DUNHAM, D and W.K. SIMPSON, 1974. *The Mastaba of Queen Mersyankh III* (Boston: MFA)

EATON-KRAUSS, M. 1990. 'The coffins of Queen Ahhotpe, consort of Seqeni-en-Re and mother of Ahmose', *CdE* 65/130: 195-205.

— 1993. *The Sarcophagus from the tomb of Tutankhamun* (Oxford: Griffith Institute).

EDGAR, C.C. 1905. *Graeco-Egyptian Coffins, Masks and Portraits* (Cairo: IFAO).

— 1907. 'The Sarcophagus of an Unknown Queen', *ASAE* 8: 276-80.

*EDWARDS, I.E.S. 1985. *The Pyramids of Egypt*[3] (Harmondsworth: Penguin).

*EDWARDS, I.E.S. and A.W. SHORTER 1938. *A Handbook to the Egyptian Mummies and Coffins Exhibited in the British Museum* (London: British Museum).

EIGNER, D. 1984. *Die monumentalen Grabbauten der Spätzeit in der Thebanischen Nekropole* (Vienna: Akademie der Wissenschaften).

EL-KHOULY, A. and G.T. MARTIN 1987. *Excavations in the Royal Necropolis at El-'Amarna 1984* (*SASAE* 33) (Cairo: EAO).

*EL-MAHDY, C. 1989. *Mummies, Myth and Magic in Ancient Egypt.* (London and New York: Thames and Hudson).

EL-SADEEK, W. 1984. *Twenty-sixth Dynasty Necropolis at Giza* (Vienna: Institut für Afrikanistik und Ägyptologie).

EMERY, W.B. 1949, 1954, 1958. *Great Tombs of the First Dynasty*, 3 vv. (Cairo: IFAO/London: EES).

*— 1961. *Archaic Egypt* (Harmondsworth: Penguin).

— 1965. 'Preliminary Report on the Excavations at North Saqqara, 1969-70', *JEA* 51: 3-8.

ENGELBACH, R. 1931. 'The So-called Coffin of Akhenaten', *ASAE* 31: 98-114.

— 1939. 'Notes on the Coffin and 'Mummy' of Princess Sit-Amun', *ASAE* 39: 405-9.

— 1940. 'Material for a Revision of the History of the Heresy Period of the XVIIIth Dynasty', *ASAE* 40: 133-65.

ENGELBACH, R. and D.E. DERRY 1942. 'Mummification', *ASAE* 41: 233-69.

*ERMAN, A. 1907. *A Handbook of Egyptian Religion* (London: Constable).

*FAKHRY, A. 1961. *The Pyramids*, 2nd edition (Chicago: University Press).

FAULKNER, R.O. 1973-8. *The Ancient Egyptian Coffin Texts*, 3vv. (Warminster: Aris and Phillips).

— 1985. *The Ancient Egyptian Book of the Dead* (London: BMP).

FILER, J. 1995. *Disease* (London: BMP).

FIRTH, C.M. and B. GUNN, 1926. *The Teti Pyramid Cemeteries* (Cairo: IFAO).

FOUQUET, D. 1886. 'Observations Relevées sur Quelques Mommies Royales d'Egypte', *Bulletin de la Societe Anthropolgie* 3: 578-86.

— 1890. *Les Mommies Royales de Deir el-Bahari. Rapport addressé a M. le Directeur Général des Fouilles en Egypte, Musée de Guiseh* (Cairo: IFAO).

— 1897. 'Note Pour Servir a l'Historie de l'Embaumment en Egypte', *BIE* 3ᵉ, 7: 89-97.

FRASER, G. 1902. 'The Early Tombs at Tehneh', *ASAE* 3: 67-76.

GABRA, S. 1928. 'Un sarcophage de Touna', *ASAE* 28: 66-79.

— 1939. 'Fouilles de l'Université "Fouad el Awal", a Touna el-Gebel (Hermopolis Ouest)', *ASAE* 39: 483-527.

GAILLARD, C. 1927. 'Les animaux consacrés a la divinité de l'ancienne Lycopolis.' *ASAE* 27: 33-42.

GANNAL, J.N. 1840. *History of Embalming* (Philadelphia).

GARDINER, A.H. 1935. *The Attitude of the Ancient Egyptians to Death and the Dead* (Cambridge: University Press).

*GARSTANG, J. 1907. *The Burial Customs of Ancient Egypt* (London: Constable).

GAUTHIER, H. 1912-13. *Cercueils anthropoïdes des prêtres de Montou* (Cairo: IFAO).

— 1930. 'Le sarcophage no. 6007 du Musée du Caire', *ASAE* 30: 1174-83.

— 1921. 'Un tombeau de Tell Moqdam', *ASAE* 21: 21-7.

— 1928. 'Un vice-roi d'Éthiopie enseveli à Bubastis', *ASAE* 28: 129-37.

GAUTHIER, H. and G. LEFEBVRE 1923. 'Sarcophages du moyen empire provenant de la nécropole d'Assiout', *ASAE* 23: 1-33.

GERMER, R. 1984. 'Die Angebliche Mumie der Teje: Probleme Interdisziplinärere Arbeiten', *SAK* 11: 85-90.

— 1986. 'Die Verwendung von Flechten bei der Mumifizierung', *SAK* 13: 95-8.

*— 1991. *Mumien: Zeugen des Pharaonenreiches* (Zurich: Artemis and Winkler).

GERMER, R., T. NICKOL, F. SCHMIDT and W. WILKE, 1995. 'Untersuchungen der altägyptischen Mumien des Ägyptische Museum der Universität Leipzig und des Museums für Völkerkunde Leipzig', *ZÄS* 122: 137-54.

GOEDICKE, H. 1955. 'The Egyptian Idea of Passing from Life to Death', *Orientalia* 24: 225-39.

GOYON, J-C. 1972. *Rituels Funéraires de l'Ancienne Egypte* (Paris: Cerf).

GOYON, J-C. and P. JOSSET, 1988. *Un corps pour l'Éternité* (Paris: Le Léopard d'Or).

GRAF, W. 1949. 'Preserved Histological Structures in Egyptian Mummy Tissues and Ancient Swedish Skeletons', *Acta Anatomica* 8: 236-50.

GRANVILLE, A.B. 1825. *An Essay on Egyptian Mummies with Observations on the Art of Embalming Among the Ancient Egyptians* (London: W. Nicol).

GRAY, P.H.K. 1966a. 'Radiological Aspects of the Mummies of Ancient Egyptians in the Rijksmuseum van Oudheden, Leiden.' *OMRO* 47: 1-30.

— 1966b. 'Embalmers' "Restorations"', *JEA* 52: 138-40.

— 1967. 'Two Mummies of Ancient Egyptians in the Hancock Museum, Newcastle', *JEA* 53: 75-8.

— 1970. 'An Account of a Mummy in the County Museum and Art Gallery, Truro', *JEA* 56: 132-4.

— 1971. 'Artificial eyes in Mummies', *JEA* 57: 125-6.

— 1972. 'Notes Concerning the Position of Arms and Hands of Mummies with a View to Possible Dating of the Specimen.' *JEA* 58: 200-4.

GRAY, P.H.K. and D. SLOW 1968. 'Egyptian Mummies in the City of Liverpool Museums', *Liverpool Museums Bulletin* 15: 28-32.

GRDSELOFF, B. 1941. *Das ägyptische Reinigungszelt* (Cairo: Archäologische Untersuchung Etudes Egyptiennes, fasc. 1).

— 1951. 'Nouvees données Concernant la Tente de Purification', *ASAE* 51: 129-42.

*GREEN, L. 1992-3. 'Mummymania', *KMT* 3/4: 34-37.

*GREENER, L. 1966. *The Discovery of Egypt* (London: Cassell).

GREENHILL, T. 1705. *NEKPOKHΔEIA, or the Art of Embalming* (London: Privately Printed).

GRIFFITH, F.Ll. 1900. *Stories of the high priests of Memphis, the Sethon of Herodotus and the demotic tales of Khamuas* (Oxford: Clarendon Press).

GRILLETTO, R. 1991. *Catalogo Generale del Museo Egizio di Torino: Materiali Antropologici e Zoologici.* (Turin: Egyptian Museum).

GRIMM, G. 1974. *Die Römischen Mumienmasken aus Ägypten* (Wiesbaden: Franz Steiner Verlag).

GROFF, W. 1900-1. 'La Momie du Roi Mer-en-ptah Ba-en-ra', *RT* 22: 136; *RT* 23: 32-8.

HABACHI, L. 1939. 'A First Dynasty Cemetery at Abydos', *ASAE* 39: 767-81.

— 1947. 'A Statue of Osiris Made for Ankhefenuamun, Prophet of the House of Amun in Khapu and his Daughter', *ASAE* 47: 261-83.

— 1955. 'Clearance of the Tomb of Kheruef at Thebes, 1957-58', *ASAE* 55: 325-50.

— 1957. *Tell Basta* (Cairo: IFAO): 97—102.

— 1967. 'An Embalming Bed of Amenhotep, Steward of Memphis under Amenhotep III', *MDAIK* 22: 42-7.

— 1974. 'Lids of the Outer Sarcophagi of Meryetamen and Nefertari, Wives of Ramessses II', in *Festscrift zum 150jährigen Bestehen des Berliner Ägyptischen Museums* (Berlin: Akademie Verlag): 105-112.

HADLEY, J. 1764. 'An Account of a Mummy', *Philosophical Transactions of the Royal Society* 54: 1-2.

HALL, H.R.H. 1929. 'Theriomorphic canopic jar-heads of the Middle Kingdom(?)', *LAAA* 16: 46-7.

HAMADA, A. 1935. 'A sarcophagus from Mit-Rahîna', *ASAE* 35: 122-31.

— 1937a. 'The Clearance of a Tomb Found at Al-Fostat, 1936', *ASAE* 37: 58-70.

— 1937b. 'Tomb of Pawen-Hatef at Al-Fostat', *ASAE* 37: 135-42.

HAMILTON-PATERSON, J. and C. ANDREWS, 1978. *Mummies* (New York: Penguin).

HAMMER III, J.E. 1987. *Se-ankh: an interdisciplinary historical and biomedical study of an Egyptian mummy head* (Memphis, TN: University Press).

HANZAK, J. 1977. 'Egyptian Mummies of Animals in Czechoslovak Collections', *ZÄS* 104: 86-8.

HARRIS, J.E. et al. 1970. 'Orthodontics' Contribution to Save the Monuments of Nubia: A 1970 Field Report', *American Journal of Orthodontics* 58.6: 578-96.

HARRIS, J.E. et al. 1975. 'Restorative Dentistry in Ancient Egypt: an Archaeological Fact', *Journal of the Michigan Dental Association* 57: 401-04.

HARRIS, J.E., E.F. WENTE, et. al. 1979. 'The Identification of the "Elder Lady" in the Tomb of Amenhotep II as Queen Tiye', *Delaware Medical Journal* 51, no.2: 39–93.

HARRIS, J.E. and E.F. WENTE 1980. *An X-Ray Atlas of the Royal Mummies* (Chicago: University Press).

*HARRIS, J.E. and K. R. WEEKS, 1973. *X-Raying the Pharaohs* (London: Macdonald; New York: Scribners).

HARRIS, J.R. 1961. *Lexicographical Studies in Ancient Egyptian Minerals* (Berlin: Akademie-Verlag).

HARRISON, R.G. 1966. 'An Anatomical Examination of the Pharaonic Remains Purported to be Akhenaten', *JEA* 52: 95-119.

— 1978. 'The Tutankhamun Post-Mortem', *Chronicle: essays from ten years of television archaeology*, ed. R. Sutcliffe (London: BBC): 40-52.

*HARRISON, R.G. and A.B. ABDALLA, 1972. 'The Remains of Tutankhamun', *Antiquity* 46: 8-14.

HARRISON, R.G., R.C. CONNOLLY and A.B. ABDALLA 1965. 'Kinship of Smenkhkare and Tutankhamun affirmed by seriological micromethod', *Nature* 224: 325.

HARRISON, R.G., R.C. CONNOLLY, S. AHMED, A.B. ABDALLA and M. EL-GHAWABY, 1979. 'A mummified foetus from the tomb of Tutankhamun' *Antiquity* 53: 19-21.

HART, G. D. et al. 1977. 'Autopsy of an Egyptian Mummy-ROM I', *Canadian Medical Journal* 117: 461-73.

HASSAN, S. 1943. *Excavations at Giza*, IV *1932-33* (Cairo: Government Press).

HAYES, W.C. 1935a. 'The Tomb of Nefer-khewet and his Family', *BMMA* 30, Part II: 17-36.

— 1935b. *Royal Sarcophagi of the XVIII Dynasty* (Princeton: University Press).

— 1950. 'The Sarcophagus of Sennemut', *JEA* 36: 19-23.

*— 1953, 1959. *Scepter of Egypt*, I, II (Cambridge, MA: Harvard University Press).

HERTZOG, C. 1718. *Mummio-Graphie* (Gothe: Reyher).

*HOFFMAN, M.A. 1979. *Egypt Before the Pharaohs* (London: Routledge and Kegan Paul).

HOFFMEIER, J.K. 1991. 'The Coffins of the Middle Kingdom: The Residence and the Regions', *MKS*: 69-86.

HÖLSCHER, U. 1954. *The Excavation of Medinet Habu* V: *Post-Ramessid Remains* (Chicago: University Press).

*HOPE, C.A. 1988. *Gold of the Pharaohs* (Victoria: International Cultural Corporation of Australia).

HOREAU, H. 1841. *Panorama d'Égypte et de Nubie* (Paris).

HORNUNG, H. 1983. *Conceptions of God in Ancient Egypt* (London: Routledge and Kegan Paul).

— 1990a. *Zwei ramessidische Königsgräber: Ramses IV. und Ramses VII* (*Theben*, 11) (Mainz: Philipp von Zabern).

*— 1990b. *Valley of the Kings: Horizon of Eternity* (New York: Timken).

— 1991. *The Tomb of Pharaoh Seti I/Das Grab Sethos' I.* (Zurich/Munich: Artemis).

HUSSEIN, M. K. 1951. 'Quelques Spécimens de Pathologie Osseuse chez les Anciens Égyptiens', *BIE* 32: 11-17.

IKRAM, S. 1995. *Choice Cuts: Meat Production in Ancient Egypt* (Leuven: Peeters).

*IKRAM, S. and A.M. DODSON, 1997. *Royal Mummies in the Egyptian Museum*, (Cairo: American University in Cairo Press).

ISKANDER HANNA, Z. 1940. 'Cleaning, Preservation and Restoration of the Silver Coffin and Cartonnage of Shashanq', *ASAE* 40: 581-8.

— 1944. 'Liquid found in the Sarcophagus of Pt3h-špss. Saqqara, 1944', *ASAE* 44:259-62.

— 1973. 'Temporary Stuffing Materials Used in the Process of mummification in Ancient Egypt', *ASAE* 61: 65-78.

ISKANDER, Z. and A. SHAHEEN, 1964. 'Temporary Stuffing Material Used in the Process of Mummification in Ancient Egypt', *ASAE* 58: 197-208.

ISKANDER, Z. and J. E. HARRIS 1977. 'A Skull With Silver Bridge to Replace a Central Incisor', *ASAE* 62: 85-90.

ISKANDER, Z. et al. 1979. 'Further Evidence of Dental Prosthesis in ancient Egypt', *ASAE* 63:104-13.

*JAMES, T.G.H. 1992. *Howard Carter: the Path to Tutankhamun* (London: Kegan Paul International).

JANOT, F. 1996. 'Instruments et la pratique des prêtres embaumers', *BIFAO* 96: 245-54.

JANSEN-WINKELN, K. 1987. 'Thronname und Begräbnis Takeloths I', *VA* 3: 253-8.

JÉQUIER, G. 1921. *Les frises d'objets des sar-cophages du moyen empire* (Cairo: IFAO).

JONCKHEERE, F. 1942. *Autour de l'Autopsie d'une Momie* (Brussels: Fond. Eg. Reine Elisabeth).

JUNKER, H. 1914. 'The Austrian Excavations 1914', *JEA* 1: 250-53.

— 1944. *Giza*, VII (Vienna and Leipzig: Hölder-Pichlek Tempsky).

*KANAWATI, N. 1987. *The Tomb and its Significance in Ancient Egypt* (Cairo: Ministry of Culture).

— 1993. *The Tombs of El-Hagarsa*, II (Sydney: Australian Centre for Egyptology).

KEITA, S. O. Y. 1992. 'Further Studies of Crania from Ancient Northern Africa: An Analysis of Crania from First Dynasty Egyptian Tombs, Using Multiple Discriminant Functions', *American Journal of Physical Anthropology* 87.3: 245-55.

KESSLER, D. 1986a. 'Tierkult', *LÄ* 6: 571-87.

— 1986b. 'Tuna', *LÄ* 6: 797-804.

KIRWAN, L.P. 1933. 'Some Roman Mummy Tickets', *ASAE* 33: 54-8.

*KITCHEN, K.A. 1982. *Pharaoh Triumphant* (Warminster: Aris and Phillips).

— 1985. *The Third Intermediate Period in Egypt (1100-650 BC)*, 2nd edition (Warminster: Aris and Phillips).

KLEBS, L. 1934. *Die Reliefs und Malereien des neuen Reiches.* (Heidelberg: Carl Winters Universitätsbuchhandlung).

KLEISS, E. 1975. 'X-rays of the Heads of Egyptian Mummies', *10th International Congress of Anatomy, Tokyo* (Tokyo): 535.

*KOZLOFF, A. and B.M. BRYAN, 1992. *Egypt's Dazzling Sun: Amenhotep III and his World* (Cleveland, OH: Cleveland Museum of Art/Indiana University Press).

KREBS, F. 1894. 'Griechische Mumienetikette aus Ägypten', *ZÄS* 32: 36-51.

KURTH, D. 1990. *Der Sarg der Teüris* (Mainz: Philipp von Zabern).

LACAU, P. 1904, 1906. *Sarcophages antérieurs au Nouvel Empire*, I, II (Cairo: IFAO).

— 1913. 'Suppressions et modifications de signes dans les textes funéraires', *ZÄS* 51: 1-64.

LACOVARA, P. 1990. 'An Ancient Egyptian Royal Pectoral', *JMFA* 2: 18-29.

LANSING, A. 1917. 'The Egyptian Expedition 1916-16', *BMMA* 12, Pt.II: 7-26.

— 1920. 'The Egyptian Expedition 1918-20', *BMMA* 15, Pt.II: 4-12.

LANSING, A. and W.C. HAYES, 1937. 'The Egyptian Expedition 1935-36', *BMMA* 32 Supp. 4-39.

LAPP, G. 1983. 'Sarg des AR und MR', *LÄ* 5: 430-4.

— 1993. *Typologie der Särge und Sargkammern von der 6. bis 13. Dynastie* (Heidelberg: Orientverlag).

*LAUBER, P. 1985. *Tales Mummies Tell.* (New York: Thomas Y. Crowell).

LAUER, J.-Ph. and D.R. DERRY 1935. 'Découverte à Saqqarah d'une partie de la momie du roi Zoser', *ASAE* 35: 25-30.

LAUER, J.-Ph. and Z. ISKANDER 1955. 'Donnés nouvelles sur la Momification dans l'Egypte Ancienne.' *ASAE* 53: 167-94.

LEAHY, M.A. 1977. 'The Osiris "Bed" Reconsidered', *Orientalia* 46: 424-43.

LECA, A-P. 1971. *La Médicine Egyptienne au Temps des Pharaons* (Paris: E. Dacosta).

— 1976. *Les Momies.* (Paris: Hachette).

*— 1979. *Cult of the Immortal.* (London: Souvenir Press).

LECLANT, J 1974. 'Fouilles et Travaux en Egypte et au Soudan 1973', *Orientalia* 43: 171-227.

LEEK, F.F. 1966. 'Observations on the Dental Pathology Seen in Ancient Egyptian Skulls', *JEA* 52: 59-64.

— 1967. 'The Practice of Dentistry in Ancient Egypt', *JEA* 53: 51-8.

— 1969. 'The Problem of Brain Removal During Embalming by the Ancient Egyptians', *JEA* 55: 112-6.

— 1971. 'A Technique for the Oral Examination of a Mummy', *JEA* 57: 105-9.

— 1972. *The Human Remains from the Tomb of Tut'ankhamun* (Oxford: Griffith Institute).

— 1976. 'An Ancient Egyptian Mummified Fish', *JEA* 62:

— 1980. 'Observations on a Collection of Crania from the Mastabas of the Reign of Cheops at Giza', *JEA* 66: 36-45.

— 1984. 'Reisner's Collection of Human Remains from the Mastaba Tombs at Giza', *ZÄS* 111: 11-18.

LEEMANS, C. 1867. *Monuments égyptiens du Musée d'Antiquités des Pays-Bas à Leide*, III (Leiden: E.J. Brill).

LEFÉBURE, E. 1889. *Les hypogées royaux de Thebes*, II (Paris: E. Leroux).

LEFEBVRE, G. 1923. 'Un couvercle de sarcophage de Tounah', *ASAE* 23: 229-45.

LEHNER, M. 1985. *The Pyramid Tomb of Hetep-heres and the Satellite Pyramid of Khufu* (Mainz: Philipp von Zabern).

*— 1997. *The Complete Pyramids* (London and New York: Thames and Hudson).

LEPSIUS, C.R. 1842. *Auswahl der wichtigsten Urkunden des ægyptischen Alterthums* (Leipzig: G. Wigand).

— 1849-59. *Denkmaeler aus Aegypten und Aethiopien*, 6vv (Berlin/Leipzig: Nicolaische Buchandlung).

— 1897. *Denkmaeler aus Aegypten und Aethiopien, Text* (ed. E. Naville, L. Borchardt and K. Sethe) (Leipzig: J.C. Hinrichs).

LEWIN, P.K. 1967. 'Palaeo-electron Microscopy of Mummified Tissue', *Nature* 213.5074: 416-7.

LEWIN, P. et al. 1975. 'Nakht: A Weaver of Thebes', *Rotunda* 7.4: 14-17.

LICHTHEIM, M. 1973. *Ancient Egyptian Literature*, 3vv (Berkeley: University of California Press).

LILYQUIST, C. 1988. 'The Gold Bowl Naming General Djehuty: A Study of Objects and Early Egyptology', *MMJ* 23: 5-68.

— 1979. 'A Note on the Date of Senebtisi and other Middle Kingdom Groups', *Serapis* 5: 27-8.

— 1993. 'The Boston/Lafayette jewel and other glass-inlaid ornaments', *VA* 9: 33-44.

LLOYD, A.B. 1976. *Herodotus, Book II, Commentary 1-98* (Leiden: Brill).

LOAT, L. 1905. *Gurob* (London: ERA).

— 1914. 'The Ibis Cemetery at Abydos', *JEA* I: 40.

LORET, V. 1898. 'Les Tombeaux de Thoutmes III et d'Amenophis II, et la Cachette Royale de Biban-el-Molouk', *BIE* 9: 91-112.

LORTET, C. and C. GAILLARD. 1902. 'Sur les Oiseaux Momifiés', *ASAE* 3: 18-21.

LORTET, C. and C. GAILLARD. 1903-9. *La Faune Momifiée de l'Ancienne Egypte*, 3vv. (Lyon: Muséum d'histoire naturelle de Lyon).

LORTET, C. and M. HUGONUNENQ. 1902. 'Sur les Poissons Momifiés', *ASAE* 3: 15-8.

LUCAS, A. 1908a. 'Preliminary Note on some preservative Materials used by the Ancient Egyptians in Embalming', *Cairo Scientific Journal* 2: 272-8.

— 1908b. 'The Results of the Chemical Analyses of Materials from the Mummies found in the Tomb of Amenophis II', *Cairo Scientific Journal*, 2: 273-8.

— 1908c. 'The Nature of the Preservative Bath used by the Ancient Egyptian Embalmers', *Cairo Scientific Journal*, 2: 421-4.

— 1910. 'The Preservative Materials used by the Ancient Egyptians in Embalming', *Cairo Scientific Journal*, 4: 66-8.

— 1911. 'Preservative Materials used by the Ancient Egyptians in Embalming', *Ministry of Finance, Survey Dept. Paper* 12 (Cairo).

— 1914a. 'The Use of Natron in Mummification', *JEA* I: 119-23.

— 1914b. 'The Question of the Use of Bitumen or Pitch by the Ancient Egyptians in Mummification, *JEA* I: 241-5.

— 1931a. '"Cedar"-Tree Products Employed in Mummification', *JEA* 17: 13-21.

— 1931b. 'The Canopic Vases from the 'Tomb of Queen Tiyi', *ASAE* 31: 120-22.

— 1932a. The Use of Natron in Mummification', *JEA* 18: 125-40.

— 1932b. 'The Occurrence of Natron in Ancient Egypt', *JEA* 18: 62-6.

— 1936. 'The Wood of the Third Dynasty Ply-wood Coffin from Saqqara', *ASAE* 36: 1-4.

— 1937. 'Notes on Myrrh and Stacte', *JEA* 23: 27-33.

*— 1962. *Ancient Egyptian Materials and Industries*, 4th edition, rev. J.R. Harris (London: Hutchinson).

LÜSCHER, B. 1990. *Untersuchungen zu ägyptischen Kanopenkästen. Vom Alten Reich bis zum Ende der Zweiten Zwischenzeit* (Hildesheim: Gerstenberg Verlag).

LYTHGOE, A.M. 1907. 'Egyptian Expedition', *BMMA* 2: 163-69.

— 1908. 'The Oasis of Kharga', *BMMA* 3: 203-08.

MACALISTER, A. 1893. 'Notes on Egyptian Mummies', *Journal of the Anthropological Institute*, 23: 101-21.

MACE, A.C. and H.E. WINLOCK 1916. *The Tomb of Senebtisi at Lisht* (New York: MMA).

*MADISON, A. 1980. *Mummies in Fact and Fiction* (London: Watts).

*MANNICHE, L. 1988. *City of the Dead/The Tombs of the Nobles at Luxor* (London: BMP/Cairo: American University in Cairo Press).

MANUELIAN, P. DER, and C.E. LOEBEN 1993. 'From Daughter to Father: the recarved sarcophagus of Queen Hatshepsut and King Thutmose I', *JMFA* 5: 25-61.

MARAGIOGLIO, V. and C.A. RINALDI 1964-77, *L'architettura delle Piramidi Menfite*, III-VII (Rapallo: Officine Grafiche Canessa).

MARIETTE, A. 1857. *Le Sérapeum de Memphis* (Paris: Gide).

— 1872-89. *Monuments divers recuillis en Égypte et en Nubie* (Paris: F. Vieweg).

— 1882. *Le Sérapeum de Memphis*, I (Paris: F. Vieweg).

MARTIN, G.T. 1974, 1989. *The Royal Tomb at el-'Amarna* I, II (London: EES).
*— 1991. *The Hidden Tombs of Memphis* (London and New York: Thames and Hudson).
MARTIN, S. 1945. *Mummies* (Chicago: Field Museum of Natural History).
MASPERO, G. 1875. 'Mémoire sur quelques Papyrus du Louvre', Notices et Extraits des Manuscrits, 25: 14-104. Paris.
— 1889. *Les momies royales de Déir el-Baharî* (Cairo: IFAO).
— 1915. *Guide du Visiteur au musée du Caire* (Cairo: IFAO).
MASPERO, G. and E. BRUGSCH 1881. *La trouvaille de Deir el-Bahari* (Cairo: F. Mourès & Cie.).
MASPERO, G., H. GAUTHIER and A. BAYOUMI 1908-39. *Sarcophages des époques persane et ptolémaïque*, 2 vv. (Cairo: IFAO).
MATHEY, 1887. 'Note sur une momie anonyme de Deir el Bahari', *BIE* 2ᶜ, 7: 186-95.
*METROPOLITAN MUSEUM OF ART 1976. *The Treasures of Tutankhamun* (New York: MMA).
MIDANT-REYNES, B., E. CRUBÉZY and T. JANIN 1996. 'The Predynastic Site of Adaima', *Egyptian Archaeology* 9: 13-15.
MIGLIARINI, A.M. 1855. 'Account of the Unrolling of a Mummy at Florence, Belonging to the Grand Duke of Tuscany', trns. by C. H. Cottrell, notes by S. Birch, *Archaeologia* 36: 161-74.
MILLER, R. et al. 1990. 'Detection of schistosome antigen in mummies', *Lancet* 335-725.
— 1992. 'Palaeo-epidemiology of Schistosoma Infection in Mummies' *British Medical Journal* 304: 555-56.
— 1994. 'Diagnosis of *Plasmodium faciparum* Infections in Mummies Using the Rapid Manual *Para*Sight-F Test', *Transactions of the Royal Society of Tropical Medicine and Hygiene* 88: 31-2.
MILLET, N.B. 1972. 'An Old Mortality: An Egyptian Coffin of the XXⁿᵈ (*sic*) Dynasty', *Rotunda* 5.2: 18-27.
— 1981. 'The Reserve Heads of the Old Kingdom', in *Studies in Ancient Egypt, the Aegean, and the Sudan: Essays in Honor of Dows Dunham on the Occasion of his 90th Birthday, June 1, 1980*, ed. W.K. Simpson and W. M. Davis (Boston: MFA).
MILLET, N.B. et al. 1977. 'Lessons Learned from the Autopsy of an Egyptian Mummy', *Canadian Medical Association Journal* 117/5f: 461-76.

MOND, R. and O. H. MYERS. 1934. *The Bucheum*, I. London: EES.
MOND, R. and W.B. EMERY 1929. 'The burial shaft of the tomb of Amenemhat', *LAAA* 16: 49-74 .
MONTET, P. 1942. 'La nécropole des rois Tanites', *Kemi* 9: 1-96.
— 1947. *La nécropole royale de Tanis* I: *Les constructions et le tombeau de Osorkon II à Tanis* (Paris).
— 1951. *La nécropole royale de Tanis* II: *Les constructions et le tombeau de Psousennes à Tanis* (Paris).
— 1960. *La nécropole royale de Tanis* III: *Les constructions et le tombeau de Chéchanq III à Tanis* (Paris).
MONTSERRAT, D. 1993. 'The Representation of Young Males in 'Fayum Portraits', *JEA* 79: 215-25.
MOODIE, R. L. 1931. *Roentgenologic Studies of Egyptian and Peruvian Mummies.* (Chicago: Field Museum Press).
MORET, A. 1912-13. *Sarcophages de l'époque bubastite à l'époque saïte* (Cairo: IFAO).
MORIMOTO, I. 1985. *The Human Mummies from the 1983 Excavations at Qurna, Egypt* (Tokyo: Waseda University).
MORIMOTO, I. et al. 1986-88. *Ancient Human Mummies from Qurna, Egypt* 2vv (Tokyo: Waseda University).
MORRISON-SCOTT, T. C. 1952. 'The Mummified Cats of Ancient Egypt', *Proceedings of the Zoological Society, London* 121.4: 861-7.
MORSE, D. et al. 1964. 'Tuberculosis in Ancient Egypt, *American Review of Respiratory Diseases* 90: 524-41.
MUHAMMED, A-Q. 1987. 'An Ibis Catacomb at Abu-Kir', *ASAE* 66: 121-3.
MURPHY, E., transl. 1985. *Diodorus On Egypt* (North Carolina: McFarland).
MURRAY, M.A. 1910. *The Tomb of Two Brothers* (Manchester: Sherratt and Hughes/London: Dulau and Co.).
MUSÉE NATIONAL D'HISTOIRE NATURELLE - MUSÉE DE L'HOMME 1985. *La Momie de Ramsès II: contribution scientifique a l'égyptologie* (Paris).
MYERS, O. H. and H. W. FAIRMAN. 1931. 'Excavations at Armant, 1929-31', *JEA* 17: 223-32.
NAGEL, G. 1949. 'Le Linceul de Thoutmes III', *ASAE* 49: 317-29.
NAVILLE, E. 1896-1900. *The Temple of Deir el-Bahari*, 6vv. (London: EEF).

NAVILLE, E. and H.R. HALL 1907-1913. *The XIth Dynasty Temple at Deir el-Bahari*, 3vv (London: EEF).
NEEDLER, W. 1950. *Egyptian Mummies* (Toronto: Royal Ontario Museum).
— 1963. *An Egyptian Funerary Bed of the Roman Period in the Royal Ontario Museum* (Toronto: Royal Ontario Museum).
NEMECKOVA, A. 1977. 'Histology of Egyptia Mummified Tissues from Czechoslovak Collections', *ZAS* 104: 142-44.
NEWMAN, R. 1990. 'Technical Examination of an Ancient Egyptian Royal Pectoral', *JMFA* 2: 30-7.
NICOLAEFF, L. 1930. 'Quelques Donnees au Sujet des Méthodes d'Excérbration par les Egyptiens Anciens', *Anthropologie* 40: 77-92.
NISSENBAUM, A. 1992. 'Molecular Archaeology: Organic Geochemistry of Egyptian Mummies', *JAS* 19: 1-6.
NIWINSKI, A. 1983. 'Sarg NR-SpZt', *LÄ* 5: 434-68.
— 1988. *21st Dynasty Coffins from Thebes: Chronological and Typological Studies* (Mainz: Philipp von Zabern).
— 1996. *La seconde trouvaille de Deir el-Bahari (sarcophages)*, I/2 (Cairo).
*NUNN, J.F. 1996. *Ancient Egyptian Medicine* (London: British Museum Press).
NUNNELLEY, L. L. et al. 1976. 'Trace Element Analysis of Tissue and Resin from Egyptian Mummy PUM II', *Paleopathology Newsletter* 12: 12-4.
OSBURN, W. 1828. *An Account of an Egyptian Mummy* (Leeds: Philosophical and Literary Society).
O'CONNOR, D. et al. 1980. *The Egyptian Mummy: Secrets and Science* (Philadelphia: University Museum).
*PACE, M. 1977. *Wrapped for Eternity* (New York: Butterworth).
PARKINSON, R. and S. QUIRKE 1992. 'The Coffin of Prince Herunefer and the Early History of the *Book of the Dead*', *Studies in Pharaonic Religion and Society in Honour of J. Gwyn Griffiths*, ed. Alan B. Lloyd (London: Egypt Exploration Society): 37-51.
PARLASCA, K. 1966. *Mumienporträts und verwandte Denkmäler* (Wiesbaden: DAI).
PARSCHE, F., S. BALABANOVA and W. PERSIG 1993. 'Drugs in ancient population', *The Lancet* 341: 503.
*PARTRIDGE, R.B. 1994. *Faces of Pharaohs:*

Royal Mummies and Coffins from Ancient Thebes (London: Rubicon).

PASSALACQUA, J. 1826. *Catalogue raisonné et historique des antiquités découvertes en Égypte par M. Jph Passalacqua de Trieste ...* (Paris: Galerie d'antiquités égyptiennes).

PECK, W. H. et al. 1976. 'Preliminary Reports on the Autopsy of PUM IV', *Paleopathology Newsletter* 16: 3-6.

PEET, T. E. 1914. *The Cemeteries of Abydos*, II (London: EEF).

— 1915. 'The Great Tomb Robberies of the Ramesside Age. Papyri Mayer A and B', *JEA* 2, 173-77, 204-06.

— 1925. 'Fresh Light on the Tomb Robberies of the Twentieth Dynasty at Thebes', *JEA* 11, 37-55.

— 1930. *The Great Tomb Robberies of the Twentieth Egyptian Dynasty*, 2 vv (Oxford: University Press).

PENDLEBURY, J.D.S. et al. 1951. *The City of Akhenaten*, III (London: EES).

PERIZONIUS, R. et al. 1993. 'Monkey Mummies and North Saqqara', *Egyptian Archaeology* 3: 31-3.

PETRIE, W.M.F. 1889. *Hawara, Biahmu and Arsinoe* (London: Field and Tuer).

— 1892. *Medum* (London: D. Nutt).

— 1894. *Tell el Amarna* (London: Methuen).

— 1896. *Naqada and Ballas 1895* (London).

— 1898. *Deshasheh* (London: EEF).

— 1901. *The Royal Tombs of the Earliest Dynasties*, II (London: EEF).

— 1902. *Abydos*, I (London: EEF).

— 1909. *Qurneh* (London: ERA)

— 1910. *Meydum and Memphis III* (London: ERA).

— 1911. *Roman Portraits and Memphis (IV)* (London: BSAE).

— 1912. *The Labyrinth, Gerzeh and Mazghuneh* (London: BSAE).

— 1913a. *Tarkhan I and Memphis V* (London: BSAE).

— 1913b. *The Hawara Portfolio: Paintings from the Roman Age* (London: BSAE).

— 1914a. *Tarkhan II* (London: BSAE).

— 1914b. *Amulets* (London: ERA).

— 1937. *The Funeral Furniture of Egypt* (London: BSAE).

PETTIGREW, T.J. 1834. *A History of Egyptian Mummies and an Account of the Worship and Embalming of the Sacred Animal by Egyptians* (London: Longmans).

— 1837. 'Account of the Examination of the Mummy of Pet-Maut-Ioh-Mes brought from Egypt by the late John Gosset Esq.', *Archaeologia* 27: 262-73.

PHILLIPS, J. 1992 'Tomb-robbers and their Booty in Ancient Egypt', in S.E. Orel (ed.), *Death and Taxes in the Ancient Near East* (Lewiston/Queenston/Lampeter: E. Mellen Press): 157-92.

PIANKOFF, A. 1955. *The Shrines of Tut-Ankh-Amon* (New York: Bollingen).

PICKERING, R. B. et al. 1990. 'Three-dimensional Computed Tomography of the Mummy Wenuhotep', *American Journal of Physical Anthropology* 83.1: 49-56.

PODZORSKI, P. 1990. *Their Bones Shall Not Perish* (New Malden, Surrey: Sia).

POLZ, D. 1986. 'Die Särge des (Pa-) Ramessu', *MDAIK* 42: 145-66.

QUIBELL, J.E. 1898. *The Ramesseum* (London).

— 1907. *Excavations at Saqqara (1905-06)* (Cairo: IFAO).

— 1908. *Excavations at Saqqara* (Cairo: IFAO).

— 1908. *Tomb of Yuaa and Thuiu (CCG)* (Cairo: IFAO).

— 1909. *Excavations at Saqqara 1907-08* (Cairo: IFAO).

— 1913. *Excavations at Saqqara (1911-12)*. (Cairo: IFAO).

— 1923. *Excavations at Saqqara 1912-14* (Cairo: IFAO).

— 1927. *Teti Pyramid, north side* (Cairo: IFAO).

*QUIRKE, S. 1992. *Ancient Egyptian Religion* (London: BMP).

QUIRKE, S. et al. 1995. 'Reawakening Resti: Conservation of an Eighteenth Dynasty Shroud', *Egyptian Archaeology* 6: 31-33.

RABINO MASSA, E. 1977. 'Arteriosclerotic Change in the Carotid Artery of a Mummy of New Kingdom Date', *Paleopathology Newsletter* 17: 12-13.

RAVEN, M.J. 1982. 'Corn Mummies', *OMRO* 63: 7-34.

RAY, J.D. 1976. *The Archive of Hor* (London: EES).

REDFORD, D.B. 1994. 'The 1992-93 Seasons of Excavations by the University of Toronto at Mendes (Tell er-Rub'a)', *ARCE Annual Meeting Toronto April 29-May 1, 1994: Program and Abstracts*: 53.

REEVES, C.N. 1983. 'On the miniature mask from the Tut'ankhamun embalming cache', *BSEG* 8: 81-3.

— 1985. 'Fragments of an Embalming-Ritual Papyrus in the Oriental Museum, Durham', *Revue d'Egyptologie* 36: 121-2.

— 1990a. *Valley of the Kings: the decline of a royal necropolis* (London: Kegan Paul International).

*— 1990b. *The Complete Tutankhamun* (London and New York: Thames and Hudson).

*REEVES, C.N. and R. WILKINSON 1996. *The Complete Valley of the Kings* (London and New York: Thames and Hudson).

REINHARD, J. 1996. 'Peru's Ice Maidens: Unwrapping the Secrets', *National Geographic* 189.6: 62-81.

REISNER, G.A. 1899. 'The dated canopic jars of the Gizeh Museum', *ZÄS* 37: 61-72.

— 1907. *Amulets* (Cairo: IFAO).

— 1931. *Mycerinus* (Cambridge, MA: Harvard University Press).

— 1936. *The Development of the Egyptian Tomb Down to the Accession of Cheops.* (Oxford: University Press/Cambridge, MA: Harvard University Press).

— 1942. *A History of the Giza Necropolis*, I (Cambridge, MA: Harvard University Press).

— 1967 *Canopics* (Cairo: IFAO).

REISNER, G.A. and A.C. MACE 1908-9. *The Early Dynastic Cemeteries of Naga-ed-Dêr* (Leipzig: J.C. Heinrichs).

REISNER, G.A. and W.S. SMITH. 1955. *A History of the Giza Necropolis*, II (Cambridge, MA: Harvard University Press).

RENSEBERGER, B. et al. 1975. 'Autopsy of PUM III', *Paleopathology Newsletter* 12: 6-14.

*RHIND, A.H. 1862. *Thebes: its Tombs and their Tenants* (London: John Murray).

RIAD, H. and Z. ISKANDER. 1973. *Mummification in Ancient Egypt* (Cairo: Egyptian Museum).

RIDLEY, R.T. 1983. 'The Discovery of the Pyramid Texts', *ZÄS* 110: 74-80.

ROBINS, G. 1984. 'Isis, Nephthys, Selket and Neith represented on the sarcophagus of Tutankhamun and in the free-standing statues found in KV62', *GM* 72: 21-32.

*— 1990. *Beyond the Pyramids: Egyptian regional art from the Museo Egizio, Turin* (Atlanta: Emory University Museum).

*ROMANO, J.F. 1990. *Death, Burial, and Afterlife in Ancient Egypt* (Pittsburgh: Carnegie Museum of Natural History).

*ROMER, J. 1981. *Valley of the Kings* (London: Michael Joseph; reissued O'Mara Books).

ROOT, M.C. 1979. *Faces of Immortality: Egyptian Mummy Masks, Painted Portraits and Canopic Jars in the Kelsey Museum of Archaeology* (Ann Arbor: Kelsey Museum).

ROTH, A. M. 1992. 'The *pss̆-kf* and the "Opening of the Mouth": A Ritual of Birth and Rebirth', *JEA* 78: 57-80.

— 1993. 'Fingers, Stars and the "Opening of the Mouth" Ceremony: the Nature and Function of the *ntrwj*-blades', *JEA* 79: 57-79.

ROUYER, P.C. 1822. 'Notice sur les Embaumements des anciens Egyptiens', *Description de l'Egypte*, 6: 461-89.

ROWE, A. 1938. 'New light on objects belonging to the Generals Potasimito and Amasis in the Egyptian Museum', *ASAE* 38: 157-95.

RUFFER, M. A. 1910a. Remarks on histology and Pathological Anatomy of Egyptian Mummies', *Cairo Scientific Journal 4.40.*

— 1910b. 'Note on the Presence of "Bilharzia haematobia" in Egyptian Mummies of the Twentieth Dynasty', *British Medical Journal* 2: 16-7.

— 1911a. 'Histological Studies on Egyptian Mummies', *Mémoires Préséntés a l'Institut Egyptien* 6.3: 1-39.

— 1911b. 'Remarks on the Histology and Pathological Anatomy of Egyptian Mummies', *Journal of Pathological Bacteriology* 15: 453-62.

— 1911c. 'On Arterial Lesions Found in Egyptian Mummies', *Journal of Pathology and Bacteriology* 15: 453-62.

— 1911d. 'On Dwarfs and Other Deformed Persons', *Bulletin de la Societe Archéologique d'Alexandrie* 13: 1-17.

— 1912. 'Notes on Two Egyptian Mummies Dating from the Persian Occupation of Egypt', *Bulletin de la Societe Archéologique d'Alexandrie* 14: 240-50.

— 1914a. 'A Tumour of the Pelvis Dating from the Roman Times and Found in Egypt', *Journal of Pathological Bacteriology* 18: 480-4.

— 1914b. 'Pathological Notes on the Royal Mummies of the Cairo Museum', *Mittheilung zur Geschichte der Medizin und Naturwissenschaften* 56.13: 239-68.

— 1918. 'Arthritis Deformans and Spondylitis in Ancient Egypt', *Journal of Pathology and Bacteriology* 22: 152-96.

— 1919. 'Food in Ancient Egypt', *Mémoires Préséntés a l'Institut Egyptien* 1: 1-88.

— 1920. 'Study of Abnormalities and Pathology of Ancient Egyptian Teeth', *American Journal of Physical Anthropology* 3: 335-82.

— 1921. *Studies in the Paleopathology of Egypt* (Chicago: University of Chicago).

RUFFER, M.A. and A.R. FERGUSSON. 1910. 'An Eruption Resembling that of Variola in the Skin of a Mummy of the Twentieth Dynasty', *Journal of Pathological Bacteriology* 15: 1-3.

RUFFER, M.A. and A. RIETTI 1912, 'Notes on two Egyptian mummies dating from the Persian occupation of Egypt (525-323 BC)', *Bull. Soc. arch. d'Alex.* 14: 240-51.

*RUFFLE, J. 1977. *Heritage of the Pharaohs* (Oxford: Phaidon).

SAAD, Z.Y. 1942. 'Preliminary Report on the Royal Excavations at Saqqara', *ASAE* 41: 381-409.

*SALEH, M. and H. SOUROUZIAN 1987. *The Egyptian Museum Cairo: Official Catalogue* (Mainz/Cairo: Philipp von Zabern).

SANDISON, A. T. 1957. 'Preparation of Large Histological Sections of Mummified Tissues', *Nature* 179: 1309-10.

— 1963. 'The Use of Natron in Mummification in Ancient Egypt', *JNES* 22: 259-67.

SAUNERON, S. 1952. *Le Rituel de l'Embaument: P. Boulaq III* (Cairo: IFAO).

SCHIAPARELLI, E. 1927. *La Tomba Intatta dell'Architetto Cho Nella Necropoli di Tebe* (Turin: Museum of Antiquities).

SCHMIDT, C. 1894. 'Ein altchristliches Mumienetikette', *ZÄS* 32: 52-63.

SCHMIDT, V. 1919. *Levende og døde i det gamle Ægypten: Album til ordnung af Sarkofager, Mumiekister, Mumiehylster o. lign* (Copenhagen: J. Frimots Forlag).

SERGENT, F. 1986. *Momies Bovines de l'Egypte Ancienne.* (Paris: L'Ecole Pratique des Hautes Etudes).

SETHE, K. 1934. *Zur Geschichte der Einbalsamierung bei den Ägyptern, und einiger damid verbundener Bräuche* (Berlin: Verlag der Akademie der Wissenschaften).

SHATTOCK, S.G. 1909. 'A Report Upon the Pathological condition of the Aorta of King Merneptah', *Proceedings of the Royal Society of Medicine* 2: 122.

*SHORE, A.F. 1972. *Portrait Painting from Roman Egypt* (London: British Museum).

— 1992. 'Human and Divine Mummification', *Studies ... Griffiths*: 226-35.

SHORE, A.F. and H.S. SMITH. 1956. 'A Demotic Embalmers Agreement', *Acta Orientalia* 25: 277-94.

SHORTER, A.W. 1935. 'Notes on Some Funerary Amulets', *JEA* 21: 171-6.

SILAR, J. 1979. 'Radiocarbon Dating of Some Mummy and Coffin Samples', *ZÄS* 106: 82-7.

SIMPSON, W.K. 1957. 'A Running of the Apis in the Reign of the 'Aha and Passages in Manetho and Aelian', *Orientalia* 26: 139-42.

SMITH, G.E. 1903. 'The Physical Characters of the Mummy of Thoutmosis IV', *ASAE* 4: 112-15.

— 1904. 'Report on Four Mummies', *ASAE*, 4: 156-60.

— 1906a. A Contribution to the Study of Mummification in Egypt, With Special Reference to the Measures Adopted During the Time of the 21st Dynasty for Moulding the Form of the Body. *Memoires de l'Institut Egyptien* 5: 1-53.

— 1906b. 'An Account of a Mummy of a Priestess of Amen supposed to be Ta-Usert-em-Suten-Pa' *ASAE* 7: 155-82.

— 1907a. 'Report on the Unrolling of the Mummies of the Kings Siptah, Seti II, Ramses IV, Rameses V, and Ramses VI in the Cairo Museum', *BIE* (5ᵉ Ser) 1: 45-67.

— 1907b. 'Report on the Unwrapping of the Mummy of Meneptah', *ASAE* 8: 108-12.

— 1908a. 'The Antiquity of Mummification', *Cairo Scientific Journal*, 2: 204-5.

— 1908b. 'The Most Ancient Splints', *British Medical Journal* 1: 732—4.

— 1908c. 'A Note on the Mummies in the Tomb of Amenhotep II at Biban el Molouk', *BIE* (5ᵉ Ser) 1: 221-8.

— 1912. *The Royal Mummies (CCG)* (Cairo: IFAO).

— 1914. 'Egyptian Mummies', *JEA* 1: 189-96.

*SMITH, G.E. and W.R. DAWSON, 1924. *Egyptian Mummies* (London: Allen and Unwin).

SMITH, G.E. and F. WOOD-JONES, 1910. *Report on the Human Remains. The Archaeological Survey of Nubia. Report for 1907-8,* 2 (Cairo).

*SMITH, H.S. 1974. *A Visit to Ancient Egypt. Life at Memphis and Saqqara.* (Warminster: Aris & Phillips).

— 1992. 'The Death and Life of the Mother of Apis', *Studies ... Griffiths*: 201-25.

SMITH, M. 1993. *The Liturgy of Opening the Mouth for Breathing* (Oxford: Griffith Institute).

— 1994. 'Budge at Akhmim, January 1896', C. Eyre, A. Leahy and L.M. Leahy (eds.), *The Unbroken Reed: Studies in the Culture and Heritage of Ancient Egypt In Honour of A.F. Shore* (London: Egypt Exploration Society): 293-303.

SMITH, S.T. 1991. 'They *Did* Take it With Them', *KMT* 2:3: 28-45.

— 1992. 'Intact Tombs of the Seventeenth and Eighteenth Dynasties from Thebes and the New Kingdom Burial System', *MDAIK* 48: 193-31.

SMITH, W.S. 1933. 'The coffin of Prince Min-khaf', *JEA* 19: 150-9.

— 1949. *History of Egyptian Sculpture and Painting in the Old Kingdom*² (Oxford: University Press).

*— 1981. *The Art and Architecture of Ancient Egypt*, rev. W.K. Simpson (Harmondsworth: Penguin)

SOUROUZIAN, H. 1989. *Les Monuments du roi Merenptah* (Mainz: Philipp von Zabern).

*SPENCER, A.J. 1982. *Death in Ancient Egypt* (Harmondsworth: Penguin).

*— 1993. *Early Egypt: the Rise of Civilisation in the Nile Valley* (London: BMP).

SPIEGELBERG, W. 1927. 'Die Falkenbezeichnung des Verstorbenen in der Spätzeit', *ZÄS* 62: 27-34.

— 1920. 'Ein Bruchsück des Bestattungsrituals der Apisstiere', *ZÄS* 56: 1-33

SPIELMANN, P.E. 1932. 'To What Extent did the Ancient Egyptians Employ Bitumen for Embalming?', *JEA* 18, 177-80.

STADELMANN, R. 1971. 'Das Grab in Tempelhof. Der Typus des Königsgrabes in der Spätzeit', *MDAIK* 27: 111-23.

STADELMANN-SOUROUZIAN, H. 1984. 'Rischi-Sarg', *LÄ* 5: 267-9.

STEINDORFF, G. 1917. 'Zwei Sarge des Neuen Reiches', *ZAS*: 53: 146.

*STIERLIN, H. and C. ZIEGLER 1987. *Tanis: Trésors des pharaons* (Fribourg: Seuil).

STROUHAL, E. 1976. 'Multidisciplinary Research on Egyptian mummies in Czechoslovakia', *ZÄS* 103: 113.

STROUHAL, E. 1979. 'Comment on the Paper of J.J. Castillos', *RdE* 31: 157.

STROUHAL, E. and M.F. GABALLAH 1993. 'King Djedkare Isesi and his Daughters', *BioAnth*: 104-118.

STROUHAL, E. and L. VYHNANEK 1974. 'Radiographic Examination of the Mummy of Qenamun the Sealbearer', *ZÄS* 100.2: 125-9.

STROUHAL, E. and L. VYHNANEK 1976. 'Results of Examination of the Mummy of Qenamun', *Acta Fac. R. Nat. Univ. Comeniane, Anthropologia* XXII: 235-9.

STROUHAL, E. and L. VYHNANEK 1979.

Egyptian Mummies in Czechoslovak Collections (Prague: Narodnivo Museum).

SUDHOFF, K. 1912. 'Agyptische Mummienmacher-Instrumente', *Archiv für Geschichte der Medizin* 5: 161-71.

SVANTE, P. 1985. 'Molecular Cloning of Ancient Egytian Mummy DNA', *Nature* 314: 644-45.

SWELIM, N. 1983. *Some Problems on the History of the Third Dynasty* (Alexandria: the Archaeological Society of Alexandria).

— 1987. *The Brick Pyramid at Abu Rowash, Number 'I' by Lepsius: a preliminary study* (Alexandria: The Archaeological Society of Alexandria).

TACKE, N. 1996. 'Die Entwicklung der Mumienmaske im Alten Reich', *MDAIK* 52: 307-36.

TACKHOLM, V. and M. DRAR 1954. *Flora of Egypt*, III (Cairo: Cairo University Press).

*TAYLOR, J.H. 1989. *Egyptian Coffins* (Princes Risborough: Shire Publications).

— 1992. 'Aspects of the History of the Valley of the Kings in the Third Intermediate Period', *ATut*: 186-206.

*— 1994. 'CT Scanning of a Mummy', *Egyptian Aracheology* 4: 15-6.

*— 1995a. 'Tracking Down the Past', *British Museum Magazine* 21: 8-11.

*— 1995b. *Unwrapping a Mummy* (London: BMP).

*TERRACE, E.L.B. 1968. *Egyptian Paintings of the Middle Kingdom: the Tomb of Djehuti-nekht* (New York: George Allen and Unwin).

THOMAS, E. 1966. *The Royal Necropoleis of Thebes* (Princeton: privately printed).

THOMPSON, D. L. 1976. *The Artists of the Mummy Portraits* (Malibu: J. Paul Getty Museum).

TILDESLEY, M.L. 1929. 'A Mummy-Head of Unusual Type', *JEA* 15: 158-9.

TITLBACHOVA, S. and Z. TITLBACH 1977. 'Hair of Egyptian Mummies', *ZÄS* 104: 79-85.

VALLE, P. della. 1674. *Eine vornehmen Römischen Patritii Reissbeschreibung* (Geneva).

VANDERSLEYEN, C. 1992. 'Royal Figures from Tutankhamun's Tomb: their historical usefulness', *ATut*: 76-84.

VANDIER, J. 1952. *Manuel d'Archéologie Égyptienne*, I (Paris: A. et J. Picard).

VARGA, E. 1961. 'Les Travaux Preiminaires de la Monographie sur les Hypocephales', *Acta Orientalia* XII: 235-47.

VARILLE, A. 1968. *Inscriptions concernant*

l'arcitecte Amenhotep fils de Hapou (Cairo: IFAO).

VERCOUTTER, J. 1972. 'Apis' *LA* I: 343.

VERNER, M. 1977. 'The Sealbearer Qenamun', *ZÄS* 100: 130-6.

*— 1994. *Forgotten Pharaohs, Lost Pyramids* (Prague: Akademia/Skodaexport).

VERNIER, E. 1927. *Bijoux et orfèvreries*, 2vv (Cairo: IFAO).

VON BECKERATH, J. 1984. *Handbuch der ägyptischen Königsnamen* (Munich/Berlin: Deutscher Kunstverlag).

VYHNANEK, L. and E. STROUHAL 1976. 'Radiography of Egyptian Mummies', *ZÄS* 103: 118-20.

VYSE, R.W.H. 1840. *Operations carried on at the Pyramids of Gizeh in 1837*, 3 vv. (London: James Fraser).

*WAGEMAN, S. 1992-3. 'A Christmas Surprise', *KMT* 3/4: 36.

WALKER, R. 1991. 'Skeletal Remains' in M. J. Raven (ed.) *The Tomb of Iurudef, a Memphite Official in the Reign of Ramesses II*: 55-76.

WALKER, R. et al. 1987. 'Tissue Identification and Histologic Study of Six Lung Specimens From Egyptian Mummies', *American Journal of Physical Anthropology* 72: 43-8.

*WALKER, S. and M.L. BIERBRIER 1997. *Ancient Faces: Mummy Portraits from Roman Egypt* (London: BMP).

WALSELM, R. VAN. 1988. *The Coffin of Djedmonthuiufankh in the National Museum of Antiquities at Leiden*, I (Leiden: Proefschrift).

WATSON, E.J. and M. MYERS 1993. 'The Mummy of Baket-en-her-nakht in the Hancock Museum: a Radiological Update', *JEA* 79: 179-87.

WATZINGER, C. 1905. *Griechische Holzsarcophage aus der Zeit Alexanders des Grossen* (Leipzig: J.C. Hinrichs).

WENTE, E. F. 1995. 'Who Was Who Among the Royal Mummies', *The Oriental Institute* 144: 1-6.

WENTE, E.F. and J.E. HARRIS 1992. 'Royal Mummies of the Eighteenth Dynasty: a Biologic and Egyptological Approach', *ATut*: 2-20.

WIJNGAARDEN, W.D. VAN, 1926. *Die Denkmäler des neuen Reiches und der saïtischen Zeit. Kanopen und Kanopenkasten* (Haag: M. Nijhoff).

*WILKINSON, A. 1971. *Ancient Egyptian Jewellery* (London: Methuen).

WILLEMS, H. 1988. *Chests of Life* (Leiden: Ex Orient Lux).

WILLIAMS, C.R. 1914. 'A Late Egyptian Sarcophagus', *BMMA* 9: 112-120.

WINLOCK, H.E. 1922. 'The Egyptian Expedition 1921-22', *BMMA* 17, Pt.II: 19-48.

— 1923. 'The Egyptian Expedition 1922-23', *BMMA* 18, Pt.II: 11-39.

— 1924a. 'The Tombs of the Kings of the Seventeenth Dynasty at Thebes', *JEA* 10: 217-77.

— 1924b. 'The Egyptian Expedition 1923-24', *BMMA* 19, Pt.II: 5-32.

— 1926. 'The Egyptian Expedition 1924-25', *BMMA* 21, Pt.II: 5-32.

— 1930a. 'A Late Dynastic Embalmer's Table', *ASAE* 30: 102-4.

— 1930b. 'The Egyptian Expedition 1929-30', *BMMA* 25, Pt.II: 3-28.

— 1932. *The Tomb of Queen Meryet-Amun at Thebes* (New York: MMA).

— 1936. 'A Discovery of Egyptian Jewelry by X-ray', *BMMA* 31: 274-8

— 1940. 'The Mummy of Wah unwrapped', *BMMA* 35: 253-9.

— 1941. *Materials Used at the Embalming of King Tut-'ankh-Amun* (New York: MMA).

*— 1942. *Excavations at Deir el Bahri 1911-1931* (New York: Macmillan).

— 1945. *The Slain Soldiers of Neb-Hepet-Re Mentu-Hotpe* (New York: MMA).

WOOD-JONES, F. 1908. 'The Examination of the Bodies of 100 Men Executed in Nubia in Roman Times', *British Medical Journal* 1: 736-7.

WRIGHT, G.R.H. 1979. 'The Egyptian Sparagmos', *MDAIK* 35: 345-58.

YACOUB, F. 1981. 'The Archaic Tombs at Tura el-Asmant', *ASAE* 64: 159-61.

— 1988. 'Excavations at Tura el-Asmant from the Old Kingdom till the Greco-Roman Period, Seasons 1965-66', *ASAE* 67: 193-211.

YEIVIN, S. 1926. 'The Mond Excavations at Luxor, Season 1924-25', *LAAA* 13: 3-16.

YOUSSEF, A. 1981. 'Notes on the Purification Tent', *ASAE* 64: 155-77.

*YOYOTTE, J. 1978. *Les trésors des pharaons* (Geneva: Skira).

ZAKI, A. and Z. ISKANDER 1943. 'Materials and Method Used for Mummifying the Body of Amentefnekht, Saqqara 1941', *ASAE* 42: 223-55.

ZIEGELMAYER, G. 1985. *Münchner Mumien* (Munich: Staatliche Sammlung ägyptischer Kunst).

ZIEGLER, Ch. 1981. 'La tombe de Sennefer à Deir el-Medineh', *Une siècle de fouilles Françaises en Égypte, 1880-1980* (Paris: Musée du Louvre): 213-7.

ZIMMERMAN, M.R. 1971. 'Blood Cells Preserved in a Mummy 2,000 Years Old', *Science* 180: 303.

— 1977. 'The mummies of the tomb of Nebwenenef: paleopathology and archeology', *JARCE* 14: 33-6.

— 1978. *A Paleopathological and Archeologic Investigation of the Human Remains of the Dra Abu el-Naga Site, Egypt* (Ann Arbor: Dissertation Abstract International).

ZIVIE, A.-P. 1980. 'Ibis', *LÄ* 3: 115-21.

— 1983a. 'Les tombes de la falaise du Bebasteion à Saqqara', *Le Courrier du CNRS* 49: 37-44.

— 1983b. 'Trois saisons a Saqqarah: les tombeaux du Bubasteion', *BSFE* 98: 40ff.

*— 1990. *Découverte à Saqqarah. Le vizir oublié* (Paris).

Sources of Illustrations

Index

club-foot 100; ills. 98-9
CM JE 37563 ill. 247
CM JE 37564 ill. 245
cocaine 95
coffin 193-243, 244, 250, 276, 288, 317-19, 322, and passim; ills. 49, 233-329; pls. XXV-XXVII, XXIX-XXXI
coffin, 'black' 38, 40, 193, 210-16, 243
coffin, 'white' 38, 193, 208-10, 238; ills. 267-9
coffin, 'yellow' 40, 41, 44, 193, 215-33, 243; ills. 293-304 passim; pl. XXVII
coffin, anthropoid 34, 35, 40, 42, 45, 47, 49, 50, 193-4, 202-4, 242-3, 261, 263; ill. 352; see also coffin, 'white'; coffin, 'yellow'; coffin, 'black'; coffin, rishi
coffin, pottery 194, 233; ills. 235, 292, 293
coffin, rishi 35, 38, 43, 45, 193, 204-8, 214, 226, 229, 235; ills. 258, 259, 263, 264, 265, 266, 278, 297, 301; pl. XXVI
Coffin Texts 17, 30, 36, 120, 143, 196, 308
coffins, manufacture of 242-3
Copenhagen, Nationalmuæet, numbered objects: 3890 ill. 381; 3909 pl. XXVII
Copenhagen, Ny Carlsberg Glyptotek, numbered objects: ÆIN 298 ill. 312; pl. XXIX
corn mummy 120; ill. 121
cowrie amulet pl. XV
crocodile 131, 136; ills. 148-9
curses 72-3

Dagi ill. 18a
Dagy 250
Dahshur 24, 83-4, 114, 116, 147, 148, 198, 281, 310, 313, 315; ills. 56, 81-3, 408; numbered monuments: L.LI/White Pyramid (Ammenemes II) 83, 167, 251, 280, 315, 318; ill.25; pls. XII, XIII; L.LIV (Ammenemes V?) 315; L.LVI/Bent Pyramid (Seneferu) 315, 320; L.LVIII/Black Pyramid (Ammenemes III) 83, 315, 318; ill. 347b; L.LVIII:1 (Hor) 84, 116, 254, 281, 315, 318, 321; ills. 203, 409; L.LVIII:2 (Nubheteptikhered) 116; L.XLIX/Red Pyramid (Seneferu) 92, 114, 315, 317, 320; L.XLVII (Sesostris III) 83, 245, 252, 315, 318; ills. 81, 331, 347a, 406, 407, 408; L.XLVII:iii ills. 406, 407
Dahshur, South 310, 313, 315; numbered monuments: A 315; B 315; C (Ameny-Qemau) 252, 254, 315, 318; ill. 348
Dakhala Oasis 311, 312
Dandara 13, 120, 311, 312, 313
Dara 311, 313
Daressy, Georges 82, 89, 102
Darius I ill. 387
David, Rosalie 95, 101

Davis, Theodore M 84, 89, 102, 324
De Morgan, Jacccues 83, 92, 102, 321
Dead Sea 117
Debeira East 311, 312
Deir el-Bahari 35, 38, 44, 45, 62, 77, 82, 88, 89, 96, 114, 160, 250, 311, 312, 315; 320-9, 331; ills. 23-4, 116, 308, 313, 378; pl. XXXI; numbered monuments: DBXI.14 (Mentuhotep II) 114, 315, 318, 321; ill. 24; DBXI.17 (Ashayet) ills. 175, 344; DBXI.23 116; DBXI.24 114; DBXI.26 114; MMA 507 (slain soldiers) 115-16; MMA 59 (Henttawy) 128; MMA 60 (Henttawy C, et al.) 89; Babel-Gasus 44, 82-3, 89, 91
Deir el-Bahari, Royal Cache: see Theban Tomb 320
Deir el-Ballas 311, 313
Deir el-Bersha 87, 114, 279, 311, 313; ill. 114; ill. XXV; numbered monument: 21 ill. 246
Deir el-Gebrawi 311, 313
Deir el-Medina 82, 124, 311, 312; numbered monuments: 1159 160; 2003 ill. 383; 2005 69; ill. 382
Deir Rifeh 86, 101, 156, 198, 311, 313; ill. 255
Den, Horus 315; ill. 10
dentistry 98
Derry, Douglas 92, 320-1
Deshasheh 95, 112, 113, 116, 139, 310, 313
Deshri ill. 342
Desqerdes 242
Dijk, Jacobus van 94
Diodorus Siculus 64, 103-4, 107, 117
Dioscorides 64
Dira Abu'l-Naga 62, 74, 311, 312, 315, 321; ill. 150; pl. XXVI
djed pillar 139; ill. 153
Djedbastiufankh ills. 106, 437
Djeddjhutiufankh pl. XXXI
Djededka 266
Djedefre 314
Djedhor ill. 161
Djedhoriufankh ill. 6
Djedkare: see Isesi
Djedptahiufankh 242, 316
Djehuty 104, 254, 318; ill. 353
Djehutynakhte 87, 114, 279; ill. 114; pl. XXV
Djer, Horus 109, 148, 155, 315, 317, 320; ills. 12, 172
Djet, Horus 315; ills. 12, 13
Djhutmose ill. 365
Djoser 22, 109, 245, 252, 315, 317, 320; ill. 14; pl. IV
DNA 100-1
dog 134
Dreyer, Günter 97; ill. 11
Drioton, Etienne 102
Drovetti, Bernardino 73, 102
drug-taking 95
Duamutef 18, 40, 256, 278, 284, 308; ills. 239, 286, 321, 363, 399, 416; pls.

XXIV, XXXV; see also Horus, Four Sons of
Dufferin and Ava, Marquess of 102
Duhig, Corinne 98
Durham, Oriental Museum 103; numbered objects: N.1988 ill. 436; N.1989 ill. 436; Un-numbered loan ill. 49

Ebers, Papyrus 98
Edfu 113, 311, 312, 313
Edgar, Campbell Cowan 102
Edinburgh, Royal Museum of Scotland, numbered objects: 1887.597 ill. 285; 1956.163 ill. 69; 1956.164 ill. 70; 1956.165 ill. 71
Edward [VII], Prince of Wales 69, 77
Edwin Smith Papyrus 98
Egypt Exploration Fund/Society 86, 88
Egyptian Research Account 86
Ehnasiya el-Medina 310, 312, 313
El-Badari 312
El-Hagarsa 95, 311, 313
El-Hawwawish 311, 313
El-Hiba 310, 313
El-Kab 311, 312, 313; numbered monument: EK 3 (Paheri) ill. 3
El-Kurru 311, 312, 315; numbered monuments: Ku.15 (Shabaka) 315, 319; Ku.16 (Tanutamun) 315, 319; Ku.17 (Piye) 315, 319; Ku.18 (Shabataka) 315, 319; ill. 435
El-Magar 64
El-Mahasna 311, 313
El-Qatta 98, 310, 313
El-Qurn pl. IX
El-Rizeiqat 311, 313
El-Rubayyat 310, 313; pl. XXII
El-Tarif 62, 311, 312, 315; named monuments: Saff Dawaba (Inyotef I) 250, 315; Saff el-Bagar (Inyotef III) 250, 315; Saff el-Qisasiya (Inyotef II) 315
El-Zir 276
embalmer 153
embalmers' deposit 105-7
embalming plaque 128
Emery, Walter Bryan 22, 89, 93
enema 133-4; ill. 143
Ennead, Great ill. 239
Ennead, Little ill. 239
Esna 86, 113, 311, 312, 313

faience 137, 142; ill. 428
Falconer, William 65
Farag, Naguib 93, 102
Faras 311, 312
Farina, Guilio 86
Farouk I 90
Fayoum 50, 52, 312
feldspar 142
fig 242
Filer, Joyce 98
fir 116
Firth, Cecil B. 88
fish 136
Fletcher, John 65

Florence, Archaeological Museum, numbered object: 2181 ill. 346
Fontaine, Guy de la 65
food offering 16
Fouquet, Daniel 92
Francis I, King 64
frankincense 106
Fustat: see Batn el-Baqara

Gabra, Sami 73
Garstang, John 86, 102
Gauthier, Henri 102
Geb 308; ill. 239
Gebel Barkal (Napata) 311, 312
Gebel el-Silsila 312
Gebel el-Teir el-Bahari 310, 313
Gebel Sheikh el-Haridi 311, 313
Gebelein 86, 194, 311, 313
Gerambe, Father 67
Germer, Renate 112
Gerzeh 310, 313
gesso 308
Giza 24, 87, 130, 102, 112, 249, 277, 310, 313, 314; ill. 337, 339; pl. V
Giza 984 98; numbered monuments: G.I/Great Pyramid (Kheops) 246, 314, 317; ill. 15; pl. V; G.II/Second Pyramid (Khephren) 74, 246, 278, 314, 317; ills. 15, 335; pl. V; G.III/Third Pyramid (Mykerinos) 74, 248, 314, 317, 320; ills. 15, 317, 336; pl. V; G2037bX ill. 173; G2220B ill. 174; G7000X 277; ill. 401; G7410 ill. 334; G7440Z 145; G7530+7540 (Meresankh III) 104, 320; G7810 ill. 340; G7820 ill. 340; LG 84/'Campbell's Tomb' ills. 319, 387
Goneim, Zakaria 92-3, 102
Graham, Cyril G. 102
Gray, P.H.K. 96
Grébaut, Eugène 82, 102
Gurob 310, 313
Gwyn, Nell 66

Habachi, Labib 102
haematite 137
Hale, J. 65
Hamilton, Duke of 71
Hammamat, Wadi 250
Hanover, Kestner Museum 88
Hapy 18, 40, 256, 278, 284, 308; ills. 239, 268, 286, 321, 322, 330, 356-7, 359, 399; pls. XXXIII, XXXV; see also Horus, Four Sons of
Hapymen (Abydos) 132
Hapymen (BM EA 23) 269; ills. 358, 386
Harageh 310, 313
Harhotpe 250
Harnakhte 90, 144, 266; ill. 377
Harnedjyotef ills. 326, 327
harpoon amulet pl. XV
Harris A, Papyrus 62
Harris, James E. 96, 98
Harsiese (A) 235, 315, 319, 330; ill. 310

un-numbered 73; ill. 69
London, University College 86
Loret, Victor 84, 89, 102
Lucas, Alfred 92, 112
lungs 278
Luxor 312
Luxor, Museum of Ancient Egyptian Art, numbered object: J.75 ills. 432-3

Maa ill. 249
Maat 140, 143, 308; pl. II
Mace, Arthur C. 102
MacGregor, Papyrus 144
Maetkare 126-7, 242, 329; ills. 27, 74, 299, 300
Maihirpri 84, 102, 170, 210, 211, 258-9; ills. 198, 270, 271, 362, 416, 417
Maillet, Benoit de 69
Manchester Museum, numbered objects: 1770 130; 4740 ill. 255
Mareis pl. XXIII
Mariette, Auguste 76, 80, 81, 88, 95, 102, 118
Marina el-Alemain 95, 189, 310, 313
Mark Antony 50
Martin, Geoffrey 94, 102
Masaharta 132, 162, 242, 329; ill. 186
Masara ill. 388
Maspero, (Sir) Gaston 78, 81, 84, 91, 102, 326; ill. 79
mastaba 22, 40, 308
mat-burial 43
Matmar 311, 313
Maya 95, 96; ill. 35
Mayer A, Papyrus 62, 63
Mayer B, Papyrus 62
Mayt 114
Mazghuna 310, 313, 315; North Pyramid 315; South Pyramid 253, 315; ill. 350
meat, mummified: see victual mummies
media 331
medical papyri 98
Medici, Catherine de 64
Medinet Habu 49, 225, 330, 311, 312, 315; ills. 46, 284, 382; numbered monument: MH 1 (Harsiese) 315, 330; ill. 310
Meidum 86, 112, 277, 310, 313, 315; numbered monuments: 9 (Ranefer) 110; ill. 111; 17 (anonymous) 111, 246; L.LXV (Huni(?)/Seneferu) 195, 315, 317
Meir 198, 378, 311, 312, 313; ills. 195, 220-2, 228
Meketaten 34
Memphis 40, 261; ills. 306, 365
Memphis 107, 132, 312; see also Mit Rahina
Men ill. 151
Mendes 49, 97, 270, 310, 312, 313, 314
Menelaeos 277; ill. 400
Menena 261
Menet 116
Menkauhor 314, 317
Menkaure: see Mykerinos

Menkheperre 89, 231, 232; ill. 301
Mentuhotep (Queen) 254; ill. 353
Mentuhotep (Steward) ill. 67
Mentuhotep II 31, 88, 96, 114, 116, 156, 202, 250, 254, 279, 315, 317, 321; ills. 23-4, 344
Mentuhotep IV 250
Merenptah 42, 96, 121, 127, 228, 252, 261, 263, 265, 266, 288 315, 326, 326, 327; ills. 41, 368-70, 371-2
Merenre I: see Nemtyemsaf I
Mereruka 249, 250
Meresankh II ill. 334
Meresankh III 104, 278, 320
Meroe 107, 311, 312
Mertseger 309
Meryet 210; ill. 5
Meryetamun (D18) 88, 92, 157, 208, 322; ills. 182, 185, 265, 266
Meryetamun (D19) 261
Meryetaten ill. 34
Meryetneith 315
Merykare 315
Merymose 212; ill. 277
Meryptah ill. 282
Mesehti ill. 250
MFA 21.301 ill. 155
Michigan, University of 111
Miller, Robert 99-100
Min 145, 175
Mirgissa 311, 312
Mit Rahina 310; see also Memphis
Mnevis 132, 309
Moalla 311, 313
models, tomb 31
Mohammed Ali 67, 73
Möller, Georg 102
Mond, Sir Robert 89, 102
monkey amulet pl. XV
Montet, Pierre 89, 92, 102
Montjuemhat ill. 42
Montjuemsaf 76, 273
Montjuhirkopshef B 265
Moodie, R.L. 96
mortuary temple ills. 16, 32
Mostagedda 311, 313
Moussa, Ahmed 93, 102
mumia 64
mummy 103-36, 309, 317-31, and passim; ill. 48
Mummy Brown paint 71-2
mummy mask 29, 41, 44, 50, 166-92, 207, and passim; ills. 44, 191-232 passim; pls. XVII-XX, XXIII
mummy-board/cover 41, 44, 47, 172-86, 230; ill. 52
mummy-cartonnage 45, 51, 171-91; ills. 209-25; pls. XXI, XXVIII
mummy-label 52
mummy-portrait 51; ill. 51; pl. XXII
Murray, Margaret 101; ill. 100
Mutnodjmet 95, 98
Mykerinos 246, 314, 317, 320; ill. 15, 317, 336, 338; p. V
myrrh 106

Nabesha 310, 313
Naga ed-Deir 311, 313; ill. 85
Naga el-Meshaikh 311, 313
Nahi (Viceroy) 258
Nakht (weaver) 100, 157
Nakhtankh 101, 156; ill. 100
Nakhte (Pelizaeus 5999) ill. 252
Nakhtefmut ill. 209
Nakhti ill. 238
Napata 45
Napoleon I: see Bonaparte, Napoleon
Napoleon III 77, 118
Napoleon, Prince 77, 118
Naqada 86, 113, 311, 312, 313
Narmer 13
natron 104, 106, 112, 113, 292, 309
Natrun, Wadi 104; ill. 103
Nauny 89
Naville, Edouard 88, 102, 114, 321
Nebamun ill. 29
Nebhotpe ill. 237
Nebkare 314
Nebkheri 316; ill. 268
Nebwenenef ill. 36
Nedjmet 329
Nefer (Giza) 108
Nefer (Saqqara) 110-11; ill. 112
nefer amulet 143
Neferefre 314
Neferirkare 314; ill. 17
Neferiyt 215
Neferkauet 89
Neferkhauet 284
Neferneferuaten: see Smenkhkare
Neferrenpet 94
Nefersemdent 156
Nefertari 88, 261, 326
Nefertiti 40, 260; ills. 34, 366a
Neferuptah 93, 202; ill. 347c
Nefri ill. 247
Nefwa ill. 245
Neith (goddess) 261, 278, 309; ills. 239, 309, 366b
Neith (Queen) 321
Nektanebo I 270, 319
Nektanebo II 66, 270, 319; ills. 388, 389
Nemtyemsaf I 81-2, 250, 315, 317, 321; ills. 78, 342
Nepherites I 49, 95, 143, 270, 314, 319
Nephthys 83, 144, 164, 175, 198, 236, 261, 264, 278, 308, 309; ills. 210, 211, 212, 239, 267, 286, 309, 318, 363, 366b, 377, 393, 431; pls. XXIV, XXXVI
Nesamun 70; ill. 52
Nesikhonsu 242, 316, 330; ill. 399
Nesitanebetashru 316
Nesitiset 61
Nesitnebtawi 126
Neskhonsupakhered ill. 316
Nesmin (i) ill. 381
Nesmin (ii) ill. 323
Nesnetjeret pl. XXXV
Nespanebimakh pl. XXVII

Nesptah 128
Nesyperennub, son of Ankhefenkhonsu ill. 308
net, bead
New York, Metropolitan Museum of Art 88, 89, 156; numbered objects: 09.180.528a ill. 345; 09.180.528b ill. 405; 14.10.2 ill. 267; 30.3.45 ill. 104; 20.3.203 ill. 170, 176-81
Nia ill. 287
nicotine 95
Ninetjer, Horus 315
Nitokris 69, 268; ill. 382
Niuserre 314; ill. 17
Niwinski, Andrej 216
Nodjmet 230; ills. 133, 143, 429
North Sinai 310, 313
Nubheteptikhered 116, 203
Nubkhaes 63
Nuri 311, 312, 315; numbered monuments: Nu.1 (Taharqa) 315, 319; Nu.8 (Aspelta) ill. 380
Nut 171, 197, 232, 238, 250, 256, 263, 309; ills. 217, 239, 271-6, 286, 305, 315, 327, 386, 395, 422

oil: see cedar oil; juniper oil
onion 106
Opening of the Mouth 16, 309
Osiris 18, 52, 83, 104, 120, 139, 140, 144, 163, 164, 174, 175, 232, 233, 277, 308, 309; ills. 73, 80, 186, 210, 211, 218, 239, 305, 400, 428; pls. II, III
Osiris bed 120; ill. 120
Osorkon I 45, 166, 185, 231, 233, 267; pl. XXI
Osorkon II 90, 185, 266, 314, 319
Osorkon III 185, 315
Oxford, Ashmolean Museum, numbered objects: 1889.1320-3 ill. 437; 1895.153-6 pl. XXXI; 1947.295 ill. 387

Pabasa 238
Paheri ill. 3
Paiwayenhor ill. 311
palaeopathology 99
Pamiu ill. 378
Paramesse 216; ill. 284
Pare, Ambrose 65
Paris, Louvre Museum 103; numbered objects: AO.4806 ill. 320; D 1 ill. 371; D 2 ill. 287; D 4 ill. 361; E 11936 ill. 238; E 13048 70; ill. 62-3; E 3942C ill. 426; N 229 ill. 204; N 338 ill. 287
Pasheredenptah 104
Pasherihoraweseb ill. 307
Passalacqua, Giuseppe 74, 102; ills. 52, 67
Pawenhatef ill. 385
Pediamun ill. 8
Pediset ill. 306
Pedismatowy ill. 318
Pedyimentet ills. 432-3
penis 121-2